D1602896

THE SIZE OF THE RISK

THE SIZE OF
THE RISK

*Histories of Multiple Use
in the Great Basin*

LEISL CARR CHILDERS

University of Oklahoma Press : Norman

Published in cooperation with the
Charles Redd Center for Western Studies,
Brigham Young University

Library of Congress Cataloging-in-Publication Data
Carr Childers, Leisl.

The size of the risk : histories of multiple use in the Great Basin / Leisl Carr Childers.
    pages cm
Includes bibliographical references and index.
ISBN 978-0-8061-4927-1 (hardcover) ISBN 978-0-8061-9313-7 (paper) 1. Land use
—Great Basin. 2. Land use—Environmental aspects—Great Basin. 3. Land use—
Government policy—Great Basin. 4. Public lands—Great Basin 5. Environmental
policy—Great Basin. I. Title. HD210.G7C55 2015

333.73'130979—dc23

2015010512

The paper in this book meets the guidelines for permanence and durability
of the Committee on Production Guidelines for Book Longevity of the Council
on Library Resources, Inc. ∞

Contents

Illustrations

⸾

FIGURES

Maps

Acknowledgments

⁓

This book would not have been possible without the support of a collection of people who believed in and actively facilitated its production. I am deeply indebted to the scholars who oversaw it as a dissertation and first helped me conceive of it as a book. David Wrobel supported my vision and unfailingly provided sage guidance and important criticism. Andrew Kirk, Greg Hise, Elizabeth Nelson, and Robert Futrell all offered key thoughts that proved most valuable, and Elizabeth Fraterrigo provided inspiration and a model for how public history can influence academic production. Thanks to Christopher Johnson, who read and reread the manuscript, to Jay Dew, Thomas Krause, and Charles Rankin for their support at the press, to Laurel Anderton for her copy edits, and to Gerry Krieg for the amazing maps. My greatest debt is to Mary Palevsky, director of the Nevada Test Site Oral History Project. Without her guidance and keen insight, I would have had a lesser project. Thanks also to the University of Nevada, Las Vegas, the University of Northern Iowa, and the Charles Redd Center for providing the necessary funding.

Historians are only as good as the archivists they work with, and I have had the opportunity to work with many wonderful people in several archives. Peter Michel, Delores Brownlee, and the staff at the University of Nevada's Special Collections in Las Vegas have my utmost gratitude, especially Su Kim Chung and Thomas Sommer, who gladly hauled an inordinate number of manuscript boxes to the reading room. Likewise, Martha Demarre at the National Nuclear Security Administration's Nevada Field Office provided access to thousands of digitized Atomic Energy Commission documents. Thanks also to Dennis McBride at the Nevada State Museum and to Susan Searcy, Chris Driggs, Elizabeth Moore, and Natacha Failler at the Nevada State Archives in Carson City for being incredibly helpful and always offering details and connections about the intricacies of Nevada politics. Jacquelyn Sundstrand, Donnelyn Curtis, and the staff at the University of Nevada's Special Collections in Reno provided help with Great Basin history. Special thanks to Tina Nappe for providing her father's photographs and offering insight into the complexities of wild horses, ranchers, and wildlife management. Thanks also to Katie Goins at the University of Nevada Cooperative Extension Northern Nye and Esmeralda Counties Office and Suzy McCoy of Nye County History Online for their assistance with key photographs. Glendon Collins and Beau McClure at the Public Lands Foundation Archives in Phoenix provided valuable perspectives on the inner workings of the BLM. Finally, thanks to Alan Kania, the staff at the Denver Public Library, and the GeoTree Center for their support.

None of this book would have been possible if not for the wonderful people who gave their oral histories to the Nevada Test Site Oral History Project and those whom I interviewed independently. In particular, Gracian Uhalde, Helen Uhalde, Donald James, Jeanne Sharp Howerton, Charles Costa, Virginia Sanchez, and Kim Townsend were incredibly open and honest about their experiences living and working in the Great Basin. They provided the foundation for the project, and my greatest task throughout the research and writing process was to better understand their experiences in the region.

Of course, the support and care provided by my family and friends has been essential. My parents and siblings, my in-laws, and a host of people whom I choose to call my friends believed in this project without fail. In particular, the Harrison and Evans families generously provided me with a place to stay in northern Nevada, Dave Harrison supplied the wonderful cover photograph, and Matt Koons made critical edits from a nonhistorian's perspective. Finally, I owe the largest debt of gratitude to Michael Childers, who has been through the process of transforming his own dissertation into a book, for patiently supporting me through this endeavor.

THE SIZE OF THE RISK

Introduction

Worrying that I might be lost, I stopped my car at the intersection of a deeply rutted dirt road and a nondescript dry wash, nearly twenty miles from the highway that had brought me to the south-central Great Basin. The wind was still for once as I got out of the driver's seat and felt the sun baking the sagebrush and surrounding sand. To the north and south, rocky gray bluffs hemmed in the dry streambed. To the east, where I had driven from, and to the west, where I was headed, I could see mountain peaks swathed in dark green. I was supposed to be on Seaman Wash Road, a main thoroughfare through Coal and Garden Valleys, which would lead me to Cherry Creek and the canyon where Adaven and the Uhalde Ranch were located. The owner, Gracian Uhalde, whose voice I had heard only a couple of times on the phone, had given me a set of instructions that included mile markers, a place called Water Gap, and a cattle gate. As I looked around, however, those landmarks seemed ubiquitous. Every one of the hundreds of valleys and mountain ranges that blanketed the area had mile markers, narrow gaps where water squeezed through, and cattle gates. After a good forty minutes of self-doubt and only a paper map to navigate by, I at last found the Uhalde Ranch. Sitting at Uhalde's kitchen table, I had a conversation that fundamentally changed my perspective on this vast desert region that most Americans are content to put in their rearview mirror.

The graying but still solid and energetic rancher spent much of our exchange describing his family and their livestock operation, what it was like

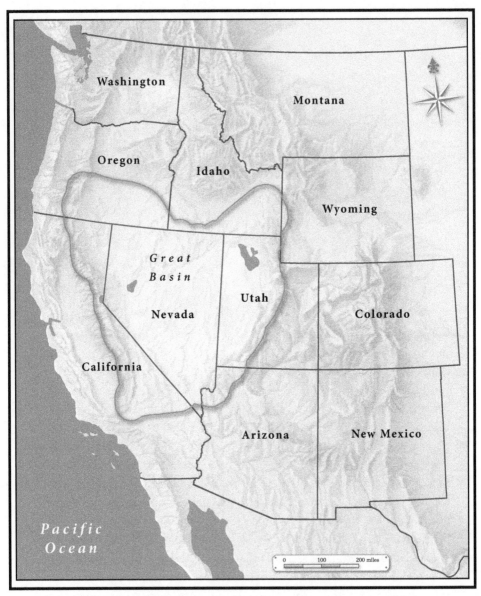

The American West featuring the approximate Great Basin boundaries. Map by
Gerry Krieg. *Copyright © 2015 by the University of Oklahoma Press*

The Great Basin featuring major towns and key ranch locations. Map by
Gerry Krieg. *Copyright © 2015 by the University of Oklahoma Press*

to live and work in one of the least-populated regions in the country, and
how troubled he was by the increasing number of conflicts resulting from
different uses of public lands that had developed during his lifetime. As a
third-generation cattle and sheep rancher, Uhalde inherited his ranch from
Basque ancestors who migrated to the Great Basin before the turn of the
twentieth century. He and his family had experienced many of the conflicts
firsthand. During our visit, he focused on explaining his frustrations with
wild horses and nuclear tests. This came as a surprise. What exactly did wild
horses and nuclear bombs have to do with the Uhalde Ranch? As I listened
more closely, I realized that his family's history was filled with stories of the

The Uhalde Ranch near Cherry Creek in the Quinn Canyon Range.
Photograph by the author.

hardships of raising livestock, watching mushroom clouds during nuclear
testing and taking cover from radioactive fallout, helping stranded mo-
torcyclists, and chasing off wild horses to protect precious grass and water
resources. It turned out that in a fundamental way, mushroom clouds and
feral equines, livestock and off-road vehicles were intertwined in his family's
life in the geography of his home. The questions that lingered with me after
the interview were how this had occurred and why.[1]

Once you know what to look for, the signs of wild horses and remnants
of nuclear testing are everywhere in the Great Basin. Evidence of cattle and
sheep ranching, outdoor recreation, and military activities is also prolific
throughout the region. The physical evidence is subtle but prolific: historic
highway signs, barbed wire fences, cattle guards, radioactive hazard warnings, bombing range notices, recreation signs and trail markers, corrals, and
the trampled earth surrounding a water hole that indicates a herd of wild
horses nearby. These signs and symbols point to a more cluttered landscape
than the wide-open spaces and dearth of population suggest. Yet, perhaps

more than other regions within the United States and because it has often been seen as an empty wasteland, the Great Basin is a perceptive hole in the nation's mental map. We may not witness all that goes on in this area, but as Uhalde described, residents there live amid a jumble of activity that constantly impacts and shapes their lives.

Because the federal government, predominantly the Bureau of Land Management, administers most of the land that comprises the Great Basin, the Uhaldes live and work within a system that blurs the line between what is local and what is national. The seemingly inconsequential populations that live in the region grapple with national interests and pressures because of their proximity to a vast concentration of public lands, more than two-thirds of the region's territory. This has made the Great Basin—its environment and its residents—a bellwether for federal land management policy and a study in the ways in which local populations influence and resist, create and reshape national trends on public lands and in how the federal government has worked (or not worked) to accommodate local interests. In particular, in this region we can see how the most influential public lands policy in the twentieth century, the multiple-use concept, was created, enacted, and transformed over time.

More than a land management paradigm, multiple use is an idea rooted in the notion that all land must have an identity and a utility. It began by default, as a means to ameliorate the amount of land that seemed to be going to waste in the last region explored and settled within the continental United States. In the mid-twentieth century, it became a critical philosophy toward land use adopted by land managers, ranchers, mining interests, wilderness and wildlife advocates, outdoor recreationists, and even the military to accommodate, promote, and sanction a multitude of ventures on public lands. Multiple use is the mechanism that has allowed nuclear testing to coexist with public lands ranching, wildlife management to sit alongside wild horse preservation, and off-road vehicle enthusiasts to share trails with hikers and mountain bikers. Today, multiple use has become an ideology, a justification, and a rationale touted by public lands users and management agencies alike to protect particular enterprises or favored activities. As a policy, multiple use is confusing and its impact stands out in high relief in the Great Basin.

Derision has underscored Americans' approach to the region. Since early exploration of the vast territory between the Sierra Nevada and Rocky Mountains, we have thought about and treated the region as a wasteland.

After a yearlong journey and many frustrating weeks of traveling through sagebrush and sand in the early 1840s, John C. Frémont called the region "a desert" and noted that "sterility may be its prominent characteristic." Frémont gave the area its name and likened its residents, whom he called "digger Indians," to its nature, speculating that their condition was due to the poor environment. His journey resulted in the first map of the Great Basin, a visual image that codified its paucity of water and resources.[2]

American humorist Samuel Clemens traveled to Carson City in the early 1860s and took a similarly dim view of the region. The Great Basin, he wrote under the pen name Mark Twain, was indeed a desert, "walled in by barren, snow-clad mountains" with "not a tree in sight" and "endless sage-brush and greasewood," lamenting that "all nature was gray with it." He had even worse to say about his journey to the capital city of the Nevada territory; crossing the Great Salt Lake Desert, he commented, "We entered upon one of that species of deserts whose concentrated hideousness shames the diffused and diluted horrors of Sahara—'alkali' desert." For more than sixty miles, Clemens and his traveling companions panted and sweated their way across its flat and cracked surface under the sweltering heat of the merciless sun. "Imagine a vast, waveless ocean stricken dead and turned to ashes; imagine this solemn waste tufted with ash-dusted sage-brushes; imagine the lifeless silence and solitude that belong to such a place," he said. All the romance Clemens felt for transcontinental travel evaporated in the dry heat—engulfed in the Forty-Mile Desert of the Humboldt and Carson Sinks, he wrote, "From one extremity of this desert to the other, the road was white with the bones of oxen and horses."[3]

As more was learned about the Great Basin, fewer people who explored or traveled in the region had anything pleasant to say about it. Robert Ridgeway, the ornithologist for Clarence King's Fortieth Parallel Survey in the late nineteenth century, had a particularly bad time exploring the marshy area near the Ruby Mountains. The scientist nearly fell off his mule before having the sense to dismount in the blazing hot midday sun. He was forced to take shelter underneath the animal's sweaty belly because there was no other shade available. Ridgeway later wrote in his report, "Upon the whole, the entire region was one of the most desolate and forbidding that could be imagined, and in these respects is probably not surpassed by any other portion of the land of 'alkali' and the 'everlasting sage-brush.' The effluvium from the putrid water and decaying vegetation of the marshes was at times sickening."[4]

While other parts of the country filled with agricultural settlement, the Great Basin remained largely undesirable despite the occasional influx of would-be gold and silver miners. General William B. Hazen, second chief of the army's Signal Service, the progenitor of the National Weather Service, thought to bring some clarity to the situation. Though he believed that the aggregate grazing capacity of the entire Intermountain West was adequate, he stated, "Farms for grazing purposes . . . will never be found here. Wherever there is unfailing water there will be an owner of it, who will control the range about it, either by cession or legal assignment, and the next water may be thirty miles away." Hazen wrote that raising livestock would be "a snare and a deception." His colleague Israel Cook Russell, a researcher with the U.S. Geological Survey, had nothing better to say, writing that the Great Salt Lake Desert, though smaller than once imagined, was "a barren waste, and fulfills all our expectations of what a true desert should be."[5]

William H. Brewer, a geography professor at Yale University and one-time mountain climbing companion of Clarence King, expressed considerable frustration about the region's persistent aridity. He wrote, "Over the whole region the actual rain-fall is vastly less than can be evaporated from the surface and this scantiness of rain-fall is the all-controlling factor as to its agricultural resources and its fitness for the homes of men. The economic foundation of civilization is agriculture, and for agriculture there must be rain in considerable quantities. . . . Crops may be grown for a time by irrigation in a rainless region, but they cannot be grown so for an indefinite period of time." Brewer argued that the soil of the Great Basin itself, the saline and alkaline content, doomed it for cultivation. Even under irrigation, "if all the water is evaporated from the cultivated soil," he wrote, "injurious salts are left behind which accumulate and finally destroy the fertility of the land and turn it back again into desert." Only the ranching industry, according to Brewer, provided some possibility of sustaining settlement in the Great Basin, but he warned that "it must ever remain a region of relatively sparse population, because of its scanty rain-fall."[6]

Again and again the Great Basin's shades of brown, gray, and olive distressed travelers and hopeful settlers who ventured across its reaches. The region's scarce water was a limitation not even the energetic Nevada senator Francis Newlands, the architect of federal reclamation, could ameliorate. The 1903 Newlands Project along the Truckee and Carson Rivers became the most important water project in the state, serving the small area around Fallon, until Hoover Dam stopped the flow of the Colorado River in the mid-1930s. It was not until the advent of automobile travel and the security of paved roads that the region experienced steady growth. Even then, few found it very attractive despite the mobility automobiles afforded. Lincoln Highway, the first coast-to-coast automobile thoroughfare, spanned the width of the desert in the early 1920s, and U.S. Highway 93, called the Great Basin Highway, bisected it along the Utah-Nevada border by the end of the 1930s. The *New York Times* reported that regardless of the federal improvements made across much of the Great Basin, "in the opinion of those who have trailed the desert, the day will never come when any considerable part of it can be reclaimed."[7]

The Great Basin resisted all conventional means to convert its vast expanse into an economic engine. By the 1930s, some hardy Mormon,[8] Basque,[9] and southern European immigrants had established ranches in small, tightly knit communities along creeks that ran dry most of the year. All of these livestock operations depended on access to the free grazing resources on public lands, those territories overseen by the federal government that were intended for settlement but had not yet been filed on. American Indian communities in the region also depended on the public domain. During the establishment of the national reservation system, most Western Shoshone and Northern Paiute tribes resisted leaving their ancestral homes for those at Pyramid Lake and Duck Valley. Even the pressure of increasing numbers of Anglo miners, farmers, and ranchers following successive gold strikes in the late nineteenth century pushed only one-third of Native peoples onto these reservations. Insistent on remaining connected to their homeland, many families lived or worked as laborers and hired help on the ranches. Derided by most Americans more than even Mormons, Basques, and immigrants from southern Europe, the Western Shoshones and Northern Paiutes maintained their presence on the land through their traditional ceremonies and practices. Although these groups maintained a clear existence on the landscape, their marginal ethnic, racial, and cultural status rendered that presence virtually invisible.[10]

By the turn of the twentieth century, the wasteland that was the Great Basin had become wasted land, a region comprising primarily public lands with little utility and without the identity afforded by private settlement. Its use for ranching by small, marginal populations and its occasional gold and silver strikes were not enough. If anything, these activities made matters worse because they did not realign responsibility for public lands. Boom and bust mining and ranching operations on the federal domain did little to contribute to the region's long-term economic and social stability. Veins of ore played out and unregulated grazing exhausted grassland resources. Land had to be someone's responsibility, someone's property, in order to ensure its maintenance over time. Congress had enacted an entire array of land disposal laws to ensure this outcome, but all of them failed miserably in the Great Basin. Even when Progressive Era reformers reconceptualized timber, grass, and scenery as valuable natural resources, rather than as aspects of nature to be freely consumed, and began protecting them with legal structures designed to conserve them for future generations and provide income to fund their management, the Great Basin's arid environment, lack of surface water, and temperature extremes prevented such laws from applying to any great degree in the region.[11]

In this absence of settlement developed "multiple use," a concept that emerged from all the various uses of public lands that occurred in lieu of disposal. Multiple use did not negate the wasteland status of the Great Basin; instead it reified the characterization. Incorporating every conceivable activity possible on public lands, multiple use broadly permitted grazing, nuclear testing, wildlife and wild horses, and a host of outdoor recreational activities, creating a variety of very different intersecting landscapes. Richard White once noted, "Despite multiple use, land cannot be simultaneously range, parking lots, and wilderness." I wanted to understand what this looked like on the ground. We tend to see these activities and the landscapes they create as distinct because their legal structures and economic functions seem so separate, but doing so precludes our awareness of their full impact. The people who live in the Great Basin, like the Uhaldes, experience all of them intertwined. The reality of multiple use, as both an idea and a policy, is a landscape filled with activities that are not always compatible. The results of their intersections are written on the region's landscape and in the lives of those who live there.[12]

This interconnectedness has exacted significant costs from the Great Basin's human population and natural environment and has tried the patience of the American public. To borrow a phrase from atomic scientist Enrico Fermi, who was instrumental in establishing a continental nuclear test site in the region, these associated costs constituted the "size of the risk." In a discussion about the probable consequences of conducting nuclear detonations in the continental United States, Fermi worked out that there was a 1 percent probability that four hundred persons in a four-hundred-square-mile area at the center of the Great Basin would be negatively affected in

some manner by radioactive fallout from the tests. This was Fermi's estimation of the potential human and environmental costs associated with a
continental atmospheric testing program. Fermi did not intend or believe
that these four hundred people would be harmed; rather, he articulated
the minute possibility that anyone living in the Great Basin would be affected by nuclear testing. In his mind, the risk of establishing a continental
nuclear test site in the region was insignificant compared to the risk to the
nation and the world of not pursuing such a program. Nevertheless, this
meant that those four hundred persons living in the Great Basin could
bear the cost of developing the nation's nuclear arsenal. In a similar manner, there have been costs associated with all the activities conducted on
public lands.[13]

It is easy to gloss over the problems of conflicting land use in the Great
Basin because so few Americans are directly affected and because the laws
governing public lands confer such great benefits to the nation as a whole.
In addition, measuring the effects of the intersecting activities on public
lands is difficult because the evidence is subsumed in the vast open space
of the region, the dialogue surrounding the conflicts is polarized and often
politically inflammatory, and the beneficent intent of every land law or
program enacted by the federal government obfuscates any negative impact
on a local scale. But the history of the Great Basin and the people who live
there is wrapped up in multiple use, and understanding it allows us to understand the ongoing reality of living in the American West.[14]

This book, as a work of cultural and environmental history rooted in
oral and public history, is an examination of the development of multiple
use, its evolution throughout the twentieth century through the lives of
those four hundred persons, the landscapes it created, and the cost of the
intersections between them. These landscapes all developed within a few
decades of each other, and the stories of their creation and intersection are
told, in part, from the perspective of a handful of those four hundred Great
Basin residents. Four main chapters detail these intersections, while three
shorter intermediary chapters following each of the main ones provide
background on the development of each landscape. In each, I highlight the
experiences of the people who lived with multiple use as well as the various
legal structures that came to articulate and govern public lands. Multiple
use is as much the product of the prior activities and needs of residents as
the demands and requirements of the federal government to make these
lands useful. It is simultaneously an embodiment of both local and national

interests. Conflicts arose from intersecting land uses when local interests diverged significantly from national ones and choices were made about whose took priority. In these situations, there was always a price to be paid, a "size of the risk." In looking at all of these costs, across the Great Basin's human and natural environments, we can also come to a better understanding of the importance and complexity of public lands management.

The first chapter begins with an exploration of how, since the late nineteenth century, Great Basin ranchers have utilized public lands for grazing livestock and how water law secured their access to and use of these ranges. The 1934 Taylor Grazing Act embraced this existing arrangement, legalized their activities, and created a ranching landscape, but the measure did not preclude settlement, wildlife management, or any other future public land use, including nuclear testing. Chapter 2 chronicles the creation of the region's bombing ranges, a designation that officially required a handful of ranchers to give up portions of their grazing ranges but that resulted in informal practices that allowed them use of some areas because of ranchers' water rights. This informal arrangement lasted until the establishment of the Nevada Proving Ground in 1951; the first atomic testing series required the absolute closure of the area. The third chapter discusses the impact of atomic testing on the lives of those who lived in close proximity to the test site. The effects of radioactive fallout seemed confined to the area near ground zero, but the intersection of ranching and atomic testing had much greater and far-reaching significance.

The subsequent chapters layer successive landscapes on top of the ranching and military constructions in the postwar era. Chapters 4 and 5 chronicle the radical increase in public land law applications and the ensuing restrictions to the land disposal process enacted by the Department of the Interior, which saw multiple use as a way to retain public lands. Many Great Basin residents perceived this as a land grab, but ranchers supported these restrictions so long as they retained their grazing ranges. In contrast, the proposed Great Basin National Park in the 1960s threatened ranchers' and miners' access, and these interests successfully defeated its creation. However, without clear definition and zoning of the region's recreational landscape, public land users such as off-road vehicle enthusiasts conflicted with ranchers and other recreationists in the vast, unregulated central part of the region.

The final chapters of the book address the most difficult aspects of multiple use. The wild horse herds that had been roaming the Great Basin for decades, which were traditionally managed by ranchers in the region, became the focus of a national preservation campaign. Chapters 6 and 7 detail how advocates who believed in their historic and cultural value lobbied vigorously for their protection, starting in Storey County, Nevada, and ending at the White House. The national movement for the 1971 Wild Free-Roaming Horses and Burros Act pitted ranchers against advocates and local interests against national ones in creating a landscape for wild horse preservation. The public outcry on all fronts and the frustration this caused federal land management agencies denoted the strain multiple use was creating.

By the end of the 1970s, these layered landscapes filled the Great Basin to the brim with activity. In 1976, the Federal Land Policy and Management Act finally allowed the federal government to retain the remaining public lands in perpetuity, but this declaration threatened to wrest the remaining semblance of local control out of the hands of Great Basin residents and make the management of public lands a purely national affair. The resulting Sagebrush Rebellion highlighted in stark relief the distance between those who lived in the region and those who governed public lands, those who relied on public lands for their livelihood and those who wanted to enjoy them.

As I found my way back through the network of dirt roads that crisscrossed the hills and playas between the Uhalde Ranch and the highway, I realized that the story of multiple use is about the land itself, and I might not like the answers I found to my questions. It is easy to take public lands management for granted and to think of it as some separate, distant undertaking. As the story unfolded, I understood it better as a collective endeavor that requires empathy and engagement at both the local and national levels to make all the different landscapes and activities work in conjunction with each other. It was hard to say for sure, but I wondered whether this was what Gracian Uhalde meant when he said: "We're at a crossroads where, you know, this way of life, I guess I see it fading out, to a certain extent. I think if you want to and you're hungry enough to hang on to it, there may be a chance."[15]

ONE

The Last Grazing District

I n the spring of 1936, a small group of ranchers from eastern Nye County
in Nevada put their names to a petition requesting that the ranges on
which they currently grazed cattle be excluded from any district organized
under the Taylor Grazing Act, the legislative measure enacted two years
prior to regulate public lands grazing. Among the signatories was Howard
Sharp, signing for his father's estate. The Sharps ranched at the southern
end of the long, narrow Railroad Valley, an unusually verdant stretch of
Great Basin desert marked by several deep springs. Forming a fairly self-
contained territory, the valley easily supported several thousand head of
cattle, providing a good livelihood for the Sharps. They, along with several
others from the surrounding area, made up the group who opposed joining
what was slated to become Nevada Grazing District 4.[1]

The White Pine County Farm Bureau, the community organizaton
overseeing the creation of Grazing District 4, which encompassed parts of
Lincoln and White Pine Counties as well as Nye County, expressed concern about the attitude of those who had signed the petition. In their investigations of the various grazing ranges in the area, agents for the farm
bureau had found the bulk of the proposed grazing district to be in serious
condition, especially "in the vicinity of the watering places." The agents
argued that these regions had become horribly denuded "on account of
climatic conditions and over-use of their summer ranges." The farm bureau
worried that other ranchers in adjacent Hot Creek, Fish Lake, Monitor,

and Big Smokey Valleys who depended on a portion of the same grazing range for their herds in winter would needlessly suffer from the lack of regulation in the region.[2]

Nevertheless, William A. Marsh, a Nye County commissioner and state senator, recommended that the farm bureau exclude, at least for the moment, Railroad Valley and the other areas delineated in the petition from any organized district. The farm bureau decided to take his recommendation and alerted Senator Key Pittman, who was working to expand the acreage included in the grazing act, of its decision.[3] Those who signed the petition represented a small but stubborn group of ranchers who believed they were in a better position to manage the public rangeland on which they relied. They believed this because they had been successfully managing that rangeland for the last thirty years to their benefit. However, over the next fifteen years, their desire to control these public lands locally ran counter to the growing necessity for federal organization and regulation of the public domain. The history of multiple use begins with this intersection and the arguments made regarding the value of the public domain by ranchers and those federal officials designated to oversee public lands. These conversa-tions demonstrate how local interests diverged from national ones and how the burden of risk fell at the feet of these families from the beginning.

Multiple use initially took shape as a solution to the problem of making productive economic use of lands that were not yet settled because of their apparent limited utility. These public lands lacked identity and did not contribute in any organized fashion to the national economy. The creation of the forest reserves in the 1890s had opened the door to federal regulation of economic activities on public lands by creating a structure in which to oversee and direct the various uses of the natural resources contained in na-tional forests. But the scope and territory of the Forest Service, established in 1906, were limited and did not encompass the majority of public lands. In addition, despite the agency's regulation of grazing resources, wildlife, and recreation and its adoption of multiple use in the 1930s, it supported primarily timber protection and harvest as a dominant use that gave forests a singular and essentially valuable identity.[4] The rest of the public lands outside the national forests, and the even more heavily managed national parks, remained open to grazing, wildlife management, recreation, mining, and any other activity that created some kind of economic benefit. None of these endeavors ranked above the others, and all were subordinate to settlement under the various land disposal laws. This was the situation on the vast majority of public lands in the continental United States, most of which were in the Great Basin, which birthed the idea of multiple use.

Because of the particular characteristics of the Great Basin's environment and the belief that its public lands were worthless, the region remained outside the realm of both settlement and direct federal management throughout the first half of the twentieth century. It was here, beginning with the Taylor Grazing Act, that multiple use developed as the solution to the remaining public lands' deficient national economic value by creating utility for land deemed essentially worthless in the broadest cultural and environmental sense of the word. At its inception, multiple use left open the possibility that the political economy of public lands could include a number of different activities, because it legitimized, at least for a time, those who came to be at the bottom of the hierarchy of land use, local residents who used public lands for themselves. The act legitimated public lands ranching until those lands could be settled and did so without interfering with mining and wildlife management. And like the Taylor Grazing Act, each successive variation of multiple use represented an accommodation of both national and local interests but placed the burden of risk on those who relied on public lands the most. As a result, many Great Basin residents, especially ranchers like the Sharps, went along with it only reluctantly, and quite a few federal officials remained mystified by their resistance.

The Sharps arrived in Nevada in the 1860s and were, like most Mormon families, missionaries and farmers. They first settled in the long, flat-bottomed Pahranagat Valley in eastern Nevada around 1865. The family's patriarch, Henry Sharp, had worked as a blacksmith in North Hampshire, England, before settling in Birmingham, where he converted to Mormonism in 1854. He immigrated to America soon after and married another English immigrant, Charlotte Morris. The Sharps migrated west to Nebraska, arriving in Deseret in 1861. After settling briefly in the southern part of the Utah territory, they moved on to Lincoln County in Nevada to take advantage of the commerce generated by the area's mining boom. Henry Sharp homesteaded 110 acres at the north end of Pahranagat Valley, near the town of Hiko at the foot of Mount Irish. His oldest son, William, mined the mountain and homesteaded 160 acres nearby, north of Alamo and twenty miles to the south of the family ranch. Henry's twin sons, Joseph and Hyrum, also settled near Alamo, at Ash Springs, where they established water rights and formed the Grove Ranch. Joseph and his son Lawrence continued their ranching operations on the Sharp Ranch at Alamo.[5]

While most of the family stayed in Pahranagat Valley, Henry's other son, George Sharp, settled near the Grant Range at Butterfield Springs on the east side of Railroad Valley. The dashing young man had ridden for several different ranch outfits before amassing enough funds to start his own. Between 1901 and 1917, George purchased several failing homestead claims adjacent to Butterfield, particularly Bacon Flat and Blue Eagle Ranch. He also obtained key water rights on the east side of the valley, including Mud Spring, Blue Eagle Well, Blind Spring, and several artesian wells near the Grant Range. Similar to the other water works owned by ranchers throughout the valley, Sharp's included pumps and pipe systems to bring water to the surface for livestock. But these improvements often drew other herds migrating through Railroad Valley, many of which had used the range seasonally prior to his arrival. On one water application, George complained that "sheep men trespass on the reserve and water their sheep" using his improvements. Besides running cattle, George also bred horses, importing well-bred animals and turning them out with nearby wild horse bands to produce hardy, smart mounts. The family grew their own fruits and vegetables, preserving the produce in glass canning jars, and kept a dairy cow to provide the family with fresh milk and butter. George's avid riding caused his death in 1934; he lost his way while out riding in cold weather and died of exposure. After his unexpected death, his sons Howard and Jim took over the running of Blue Eagle Ranch.[6]

The Sharp family had established their ranching operation in the last moment ranchers were able to run livestock in Railroad Valley, or anywhere else in the Great Basin, without any federal oversight. Where once ranching had occurred predominantly in places rich in pasture and water, the growth of the farming industry on the best lands had pushed livestock production to the most desolate areas, where cattle and sheep herds ate up the sparse vegetation and a significant amount of water pumped from underground stores was required to survive. Any competition for these scarce resources led to conflict. This was an outgrowth of the land disposal process, which had prioritized agricultural settlement, via the 1862 Homestead Act, over all other settlement; but it depended on an abundance of arable land. Ranching was an acceptable substitute for farming if it led to private land ownership—the Stock-Raising Homestead Act of 1916 facilitated this possibility; but the trouble with land in the Great Basin was that it was ranched but not privatized. It was not being properly managed or fully contributing to the local, state, or national economy.

Blue Eagle Mountain rises nearly a mile above the Butterfield and Blue Eagle Ranches in Railroad Valley. This 1964 view from the meadows at Butterfield shows the original ranch. On the right is the new ranch, which George Sharp built just after the turn of the twentieth century. Photograph courtesy of Jeanne Sharp Howerton.

Available land had been one of the nation's greatest assets throughout the nineteenth century, and the disposal of this land had significantly influenced the nation's development and identity. But increasingly, the remaining arid lands proved impossible to settle. In the decades on either side of the turn of the twentieth century, two public lands commissions attempted to resolve the question of what to do with the remaining public domain. In 1881, the first land commission to study this problem, under the auspices of the U.S. Geological Survey, included the agency's first two directors, Clarence King and John Wesley Powell. The commission argued that the federal government should "part title direct to the desert land" because "if granted free of acreage in sufficient quantity, these lands may be developed by private interests." One of the members of the commission, Thomas Donaldson, a former General Land Office employee familiar with the frustrations of the land disposal process, further commented that "the largest portion of the remaining public domain, is at present, a common—herders, woodcutters, lumbermen, and prospectors roam over it at will, most of them unable to acquire title under the present laws to what they require for their actual wants, and public benefit."[7]

In 1903, President Theodore Roosevelt organized a second public lands commission to address this problem. The Congressional Public Lands Commission of 1904 used the same language to describe the marginal nature of the remaining public domain, most of which by then was located in the Great Basin, and highlighted the increasing problem of multiple, conflicting ranching operations on public lands. The commission reported that the "general lack of control in the use of public grazing lands has resulted, naturally and inevitably in over-grazing and the ruin of millions of acres of otherwise valuable grazing territory. Lands useful for grazing are losing their only capacity for productiveness, as, of course, they must when no legal control is exercised." Through their unregulated use of public lands grazing resources, ranchers were not only taking for free what they did not own, they were wasting what little productivity these lands contained. The commission recommended, and Roosevelt agreed, that a formalized leasing system be established to streamline range access and prevent ranchers from overlapping their use of the range, which had led to conflicts like the Johnson County War in Wyoming. Many western ranchers had already taken to illegally fencing grazing areas they considered their rightful range to fend off newcomers. Roosevelt urged Congress to pass legislation to provide for federal range oversight similar to that which the government had provided since 1891 for timber resources. However, he argued that "local control of the range should be in the hands of western men familiar with stock raising, and there should be a full local hand in the management of the range." Roosevelt stated, "There is no need at present that the government should get a net revenue from grazing on the public range, but merely enough to pay for administration and development."[8]

The Progressive notion of federal regulation of rangeland resources had its origin in the new land economics developed by Richard T. Ely. Rejecting the laissez-faire economic model that spurned government intervention of any kind, Ely advocated federal or state involvement in managing natural resources, utilities, and other aspects of the American economy in the interest of public welfare. Along with Frederick Jackson Turner, his former student at Johns Hopkins University and now his colleague at the University of Wisconsin in Madison, Ely was concerned about the economic, social, and related political consequences of the closing of the frontier, as declared by the U.S. Census Bureau, and the subsequent cessation of the land disposal process. Turner expressed his concern in his 1893 essay "The Significance of the Frontier in American History," arguing that the end of westward expansion, which had been predicated on the availability of good, inexpensive farmland, meant the end of the nation's social and economic stability. Efforts to make the public domain "a source of revenue," Turner wrote, had been "in vain." Referring to the political consequences bred by the frontier, Turner remarked that western individualism had "allowed a laxity in regard to governmental affairs" that if left unchecked, produced economic crises. Ely articulated his concerns, driven by what he perceived to be the dearth of desirable land, by arguing that without the abundance of free land, which had "kept up the wages of labor" by encouraging Americans to own and work land instead of seek jobs in manufacturing, the nation had to remake its economy to compensate for the inevitable growth of the available urban workforce, which would severely lower wages.[9]

Ely advocated federal involvement in administering the remaining public domain, an unpopular idea among neoclassical economists of the time who opposed government involvement in any economic sector. Ely, like other conservationists of his era, reasoned that federal oversight of the nation's remaining public lands and its natural resources ensured "the preservation in unimpaired efficiency of the resources of the earth, or in a condition so nearly unimpaired as the nature of the case, or wise exhaustion, admits." He agreed with his other colleague at the University of Wisconsin, John R. Commons, that the most valuable quality of land was its ability to furnish "room and situation." But, he argued, "not all space is valuable." Yet to Ely and the other economists of his generation, "idle land is never neutral." Letting land go to waste was every bit as wasteful as overusing natural resources. What, then, was the political economy of public lands? Ely recommended that the federal government use a process of land zoning or classification to determine the best use of public lands and their natural resources to prevent the continued "misuse of the soil on the public domain."[10]

But despite his Progressive mind-set toward the management of public lands and natural resources, Ely did not disagree with the fundamental premise of utility embedded in both neoclassical economics and the new land economics. Rather, he differed as to the means by which utility could be achieved. Where neoclassical economists held that the perpetual balance between individual self-interest and sacrifice "brought the best good for all of society," Ely believed that the public good depended on the support of governments that fostered scientific and technological innovation to assist the individual. He supported a system that promoted individual access to public lands to create economic opportunity and efficient use of natural resources through conservation and federal management. The creators of the nineteenth-century land disposal policies had argued that their laissez-faire approach accomplished the same objective through privatization. In either case, the goal remained the same: to use public lands to serve the interests of both the individual and the nation.[11]

But the Great Basin posed an interesting challenge to both land disposal and conservation. Lying in the rain shadow of the Sierra Nevada, the Great Basin receives, on average, between three and twelve inches of precipitation annually, depending on elevation. Because of the region's aridity, temperatures regularly run in the extremes—below-freezing temperatures in the winter and at night and above one hundred degrees Fahrenheit in the blazing summer sun. Dry playas, dunes, and powdery clays produce fine particulate matter that can coat the entire area. The region lacks the widespread and consistent water and forage resources that would enable even small-scale agriculture to be functional year after year, even with irrigation. Ranching has been a better option than farming, provided livestock have plenty of room to roam for forage and consistent access to small, regular, if artificially developed, water resources. Since the 1880s, the ranching industry has dominated the agricultural development of most of the region. The Humboldt River valley, from its three forks near Elko to its sink north of Fallon, fostered the first operations. All the valleys to the north and south of the Humboldt, including the Pine, Ruby, Paradise, Reese River, and Quinn River, had enough water and forage for browsing cattle and sheep, and the nascent industry expanded throughout these areas. The Central Pacific Railroad, which ran from Salt Lake City to Sacramento, ensured that Great Basin ranchers had meat markets from California to the Midwest. But those who chose to live in the Great Basin did not amass the same level of wealth as the iconic Texas and California ranchers. If they could have purchased more than the small properties that anchored their operations, they would have. These ranchers relied on the "unallotted commons," the public lands surrounding their homes that had no federal or private designation, for grazing resources. In lieu of acquiring these lands, water rights became ranchers' only means of securing these ranges.[12]

Acquiring water rights for wells and small-scale irrigation development was fundamental to ranching in the Great Basin and became more important as livestock operations moved south into the drier sections of the region. In summer, livestock browsed the native sagebrush and grasses, but in winter, especially after the devastating freeze of 1890, herds required hay to survive. Ranchers created irrigation systems and used them to cultivate enough hay to see their stock through the cold winters. But irrigated hay production required a delicate application of water to the region's alkaline soils. Too much irrigation, and unwanted salts drained into the lowest-lying lands, rendering them unproductive. Too little water, and the soil became laden with hard minerals that also decreased production. Irrigated hay crops led to an overall increase in the production of livestock through-out the Great Basin, but when water supplies ran short or were depleted, the entire industry was in danger of collapse.[13]

For Great Basin ranchers, water rights were the most important aspect of their operations. Without an adequate number of flowing rivers and streams, groundwater proved critical to settlement and economic development. The state controlled the allocation of this water and so state water law, Nevada's in particular, implemented and enforced by the state engineer, determined water rights. The state legislature enacted Nevada's first water statute in 1866, and by the 1920s, the water statutes delineated two criteria by which the state engineer was allowed to grant water rights: prior appropriation, defined as "first in time, first in right," and beneficial use, which was determined by the use of water in making economic contributions through agricultural and industrial production or through domestic and municipal use. The state engineer's office issued certificates to validate water rights and recorded vested water rights, those that demonstrated beneficial use of surface water prior to 1905 and use of underground sources prior to 1913. Once granted, a water right could be lost only by abandonment or forfeiture if the water was not used for five consecutive years.[14]

To those who wished to maintain a livelihood in the region, vested or certified water rights, even more than land patents, were essential to their success. There were cautionary tales of those who got squeezed out of accessing nearby grazing range because they had not secured water rights. Hubert Grant Welch, born in the booming mining town of Pioche in 1912, lived on a ranch east of the Quinn Canyon Range near Cherry Creek. His father, Green Berry, and his brother Albert had homesteaded 160 acres each along Pine Creek in Garden Valley. They then secured the water rights to Pine Creek and Carpenter Spring and constructed ditch diversions from Cottonwood Creek for irrigation and stock watering. In 1920, Welch patented a small homestead of thirty-three acres along Pine Creek and secured a water right for domestic purposes and irrigating hay fields. Welch applied for several other rights for stock-watering purposes, but the state engineer denied him based on how those rights negatively affected other livestock operations with established water rights in the same region. Denied access to water across a wide enough territory to raise livestock, Welch turned to prospecting in the mountains nearby.[15]

To clamp down on the unauthorized use of water resources, in 1925, the Nevada state legislature passed the Stock Watering Act, which declared the use of water for livestock grazing on public rangeland a beneficial use of that water and determined that previously established development and use of watering holes on the public range for that purpose constituted a water right recognized by the state engineer. The legislative measure made water rights the anchor for an alternate form of land ownership; instead of owning the land outright, Great Basin ranchers merely legitimized their water usage with the Nevada state engineer's office, which converted prior usage into a water right and the grazing range into liminal property. This unprecedented acknowledgment of water in lieu of land as ranch property sanctioned ranchers' presence on public lands. The state engineer's office rationalized the act as a means by which "range control could be indirectly accomplished, in a measure at least, through administration of water re-sources, over which the State exercised unquestioned control." State legisla-tors hoped it would establish order and stability on the rangeland.[16]

An additional statute, passed in 1927, gave Nevada's district courts ju-risdiction over the supervision and control of the orders of determination, which distributed the water rights according to the decisions made by the state engineer's office and gave priority to those ranchers who owned a base property nearby. The great benefit this new law provided, in addition to helping stabilize the livestock industry by regulating range access, was a more consistent means by which to collect the property taxes charged per head of livestock. If the state engineer's office knew who owned the water, it knew who owned the livestock or who had leased the area for grazing and could conduct accurate head counts, a feat that had heretofore been relatively impossible. The law also precluded transient herds, not specifi-cally cattle or sheep operations, but those who lacked adequate water rights, by denying them access to water and grazing within three miles of exist-ing properties. As ranchers consolidated their water holdings, this left little room for these nomadic herders to graze their animals.[17]

Two years later, in 1929, Elko County district judge E. P. Carville, who later served as Nevada's governor, ruled in favor of granting water rights to livestock owners "whose animals have continuously watered themselves at water holes or running streams" and have "thereby acquired by usage a valid right to such streams and water holes, without having filed upon their waters and without having diverted them by means of pipe lines, ditches or other physical works."[18] This decision resonated throughout the Great Basin, as it recognized priority of water use regardless of whether any investment had been made in the development of the water supply at the site. Vernon Metcalf of the Nevada Livestock Association declared that "the welfare of the big majority of the livestock interests of Nevada," particularly the northern sheep operations, depended on Carville's decision.[19]

State engineer George Malone, who had overseen this transformation in Nevada state water law, worked diligently to create a state range map that delineated "the boundaries of the range rights claimed by the various stockmen and ranchers of the state of Nevada." The importance of clearly establishing water rights, along with the essential nature of developing water resources, underscored the entire livestock industry throughout the Great Basin. Those ranchers who had legal water rights controlled the public ranges surrounding them. The Stock Watering Act of 1925, the 1927 statute, and the Carville decision allowed the state government to solidify range control in Nevada and throughout the region. The key for ranchers, however, was to file for certificates and proofs of appropriation of their water rights with the state engineer's office as soon as possible after 1925. The Sharp family at Blue Eagle Ranch did just that; they vested their water rights, which they had acquired in the first two decades of the twentieth century. However, they did not control all the water rights or all the ranges they used.[20]

Not everyone benefited from this early attempt to organize the Great Basin rangeland. The Western Shoshone were virtually left out of the process and divorced from their ability to irrigate and cultivate farmland and raise livestock. In 1917, Congress authorized the creation of small Shoshone colonies adjacent to several Great Basin towns such as Elko and Ely, in places where many Western Shoshones lived and worked to increase their landholdings beyond the tiny Duck Valley Reservation. A handful of non-reservation Shoshones filed land claims, if they met the stringent requirements of the Indian homestead act and received public land allotments under the General Allotment Act, but few could file under the Homestead Act or secure water rights because they were not citizens. Without citizenship, they could secure neither land nor water. This left the Western Shoshone to work other people's ranches with little hope of achieving economic stability at a very precarious time.[21]

The 1920s were a tough time for the agricultural industry. Two decades after the public lands commission report, Benjamin Hibbard, another former student and colleague of Richard T. Ely at the University of Wisconsin, believed that the nation's depressed agricultural economy was a direct result of inadequate public lands policies and federal encouragement of farming in submarginal regions. Of the remaining 186 million acres of "unreserved and unallocated" public domain, Hibbard wrote, some of the "mountain peaks, alkali plains, and plateaus covered with rocks" could be ranched, though very little of such land could be irrigated. Ranching thus offered a better alternative for economic development on the remaining public lands. Hibbard, who agreed with Ely's land economics, criticized the federal government for not producing "a conscious, workable, vigorous land policy." In his opinion, the premise that "land should be made private property as rapidly as possible" had actually impeded earlier attempts at disposal. He argued that areas with timber stands and grazing resources were the least suited to operate in a capitalist system ruled by laissez-faire and private ownership; timber, he wrote, "can hardly succeed without a large measure of public ownership and management," though ranching "might, but has not yet done so in a marked degree."[22]

He attributed increasing range degradation to inadequate legal structures and the problem of uncertain administration: "The range has been treated as booty rather than as property," such that "a short-time view is preferable to a long-time view in range management." Hibbard did believe that there were successful grazing operations under state and private ownership, mainly in California and Texas, a model that he argued could be applied to the more arid regions of the Intermountain West. But instead, he advocated a comprehensive land policy, created and administered by the federal government, that would promote mineral development and find a suitable and regulated use for the leftover public lands that provided a means of both private ownership and federal oversight.[23]

But federal control was a hard sell during the interwar years. The Hoover administration made a serious attempt to rid the federal government of the remaining public lands in the American West that had not been given national park or national forest designation. In a letter addressed to the governors of the western states, written just as cattle prices finally began to climb out of their depressed state and only months before the stock market's collapse, Hoover made a tentative proposal to transfer the surface rights of these lands to the states. He argued that "the most vital question in respect to the remaining free public lands for both the individual states and the nation is the preservation of their most important value . . . grazing." He believed "the grazing value of these lands is steadily decreasing due to overgrazing and their deterioration, aside from their decreased value in the production of herds, is likely to have a marked effect upon the destruction of the soil and ultimately upon the water supply." Since the lands brought in no revenue and since the federal government appeared unequal to the task of satisfactorily managing these lands, the best course of action seemed to require the states to handle their administration and possibly transfer title to the stockmen who used the land. Ranchers in the Great Basin wholeheartedly agreed.[24]

Initially, the western governors, including Nevada's Frederick Balzar, expressed their approval of the plan, as did the chair of the Senate Committee on Public Lands and Surveys, Nevada's Gerald P. Nye. Each supported Hoover's appointment of another public lands commission to study the matter. However, several western representatives worried that a land transfer would burden the states with "worthless land" and deprive them of valuable oil and mineral rights and essential federal highway funds.[25] Agreeing, Utah governor George Henry Dern reportedly commented, "Without the forest lands and the minerals, the land would be more of a liability than an asset to the States which would have to administer it." He argued that the wealth of public lands was really in their timber and mineral resources. One Utah newspaper put the problem this way: "The surface rights on this public owned land is practically worthless except for grazing purposes. It is an established fact that all such lands suitable for grazing are now grazed to the limit. The transfer of ownership would not provide forage for one single extra sheep." The mining industry also took issue with the proposal. Miners expressed concern about different governments administering the public domain because it "would create hardships for mining men" and could produce confusion with the existing mining law.[26]

In October 1929, the public lands commission, under the direction of James R. Garfield, former secretary of the interior under the Roosevelt administration, began its work. The Committee on the Conservation and Administration of the Public Domain included many westerners, but one of the most significant members was Nevada state engineer George W.

Malone. Along with William Peterson of Utah and I. H. Nash of Idaho, Malone represented the Great Basin and understood from grappling with water rights and range issues firsthand the problems of grazing in the region. Malone immediately met with the members of the Nevada Livestock Association, the representative body of livestock operators who ranched throughout the area, to ascertain their perspective on the issue. The seriousness of the committee's investigation could not be overstated; as one paper reported, "Nevada contains nearly one-third of all the federal lands— ninety per cent of the state's area being public domain." Because the state's cattle and sheep industry was rooted in securing grazing rights to these lands, many felt a wrong decision could cause "heavy expense and trouble to the business for many years to come." In anticipation of regulating the region's range resources in addition to water rights, the state had organized a range commission "to decide upon the laws and best practices most beneficial to the livestock industry as a whole."[27]

Members of the Nevada Livestock Association recommended to Malone that ranchers be extended permanent grazing rights on the ranges they used, which they could sell or transfer like water rights or mining claims. Since virtually none of the land in question was fit for homesteading, a fact evident to ranchers because the public lands on which they ran their cattle had been "open to homesteaders for many years" and had "not been entered," it was therefore "fit for grazing and mining only." The organization argued that such a land right would stabilize ranch investments, encourage ranchers to make range improvements without fear of infringement from other users, and legalize the "situation which has prevailed since the beginning of stock-raising land settlement in the state."[28]

At the close of the meetings, most attendees agreed that "unless the system of range control is changed the livestock business in Nevada is doomed. The rancher must not only have control of the water but must control the range." Though many supported President Hoover's proposal, ranchers argued that regardless of which government administered public lands, "control of the range must go direct to the rancher who has established his right by use of the range." They also reiterated that purchase of these ranges was impossible "owing to the inability of stockmen to pay taxes upon them." These sentiments did not fall on deaf ears; Malone was in an excellent position to assist public lands ranchers both as a member of the president's commission and as state engineer. Malone urged the ranchers to be of one mind on the issue and assured them that their water rights controlled their range usage and that he would not grant water rights to anyone other than traditional range users on their customary grazing range.[29]

Public lands historian Karen R. Merrill has argued that the response of organized ranchers to Hoover's proposal to turn the surface rights of the remaining public lands over to the states represented a significant shift toward states' rights sentiment. This was generally true in the western states; most ranchers at the time preferred state control to federal control, especially if it meant avoiding Forest Service regulation. But in the Great Basin, specifically in Nevada and Utah, states that had sold their lands to private owners at premium prices to generate revenue, most ranchers could not afford to purchase their grazing ranges outright and did not stand to benefit in any way from state control of public lands. In Nye County, Nevada's largest administrative unit and the one containing nearly 100 percent public lands, rancher, county commissioner, and state legislator William A. Marsh worried that state ownership of public lands would make the county "a vast grazing domain for a few large livestock companies," crowding out landowners who ran stock operations on a much smaller scale. Nye County was the traditional winter range for many of the state's northern sheep operations, most of which predated white settlement in the area. But ranchers in the county relied on access to their proximate ranges year-round, since the region lacked the essential water to irrigate pastures.[30]

The problem was that ranchers who owned land and water in Nye County were latecomers to the state's livestock industry. Although they owned property, the northern sheep herds had the right of customary use on Nye County ranges during the winter, a situation that depleted the range for resident ranchers. Marsh favored local control with federal oversight because the federal government was more likely to recognize the property rights of ranchers in Nye County over the usage rights of northern sheep ranchers, whereas state control would most likely mean large livestock operators would dominate range-use decisions.[31]

Marsh had a legitimate concern. Ranchers, especially those in the comparatively fertile Elko County, had political power that was disproportionate to their numbers—only about 5 percent of the state's population participated in the industry and yet they controlled most of the water rights in the state. But in Nye County, this kind of regulated use threatened the small ranchers who believed that the proximity of their properties to the range essentially gave them the right of use above those who had established traditional water and range rights through their historic use.

Ultimately, Nevada and Utah ranchers were concerned that the states, if granted the surface rights to public lands, would simply sell them as they had sold most of their lands prior to that time. However, as the failure of land disposal laws in Nevada had demonstrated, its public lands were "invariably worthless as homesteads." In fact, the bulk of public domain remaining in the Great Basin in the late 1920s was "not of such nature that would inspire a person to pack up his belongings and rush out to homestead." Ranchers could not afford to purchase their grazing ranges outright and pay property taxes on both the land and livestock. They supported only a scenario that granted them continued and permanent access to their grazing ranges at low or no cost. Permanent water rights and permanent grazing rights allowed ranchers to benefit directly from any water and range improvements they made. These measures also provided the security for acquiring the farm loans necessary for continuous operation through poor production years, because in most cases the ranch property was worthless without the range.[32]

Western states came to agree with the position of Great Basin ranchers and favored some kind of loose federal oversight with greater local administration. None of the eleven states were capable of funding the range conservation programs necessary to improve their degraded condition unless they charged significant grazing fees. What almost all ranchers seemed to want was federal administration using federal funds with local decision-making powers that would ensure operators a place on the public rangeland they had used historically. At the end of 1929, the Nevada Livestock Association passed a resolution pronouncing that Hoover's plan to turn the surface rights of public lands over to the states was not a "practical solution fitted to Nevada conditions." Nevada state engineer and public lands commission member George Malone actively opposed any sort of dual range control in which the state administered the grazing range and the federal government retained title, arguing that such a situation would lead to "interminable disputes."[33] Instead, he favored the status quo.

The tentative report of Hoover's public lands commission at the end of 1930 recommended that the federal government retain the subsurface rights in the public domain as well as the lands already reserved in national forests, reclamation projects, and American Indian reservations. It suggested that those states desiring to manage grazing rights on the public domain within their borders could apply for a transfer of the surface rights within ten years. With reference to grazing regulation, the commission recommended that the states regulate the range themselves, and if they were unable to do so, it suggested that the federal government create "a national range to be administered by the United States." This pleased no one. Colorado's representative on the commission, C. J. Moynihan, opposed the report, angrily arguing that its recommendations abrogated local control and made the federal government the American West's "permanent landlord."[34]

Nevertheless, by 1931 a federal grazing system to accommodate ranching in a region deemed worthless for much else was the most likely course of action to ensure occupancy and use of the remaining public lands. Those lands ranchers in the Great Basin used for grazing may have been of little value without the mineral rights, but they were of great value to individual ranchers. In addition, the marginal forage they offered, while sparse compared to that of more fertile ranges, provided the basis for the only agricultural production possible in the Great Basin—livestock. And while the livestock industry throughout the region, especially in Nevada, was fundamentally important to the area's economics, it was merely a fraction of the overall livestock production in the country.[35]

Time was running out for public lands ranchers. In the early 1920s, overproduction in all agricultural sectors significantly depressed farm prices, though lowering production had helped stabilize the livestock industry. Between 1925 and 1929, livestock prices increased slowly, seemingly indicating that the depression in the livestock industry was over. When the summer rains of 1929 deluged much of the Great Basin, to the delight of ranchers, the region experienced a bumper range and hay crop. But in 1930, the Great Depression hit the livestock industry with full force and prices dropped to 50 percent of their peak value a decade earlier. To make matters worse, the drought that accompanied the economic crisis devastated grazing resources. Ranchers across the country faced collapse, but those in the Great Basin, already living with scarce water and increasing range competition despite the efforts of George Malone, Nevada's state engineer, to regulate the resource, faced the worst conditions since the prior collapse of the industry in the late 1880s, when ranchers suffered cattle losses of over 95 percent.[36]

Something had to be done. By 1934, one of the driest years on record, ranchers in the region were desperate for federal assistance. As failed homesteaders defaulted on their land claims and ceded hundreds of thousands of acres back into the public domain, the burden of the remaining public lands threatened to overwhelm Great Basin and other western states. The Drought Relief Service, created in spring of that year, began purchasing cattle across the country in drought-stricken areas, destroying those unfit for human consumption and hauling the rest to regions short of food. In Utah, the federal government purchased 85 percent of the ranchers' cattle in Beaver County. The numbers of sheep dropped dramatically in Tooele County, where the Grantsville Dust Bowl, a smaller version of that which plagued the Great Plains, threatened to decimate both the sheep and human population southwest of the Great Salt Lake. From Box Elder to Iron County, at least two-thirds of the cattle and sheep herds as well as the alfalfa crop failed. Similar problems existed in the other Great Basin states, including Nevada, where the federal government purchased more than twenty thousand cattle for slaughter. As the costs of failure began exceeding the meager economic gains provided by public lands ranching nationally, a federally managed grazing range seemed a better and better idea.[37]

Conversations about federal regulation of public lands range resources took on a new sense of urgency because of the drought. Many livestock interests in the Great Basin had supported the failed Colton Bill, the alternative to the recommendations of the Hoover commission report, which would have created locally controlled but federally owned grazing districts. When Representative Edward T. Taylor, a Democrat from Colorado, and several other supporters introduced a similar measure to Congress in 1933, the bill also received the support of most ranchers in the Great Basin states. However, Wyoming, Arizona, and a handful of Nevada ranchers maintained consistent opposition to any kind of federal control on principle, and many other residents in these states clung to the hope that someday the remaining public lands could be farmed. These people believed that if the federal government actively managed such lands, then "the hope of expanding the agriculture within those [public lands] States, except in isolated instances and through reclamation, finally [would] be dashed."[38]

Taylor's grazing bill passed the House of Representatives on April 11, 1934. The following month, ranchers throughout the Great Basin held several meetings to discuss the measure and displayed a variety of opinions about the legislation. At discussions in Elko, Lincoln, Nye, and Eureka Counties in Nevada, some indicated their opposition to federal management, which they believed would preclude their existing range usage. But cattlemen in White Pine County "favored the plan to transfer control of the range lands [to a federal grazing service] providing that it is amended to protect customary use rights and to provide for the formation of grazing districts." Nevada governor Morley Griswold echoed this sentiment, as did state engineer George Malone, who again went to Washington, D.C., to negotiate on behalf of ranchers. The state range commission resolved to approve the Taylor Bill provided that it was amended to "recognize customary range use," that grazing permits conformed to "the requirements of the federal land bank, so as to enable loans to be granted over a complete ranch," that fees were "limited to the actual cost of range supervision and improvement," and that "grazing districts be established only by consent of a majority of the stockmen concerned."[39]

Nevada senator Pat McCarran explained the necessity of these measures when the Taylor Bill arrived in the Senate. He reiterated that in Nevada, where there was very little cultivated land on the tax roll, the state was "dependent for its income on the taxing of personal property including the herds using the public domain." Reducing the number of livestock reduced the income of Nevada. Only measures that guaranteed some kind of stability in the livestock industry of the region would ameliorate the problem. In addition, McCarran pushed for stipulations in the act that would allow ranchers to factor the value of their grazing allotments into the worth of their property for loan purposes—effectively placing value on land that had previously had none—and ensure that they would be guaranteed renewal of grazing permits provided they complied with range rules and regulations, which included who could run livestock and where, but did not limit the number of animals.[40]

McCarran's colleague, Nevada senator Key Pittman, hastily tried to secure these measures in the bill but reminded Nevada ranchers, who seemed reluctant to accept some of the more restrictive aspects of the proposal, "If we do not pass some grazing act containing as much protection to states [water] rights and stock raisers as possible then the President will issue a proclamation and turn over the public lands to the Secretary of the Interior to regulate and control as he sees fit for grazing purposes." Unlike the Hoover administration, Franklin D. Roosevelt and his secretary of the interior, Harold L. Ickes, took a much stronger position on regulating public lands. Pittman argued that under a federally granted license, ranchers would have the legal legitimacy and protection they had heretofore lacked.[41]

At the same time the Senate was debating the Taylor Bill, choking yellow dust from the West reached the steps of the nation's capitol, and ranchers throughout the Great Basin began to panic. Winter precipitation over the past several years had consistently decreased. Acute drought conditions already existed in Eureka, White Pine, Nye, Lincoln, and southern Elko Counties in Nevada. Livestock were reportedly dying "like flies" and only 30 percent of the offspring during the lambing season had survived.[42] Roosevelt and Ickes argued that the controls the Taylor Bill instituted on public lands were necessary to stabilize the western range livestock industry in light of the drought and the overuse of public rangelands in general. By mid-June, the bill passed the Senate and most of its opposition ceased.[43]

President Roosevelt signed the Taylor Grazing Act on June 28, 1934. The new law initiated a system of oversight "to stop injury to the public grazing lands by preventing overgrazing and soil deterioration, to provide for orderly use, improvement, and development, to stabilize the live stock industry dependent upon the public range, and other purposes." But despite its focus on regulating grazing on public lands, the act was the first multiple-use public lands management tool. The Taylor Grazing Act promoted "the highest use of public lands *pending its final disposal*" and left room for other uses such as hunting and fishing. In essence, it recognized that livestock production was a good stopgap along the way to the ultimate purpose of public lands, their privatization. However, at the same time, the act presumed that these lands might not be suitable for "final disposal" and prescribed one alternative for them for as long as an alternative was needed.[44]

The act authorized the secretary of the interior to establish grazing districts on no more than eighty million acres of the public domain at the voluntary request of ranchers who desired federal oversight to assist them in conserving and using the range. The broad stipulations of the act had widespread ramifications throughout the livestock industry, from the smallest operator to the largest company. The act also required procedural clarification before its stipulations could be implemented in the field, so the Department of the Interior arranged for a series of hearings across the western states to survey the variety of regional needs. Assistant Secretary of the Interior Oscar L. Chapman reported consistent cooperation and an increasing number of applications for the establishment of grazing districts at the hearings. Chapman noted, "Ranchers throughout the West realize that the vast public ranges which are being overgrazed and depleted must be protected and restored or they will soon be replaced by acres of desert land."[45]

In the fall of 1934, Secretary Ickes established the Division of Grazing to oversee the creation and administration of grazing districts. Of the twenty original division employees, nine worked for the U.S. Geological Survey, seven worked for the General Land Office, three worked for the Forest

Service, and one, director Farrington R. "Ferry" Carpenter, was a Colorado rancher and Harvard-educated lawyer. Half of them lived and worked in the Great Basin.[46] Carpenter appreciated the tenor of the grazing act and its emphasis on coordinating range regulation with local livestock associations. He was also satisfied with the priority it gave grass in conservation of practices and was particularly concerned with the state of grazing conditions in Nevada, which were, in his estimation, "intolerable." Nevada ranchers wholeheartedly agreed, as did Oregon, Idaho, and Utah stock operators who ranged across state borders. They considered Nevada's grazing ranges primary to public lands ranching but agreed that the general condition of this range was poor.[47]

Unsurprisingly, Nevada ranchers elected the experienced state engineer George W. Malone to attend regional meetings discussing the creation of grazing districts and grazing policy. Considering his position of power within the ranching industry in the state and his previous experience in working with federal representatives, Malone was the logical choice. John Robbins, a state senator from Elko County, and former governor Morley Griswold joined him at the national convention. Even Carpenter noticed Malone's unique position, commenting that as the state's engineer, he controlled the water and therefore the public lands. Malone's opinions were of critical importance at this early stage. Malone estimated that "wide latitude in administration" was "necessary to meet local conditions, with particular reference to the Nevada situation." In his opinion, a system of valuation that connected the grazing range to the ranch headquarters and ranchers' water rights was the only way to secure consistent access to credit and ensure the industry's stability. Malone, as he had demonstrated before, understood the necessary criteria in determining range assignments in the Great Basin.[48]

In Arizona and New Mexico, states that used water alone to control range access through development of wells that provided surface water where there was none, ranchers relied solely on water rights to secure range access. In these warmer climes, livestock could find feed most of the year on a single range so long as they had water. In the northern and mountain states, such as Colorado, Wyoming, and Montana, ranches had to include a large enough base property to produce hay to feed livestock during the cold winter months. These ranchers controlled range access through ownership of a base property, and water rights tended to be riparian or surface rights rather than underground. This seemed to be the model the Department of the Interior understood best. But in the Great Basin, ranching and range control worked differently. Ranchers in this region utilized summer and winter ranges controlled by both base properties and water rights, some surface and some underground. Malone believed that "the livestock man will protect and build up his range unit if he can control it," and this was critical to the successful operation of ranches in his state. The entire ranching operation, as he understood it, had to be based on "land holdings and water rights" so that "complete units can be preserved."[49]

For Malone, the outcome of constructing grazing districts and regulating public rangelands had to allow ranchers to maintain the entire ranch "unit": grazing range, headquarters, and water rights. Clel Georgetta, a former president of the Utavada (Utah-Nevada) Wool Growers Association and onetime Nevada state assemblyman, agreed. Georgetta and many other ranchers present in Denver at the first grazing district organization meeting in 1935 were concerned that grazing permits would be granted on the basis of land ownership instead of a formulation of property ownership that included water rights "the same as land." In general, ranchers at the meeting worried that eastern bureaucrats who resented westerners profiting off public lands without adequate payment would end up governing grazing on the public domain.[50]

They were right to be concerned. After passage of the Taylor Grazing Act, Secretary of the Interior Harold Ickes chastised public lands ranchers for their complaining and reluctance. He accused them of "destroying their own livelihood through short-sighted competition for grazing for their flocks and herds." Pointing out how overgrazing caused erosion and depletion of water supplies, Ickes was key to pushing forward the plans to administer the act. But Georgetta had a difficult time trusting him, saying Ickes was "ignorant of livestock problems of the west and . . . unwilling to learn." The ranchers who attended that first meeting believed that Ickes refused "to consider possible solutions to pressing problems that exist, which if unsolved, will exterminate much of the livestock industry."[51]

After the initial meetings, Malone wrote Nevada governor Richard Kirman that he believed he had impressed upon the nascent Division of Grazing the importance of creating a credit structure, stable livestock units, and a local board to assist in authoring the range regulations with respect to local conditions. He had tried to find a sympathetic ear in Ferry Carpenter, who oversaw grazing administration, arguing that "the livestock owners themselves, with a period of 60 years' experience in this area behind them, are better able to assist in outlining the necessary principles and policies than any other agency." Fortunately for the ranchers, the agency's first director found Malone's insights compelling.[52]

Carpenter agreed with Malone's recommendations. He understood that "in Nevada, the man who did not develop water on the range in 1926, ran on there as a criminal," because "that was their range rights." In the rules for the issuance of grazing permits, Carpenter, in consultation with western ranchers at regional meetings held throughout 1935, created a hierarchy of range use based on land ownership, water rights, and prior use to determine which ranchers received permits under the Taylor Grazing Act. Carpenter provided a list of clarifying definitions to aid in determining who got range access. He defined *property* as "land and its products or water owned or controlled within or near a district, which according to local custom is used in connection with livestock operations"; *dependent property* as "property whose proper use requires supplemental public land range"; and *commensurate property* as "property which has livestock carrying capacity to supplement the public range land." Other concepts included the idea of *near* as "close enough to be used in connection with public range in the district in usual and customary livestock operations," but not *adjacent* or next to such public range, and *prior use* as "use of the public land range according to local custom for grazing livestock prior to the year 1935." He ordered that *recent use* and *consecutive use* also be given consideration. Ranchers with long-established use of the range and adjacent dependent commensurate property were the first to receive permits for range access.[53]

Carpenter told those who did not meet the requirements for the first tier of permits that "after residents, bona fide settlers, and occupants within or immediately adjacent to grazing districts who have dependent commensurate property are provided with range," other applicants with near dependent commensurate property with some prior use, applicants with prior use but without adequate commensurate property, and applicants with dependent commensurate property but without prior use could apply, in that order. Decisions regarding range use were not to exceed 1934 levels of livestock and would be lowered if the capacity of the range required it. Carpenter issued no long-term permits in the initial permitting process, but only temporary licenses with no fee attached. He announced that there would be no fees until the range had been properly classified and adjudicated and the values of the ranch units properly determined so that fees could be set. Most importantly, Carpenter banned interstate movement of livestock because it "created a danger similar to that of the nomad sheepman, who commercializes pasture lands without any overhead expense," creating the basis for state grazing districts.[54]

Nevada ranchers initially petitioned for eleven different grazing districts, an area that covered the entire state, to run ten thousand cattle and eighty thousand sheep. Other western states made similar requests but not across an area that covered their entirety. Most other requests for grazing districts radiated out from the Nevada range to encompass the entire Great Basin. Those made outside the region in Colorado, Wyoming, Montana, and New Mexico were smaller and more concentrated. Nevada ranchers met in Reno in January to elect twenty-eight representatives in equal numbers from the cattle and sheep industries to form the state's first advisory committee to begin "drawing the lines for the lands which [should] properly be included in grazing districts and excluding those public lands, which, because of their character or isolation should properly be left out of the grazing districts." The other states involved followed suit.[55]

Unlike the states' internal political boundaries, grazing district boundaries followed the natural landscape and traditional ranching patterns and often included concentrations of common cultural and economic groups. In Nevada, one group of ranchers, predominantly Mormon, proposed that the East Central Nevada Grazing District include southeast Elko County, southern Eureka and Lander Counties, northern Nye and Lincoln Counties, and all of White Pine County, an area particularly suited to browsing both cattle and sheep. Another group proposed including southern Lander and Eureka Counties and all of Nye and White Pine Counties in a district. According to those ranchers, "this area was designated as such because it is particularly adapted to the growing of feeder livestock and stockmen in the district have many interests in common." Proposed as the fourth Nevada grazing district, this central range included cattle ranchers only. In northern Nevada, the Producers Livestock Marketing Association of Salt Lake City solicited ranchers in this area for membership in another district. The association had convinced ranchers in Utah, Idaho, and Wyoming to join, and if Nevada ranchers also joined, the grazing districts in these member states stood to gain increased access to meat markets and credit lines.[56]

However, the eighty-million-acre limit on the total amount of land set in the Taylor Grazing Act precluded creating too many grazing districts. Division of Grazing director Farrington Carpenter focused on "areas in which range administration was most urgently needed" and in which "the lands are conveniently located for administration." By the fall of 1935, the Division of Grazing had authorized thirty-four districts in high-use, high-demand areas. Utah received all its proposed grazing districts on the fertile Wasatch and Sevier Plateaus and the eastern rim of the Great Basin. Oregon and Idaho ranchers gained districts adjacent to those in northern Nevada, though Carpenter authorized only one of three proposed districts in Idaho. In Nevada, the director allowed two of the proposed five districts, one that included all of Elko County and the portions of Eureka and Lander Counties north of the Humboldt River, and one that encompassed the entirety of Humboldt and Pershing Counties and all of Washoe County north of the Truckee River. Ranchers in the central and southern parts of the Great Basin, where the ranchland was marginal and too inconvenient to administer, worried that those outfits eliminated from the two districts would move south to the unorganized range, making the region "the dumping ground for transient livestock, both cattle and sheep, from surrounding districts in Nevada, Utah and California."[57]

Nevada senators Pat McCarran and Key Pittman worked diligently in Congress to create an amendment to the Taylor Grazing Act that would increase the acreage by about sixty-two million acres to include all requests for range organization. Secretary of the Interior Harold Ickes and President Franklin Roosevelt, however, disagreed with the changes. Ickes believed increasing the acreage would cause "the despoilment of the remaining public domain in the name of conservation or set the stage for the abandonment of homesteads by small owners under pressure from the livestock interests." In addition, besides including an acreage increase, the proposed amendment would ensure that ranchers could include their grazing rights as an asset on credit applications, mandate that the federal government exchange public lands with states at their request, allow users who owned or occupied tracts adjacent to those otherwise considered discontinuous to lease them, and employ local personnel to enforce grazing regulations. According to Ickes, the amendment gave an advantage to existing large livestock operators and did little for the "small stockman and homesteader." President Roosevelt agreed and vetoed the bill on those grounds.[58]

Both Ickes and Roosevelt misunderstood the Great Basin environment and its political economy. On the eighty million acres of organized range, ranchers seemed productive and content. There seemed no overriding national need to add more acreage to the grazing reserve. However, the Great Basin range had barely been organized and the entire central portion of

Nevada had no federal grazing oversight of any kind. Ranchers in this part of the region could not successfully remain outside the system.[59]

Those in White Pine County, southern Eureka and Lander Counties, and northern Nye County proposed organizing outside the Taylor Grazing Act system to protect their range rights against predicted incursions by displaced range users to the north and east. White Pine County ranchers were particularly disappointed their grazing range had not been included in the eighty million acres; they had consistently supported range organization and were the first in the state to petition for a district under the Taylor Grazing Act. In a letter to Nevada senator Key Pittman, the White Pine County Farm Bureau, based in Ely, pleaded that "following several years of drought and misuse of the range the forage crop on this area has become denuded to such an extent that our livestock population has decreased seventy per cent in cattle since 1925 and fifty per cent in sheep since 1929." The organization reminded Senator Pittman that it had "heartily supported range legislation" to protect and conserve forage resources in an area "suited only to the growing of range sheep and cattle and the production of forage, small grains and root crops." Ranchers in that part of Nevada surrounded by the northern and western grazing districts and national forests stood to "take the blunt [sic] of any misuse of the range which might, in the future, come about by improper range management on these unregulated ranges."[60]

Soon after, ranchers in Lincoln, Clark, Churchill, Mineral, and Esmeralda Counties likewise proposed organizing two additional districts. Division of Grazing director Farrington Carpenter assured them their organization would be recognized, though not regulated, by the Department of the Interior. Unhappy with Carpenter's response, the Nevada Livestock Association proposed repealing the legislation unless "the Department of Interior lives up to the representations of the act," providing oversight and regulation on all rangeland, and enlarging the acreage to include these additional districts. By early 1936, senators from several western states were again pushing for an increase in the acreage limit to regulate grazing in these areas, and even Secretary Ickes was willing to consider it.[61]

Skeptical about central and southern Nevada's ability to support even a meager livestock industry, Senator Key Pittman remarked in a letter to Nevada governor Richard Kirman that even he "had doubts as to whether the land around Las Vegas should be included in a grazing district." Many others, including Carpenter, had reservations about the whole area. Carpenter had not recommended any of these three districts as part of the eighty-million-acre grazing district withdrawal. He was mystified by ranchers who fought intensely for access to meager amounts of rangeland; he found "the drier the land is and the more worthless it is, the harder stockmen fought for it." Some of the ranchers in the organized parts of the Great Basin agreed with Carpenter and Pittman. But, by July, Congress had lifted the acreage limit through the first amendment to the Taylor Grazing Act and increased the acreage to 142 million. Out of a total of 163 million acres of unreserved and unallocated public lands, nearly 90 percent was now grazing range. Soon after, Congress increased the grazing district acreage, the Division of Grazing authorized Nevada districts 3, 4, and 5, the remaining two districts in Idaho, and those in southern Wyoming. However, none of these areas included the nearly twenty million acres of rangeland in the very center of the Great Basin, in southern Eureka, Lander, and Lincoln Counties, and in Nye County where ranchers had petitioned for their exclusion.[62]

To those living in the northern and eastern Great Basin who were frustrated by competing livestock operations poaching their locally regulated grasslands, the federal government was a welcome arbiter. But to those in the center of the region, it represented an unprecedented intrusion into their use of the public domain. The central Great Basin had very few ranchers and they had succeeded in dividing the rangeland among themselves, supported by the state engineer's office, which managed the water rights and resolved any conflicts. Since the area was much drier and ranchers there strictly controlled its water resources, the likelihood of nomadic herds poaching the range was less. Much to the dissatisfaction of ranchers in this area, the Forest Service had begun issuing permits to them in 1906, charging them for use of the grazing resources on the national forests, and regulating their livestock numbers. By giving the Department of the Interior authority to regulate grazing districts under another set of rules, ranchers faced having their entire operation regulated, permitted, and taxed.[63]

To soften this, the Department of the Interior's Division of Grazing intended to operate on the principle of home rule. The few administrators from the agency relied on the local grazing advisory boards to manage a grazing district's permits. As a result, the new grazing regulations did not really disrupt the status quo, mostly facilitating ranching as it had previously existed. The Forest Service and its stricter grazing regulations, developed from its nascent research in range management, seemed much more intrusive, though as Nevada governor Richard Kirman stated, most ranchers in the Great Basin had "very little complaint about the government supervision of the forest ranges" after thirty years of Forest Service regulation. Kirman and Division of Grazing officials believed that ranchers initially opposed to organized districts and the permitting process would eventually come around. However, during the late 1920s, ranchers had vigorously complained that the Forest Service policies were unsuited to the special conditions in Nevada and the rest of the Great Basin where there was very little timber and crucial summer grazing range in the national forests. Vernon Metcalf, then secretary of the Nevada Livestock Association, argued that "existing forest service range policies [were] in exact opposition to state policy"; grazing permits were temporary and did not recognize the permanency afforded ranchers by the stock watering law.[64]

Similar complaints surfaced about the new grazing regulations by the 1940s. Farrington Carpenter, the Division of Grazing director, announced to ranchers operating in unorganized areas that unless they formed grazing districts, made possible by the congressional increase in acreage under the Taylor Grazing Act, they would be subject to leasing contracts potentially more expensive than permits. Section 15 of the act authorized the secretary of the interior to lease vacant, unallocated, and unreserved lands not included in a grazing district for grazing purposes. However, where the agency granted permits for up to ten years based on a fee structure developed in consultation with the local grazing advisory boards, leases were more expensive and granted for a much shorter period. In light of this, some ranchers in central Nevada who had initially resisted organizing a grazing district began to rethink their position. In 1940, responding to pressure from the Division of Grazing, recently renamed the Grazing Service, some ranchers in Nye County made a petition to organize into a grazing district. However, the number of ranchers in the area "opposed to the formation of the grazing district" offset the request. For the next decade, most ranchers there, including the Sharp family, consistently voted to remain unorganized.[65]

The Sharp family lived near Tonopah in central Nevada, an area purportedly suffering from such critical range depletion that the Grazing Service considered it to be beneath even the marginal quality of most ranges for livestock production. Ranchers in this area continued to oppose any type of organization or government regulation. George Sharp's son Jim, who took over the Blue Eagle Ranch after his father's death in 1934, struggled to understand the necessity of federal range oversight. Always conscientious

In 1942, the Nye County Farm Bureau was organized to better manage the open range where ranchers grazed their cattle and sheep. President Jim Sharp is signing the charter, joined by other ranchers. John Ahern (county agent) and Joe Williams (Hot Creek) are seated at the end of the table, while Joe Clifford (Stone Cabin) and Wes Blair (Angleworm) stand third and fourth from the left. Others present include members of the American Farm Bureau Federation. Photograph courtesy of the Sharp Family Photo Collection.

about improving his ranching methods, the young cattleman worked to improve his herds and maintain quality grazing resources. But where Sharp saw sagebrush-covered slopes perfect for browsing cattle, Grazing Service officials saw denuded hillsides. In Sharp's mind, the Grazing Service's vision of the Great Basin environment created a void that only grass could fill, but that was not a realistic interpretation of Railroad Valley's grazing resources. Worried as to the application of the act to Blue Eagle Ranch, in 1942 he joined the newly formed American Farm Bureau Federation chapter in Nye County—a local organization chartered to oversee grazing in the area in lieu of the Grazing Service—and was elected its first president. For the moment, the isolation of Railroad Valley and the small number of ranches it contained sheltered the Sharps from federal oversight, but it remained to be seen how long the agency would overlook their maverick status.[66]

From 1935 until 1943, the handful of ranchers in this region were not required to pay for either permits or leases, running livestock on the unallocated commons essentially for free. Conceivably, the Grazing Service had "overlooked" the area, but these ranchers had also actively chosen to oppose any federal regulation of the grazing range in their area beginning in 1935 by voting to forgo organization under the Taylor Grazing Act. But their position was tenable only so long as federal oversight was neglected. On May 18, 1943, Assistant Secretary of the Interior Oscar L. Chapman posted a public notice for the parts of Nye, Esmeralda, Eureka, Lander, and Lincoln Counties not already organized into grazing districts. He also announced public hearings in Tonopah and Alamo that would organize the area into one or more grazing districts. Immediately, virtually all the ranchers in the area sent their protests to Senator Pat McCarran and the former state engineer George Malone, now a senator himself, and Governor Vail Pittman, who convinced the secretary of the interior to postpone the initial hearings. The ranchers reasoned that the act of organizing would create additional hardships for them during the war effort and that there was "no emergency calling for a grazing district in this area." This argument earned them a short reprieve, but by 1945 and the end of World War II, the pressure was on again. The Sharps and several other families in Railroad, Reveille, Stone Cabin, Garden, and Pahranagat Valleys signed a petition appealing to Senator Pat McCarran, requesting that he prevent their graz-ing range from being organized into a grazing district.[67]

Despite the efforts of these ranchers, the Department of the Interior worked tirelessly to bring all rangeland under federal administration. Rather than being voluntary, grazing district organization was, in the end, compulsory. Much of this had to do with the changing culture of the Grazing Service and the Department of the Interior as well as the creation of the Bureau of Land Management in the mid-1940s. In 1938, Secretary of the Interior Harold Ickes fired Ferry Carpenter, whom he had never liked, and replaced him with Richard H. Rutledge, a Forest Service range expert committed to establishing efficient conservation practices, as the director of the Grazing Service. In 1944, Clarence Forsling, also a former Forest Service range management expert who had worked extensively in the Great Basin, sought to bring more professional control and oversight to the Grazing Service as the new director following Rutledge. Where ranchers had been allowed a significant amount of "home rule" through their initial role in establishing the grazing districts and through their continued management via the grazing advisory boards, both Rutledge and Forsling sought to tighten regulation of public lands. This certainly suited Secretary of the Interior Harold Ickes's vision of federal control over public resources.[68]

Then in 1946, the federal government restructured its land management agencies. Ranchers throughout the American West hoped the Forest Service, in the Department of Agriculture, would be transferred to the
Department of the Interior and one department would handle all grazing
operations. To those who depended on using public rangelands, the Forest
Service problematically prioritized grazing range well below timber cultivation and did not issue long-term grazing permits to ranchers. Instead,
however, the federal government merged the General Land Office (GLO)
with the Grazing Service to form the Bureau of Land Management (BLM)
and placed Fred Johnson, the GLO commissioner, at the helm. Johnson's
appointment spoke volumes about the priorities of the new agency. Ranchers had hoped a "livestock man" would run the BLM and give them greater
status in the hierarchy of land management; Nevada ranchers in particular
were steamed at Secretary Ickes's decision. But with Ickes's retirement in
early 1946, the problem was now in the hands of the new secretary, Ju-
lius A. Krug.[69] The following year, Krug applied even greater pressure to
ranchers in central Nevada. Krug issued an ultimatum that required them
to either "declare for formation of a grazing district under the Bureau of
Land Management or become subject to lease application under section
15" of the Taylor Grazing Act by the end of 1947. Either way, under this
ultimatum, ranchers were going to have to submit to the administration of
public rangeland under the federal government and pay for their use of it.[70]

In another attempt to organize locally and stave off formation of a grazing district and subsequent federal oversight, in early 1948, before Krug
could act on his ultimatum, ranchers in Nye County formed the Central Nevada Livestock Association. Jim's brother Howard Sharp joined the
newly created organization and stockmen from Nye, Lander, Eureka, and
Esmeralda Counties called a meeting in Tonopah. In a last-ditch effort, they
voted to request a yearlong postponement of federal oversight in order to
thoroughly study the matter and make an informed decision, complaining
that a large portion of the unorganized area was "absolutely useless for grazing purposes." The state's leading newspaper in Reno reported that "had it
not been for pressure brought to bear in the interior department by eastern senators who imagine the stockmen are fattening their pocketbooks at
the expense of the federal government it is unlikely the department would
have molested the stockmen ranging cattle over the usable portions of the
12,000,000 acres involved."[71]

By December 1948, on the advice of Senator Pat McCarran that their
time had run out, ranchers in central Nevada voted to organize a grazing

district in preference to taking Section 15 leases, fearing federal prosecution and fines. This decision, however, came in the middle of a bad winter that blanketed much of the Great Basin in deep, windblown snowdrifts. In January 1949, livestock operators requested that Governor Vail Pittman declare a state of emergency in Nevada. Ranchers in Utah, Wyoming, and Montana had already required significant assistance, and some operators had lost nearly 50 percent of their herds that winter. Federal oversight from this perspective seemed less onerous because it came with much-needed assistance. Although the Section 15 leases would have ensured less oversight, ranchers believed permits granted through the grazing districts were far more secure in the long term.[72]

Yet the ranchers who had petitioned to be excluded from grazing district organization did not fully understand why the Department of the Interior was forcing them into a grazing district. Still reluctant to accept federal administration, they felt that there was "no reason in the world why the government should force the stockmen using these 12,000,000 acres of desert land to accept federal regulation." There was "no doubt" the "best possible use" was being made of the land under the current arrangement. They thought the land was worthless, "practically desert; only the fringe of which where there is water, may be considered good grazing land," and once again argued that the "bulk of it is absolutely useless for any purpose other than mining—and little of it can be designated mineral land." With the backing of Senator George Malone, ranchers argued that once the federal government charged them for the use of "these desert acres," they would be forced out of business. They countered that the government was "receiving more in the form of income taxes; the state and the counties involved are receiving greater revenue, and more badly needed beef is being raised, than could possibly accrue to these varied interests under any form of control the government could devise." Why, they wondered, make them organize into a grazing district?[73]

Marion Clawson, a bespectacled Nevadan who had earned his doctorate in economics at Harvard University, became Krug's new director of the BLM in 1948 and provided these Great Basin ranchers with an answer. Clawson was deeply interested in making public lands administration more efficient. He worked to seamlessly merge the Grazing Service and GLO and make the BLM a thorough manager of public lands. In addition, he was a proponent of multiple use, which he maintained was written into the Taylor Grazing Act itself because it situated public lands grazing alongside hunting and fishing. As the demands of public lands users changed with the nation's shifting economic and social conditions, the BLM, according to Clawson, was obligated to respond. That meant that those outside the Taylor Grazing Act could no longer remain so. Clawson believed "the responsibility to place the public domain suitable for grazing purposes under administration" was consummated with this effort and only once the last grazing district was organized would this responsibility be fulfilled. He warned the ranchers, as had his superiors, that the areas not included in the final grazing district would be subject to Section 15 leases, a situation none of them wanted. In 1950, the BLM announced a public hearing in Tonopah to set the Battle Mountain District grazing allotment boundaries. Ranchers continued to hold out hope that despite the government's "upper hand in [the] matter of forcing stockmen to form a grazing district," they would still gain a reprieve. They hoped grazing administrators would "recognize the barrenness of [the] bulk of the land it is proposed to organize into the new district, and will make proper allowances for this fact."[74]

In early 1951, after considering the concerns of central Nevada's ranchers, the BLM announced the formation of the sixth grazing district in the state and the last one with the federal grazing system. This "sudden announcement" came as a surprise to ranchers; they had thought that "at least an additional meeting would be held before any final action was taken." But their cooperation was not necessary. In a desperate attempt to stave off organization and fee implementation indefinitely, they petitioned Nevada governor Charles Russell to make an appeal to Krug's replacement, the new secretary of the interior, Oscar Chapman. Citing greater wool and beef demand and potential economic upset to a valuable state industry, Russell protested the district's establishment "against the wishes of the great majority of the stockmen involved."[75]

Ranchers in the last grazing district wondered what the BLM could possibly gain from managing the area at a financial loss. But Secretary Chapman, who had dealt with ranchers across the West during Harold Ickes's tenure, believed that in forcing the organization of this district he was "taking the right action in order to secure more efficient and economic use of grazing lands and preserve lands from overgrazing." Yet the economic value of the central Great Basin was not really a deciding factor in bringing the last of the public rangeland under federal administration. The grazing fees collected in that area would be pennies on balance with the revenue collected in other grazing districts. In fact, when the Grazing

Marion Clawson, circa 1950. Photograph courtesy of the Public Lands Foundation Archive.

Service organized the districts in Nevada, of the more than 300,000 cattle in the state, Nye County contained only 18,500, and of the more than 800,000 sheep in the state, it contained only 31,000. The central part of the state had once had significant cattle and sheep production during the early 1920s, but by the mid-1930s, livestock numbers had plummeted to half of their peak. In addition, BLM director Marion Clawson ranked Nevada last among public rangeland states in cattle and sixth to last in sheep. Those numbers amounted to the Nevada livestock industry contributing a little over 1 percent to the national cattle industry and 3 percent to the national sheep industry.[76]

The BLM was not concerned about the revenue from the sixth grazing district or about the area potentially costing more to administer than the government would receive in fees. Overgrazing was not an issue either. The Central Nevada Stockmen's Association, the area's most recent group created to stave off grazing district organization and federal control, stated that ranchers "had made every effort to conserve the range they use" and that there had been no instances of range abuse or overgrazing.[77] The impetus for the BLM to bring the area around Tonopah under federal administration came predominantly from the desire of the federal government to oversee the nation's public lands in order to make their economic production more efficient as a whole through the central administration of range management.

But beyond Clawson's desire to place all range under federal control, the other motivation behind the organization of the sixth grazing district in Nevada was the security required to protect the newly established nuclear testing program and the potential danger it posed to ranchers in the area. In late 1950, the Atomic Energy Commission (AEC) announced its intent to establish a permanent presence in central Nevada at Frenchman Flat in Nye County, considered by the government, nuclear scientists, and the military to be the most isolated and favorable site for a continental nuclear test site. The new Nevada Proving Ground was enclosed within the Las Vegas and Tonopah Bombing and Gunnery Ranges. All the areas to the north and east, spanning Tickaboo, Kawich, and Emigrant Valleys; Yucca, Frenchman, and Cactus Flats; Pahute Mesa; and as far as Ralston, Big Smoky, Monitor, Stone Cabin, and Little Fish Lake Valleys, were considered too dangerous for civilians to occupy during military activities. Since its establishment in the early 1940s, the U.S. Air Force had required that ranchers and prospectors stay out of the area when it conducted bombing missions.[78]

Operating predominantly in Frenchman Flat, but with potential hazard to ranchers in adjacent valleys including Hot Creek, Railroad, Coal, Garden, White River, and Pahranagat Valleys, the AEC published notices of dangerous operations being conducted in the area. Both the air force and the AEC were concerned about trespassers and announced publicly that their safety could not be guaranteed. "Every possible effort," the AEC announced, "is being made to clear all persons and all livestock from the area." The BLM's insistence on the sixth grazing district served the AEC's desire to clear the testing range. Ranchers in central Nevada strongly objected to what they believed was "arbitrary action on the part of the Department of Interior," but BLM director Marion Clawson responded that the ranchers' opposition had no significance. This was certainly true in the face of nuclear testing. Still, nearly two hundred ranchers continued to protest until Secretary of the Interior Oscar Chapman refused their requests.[79]

Meanwhile, the AEC began to remove ranchers' livestock and any miners who lingered on what had now become AEC property. Officially, only one unnamed rancher from Las Cruces, New Mexico, held a grazing permit on the range, and the AEC relocated his livestock to the northeast. The organization suspected that several miners were working mining claims

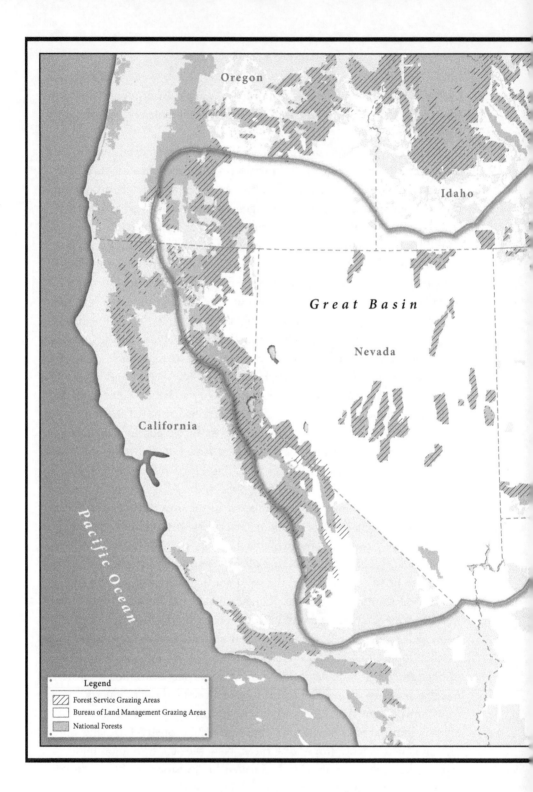

Oregon

Idaho

Great Basin

Nevada

California

Pacific Ocean

Legend
Forest Service Grazing Areas
Bureau of Land Management Grazing Areas
National Forests

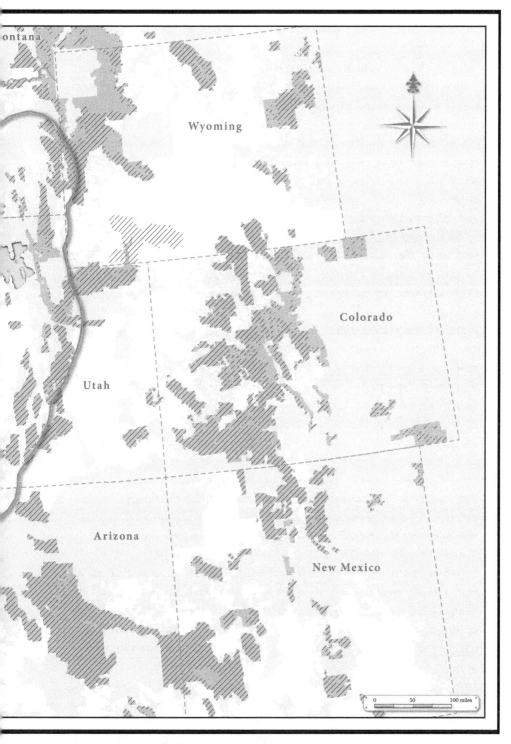

The Great Basin delineating the areas where the Bureau of Land Management
and the Forest Service permit public lands grazing. Map by Gerry Krieg.
Copyright © 2015 by the University of Oklahoma Press

"illegally" in the mountain ranges surrounding Frenchman Flat and advised civilians of the dangers when entering the new test site. The military continued to warn ranchers to stay off the bombing range during any military or AEC scheduled operations, while the AEC's test preparations rapidly moved forward. By January 1951, with the official announcement of the new continental test site, the AEC conducted patrols and restricted the air space above the range, including ranchers who had taken to using small airplanes to locate stray cattle in the area, to ensure that absolute security and secrecy protected the tests.[80]

By the end of May, the AEC had conducted the first round of atomic tests at its Nevada Proving Ground, completed a series in the Marshall Islands at the Pacific Proving Ground, and was preparing for another series in Nevada that fall. Evidence of the correlation between organizing the last grazing district and the start of the nation's nuclear testing program appeared in one of the regional newspapers. Though the issue was not important enough to warrant headlines on the front page, two articles appeared side by side on the first page of the second section, which covered matters of regional importance. Next to the article entitled "Chapman Turns Down Plea to Delay Grazing District" ran the telling title "More Atomic Tests Planned." In the first article, Secretary of the Interior Chapman declared that "all factors were considered," but that the "orderly and systematic use of the range" was of greater importance and benefit. In the adjacent column, Captain Caroll L. Tyler, head of the Los Alamos Scientific Laboratory's Santa Fe operations, the group responsible for the tests in Nevada, declared, "We are proceeding to permantize [sic] and will conduct future tests there [at the Nevada Test Site] and may be required to advance the nuclear weapons program."[81]

While atomic bombs detonated across the desert playa at Frenchman Flat, the last grazing district elected its first officials in October and the Sharps filled out their grazing applications. The BLM organized the last grazing district at the same time the nation's nascent continental nuclear testing program began. In the same moment that the entire Great Basin became devoted to the ranching economy, the mushroom cloud also became a prominent fixture on the region's range. Solidifying the presence of the livestock industry on public lands through the Taylor Grazing Act was of great benefit during the Great Depression, when preventing the collapse of the industry proved crucial, and during the two World Wars, when increased livestock production was essential to support the war effort. The act in essence softened the wasteland status of the Great Basin and legitimized the presence of public lands ranchers.[82]

But the Taylor Grazing Act was only a single law designed to serve a single constituency on public lands. It legalized and regulated what ranchers in the Great Basin and the greater American West had been doing for decades on the remaining public lands and ensured them a legitimate place. However, it was not an instrument that purported to govern the entirety of these lands. It left room for mining, wildlife management, and other possible activities. Though grazing might have ranked as the highest use in the mid-1930s, determining the best use of public lands was a dynamic process. During Marion Clawson's tenure as the second BLM director, grazing had already become "perhaps the lowest use in the scale of values on public lands." This did not mean that grazing would "produce the least income" or that it would be "restricted to a small area," but that other public lands uses were "probably superior to grazing in the general social interest and must take precedent over grazing." J. Russell Penny, a Harvard University–trained range conservationist, and the other authors of a 1953 article published in Richard T. Ely's *Land Economics*, agreed that "rarely, if ever, is any part of the public lands within grazing districts used solely for grazing by livestock." They argued that "generally multiple uses do not conflict appreciably," but when they did, "the most beneficial use or uses" would take priority. As much as possible, though, Clawson and his agency worked to "balance one use against another" in order to achieve "the most desirable combination of uses in a multiple-use area." This was not quite the same version of the Forest Service's vision of multiple use, but it was close enough for Clawson to argue that multiple use now governed public lands.[83]

As the twentieth century progressed, these other endeavors often took precedence over ranchers' access to public rangeland. Conforming to the changing demands made of public lands proved difficult for those who depended on a consistent and stable system of access to range resources. To the Sharps, after five decades of managing the range themselves, adapting to the varying environmental conditions and making their own improvements to sustain their operations, it was hard to see how the BLM could be of any help at all. Used to negotiating risks such as herd depletions from disease, harsh winters, range fires, and drought, they now had to grapple with the fact that their use of public lands was merely one of the many potentially good uses of the Great Basin.[84]

TWO

A Backyard Workshop

A decade before the first atomic bomb detonated above the cold desert, the Second World War had prompted the federal government to begin reordering its priorities on public lands. But the establishment of military activities in the region proved highly problematic and far riskier than grazing. The remaining public lands in the Great Basin, despite their organization into grazing districts and their potential attractiveness to would-be homesteaders, turned out to be perfect for hazardous military training and testing. In early 1940, the Department of the Interior reported to the War Department that the entire region in western Utah and central Nevada consisted of unallocated and unreserved public lands that were more than 90 percent unpopulated. Officers with the Army Air Corps survey group were impressed by the area's "utter desolation and emptiness." Politicians in the region eagerly embraced the opportunity to increase populations, improve the economy, and structurally transform the area by encouraging the growth of vibrant urban centers.[1]

Initially, two sites in the Great Basin competed for the chance to be designated a bombing range to train pilots and test weapons. The proposed Wendover Bombing Range, comprising 5,800 square miles of dry lakebed near the town of Wendover in western Utah, allowed pilots to practice bomb drops under a variety of conditions without severe restrictions. Most Utahans hoped that the bombing range, only one hundred miles from Hill Field, just north of Salt Lake City, would make their major military base "more valuable, giving added assurance of its permanence and full development as an important unit of the nation's air defense system." Similarly, the majority of Nevadans hoped for the same results for the suggested Tonopah Bombing Range, a 5,400-square-mile expanse of public domain near Tonopah. The state's congressional delegation promoted the selection of the site in Nye County based on its "economic and natural advantages." Representative James G. Scrugham and Senators Pat McCarran, Key Pittman, and Berkeley Bunker outlined multiple valuable assets of the site: the area was centrally located and in the "most sparsely populated" part of the country; there was plenty of space for base construction; it had a good airport that was already being used by the military; the federal government managed the land and it was "not usable for any other purpose"; it posed no hazard to private property; and, most importantly, there was no local opposition. These same politicians had helped push the Taylor Grazing Act through Congress only six years before, and the area they discussed had not yet been organized into a grazing district.[2]

Residents in Nye County were deeply disappointed when the military initially preferred to establish the bombing range in Utah rather than in their state. Nevertheless, Nevada continued to lobby the Department of War for a bombing range, which county officials hoped would pump important dollars into the local economy. This income, they believed, would stimulate growth of Tonopah and facilitate the tourism industry in the area, which had begun with improvements to the transcontinental Highway 6 that ran right through the center of town. Considering that Tonopah had only 2,449 residents, and only 3,562 resided in Nye County as a whole, any influx of population and business would bring with it important tax dollars. The state's efforts paid off. The military quickly determined that a second bombing range at Tonopah would allow for advanced training for pilots and gunners coming from the Las Vegas Army Air Field, slated for operation in early 1941. Instead of one bombing range in the Great Basin, the military got two before the nation even entered the war.[3]

Despite popular political portrayal of these areas in the Great Basin as empty landscapes, ranchers did graze there and some had permits. Although the Grazing Service considered the permits temporary, pending final adjudication of the grazing range, they were nonetheless critical to ranching families' livelihood. Establishment of these bombing ranges required removal of livestock operations on several million acres of public lands in western Utah and central Nevada to protect the more secretive aspects of weapons development and to ensure ranchers' safety. At the very least, the military sought restriction of ranchers' access to roads that traversed the bombing ranges and connected various grazing allotments. Unlike the political delegations from Utah and Nevada, those who ran cattle and sheep in the area were less eager to support establishment of these bombing ranges. In the case of Wendover, seventy-five ranchers in Utah petitioned the Grazing Service to reduce its size to protect their winter grazing rights.[4]

The commander of the Army Air Corps complained bitterly to the Salt Lake City Chamber of Commerce about these ranchers' opposition, stating that the original size of the Wendover range, critical to military operations, was "materially reduced due to concerted action of sheep grazers through the Grazing Service of the Department of the Interior," and that this was causing serious delay in the use of the range for pilot training. In addition, many of those with grazing rights also had private holdings, particularly water rights, within the proposed bombing range, and the Department of the Interior required the Department of War to acquire this property before the range could become fully operational. This further delayed the start of operations at the Wendover Bombing Range. The Salt Lake City Chamber of Commerce and the military petitioned Utah's congressional delegation to pressure the Department of the Interior and the Grazing Service to cooperate with the military to get the public lands withdrawal approved and the Wendover range up and running. Representative James W. Robinson, recently appointed as chair of the House Public Lands Committee, assured the Department of War and the anxious citizens of Utah that he would do everything in his power to resolve the dispute. However, Robinson acknowledged that the seventy-five stockmen impeding the development of Wendover "had grazed their sheep there for many years" and required serious consideration.[5]

On behalf of the ranchers, James A. Hooper, secretary of the Utah Wool Growers Association, argued that the withdrawal of these lands for the bombing range constituted "a definite hardship on the stockmen who have continuously used said areas or who may have been transferred to such areas by the Grazing Service." Hooper advocated that the ranchers affected be granted licenses somewhere else as compensation. However, this was easier to accomplish on paper than in practice. It was nearly impossible for the Grazing Service to reduce other ranchers' livestock numbers and reorganize existing range use in the area to accommodate a greater number of users in a smaller territory, even on a temporary basis. Grazing ranges reflected historic use of particular areas of public lands by specific ranchers. More importantly, they were contingent on ranchers' ownership of site-specific water rights, a type of property right that could not be abrogated without lengthy procedures. Hooper urged Utahans to protest the withdrawal of land for a bombing range, arguing that the measure of its importance as grazing range was not in its resident population, but in the numbers of livestock it supported. No one in Utah, however, wanted to be seen as unsupportive of the war effort.[6]

Establishing the Dugway Proving Ground, an additional site near Wendover proposed in 1941 by the army's Chemical Warfare Service to test chemical and biological weapons, proved only somewhat easier. The military and Grazing Service stated that restricting the area for army operations would have "only a negligible effect on grazing operations." Only a small number of livestock had grazed the dry reaches of the southern Great Salt Lake Desert. The Grazing Service assured these ranchers that their livestock could be temporarily absorbed into other grazing districts for the duration of the war, though this did not really matter for so few animals. By March 1942, the military activated the Wendover and Dugway ranges, and within a year, the economic windfall that construction of the two bases brought Tooele County overshadowed any hardship suffered by a few individuals. Congress amended the Taylor Grazing Act that July to require the payment of compensation to ranchers for their lost or decreased grazing permits, and because the withdrawal of this land was not considered permanent, many ranchers chose to lease it to the military. The isolation of the bombing ranges made Wendover the perfect choice to train the B-29 crews designated to drop the first atomic bomb on Japan, and Dugway the ideal location to test incendiary and chemical weapons designed to win the war.[7]

In Nevada, the isolated central Great Basin offered a similarly remote setting, especially the area around Tonopah. The creation of the Tonopah Bombing Range was an important economic asset to Nevada and, as in Utah, its designation affected ranchers in the area. Former Nevada senator Key Pittman lobbied President Roosevelt about the matter before the senator's death. Representative James Scrugham and Senators Pat McCarran and Berkeley Bunker, Pittman's successor after his unexpected passing, assured the military in late 1940 that the bombing range project in their state would not be held up and sent notice to ranchers that "satisfactory adjustments" to their grazing rights would be made. McCarran in particular looked to use the Great Basin's wealth of public lands to facilitate economic development in his state using federal dollars, and the rapidly expanding defense industry provided ample opportunity. Besides facilitating development of the Tonopah Bombing Range and the related growth of that community, the senator also secured construction of the nation's largest magnesium plant at a site just east of Las Vegas. McCarran deemed the economic boon the defense industry brought to Nevada essential to the growth of the state. Despite his previous efforts to support ranchers' access to public grazing range, he expected them to move over and make room for the military.[8]

Ranchers in Nevada, like those in Utah, resisted the restrictions that resulted from the presence of the military. Several petitioned the federal government to exclude their grazing areas from the Tonopah Bombing Range boundaries, but the Department of War needed the space. Eleven ranchers gave up portions of their grazing range to make room. In addition, six other mining claimants faced condemnation procedures that terminated their mining patents. Many of these individuals held out hope that they could reach a cooperative agreement with the military that would allow shared use of the range, but the Department of War considered the intersection of bombs and civilians too dangerous. In the interest of national defense, a pressing matter after December 7, 1941, suspension of a handful of grazing rights and denial of a few water rights seemed a small sacrifice. Almost immediately, the Department of the Interior began proceedings to condemn mining claims and suspend grazing rights within the proposed range. In early 1942, the military activated the Tonopah Bombing Range, much sooner than ranchers expected and sooner than even the army anticipated.[9]

Nevertheless, some ranchers' cattle continued to graze the area and some miners did not relinquish their claims. In late 1942, Nevada senator Pat McCarran and the Committee on Public Lands and Surveys held a public hearing in Tonopah to assess the persistent problem of those who refused to vacate their properties and grazing ranges encompassed within the Tonopah Bombing Range. At the hearing, William Fallini, a local rancher, testified that although his family held no patented land inside the bombing range, their primary winter grazing area was inside its boundaries. In addition, the northern boundary of the bombing range ran right through Cedar Pipeline, one of their major water improvements, at the south end of Reveille Valley.[10]

The Fallini family had lived in the Tonopah area for decades before the advent of World War II. Giovanni Battista Fallini, an immigrant from the

Twin Springs Ranch, circa 1951. Photograph courtesy of Helen Fallini, Nye County History Project, and Nye County History (https://nyecountyhistory.com/).

Swiss-Italian borderland, had homesteaded 150 acres at Eden Creek and established corresponding water rights there and at Crystal Spring in the Kawich Range to the west. The elder Fallini had arrived in Nevada in the 1870s, working odd jobs in the boomtowns of Eureka and Tybo. By 1900, he had moved south to Reveille, a mining district established in 1866 that had a productive mill operation, where he ran a small grocery store and built a stone house at Eden Creek. He took any extra work he could get and used the funds to buy cows and calves, building his herd one animal at a time.[11]

In the 1930s, Giovanni's sons, William, Raymond, and Joseph (Joe), moved the family's ranching operations from Eden Creek north to Twin Springs, at the center of the Fallinis' livestock range, in order to better oversee their herds. The Fallinis purchased property near Warm Springs held by Herman Reischke, a prospector from the Reveille Range and owner of the Last Chance mine, and a substantial portion of the United Cattle and Packing Company's spread in southern Railroad Valley. As owners of one of the larger ranching operations in the area, the Fallinis controlled a number of water rights. In addition to Eden Creek and Twin Springs, they had rights at major springs and in underground sources in the southern end of Railroad Valley, and in the Reveille, Penoyer (Sand Springs), Kawich, Stone Cabin, and Hot Creek Valleys. The family ran several thousand head of cattle, driving them on the ground to the shipping facilities in Tonopah until the advent of truck hauling in the late 1930s made delivering herds faster.[12]

The Fallinis cultivated a garden and fruit trees and canned much of the produce for use during the winter. They corned and jerked some of the beef they raised for their own use and went to Tonopah twice a year to get other foodstuffs such as flour, sugar, coffee, and dried fruit, which they ordered through the mail. Their ranch, like others in the region, operated on a seasonal schedule. The calving began in the late winter and early spring. In July they rounded up their cattle herds and separated out those destined for sale and shipping and grazed the remaining animals the rest of the summer on ranges in the higher elevations. They weaned the calves in the fall and turned the herds out onto the winter range until the calving began again the following year. Every member of the family helped out with the ranch chores, but they also hired local Western Shoshones for seasonal work such as roundups and branding. Several of these individuals worked for the Fallinis for decades. Winters were tough if the weather was particularly cold—feed could run short, forcing them to buy expensive supplemental hay, and water sources often froze—hence the importance of the family's access to Cedar Pipeline and the southern grazing range.[13]

Although Senator McCarran was sympathetic to their difficulty at the hearings, he reminded William Fallini and the other ranchers present that the bombing range was a boon to the community and that "the people of this section wanted the bombing range put in." All the Fallinis could hope for was that the army would let them continue running their herds on the public rangeland contained within the bombing range and would merely confine their access to the animals during certain specifically designated times.[14]

Combined use of these public lands by ranchers and the military was possible, but difficult to implement and subject to the discretion of military commanders. The Fallinis expressed willingness to continue their livestock operations on the bombing range at their own risk and without miles of fencing and a dramatic increase in costly manpower; their cattle would simply continue to forage in the area until they met a natural barrier such as Pahute Mesa. The military seemed unwilling to facilitate Fallini's request.

Cattle branding at Twin Springs, circa 1940. A kneeling Ray Fallini marks the calf's ear while Joe Fallini sits atop the horse. Photograph courtesy of Helen Fallini, Nye County History Project, and Nye County History (https://nyecountyhistory.com/).

Disheartened by the outcome of the hearings, Fallini quipped that the "Indians" in Nevada had starved and drily stated, "I guess we will too."[15]

Ranchers who lost their range access and personal property hoped that the withdrawal of public lands for military use would end with the war's conclusion in 1945. The original withdrawal orders had only been for five years, and residents who held grazing rights or mining claims or both on the range were eager to resume their normal operations.[16] But in 1946, the Department of War filed suit in federal court to continue its use of the bombing ranges in the Great Basin to test captured experimental weapons in Utah and Nevada.[17] After a brief period of deactivation, in 1948 the Tonopah Bombing Range and the Las Vegas Army Air Field consolidated and the newly created air force established a permanent pilot training program headquartered on the northern edge of Sin City.[18]

By that point, the Atomic Energy Commission (AEC), the agency responsible for overseeing the nation's new weapons technology, was quietly pursuing the establishment of a test site within the United States. Nuclear testing in the Pacific Islands had become an expensive proposition and was too slow to be effective for small tests. Because of the radioactive fallout issue, the North Carolina coastline, the AEC's top site in the Southeast,

seemed a better choice until further investigation revealed the only unin-
habited areas consisted of "dunes or marshes," features not conducive to
conducting tests. In contrast, several sites in the American West, especially
the Southwest, proved more attractive, considering the region's aridity and
low population density. In New Mexico, Nevada, and Utah, in particular,
vast stretches of undeveloped desert were already devoted to military weapons testing at White Sands, Tonopah, and Dugway. In its explorations of
these areas, the AEC noted that ranchers in proximity to these ranges had
signed lease agreements turning their private property, water, and grazing
rights over to the military for five years during the war, and many had
signed additional agreements lasting through 1951. Bringing the testing process closer to Los Alamos in New Mexico and key military bases there and
in the Great Basin most certainly would facilitate the testing process.[19]

Not everyone, however, was convinced that a continental nuclear test
site was a viable idea. David Lilienthal, the AEC chairman, agreed that
"the ease of access to a continental site would allow greater flexibility in the
preparation for and conduct of these tests and would facilitate the participation of scientific and technical people." However, in his estimation and
that of many others, the cost savings were offset by the potential expenditures required to maintain appropriate "safety and security measures that
would be required at a continental site." In addition, Lilienthal believed a
continental site would likely create domestic and international relations
problems, presumably because of radioactive fallout. But, according to the
chairman, "the magnitude of these problems could in time change, as in the
event of a national emergency." His words proved prophetic in 1949, when
the Soviet Union tested its first atomic weapon.[20]

In the interest of pursuing a continental nuclear test site, the Armed
Forces Special Weapons Project (AFSWP), the newly organized Department of Defense's counterpart to the AEC's Military Liaison Committee,
delineated the parameters such a test site would have to meet in a report
that synthesized all the known environmental factors that influenced the
testing process, including humidity, wind, likelihood of precipitation, and
population. The investigation narrowed the possibilities for a continental
nuclear test site to two regions: the nation's Southeast and Southwest. The
report stated that "for purposes of planning and logistics . . . the arid southwest is more favorable as a location for atomic test sites than the humid
southeast" because of the greater percentage of days with favorable climatic
and meteorological conditions and the low population density. AFSWP

investigators were especially concerned that "a certain amount of radioactive waste [would] fall out of the atmosphere to the eastward of continental sites following atomic tests." But, after studying the fallout figures from the Pacific Proving Ground, they determined that it would probably "not harm the population, the economy nor the industry of the nation." In examining their choices, the AFSWP and AEC realized that the site in Nevada was perfect. The very conditions that had rendered it a wasteland were the region's greatest assets.[21]

In August 1950, a dozen of the leaders in the nation's nuclear testing program, including Enrico Fermi, Alvin Graves, and Edward Teller, met at Los Alamos to discuss the primary obstacle to establishing a continental test site: the radiological hazards associated with a testing location. These men used a calculation called the hazard factor, their mathematical description of the environmental impact of testing on a region using an equation that added the ratios of the population at a given distance from the detonation to the square of that distance, to illustrate the potential radioactive fallout problem in any given area around ground zero. In their experience, other effects of detonations such as the force of the blast and thermal radiation, or heat, had "much smaller danger radii," so that reduced test sizes, smaller than those conducted in the Marshall Islands, were relatively safe beyond twenty miles. Given that the prevailing winds in the Great Basin and desert Southwest in general blew predominantly west to east and south to north, and that Salt Lake City, the largest urban area in the Great Basin, was only one hundred miles west of Dugway, the scientists felt the Utah site was not feasible. The Tonopah range in Nevada, however, proved three times more favorable than even the New Mexico site at White Sands, where Los Alamos had conducted the Trinity test.[22]

The Los Alamos scientists planned for meteorologists to determine the days on which tests would take place, in appropriate weather and wind conditions, avoiding rain at all costs, a condition they presumed to be "the only cause of fall-out." They believed smaller particles would remain suspended long enough to shed radioactivity that exceeded the supposed safe level. Los Alamos lab personnel had collected much meteorological and fallout-monitoring data during the Pacific tests over the past five years, and this database allowed Fermi, Graves, Teller, and the others to determine a conservative threshold for a rapidly administered integrated radiation dose. They set this amount at half the maximum recorded at the Trinity site and determined that this was the level of exposure from which the human body could recover. The scientists believed their estimation was reasonable considering that despite the Trinity site's higher hazard factor and the unfavorable meteorological conditions in which Los Alamos had conducted the test, the detonation had resulted in "only unimportant radiological effects." In general, they assumed that radiation exposures up to that point were safe.[23]

Beyond the hazard factor, scientists considered the proximity of the population in Nevada to the testing site from another angle. The distance between Las Vegas, the closest city to the potential ground zero at Frenchman Flat, and Tonopah, at the northern boundary of the Tonopah Bombing Range, was roughly two hundred miles. Given that north-south boundary, the scientists determined that the territory within a radius of one hundred miles from ground zero to the east of that boundary was the primary area in which radioactive fallout would occur. They believed fallout there could be safely managed if tests ranged between twenty-five and fifty kilotons of TNT equivalent. This is what the scientists designated the "sector of safety." In their understanding, very little human activity went on in this area since the military had already designated it a bombing range and had curtailed civilian access. From Frenchman Flat, one hundred miles stretched almost to Tonopah and Highway 6 in the north and to Saint George to the east. This sector of safety included the tiny communities of Carp, Elgin, Rachel, Alamo, Hiko, Caliente, Adaven, and Moapa. In a clear rationalization that revealed their astounding ignorance of the region and its environment, these scientists and the AEC in general believed that the population density in these places was so small that monitoring them would require "very little logistic effort."[24]

Between one hundred and three hundred miles from Frenchman Flat, an area covering roughly forty thousand square miles and including Tonopah and Saint George, Enrico Fermi estimated that there was only a 1 percent probability that 1 percent of the population in that area would receive a radiation dose similar to the higher levels registered after the Trinity test. Assuming a population density of one person per square mile in this second area, Fermi determined that four hundred persons could be exposed at this level. This, according to Fermi, was "the size of the risk" of conducting a continental nuclear testing program. In the opinion of the other scientists present at the meeting, none of whom knew the Sharps, the Fallinis, or any of the other families who comprised the size of the risk, Fermi's estimate that there was a 1 percent chance that four hundred people would be exposed was too high. Most felt it was "not a probability that anyone will be killed, or even hurt."[25]

By the end of the year, the AEC, Los Alamos, and the Department of Defense considered the Nevada site "so superior to any other under consideration as to render it unnecessary to go into detail on those other sites." Given the necessity of nuclear weapons testing to the nation's national security, and embracing the assumption that the area was still a wasteland and an empty quarter, the AEC deemed testing in Nevada essential and began to set up operations.[26]

Between late January and mid-February, the AEC detonated five small experimental devices on Frenchman Flat as part of Operation Ranger, dubbed the "Hurry-Up Operation" by the Los Alamos Test Activities Branch because of its short-order organization. The largest detonation amounted to twenty-two kilotons, well under the AEC's self-imposed twenty-five-kiloton limit, and all of the tests were dropped from airplanes and exploded above the ground to reduce the size of the fallout cloud.[27] The organization worked to ensure that the proper officials in Nevada's government were on board with the testing program and that planned tests would not produce any significant radioactive fallout beyond the immediate vicinity of ground zero and well within the planned hundred-mile geographic limit.[28]

During Operation Ranger, Governor Charles Russell's office in Carson City received only one complaint; a rattled Las Vegas resident wrote that the shock wave nearly knocked the roof off her house. She felt that the AEC could not ensure her safety "in a locality when atomic tests, even of a limited nature, are made from day to day, especially in a mountainous area like the country around Las Vegas, where the fissionable material could be drawn together between the mountain ranges, or sucked into a valley, such as the one in which Las Vegas is placed." The governor's office wrote the AEC that the receipt of only this one complaint was evidence that the general public had "accepted your testing program in the spirit in which they should." The governor was confident the hazards associated with continental nuclear testing would be no threat to the state's residents, believing the AEC would work diligently to minimize any risks.[29]

The AEC and Los Alamos scientists, after several years of successfully conducting nuclear tests, believed they understood the effects of radiation exposure and could minimize its impact on the test site and the surrounding population. After the Ranger series, the AEC announced that routine checks on radiation levels in areas surrounding the test site indicated they were insufficient to injure human or animal life. Dr. Thomas Shipman, head of the AEC's nascent radiological safety group at Los Alamos, which was created to monitor radioactive fallout, even sent an amused letter to a doctor in California who said he had two patients claiming they received burns from radioactive fallout while hiking in the mountains near Sacramento. He wrote, "The case was rather too absurd to dignify with further attention," as fallout would have had to circumnavigate the earth before reaching them. "I am afraid," Dr. Shipman stated, "that Mrs. Gipson and her son-in-law either got a garden variety case of sunburn or possibly made the acquaintance of some poison oak or some similarly irritating plant."[30]

Some civilians expressed their concern to reporters; one Las Vegas housewife complained, "What are they trying to do—make us click like Geiger counters?" A spokesperson from the Federal Civil Defense Administration (FCDA) grimly stated that if the effects of the tests were not spent in the sixty miles between Frenchman Flat and Las Vegas, "then God help us all." Nevertheless, in general the AEC was satisfied with the lack of public concern and the general support of an all-out testing program. Carroll L. Tyler, the AEC's Santa Fe Operations Office manager, wrote Governor Russell that his "matter-of-fact acceptance of the tests, and a similar approach on the part of officials and of news media in southern Nevada, helped develop a calm and sane public attitude which contributed materially to the conduct of our operations." Tyler remarked that "to those of us who know the West, such a reaction was not surprising, but it was nonetheless remarkable." Pleased with these circumstances, Tyler indicated that the AEC was moving to "permantize [sic]" the test site since its physical and "human relations" environment were highly conducive to the testing program. Russell responded, "I believe that you can rest assured that in your future program, the same co-operation will be forthcoming in every respect from the State of Nevada."[31]

The ease of the smaller tests allowed Los Alamos scientists to fine-tune their understanding of acceptable meteorological conditions, desirable detonation elevations, and permissible radioactive doses. Rather than work more conservatively, Los Alamos scientists saw how to operate closer to their self-imposed environmental limits. In late 1951, the AEC conducted a second series of tests, in back-to-back operations called Buster-Jangle, on Yucca Flat, about fifteen miles from Frenchman Flat, a sufficient distance farther north to prevent any recurring structural damage in Las Vegas. This operation consisted of four small detonations, one explosion slightly bigger

Operation Buster-Jangle, Easy shot, detonated November 5, 1951, on Yucca Flat. Photograph courtesy of the National Nuclear Security Administration/Nevada Field Office.

than the Trinity test, an underground detonation, and a larger thirty-one-kiloton test conducted on November 5, designated Easy. Besides testing the improved design initially developed in the Ranger series, the second set of continental tests allowed the military to expose troops and equipment to the potential conditions of nuclear warfare. It also used rats, dogs, and sheep to collect data on injuries resulting from blast and radiation exposure. The AEC reminded Nevada residents that radiation-monitoring teams would canvass the local area and warned the general public that slight increases in radiation levels could occur in other sections of the country. As with Operation Ranger, the AEC expected radioactive particles to concentrate within a hundred-mile radius from ground zero and announced that these tests were harmless.[32]

Scientific data showed that the first series of continental tests had produced no radiological safety problems of any consequence; likewise, the second series in 1951, which involved troops entering the ground zero area after detonation, had caused no hazard to their or the public's health. In fact, the first year of testing in Nevada was so successful and the national imperative to develop nuclear weapons in order to remain internationally dominant so strong, the AEC worried less about the effects radioactive fallout had on the environment and instead began pushing the boundaries of the testing process. The agency began creating and promoting a large-scale testing operation on its new test site. Nevada state officials were delighted; the potential job opportunities this afforded Las Vegas and other communities promised to be an economic windfall to the state. The AEC's "backyard workshop" was now fully operational.[33]

THREE

Mushroom Cloud on the Range

In the late fall of 1951, eight months after Operation Ranger, the first continental nuclear testing series, and just before the second series, Operation Buster-Jangle, was set to begin, Floyd Lamb, a rancher in Alamo and a commissioner for Lincoln County, wrote a troubled letter to the Atomic Energy Commission. Something unusual and unsettling had prompted Lamb to write the AEC, something that was not within the ordinary framework of his life at the ranch. In this letter, Lamb expressed concern about the "danger which might exist for his livestock on his range adjacent to the Nevada Test Site." Lamb had water rights and permits to graze the summer range very near Frenchman Flat and ground zero. Floyd and his uncle Carleton Lamb, operating as the Willard Cattle Company, had subleased some of their grazing range to the Department of War during World War II, but their cattle still ranged across the unfenced boundary into Kawich, Tickaboo, and Emigrant Valleys. This was very close to where the AEC had detonated five atomic tests.[1]

In his letter, Lamb was not specific as to the oddities he had witnessed in his cattle, but he wrote with purpose and authority to the distant AEC office, appealing to people he had never met. A staff assistant for testing operations responded to Lamb's inquiry, placing a phone call to the ranch that was answered by Lamb's wife, Eleanor Schofield Lamb. After asking for her husband, the staff assistant assured Eleanor that the AEC "recognized the interests of people in areas adjacent to the test site," and that it was "taking every possible precaution for their welfare and for the protection of their property." The AEC official informed the Lambs that "if their cattle were on their own range and did not stray onto the test site area there should be no particular cause for concern in connection with the planned operations."[2] The staff assistant thought the Lambs were concerned about their cattle accidentally straying onto the test site during an active detonation. In reality, Floyd Lamb was asking if there was anything they should know about exposure to radioactive fallout.

This interaction was the first of many in which the vocabulary and procedures the AEC used to frame and control the nuclear testing program obscured the realities of the testing process in areas around the test site. Where the AEC desired to calm public concern and continue the testing program unopposed, ranchers such as Floyd Lamb wanted to gather information that would help them maintain the stability of their herds. This meant that that officials and ranchers often talked past and regularly misunderstood each other, which led to frustrated and tense situations. It also meant that through the course of its interactions with local residents, it became easier for the AEC to dismiss ranchers as uneducated nonexperts and ignore their concerns. This obfuscated the damage created in the bodies of local residents and their animals, and in the environment of the Great Basin, from exposure to the radioactive fallout produced by nuclear tests. In addition, testing itself functioned within an increasingly complex and self-perpetuating bureaucratic framework, which created no incentive to listen.

The success of the nuclear testing program in 1951 allowed AEC officials and Los Alamos scientists, who believed they had established a workable system in which to conduct tests, to relax. Detonating fission devices in the Great Basin had produced no negative effects or public outcry during the first series. This gave the AEC a sense of security that would be difficult to shake in later years, despite some scientists' acknowledgment at the time that they still had much to learn regarding the effects of radiation exposure. When evidence of exposure to radioactive fallout did manifest in livestock surrounding the test site, it caused a rift between the scientific experts and ranchers in the region as to what exactly the effects of radioactive fallout were and who had the authority to determine those effects. Whereas the nation's nuclear scientists believed they understood, as much as anyone could, radiation and its impacts on biological life, ranchers believed their experience managing the bodies of their animals and the range on which they lived made them the experts in the field.

Despite efforts to remove livestock from the Tonopah Bombing Range, cattle still grazed in the region, particularly on the area's northern and eastern edges. Testing and military training had actually proceeded without clarification of the status of property within the site, including mining claims and water improvements used to support cattle herds. These issues continued to linger past World War II and into the Cold War. The AEC had wanted to construct a 125-mile barbed wire fence along the boundary of the Nevada Proving Ground, but the expense proved prohibitive. Local newspapers during the 1940s had warned residents to stay off the bombing range during periods of intense activity, but cattle often strayed onto the area and had to be collected regularly. In 1945, for example, "G.I. Cowboys" helped a rancher near Tonopah collect his errant animals off the bombing range in late winter and early spring.[3] Military officials and the AEC expressed concern for ranchers' welfare and constantly urged them to steer clear of the testing area unless otherwise notified, regardless of the movements of their livestock. Nevertheless, the air force in particular annually accommodated roundups of local herds rather than eradicating any animals that appeared on the wrong side of the bombing range.

These warnings stemmed from concern over protecting individuals from blast effects, the most immediate and damaging aspect of detonations, stemming from the shock wave and heat that emanated from ground zero. Damage from blast effects had surfaced during Operation Ranger, prompting a rash of damage claims filed against the AEC. In early 1951, residents of the southern Great Basin, particularly in Las Vegas, filed 200 claims for broken windows and damaged roofs, which totaled $15,000 once paid. These claims required verification by AEC officials, although initially the agency probably paid on more claims than actual blast effects justified. As the AEC became more practiced at verifying this kind of damage, the number of claims paid decreased. After the Buster-Jangle test series later that year, the AEC paid on only 118 claims, refusing to compensate Las Vegans for every marred roof or cracked window.[4]

Reports of damage from exposure to radioactive fallout were another matter entirely for the AEC officials. After the Ranger series, the Eastman Kodak film and camera company detected small amounts of radiation after a snowfall in upstate New York had threatened to ruin its stored product. An important supplier of film badges used by testing personnel to determine individual radiation exposure levels—by measuring the degree to which the film darkened upon development—Kodak felt its concern

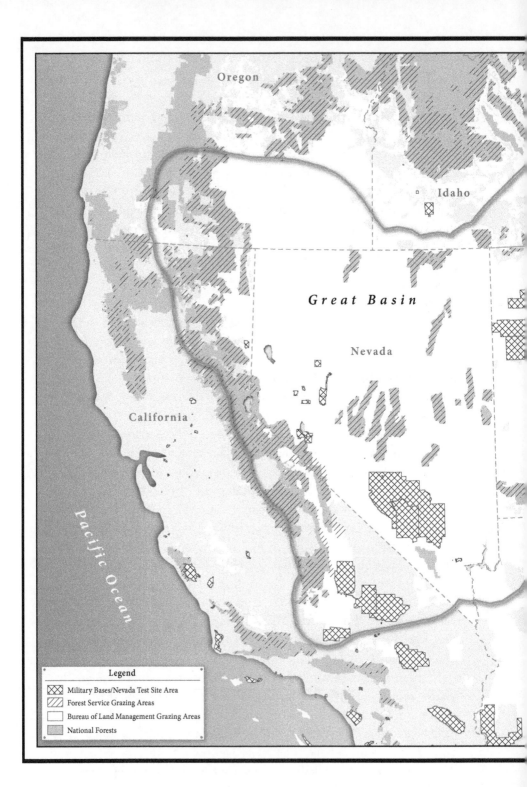

Legend

Military Bases/Nevada Test Site Area

Forest Service Grazing Areas

Bureau of Land Management Grazing Areas

National Forests

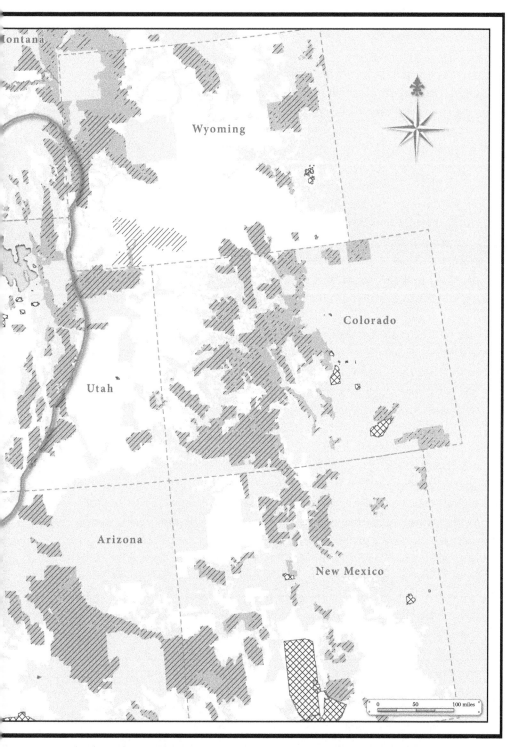

The Great Basin delineating the location of the Nevada Test Site and the region's major military installations, overlaid by the areas in which grazing is permitted. Map by Gerry Krieg. *Copyright © 2015 by the University of Oklahoma Press*

warranted a response. Shields Warren, a contractor with the AEC's Division of Biology and Medicine, the agency responsible for early monitoring programs, determined that "because of the Film Industry problem, as well as other potential problems," it was necessary to "have data on fall-out from the [radioactive] cloud at least to the Atlantic Ocean."[5] This effort was an important step in understanding radioactive fallout patterns.

But the AEC was not overconcerned about exposure to radioactive fallout since the radiation levels were very, very low compared to the area around ground zero. After the Buster-Jangle series, a monitoring station in southern California at Downey recorded increases in radiation over background readings in late November 1951. Radiation monitors working from a lab set up at the North American Aviation facility used Geiger counters to chart readings ranging from less than one milliroentgen per hour taken from a dog's foot to ten milliroentgens per hour on sampled vegetation. This level of radiation exposure—not to be confused with radiation dose, which is measured in terms of the amount of radiation actually absorbed— approached the limit of safe exposure, but only if the exposure had continued at the same level over the course of an entire day. An exposure of this type would cause no measurable damage at all.[6]

Nevertheless, popular articles on the effects of radiation exposure during 1951 portrayed its impact as a little less safe. Stories in national newspapers led with titles such as "Corn Freaks Grow from Atomic Tests" and warned against massive internal bleeding, highlighting the frightening nature of extreme exposure effects. The "Corn Freaks" article reported that in a California Institute of Technology study, corn seeds were subjected to gamma radiation in the Marshall Islands during the 1946 tests and then planted and harvested through five generations; they produced corn that was "dwarfed, twisted, frail or partly sterile." In another study at the University of California at Los Angeles, researchers determined that exposure to X-rays caused ferritin, a protein that transports iron throughout mammal bodies, to be released in larger-than-normal quantities, causing internal hemorrhaging. This information, coupled with movies such as *The Beast from 20,000 Fathoms* and other atomic horror stories, meant that no amount of radiation exposure sounded safe.[7]

These articles and fictional stories called to mind images of misshapen and twisted bodies swollen with blood, monsters from the deep created by nuclear testing, and alluded to the horrifying potential problems that could occur if humans or the environment were exposed to certain levels of radiation. But in reality, from the AEC's perspective, nothing they discussed compared to the damage the atomic bombs had produced at Hiroshima and Nagasaki. Neither were these popular depictions of radiation and radioactive fallout a realistic reflection of the actual levels that had been produced by the tests in the Pacific only a few years prior.[8]

Radioactive fallout may not have been the major concern of the staff assistant who called the Lamb family, but it was probably the most important issue for Floyd Lamb. A third-generation Mormon cattle rancher, Lamb closely watched his herds and grazing ranges for potential trouble. His grandfather, William S. Lamb, had arrived in Pahranagat Valley in the 1910s and with his son William (Billy) Granger Lamb had homesteaded 164 acres just south of the small settlement at Alamo. The two filed for water rights in the adjacent Coyote Spring and Tickaboo Valleys in addition to Pahranagat Valley to control their proximate grazing range. Billy rode for other livestock outfits in the area, worked as a janitor at the Alamo schools for a while, and served as a general handyman for the town. In 1939, he died trying to save a young boy on a runaway horse at a rodeo in Fallon.[9]

Billy Lamb's untimely death left his oldest son, Floyd, in charge of the ranching operations, with brothers Ralph, Sheldon, Darwin, and Larry and his uncle Carleton Lamb to help. In the late 1930s, the hard-working rancher married Eleanor Schofield, whose grandfather, William Jonah Schofield, in the 1910s had owned the Buckhorn Ranch at Crystal Springs at the north end of the valley near Hiko. Like the Lambs, the Schofields owned water rights in Pahranagat Valley and Hiko Springs and in nearby Tickaboo Valley. Floyd's first outfit, the Buckhorn Land and Cattle Company, had been compiled in part from the old Schofield holdings, and he ran his livestock south and west of Alamo across the Pahranagat Range into Tickaboo and Emigrant Valleys. He also formed the Willard Cattle Company with his Uncle Carleton and expanded their water rights into Kawich Valley, where several other ranchers also had their herds. At the same time, the nation's military carved the Tonopah Bombing Range out of the region, and a good portion of where the Lambs grazed their cattle intersected with where the Army Air Corps dropped their bombs. A lease agreement allowed the military to use the grazing range for bombing activities during and after the war, but this did not necessarily prevent the Lambs' cattle herds from grazing the same areas. Less than a decade later, however, the Lambs' livestock foraged in places adjacent to the Nevada Test Site, the primary area for nuclear testing.[10]

Floyd Lamb, circa 1957. Photograph courtesy of the
Nevada State Archives.

The impetus for Floyd Lamb's letter came from something he saw in his
cattle that was well out of the ordinary. Floyd and Eleanor Lamb lacked the
scientific vocabulary to discuss the phenomenon they witnessed after the
Ranger series, but asking the AEC about the "danger" of testing hinted at
their line of thinking. In her phone call with the staff assistant, Eleanor "expressed anxiety regarding the welfare of their livestock" and a deeper concern about the welfare of her husband, who spent most of his time looking
after their cattle scattered across the grazing range. Missing her point, the
AEC official assured her that "prior to an operation the entire major area
is checked by air, and operations are delayed if necessary to assure that any
persons in hazardous areas are removed."[11] Eleanor relayed the exchange to

her husband, and the dissonance of her conversation must have resonated with him.

The assurances provided by the AEC did not address Floyd Lamb's concerns, and a few months later, in January 1952, he notified the Las Vegas Field Office that almost forty of his cattle had developed skin sores, particularly on their legs, and were losing hair. Carroll L. Tyler, the manager of the AEC's Santa Fe Operations Office and the test director for the Buster-Jangle series, sent a brief but urgent and unsettling teletypewriter exchange message to John C. Burgher, director of the AEC's Division of Biology and Medicine, about the matter: "Floyd Lamb a rancher at Alamo Nevada has reported to field manager that about forty cattle have developed skin sores particularly on legs and are losing hair. He attributes to test activities. Claim has not been made but we feel investigation should be made to determine if tests [sic] activities are responsible. Has been advised to have private veterinary look at cattle. Request advice of your office as to possibility that these symptoms result from radioactive poisoning, and any suggestions as to course investigation should follow."[12]

This singular complaint by Floyd Lamb had a powerful ripple effect on continental nuclear testing. At least at this point, AEC officials were willing to entertain the idea that Lamb's cattle might have been affected by exposure to radioactive fallout. This was the first complaint to the AEC that had elicited this type of response. But the agency's willingness to consider radiation exposure disappeared rather quickly in the face of other, more pressing issues.

In early 1952, Los Alamos and the AEC were concerned largely with the production of another test series, Operation Tumbler-Snapper, scheduled for April and May of that year. In the first two test series, detonations Fox, Dog, and Easy had each yielded twenty-two kilotons of TNT equivalent and had distributed a small but measurable amount of radioactive fallout in the direction of Las Vegas and Mount Charleston, the tallest peak in the southern Great Basin located in the Spring Mountains a few miles northwest of the city. Readings indicated that radiation levels were well below the AEC's permissible limits.[13]

The exposure standards that the AEC adopted for the new test series in the region around the test site, known as offsite, were basically the same as those of the earlier test series, even to the extent that the AEC reactivated the same monitoring system it had previously used. This system included monitoring the area from ground zero, on either Frenchman or Yucca Flats, outward to a radius of one hundred miles, the so-called sector of safety. Monitors also canvassed the area in a radius between one hundred and two hundred miles outward from ground zero. Radiation monitoring in this second area was not as imperative since most tests were air-dropped and exploded at least one thousand feet above the ground, generating only a small amount of radioactive particulate matter. Even less of a concern was the area beyond a radius of two hundred miles from ground zero. In the case of tower, surface, or underground detonations—these types of detonations had occurred in the Buster-Jangle series in 1951—monitoring in these zones was more important because more radioactive particulate matter occurred than in tests that had been dropped from planes. The AEC scheduled monitors to canvass these zones but did not expect any hazardous levels of fallout in the next test series since it consisted of airdrops and tower detonations only.[14]

One of the persistent problems that plagued the AEC was the public's "unfounded fear [of damage to humans, animals, crops, and property] from radiation exposure and testing." AEC officials constantly worried that unreasonable public paranoia about radioactive fallout "might hinder testing, even threaten use of the Nevada Proving Ground." To assuage this fear, the commission arranged for hundreds of civilians, congressional representatives, civil defense personnel, and the press to witness one of the Tumbler-Snapper tests conducted in late April 1952 and see for themselves the awesome, but safely controlled and contained, detonation.[15]

Observers and troops were present at the largest of the Tumbler-Snapper series, a test named Charlie that yielded thirty-one kilotons. Gene Sherman, a *Los Angeles Times* reporter, poetically described the event as "blazing atomic fury" in which the "searing sun, unshielded by clouds, was blacked out at the instant of the unworldly incandescence of the initial flash." So massive was Charlie's mushroom cloud, it was seen by observers on Mount Wilson near Los Angeles. By the end of Operation Tumbler-Snapper, the AEC reported that in total, the three continental test series had provided scientists with valuable information about atomic processes and had immeasurably facilitated the military's development of tactical nuclear weapons for the nation's defense, demonstrating the enormous value of the continental test site's desert laboratory. Civil defense officials were not quite as content with the outcome of Tumbler-Snapper. They had hoped that the eyewitness accounts of this latest series would shock a lethargic public out of its complacency about the very real possibility of nuclear war. Instead, by mid-1952, Americans generally viewed the tests as a curiosity and tourist attraction; seeing a nuclear explosion actually carried more appeal than the pools and casinos of Las Vegas.[16] Nevertheless, the AEC's attempt at a public relations campaign had worked—most Americans were not particularly worried about exposure to radioactive fallout.

The AEC's Division of Biology and Medicine, however, was anxious after Tumbler-Snapper. Several possible problems with radioactive fallout and the local population offsite had surfaced as the operation ended. These concerns appeared in a draft press release that was not publicly distributed, in which the agency indicated that the May 7 test, the twelve-kiloton Easy shot, had elicited reports from people who owned instruments capable of measuring radioactivity of "radioactive dust blowing through or falling in their home communities following tests." The release stated that "the movement and extent of this radioactive material" was "followed with utmost care by members of the test organization and other Atomic Energy Commission representatives." The draft press release indicated that radioactive material had been distributed thousands of miles away from the test site and had caused problems at the Eastman Kodak plant in Rochester, New York, again exposing thousands of dollars worth of film. But, it declared, the amounts were "so small as to be of no consequence" in terms of human and environmental health and safety. The author of the press release was fundamentally worried that the public did not understand the extent to which the AEC worked to ensure that no harm came to "humans, crops, livestock, wildlife, or water supplies."[17] Although this press release addressed the issue of radioactive fallout directly, such a candid statement from the AEC was not the way the commission usually alleviated public concern, especially in offsite areas.

The AEC walked a fine line in terms of public relations with locals. In the middle of Operation Tumbler-Snapper, the eleven residents of nearby Groom Mine, only twenty miles northeast of ground zero at Yucca Flat, had been evacuated just before the Easy test. Twenty-five miles farther in the same direction, Thomas N. White, the radiation monitor assigned to the area, estimated radioactive fallout at Lincoln Mine, a small community of about forty-five near Tempiute, close to the gamma radiation exposure limit soon after the detonation.[18] This fifth test in the Tumbler-Snapper series produced the greatest radioactive fallout readings since the Trinity test in 1945. The eleven-kiloton Fox test on May 20 also produced heavy fallout to the northeast, again affecting Groom Mine and the Tempiute area. Daniel Sheahan, a resident of Groom Mine, expressed grave concern at the AEC's indication that "the mine area would receive contamination after each shot and operations would probably be interrupted weekly." He said officials had led him to believe in the "strong possibility that heavy contamination in the mine area would result from test operations," and that "there would be a build-up of contamination which might necessitate evacuation for a considerable period of time."[19]

Residents in Salt Lake City also expressed their concern about the May tests. The Easy shot had spread radioactive "dust" throughout the Salt Lake area, though AEC monitors notified state health commissioner George A. Spendlove that the levels were not dangerous and that by the following day they had diminished significantly. However, one uneasy individual, who seemed affiliated with the scientific community, wrote the editor of the Salt Lake City paper that the AEC should have been more careful about the turbulent meteorological conditions that spread radioactive fallout over the city. The author of the piece stated, "We don't know enough about radioactivity to be absolutely sure of its dangers." An AEC official from the New York Operations Office penned a response that defended the concept of safe doses of radiation, arguing that the AEC allowed its personnel to receive a threshold dose of up to thirty times the radiation level received by Salt Lake City residents after the May 7 test. In addition, the official pointed to the network of monitors deployed throughout the country who were tracking and measuring radioactive fall-out and emphatically insisted that "at no time has radioactivity from AEC test operations been harmful to any human, animal, or crop." The AEC official thanked the Utah press for "the level-headed way" it approached the "very difficult task of explaining in understandable terms just what the levels of radioactivity resulting from the May shot meant to persons residing in the area."[20]

Unlike ephemeral Geiger counter readings and reports of dust floating around, the bodies of Floyd Lamb's cattle still posed a significant and substantial problem. For the first six months of 1952, the Lamb family followed the AEC's suggestion and sought the opinion of a private veterinarian in the area, probably from Las Vegas. At the same time, the organization's officials distributed Lamb's allegation that his cattle had radiation poisoning throughout the agency's hierarchy and requested advice on how to proceed with an investigation.[21]

In early August, Thomas L. Shipman, now head of the Los Alamos Health Division, which oversaw the radiation safety group, wrote Alvin C. Graves, leader of the lab's Test Division, that "we are certainly not in a position to state categorically that these cattle might not have been damaged in this way [by exposure to radiation], and I feel that the implications of the situation are serious enough to warrant prompt and full-scale investigation." Shipman recommended that Los Alamos send a group to Alamo, Nevada, that included the lab's veterinarians, Robert E. Thompsett and Harry O. Whipple, who were familiar with the cattle that had been exposed to radioactive fallout at Trinity; radiation monitor Thomas N. White; and two others familiar with the area to investigate the situation. Shipman warned, "If these cattle actually were injured by radiation, I see little choice except to tell the truth and shame the devil."[22]

The investigation into the problems with Lamb's cattle proceeded in several parts. In addition to the local veterinarian examining the animals, the AEC arranged for Edward E. Maas, the Department of Agriculture's lead field veterinarian in Nevada, to ascertain whether the damage to the livestock was from an "ordinary disease." This seemed unlikely; ongoing concerns about the transmission of foot-and-mouth disease from Canada and Mexico had made ranchers, livestock officials, and veterinarians hyper-diligent about watching their animals for blisters and other signs of irritated skin. In addition, Nevada State Department of Agriculture veterinary inspector John L. O'Harra and a practicing veterinarian from Ely had just publicly reported on a separate investigation into the deaths of fourteen cattle one hundred miles north of Alamo at Lund, and they had no real answers as to the cause. It was left then to a radiation expert, who proceeded to verify that the "distribution and intensity" of radioactivity could have caused the damage. This seemed more probable because there had been some fallout in several different locations, including where the Lamb cattle had grazed, during each of the test series to date.[23]

But Shipman and other AEC officials indicated that they were confused as to when exactly the cattle had demonstrated signs of damage. Floyd Lamb had told officials that his herd had developed significant sores on their legs and were losing their hair between the first and second test series, but after the third test series, Lamb reported that his cattle experienced a "loss of hair and ulcerations down the middle of [their] backs."[24] Shipman acknowledged that Lamb's descriptions sounded "suspiciously like the descriptions of the Trinity cattle" but did not know whether these were separate or related incidents or even the same herds.[25]

At this point, the AEC's tentative position on the matter was that Floyd Lamb had asked its help in determining the cause of his cattle's problems because his herds grazed close to Frenchman and Yucca Flats and because "on several occasions during the spring 1952 test series, range cattle were found inside Yucca Basin," since there were no fences between the grazing range and the testing range. There was, the agency privately acknowledged, the "possibility that some of Mr. Lamb's cattle through proximity to our firing area were exposed to some degree of residual radiation."[26]

The investigation of Lamb's cattle progressed throughout late summer 1952. On August 13, upon inspecting Lamb's cattle that were grazing in Kawich Valley, Thompsett, Whipple, and White reported that of the 150 animals observed, at least half exhibited sores on their backs. These lesions, similar to those seen in the Trinity cattle though of less intensity, looked very much like radiation burns. Since radioactive fallout from the recent tests in June had been measured in Kawich Valley, it was likely that radiation exposure had caused at least some of the damage to Floyd Lamb's cattle. However, no one could verify for certain that the cattle had been in Kawich Valley at the time of the test, and this explained only the current sores on the cattle's backs, not the earlier sores on their legs.[27]

Regardless of which tests had caused what damage, the investigators were fairly sure that the animals had not suffered any permanent damage. Their primary objective focused on whether their value at market would be impaired by fears of contamination. Floyd Lamb was particularly concerned about this point, and Los Alamos, despite believing that little additional information would be gained from further study of Lamb's cattle, supported a continued investigation to "convince the present owner and possible purchasers that careful studies were made of the cattle injured," presumably in order to settle the public's fear of radiation damage.[28]

To get control of the issue, the AEC issued a public announcement in Las Vegas about the entire incident in late August. The commission's statement indicated that Lamb's cattle had indeed been exposed to a small amount of "radioactive dust" and reminded the general public that the potential for radiation exposure within the test site and in areas surrounding it was great. The AEC said it had repeatedly made this danger known, especially to ranchers. The statement assured readers that no human exposure would occur unless members of the public disregarded the official warnings and wandered into prohibited areas.[29] This was an unprecedented public acknowledgment from the AEC and the first and only time the agency admitted that animal life, human or otherwise, had been exposed to radioactive fallout offsite.

Presumably, this gave the Lamb family a basis on which to file a claim for compensation. With reference to a potential filing from the rancher, the AEC's assistant general counsel advised the Las Vegas Office that the family could make a damage claim only if a more detailed investigation was made of their cattle. These results would then be compared to studies of the Trinity cattle, with adjustment made for the proportional amount of radioactive fallout measured in Kawich Valley versus that at White Sands. The general counsel also indicated that Lamb would have to verify that his cattle were in the area and that he could legally graze there.[30] This was the bureaucratic loophole in Lamb's claim.

The general counsel's office requested that the Department of Defense, via the air force, provide information on Floyd Lamb and the Willard Cattle Company's grazing rights. The lease agreement the air force delivered to the AEC's general counsel proved problematic for Lamb. Last signed in 1946 and amended twice in 1951 to extend the lease period to 1967, the agreement indicated that Floyd and Carleton Lamb, doing business as the Willard Cattle Company, had leased "all real property, water rights, whether acquired by vested right or appropriation, all interest . . . in grazing rights within the Tonopah Air Force Base and the Las Vegas Air Force Base" to the federal government for its "unrestricted use" as a "bombing and aerial gunnery range" for one dollar per year. The lease agreement indicated that the air force would have concurrent use with the Lambs but that before entering their grazing ranges, the Lambs needed to obtain written permission from the air force. In the agreement, the Lambs assumed all risks of concurrent use of the range and waived any claims of damage against the government.[31]

Even though Floyd Lamb's cattle were probably in the area and they were most likely damaged by exposure to radioactive fallout, none of that would result in payment on an actual claim if the lease agreement between the Lambs and the air force also extended to the AEC, which had leased its land from the military. From Lamb's perspective, the AEC was liable for the financial loss he anticipated taking on the cattle upon their sale, since the agency's investigation had found, and officials had publicly announced, that radioactivity from the atomic tests had damaged the animals—more even than the originally reported forty head.

In anticipation of this, Lamb notified the AEC that he intended to sell his herd in the fall and waited for its response acknowledging this deadline. But according to the agency, Lamb had to submit a formal claim form for damages before any compensation could be given him. Seth R. Wood-ruff, manager of the Las Vegas Field Office, emphasized to Carroll L. Tyler, manager of the lab's Santa Fe Office, that the AEC had given Lamb no assurances that it would pay him at all for the "alleged loss in value of his cattle." In his reply, Tyler corrected Woodruff, saying that since the cattle had suffered only temporary damage, which affected their skin and not the quality of their meat or reproductive capabilities, there was no need to delay Lamb's sale of the cattle. He directed Woodruff to remind the rancher of the temporary nature of the damages his cattle had suffered and to let the rancher make up his own mind about when to sell his cattle.[32]

The letter Woodruff sent to Lamb emphasized the temporary nature of the radiation damage, especially relative to the more severe consequences suffered by the cattle exposed during the Trinity test in 1945. Floyd Lamb responded in a hand-delivered letter to the Las Vegas Field Office, re-minding the AEC that it had admitted that his cattle had been harmed by "atomic radiation" and verifying that his normal buyer, his wife's brother William U. Schofield, Jr., who owned a dairy in Alamo, would purchase the cattle only at half the going market price. Lamb wrote, "I feel that I have suffered severe financial loss, therefore, I request a settlement should be made just as soon as possible." For Lamb, temporary or not, the radia-tion damage to his animals caused his regular buyers, Schofield and two other locals, J. A. Hail and Wilson Stewart, to significantly drop their pur-chase price, costing him more than $3,000.[33]

Lamb asked that the AEC conduct a joint investigation with him to de-termine the exact number of cattle under consideration in his claim. Joe B. Sanders, Woodruff's assistant in the Las Vegas Field Office, recommended to Tyler that they conduct the roundup with the Lambs. This would save Los Alamos and the AEC "considerable expense," since the agency would have to undertake a roundup anyway for an investigation. At this point, for all intents and purposes, Sanders at least assumed that Floyd Lamb's claim, as a rancher and a Lincoln County commissioner, was valid, in its form as a letter and in its request. Sanders asked Los Alamos for instructions as to how to proceed.[34]

Within the AEC, however, Lamb's letter caused a flurry of preventive ac-tion. The general counsel appraised the U.S. attorney in Reno, Miles Pike, that Floyd Lamb "may initiate an action in the United States District Court for damages resulting from the exposure of some of his cattle to radiation." They advised Pike that the AEC was authorized to settle claims of $1,000 or less administratively, but that amounts in excess of that limit would have to be filed with a federal district court. Since Lamb's claim indicated damages in excess of $3,000, the matter would "have to be pursued in the courts if more than twenty head of cattle [were] affected."[35]

The general counsel advised the Las Vegas Field Office of this situation. Woodruff wrote Floyd Lamb that "although I have no doubt that you intended by your letter to present a claim to the Commission for damages alleged to have been sustained by you as a result of the exposure of certain of your cattle to atomic radiation, your letter cannot be regarded by the Commission as constituting a claim for damages because it does not set out the specific amount of money claimed by you." He acknowledged that Lamb probably would not be able to determine the exact amount until the joint roundup Lamb had recommended was undertaken. Woodruff advised Lamb that the AEC was authorized to settle only claims of $1,000 or less and that claims in excess of that amount had to be filed in a federal court. He also sent the appropriate forms to Lamb if the rancher decided to file for an amount less than the $3,000 mentioned in his letter. Woodruff suggested Lamb hire an attorney to assist him in this matter.[36]

The roundup of Floyd Lamb's cattle occurred on October 25, 1952, more than one year after Lamb's initial letter of concern had reached the AEC. The consensus of the AEC officials involved was that of the four hundred animals on the grazing range in and around Kawich Valley, "it appeared that 102 head of cattle had been affected by radiation fallout resulting from atomic tests." Of that number, Floyd Lamb owned 53, his uncle and partner, Carleton Lamb, owned 30, and 19 were owned by another member of the Lamb family. The inspectors organized the animals into four categories of damage: three-quarters of the cattle displayed scarring from radiation burns as white hair, a dozen had minor skin lesions, about ten exhibited denuded areas, and one cow, "an unsightly animal," had severe skin injuries.[37] This provided the Lambs with definitive analysis of their cattle's injuries.

But where the investigators differentiated the less impacted animals from the more severely injured ones, the buyers of the cattle did not. At half the market price normally commanded by Lamb cattle, all three claims amounted to over $1,000 each. But Floyd Lamb and the others were reluctant to hire an attorney because of the time and expense involved. The Lambs, eager for an informal solution, indicated their preference to drop their claims to the thousand-dollar limit and settle them administratively with the AEC. They asked those officials present at the roundup, Los

Alamos veterinarians Robert E. Thompsett and Harry O. Whipple, personnel officer W. B. Creamer, and a federal attorney, what their course of action should be in finalizing their claim.[38] In Great Basin ranching communities, this was a reasonable expectation. These kinds of negotiations were common practice and often saved everyone time and money.

But the Lambs were looking for an informal settlement to a formal problem couched within a highly bureaucratic system. The AEC's general counsel deemed the lower claims inequitable because "three claimants would be claiming identical sums for damage to a different number of cattle in each instance." Additionally, a lower claim meant that "Floyd Lamb would be willing to settle for $1,000.00 without the advice of counsel" despite his assertion that his damages were larger than that amount. To the AEC's lawyers, this was an improper and unacceptable manner in which to file a claim. Finally, the Lambs had yet to actually prove monetary damage and locate liability with the AEC, something that could happen only with the sale of the cattle. In addition, the release of liability in the Lambs' lease with the federal government for damage to their property on the bombing range could exempt the government in the case of radioactive fallout caused by atomic testing. Federal attorney Miles N. Pike urged Lamb to engage an attorney and file a lawsuit in federal court.[39]

In January 1953, the Lambs retained a lawyer and "expressed the intention of suing the Government . . . for radiation injury to their cattle." Floyd Lamb had understood the subtext of his multiple and frustrating conversations with AEC officials; if he wanted to be successful in making a claim for damages, he had to participate in the formalized claims process as determined by the commission and the nation's legal structure. However, entering into a formal suit against the federal government did not ensure Floyd Lamb's success; rather, it hurt his chances of a successful claim because it made the process more about liability than about acknowledging the source of the damage. But the AEC would make no informal settlement, no matter how much such a measure might simplify the process and produce a fairer result for the claimants. In addition, the agency also had the problem of setting precedent. Up to that point, the only claims of damage had been to structural property from the detonations' blast effects.[40]

Once Floyd Lamb agreed to participate in the formalized claim system, the standard legal process prohibited any informal exchange of information and assistance. The AEC refused to share the information contained in Robert E. Thompsett's report on the October 25 inspection, which clearly stated that the Lambs had "a very legitimate claim," but did not define the extent or dollar amount. Las Vegas Office field manager Seth R. Woodruff wrote Lamb's attorney that any information regarding the case had to be obtained from the U.S. attorney in Reno. At this point, Floyd Lamb's cattle case began to devolve. The adversarial nature of litigation made it impossible for the claim to remain independent of other issues, especially the release of liability clause in Lamb's lease with the federal government, which the AEC's general counsel hoped to use against Lamb in court. As a result, the Lambs were forced to again seek other avenues of assistance to avoid suing and losing. Fortunately for him, Floyd Lamb was well connected.[41]

Unknown to the AEC until early 1953, Floyd Lamb's claim actually involved Nevada lieutenant governor Clifford A. Jones, a lawyer and businessman from Clark County who owned an interest in the rancher's livestock operation. The rancher and state official sought the assistance of Nevada senator Pat McCarran, who worked to help Lamb receive payment on his claim through passage of a special congressional bill, Senate Bill 3355. Throughout the first part of the year, the AEC frantically worked to oppose passage of the measure in Congress, warning potentially sympathetic senators that Lamb had "neither filed a claim with the Commission" nor appropriately "instituted action in the Federal Court under the Federal Tort Claims Act." The AEC's general counsel made it known that "an undesirable precedent would be established if the Commission approved a bill for special relief where no effort has been made to obtain administrative settlement or to pursue available legal remedies." This forced Lamb back into the very situation he was trying to avoid. Meanwhile, he sold some of his cattle; Francis Taylor of the Warm Springs ranch near Moapa purchased thirty head at the current market price with the provision that "Lamb would have to make them good if anything happened to them."[42]

However, by March 1953 and the start of the new testing series, Operation Upshot-Knothole, Floyd Lamb's claim was no longer a major concern for the AEC. Nor was it the last time Lamb experienced the damaging effects of radioactive fallout. The entire situation became severely complicated. Los Alamos, the AEC, and the military had consistently conflicted over the types of tests conducted, the purpose of testing in general, and the use, in particular, of the continental test site in the Great Basin. The testing process had become packed with experimental procedures, military effects, civil defense projects, troop training, and public outreach. At the same time, these competing interests all lobbied for bigger tests. Scientists and military designers pushed the boundaries of test yields, making them larger and larger—the new norm became more than thirty kilotons for tower tests and around fifty kilotons for detonations dropped by bombers. Even the name of the place changed from "test site" to "proving ground." Los Alamos scientists complained that the emphasis on the military aspects of continental tests threatened to take over the entire purpose of the test site. Rather than a small-scale site in which to conduct essential experiments in preparation for the larger, more developed operations in the Pacific, the Nevada Proving Ground was swiftly becoming necessary in its own right for civil defense effects, troop indoctrination, and, most importantly, weapons development—activities that could not be conducted in the Pacific. As such, Los Alamos scientists and the AEC struggled with the environmental and geographic constraints present at the continental test site, especially when developing the larger, more deadly thermonuclear weapons.[43]

In addition, the AEC was regretting its public admission about the exposure of Floyd Lamb's cattle and growing increasingly careful about the general perception of continental nuclear testing. When the commission's Division of Biology and Medicine requested permission to purchase some of Floyd Lamb's cattle for further examination, both Carroll L. Tyler of Los Alamos's Santa Fe Office and Kenneth E. Fields of the military's AEC office refused because they felt "a serious public relations problem would be unavoidable were we to procure the cattle" during an ongoing investigation.[44]

Tyler was fundamentally concerned that the radiation monitors deployed by Los Alamos's "Rad-safe" program, who canvassed the area measuring fallout between the test site boundaries and offsite communities, were uniform in their response to inquiries about damage from exposure to radioactive fallout. Most of these personnel had been newly assigned to the test site by the Public Health Service and lacked the knowledge gained in the previous series by military monitors. To this end, the AEC planned an entire public education campaign in conjunction with Upshot-Knothole in which it blanketed scientific and medical publications and the national news media with information that demonstrated its command of nuclear testing and reassured the public of its guardianship. The AEC hoped to "help achieve public understanding that continental tests have contributed materially to the total atomic defense position and that they are economical

Carroll Tyler, test manager for the Upshot-Knothole series, talking to reporters at News Nob, March 17, 1953. Photograph courtesy of the National Nuclear Security Administration/Nevada Field Office.

to manpower, time and money, so that the public will accept both the necessity for a continental site and the degree of inconvenience or hazard which may result."[45]

Despite these efforts, the Upshot-Knothole series posed significant problems from the beginning, especially in terms of public relations. Rather than dropping the devices from aircraft, Los Alamos scientists engineered the majority of the tests to detonate on towers, which drafted more radioactive ground particles into the fallout cloud. According to Los Alamos, because of the size of the detonations in this new series there was a real possibility that in the areas within a radius of one hundred and two hundred miles from ground zero, "people living around NPG may receive a greater total dosage than that normally authorized for test personnel." Test planners recommended that the number of radiation monitors be tripled and stationed in populated areas such as Lincoln Mine, Tonopah, and Ely to advise residents when to seek shelter.[46]

To preempt the potential problems posed by Operation Upshot-Knothole, the AEC published a report on continental weapons testing and safety. In the pages of this rare public disclosure, the commission dismissed controversial features of continental testing by making them routine, saying that it was "impossible to confine the effects of the explosions entirely to the proving ground," that radioactive particles "may fall back to earth virtually anywhere within the United States," and that fallout had already "caused a degree of public concern in some communities." But, the agency asserted, experience to date with continental testing indicated that atomic tests could be held at the Nevada site "without serious hazard to persons, animals, crops, property, or industry." The expert use of instruments by radiation monitors and the proper explanation of facts, the AEC argued, were key to dispelling fear; the publication reiterated that "no person has been exposed to a harmful amount of radiation from fallout." The AEC acknowledged that "the manner in which the particles descend through various layers of the atmosphere . . . is not well understood," and that radioactivity produced by an atomic explosion "can present a safety hazard outside the proving ground under certain conditions."[47]

According to reporters, the first detonation in Operation Upshot-Knothole, the Annie shot conducted on March 18, was "the most powerful single shot of its kind ever fired in either real or simulated warfare . . . a shot seen and heard by millions in all parts of the country over television and radio." The Annie test, called Operation Doorstep by the Federal Civil Defense Administration, resulted in the famous series of eight high-speed photographs showing the decimation of a typical American home by a nuclear bomb. Courtesy of the nation's major networks, nearly eight million Americans watched the detonation; it was the first time the public had ever seen an actual test on their television sets.[48]

As the series progressed throughout the remainder of March and into April, AEC press releases indicated that the main fallout clouds in the March and April tests passed northeast over Groom and Lincoln Mines, southeast over the desert between Las Vegas and Mercury, and southwest over Death Valley. They reported that the fallout levels were not high enough to be considered hazardous. Nevertheless, scientists conducting animal surveys noted radioactive contamination in cottontail rabbits, mice, and kangaroo rats that had ingested exposed plants, but they also noted that these amounts were smaller than they had expected. This led one radiation monitor to facetiously suggest that "maybe the animals were too astonished to inhale following the shot." Despite their confidence that all was well, by June, the rabbits had started dying.[49]

The Simon shot, detonated on April 25, created additional problems. At midmorning the fallout cloud was headed southeast toward Mesquite over two major highways, and the AEC ordered vehicles along State Route 91, the old highway into Saint George, and State Route 93 toward Ely to stop for decontamination procedures. Purportedly, very few cars required decontamination washes.[50] However, two trucks in Alamo, an empty cattle truck and a milk truck, registered radiation levels that prompted a monitor to recommend thoroughly washing each truck before reusing it.[51] In addition, the Utah State Highway Department's scale facility on Highway 91 just before Saint George showed readings high enough for the radiation monitor in the area to suggest that the state agency tell truckers coming north on the highway into Saint George to "get their trucks washed inside and out at their earliest convenience." Almost all the vehicles headed north on that route caused "the survey meter to register off-scale."[52]

This was the first time the AEC had publicly recommended decontamination procedures after a continental test.[53] Monitors told the residents of Alamo, Saint George, and the little towns in between that their vehicles had been exposed but there was no danger to their health. The bulk of the agency's expenditures on radiation monitoring, an ever-growing concern as the testing process became more expensive, occurred in conjunction with maintaining exposure levels for personnel and offsite residents below the allowed maximum. Decreasing the maximum exposure level to ensure the public's safety was a logical adjustment to prevent this situation from happening again, but doing so would not only cost the AEC more money, according to Division of Biology and Medicine director John Burgher, it would also "effectively deny continued operation of the NTS."[54] More importantly, however, the Simon test and its aftermath indicated the extent of officials' frustration with the limitations on the size of tests and the agency's pragmatic position on establishing the level of radiation doses relative to minimizing exposure to populations living in the adjacent areas.

From the AEC's perspective, radioactive fallout happened as a routine result of the testing process. It affected offsite populations because of the agency's imperfect understanding of fallout patterns, cloud dispersal, and weather. Therefore, its efforts were better spent minimizing not fallout, but the negative impact fallout had on the public's perception of nuclear testing. This was the agency's hubris. Carroll L. Tyler, the test manager for the series, stated, "It must be recognized that it is impracticable to conduct, with sound economy of effort and money and with maximum utilization of the proving ground toward expeditious forwarding of weapons development, a series of tests, conditioning each shot on weather, atmospheric and technical characteristics which insure no possible radiation or blast hazard to any persons or communities." Tyler argued that the set limit on radiation exposure imposed "a serious and perhaps unrealistic limitation upon an expensive, important, and onerous operation."[55]

After the Simon test, the AEC conducted four more detonations throughout May and early June. Two tests, the airdropped Encore on May 8 and Climax on June 4, yielded twenty-seven and sixty-one kilotons, respectively.[56] The highly publicized and eagerly anticipated Grable experiment, designed to test the viability of an atomic cannon, yielded fifteen kilotons on May 25.[57] But the thirty-two-kiloton tower test on May 19, designated Harry, caused the greatest uproar. Though both were tower tests, the Harry shot was smaller than Simon and should not have produced as much radioactive fallout. But, despite the best meteorological predictions, during the detonation the wind shifted just enough to cause a major fallout pattern east and north of the test site. The Harry test produced the most significant amount of radioactive fallout to that point in the communities surrounding the test site.[58]

This was exactly the situation the AEC had hoped to avoid. As with the Simon test, the organization believed it was more a public relations problem than an actual radiation exposure event. Regional and national newspapers carried stories of "closed" Nevada and Utah towns as residents stayed indoors per the agency's warnings.[59] Several southern Utah residents wrote the editor of the *Salt Lake Tribune* demanding information on the effects of exposure and wanting to know why Saint George residents were warned to stay inside if there was no hazard from radioactive fallout. To make matters worse, Utah representative Douglas R. Stringfellow wrote the AEC that he was "greatly disturbed" over recent reports "concerning the atomic tests being conducted at Yucca Flats in Nevada." "The explosion which occurred on Tuesday, May 19," he wrote, "especially aroused bitterness and anxiety among residents of St. George in southern Utah, who were ordered by the A.E.C. to remain indoors from 9:00 A.M. until after noon because of the danger from radioactive clouds which centered in that area." Stringfellow explained, "I am sympathetic to the need for atomic research but I cannot condone practices or policies which unduly threaten or cause harm to either our civilian populace or our men in uniform."[60]

AEC testing personnel faced sharp criticism from their superiors on the commission for a time for their handling of the events, but the problems produced by the Upshot-Knothole series seemed at an end once the fallout cloud passed.[61] However, despite the efforts of radiation monitors, there were too few of them to check everywhere, especially in the spaces between the major highways. Monitors at Groom and Lincoln Mines routinely evacuated residents, but they could not observe all the effects of exposure to radioactive fallout as they happened. In particular, the Sheahan family at Groom Mine caused Thomas L. Shipman of the Los Alamos Health Division some concern. Shipman stated, "It was probably more good luck than good management that the Groom Mine area itself did not receive a higher dose than it did." Nevertheless, the AEC's Division of Military Applications argued that the commission had not "subjected Groom Mine personnel to any real danger from fallout."[62]

Radiation monitors and the AEC relied on the people injured to come forward and present their cases to the very institution that had perpetrated those effects and whose personnel were not entirely sympathetic to them. This put both the residents in areas adjacent to the test site and the AEC in an untenable situation. Injured persons lacked the scientific and medical language to articulate their symptoms and those of their animals, and AEC personnel, though many were sympathetic, lacked the proper objectivity to judge their cases. The gap between locals suffering injuries and the AEC's ability to adequately investigate their claims became especially apparent after the Harry test when reports of damage from exposure to radioactive fallout dramatically increased.

In the days and months that followed Harry, a flood of accounts claiming damage from exposure to radioactive fallout reached the AEC. Reports of massive sheep deaths arrived around June 2 about animals that had ranged in Lincoln County east of the test site before heading to their summer range in Utah. The dead sheep numbered more than one thousand ewes and two thousand lambs throughout eastern Nevada and western Utah. The herds belonged to Mormon families in Cedar City, including Lillian W. Clark, David Bulloch, Douglas Cory, A. C. Seegmiller, Nelson Webster, T. Randall Adams, the Lambeth brothers, and the Higbees. Most of these individuals were related by blood or marriage to the Mormons in Pahranagat Valley. The *Salt Lake Telegram* called the Santa Fe Operations Office to check on the story, as did other regional newspapers. All the animals exhibited scabs, lesions, and burns similar to those caused by exposure to radioactive fallout, and the injuries could have been present as early as the first test in the series. Within several days, a cadre of veterinarians, along with AEC personnel, quietly examined the animals and began running extensive tests on tissue samples in order to determine whether radioactive fallout had caused the deaths.[63]

On June 14, the story broke nationally when the *NBC Evening News* featured a Utah sheep rancher who stated his herd had been ill since April. The AEC faced a snowballing public relations problem, since "definitive findings" on the sheep deaths would not be available anytime in the near future. To prevent too much public concern and to control the flow of negative information, the agency announced an abeyance in activity at the proving ground for twelve months and planned no public meetings until investigators released their report.[64]

In the meantime, officials proceeded with their investigation of the problem. Paul B. Pearson, director of the Biology Branch of the Division of Biology and Medicine, led the inquiry. Initially, the sheep's skin lesions and the wool they shed in clumps seemed to be produced by beta burns from exposure to radioactive fallout. But by midsummer, AEC personnel had introduced another possible cause. The Nevada Operations Office distributed articles among its staff about a sheep-killing weed, complete with wrenching photos of sick and dead sheep on an abandoned ranch, which detailed the region's severe drought conditions in the early 1950s. These articles insinuated that the sheep, prompted by malnutrition produced by poor range quality, had suffered a fatal reaction after ingesting one or more noxious weeds. John O'Harra, a state veterinary inspector, fueled this line of inquiry by providing a report on the region's abysmal range conditions. In light of this new information, the AEC brought in a second team to examine the sheep, including a plant toxicologist from the Department of Agriculture's Bureau of Animal Industries. The toxicologist reported there was no evidence of any "infectious disease or poisonous plants . . . the skin lesions on the face and back were somewhat similar to those seen following photosensitization, but since black [faced] animals were reported to be similarly affected, this can be ruled out." However, he stated, "the shedding of fleece is quite common in sheep that have been maintained at a low nutritional level." This alluded to the region's ongoing drought and gave AEC officials an alternative to fallout: poor range quality.[65]

The primary weed that AEC investigators thought was involved in the sheep deaths and that signified the poor range quality of the Great Basin was *Halogeton glomeratus*, a variety of Russian thistle pervasive in overgrazed areas of the region since 1935. The Bureau of Land Management was in the midst of waging an ongoing war against the plant, a campaign it had begun in 1950, when drought began to severely disrupt grazing operations. Halogeton was particularly problematic during dry years since hungry livestock often ate abnormal amounts that often proved fatal. Accounts of ranchers watching their entire herds die hours after eating halogeton constantly worried livestock operators in the region. Suppressing the noxious weed and reseeding rangeland to prevent its spread was a critical range management program fully supported by the BLM and ranchers alike throughout the decade.[66]

The bad drought years in the early 1950s made the war on halogeton a losing proposition. In particular, Lincoln, Nye, and White Pine Counties in Nevada suffered from lack of rainfall; even in good years, this area had little water. In 1953, Floyd Lamb reported more than two hundred cattle were dead at midsummer; he gathered his animals off the range as quickly as he could but continued to experience losses despite improving their feed. Other ranchers' cattle suffered a similar fate, and sheep operations did not fare any better. The drought was so bad, Nevada governor Charles Russell got President Dwight D. Eisenhower to declare a state of emergency and provide federal funds to assist ranchers in supplementing their livestock feed to combat the problem.[67] Where radioactive fallout ended and halogeton poisoning began was anyone's guess.

During the investigation of the sheep deaths, the inquiry's leader, Paul B. Pearson, discredited the strongest evidence, presented by veterinarians Robert E. Thompsett and Robert H. Veenstra in their report, which implicated radioactive fallout as the most likely source of the damage. Veenstra felt that the abnormal levels of the isotope iodine-131 (I-131) found in the sheep's thyroid glands were the result of exposure to radioactive fallout. Pearson, however, insisted that Veenstra had falsely correlated these abnormalities with an elevated level of I-131. Experiments at Hanford, Pearson insisted, had shown that sheep could tolerate several times the calculated level of exposure without demonstrating any effects. Thompsett believed that grazing in radioactive brush had caused the facial lesions on the sheep. In contrast, Pearson insisted that beta burns in laboratories had produced lesions that had not healed and that these were inconsistent with the healed lesions exhibited by some of the Utah sheep. But Veenstra and Thompsett continued to insist that radioactive fallout had contributed to the deaths of the sheep and that they were not wrong. By the spring of 1954, many Utah sheep still had unhealed lesions, much of their wool had grown back more like actual hair, and the lambs that had survived the year had not matured to a normal size and were faring poorly.[68]

Pearson's reliance on laboratory experiments to set a baseline of what constituted damage from radioactive fallout and what did not conflated the laboratory with the natural environment. Damage produced by radioactive fallout in the environment could not be replicated in the laboratory because of the complex character of the natural system. But that same complexity made it impossible to separate the damage from radiation exposure from any damage caused by drought conditions and ingestion of halogeton. Because drought and halogeton were present on the Great Basin range, Pearson preferred the other investigators' response, which had focused not on the effects of fallout on the sheep but rather on what ultimately caused the sheep to die. This meant taking into consideration noxious weed consumption and malnutrition because of drought conditions. In August, AEC investigators, under pressure from the commission's leadership to resolve the sheep issue, held a conference on livestock losses in Salt Lake City so that the investigators could present their report to the public. The results discussed reflected this particular path of investigation, which did not directly implicate exposure to radioactive fallout as the cause of the sheep deaths.[69]

After the conference, the ranchers, unhappy with the official report and suspicious of the AEC's treatment of Thompsett and Veenstra's evidence, filed suit in court against the agency. The sheep ranchers believed the AEC blamed them for the deaths of their own animals and had treated them as "mostly uneducated, and untrained, . . . not capable of detecting trouble until the actual deaths of the animals." Unlike the investigation of Floyd Lamb's cattle, the AEC's formal investigation of the sheep fatalities was not actually about whether the damage to the sheep was caused by radioactive fallout. The sheep case instead focused on the expertise of different kinds of witnesses and laboratory-determined effects of exposure to radioactive fallout.[70]

The precedent the AEC set in its investigation of the sheep deaths affected other concurrent sheep, cattle, and horse inquiries in Nevada. Besides the ranchers in Utah, the Stewart family—including Cornell and his brother Daniel, who was the Mormon bishop at Alamo; Daniel's son Cordell (Dell); and their cousins who ran the Stewart Brothers Ranch—had reported their damages. In early June, one of the Stewarts contacted AEC officials about their horses, suffering from lesions and blindness, and cattle with similar symptoms that had manifested within six months of the last test series. In addition, several head of their cattle had died near Papoose Lake, about fifteen miles northeast of Yucca Flat.[71] The investigations into their reports produced results similar to those of the Utah sheep cases. Officials said the Stewarts' cattle demonstrated some damage from exposure but had died from malnutrition due to the same poor range quality that caused the demise of the Utah sheep.[72] The Stewarts were not convinced that their cattle had not been damaged by exposure to radioactive fallout, but further investigation produced the same outcome, and laboratory experiments could not replicate the damage. The AEC believed the problem was related to uncontrolled growth of surface tissue, tick-borne fatal anemia, and low levels of magnesium from either the ingestion of noxious weeds or the presence of bacteria. Another similar investigation of cattle deaths near Mesquite and Littlefield off Highway 91 between Las Vegas and Saint George blamed red water disease.[73]

Surprisingly, the AEC proved more amenable to damage claims for injury to horses. Investigators told the Stewarts that twenty of their Quarter Horses had received beta burns and developed severe lesions, even blindness, from radiation exposure.[74] The ranchers were able to claim their horses for the difference between their current value based on their recent incapacity, and their previous value. Horses that had lesions on their backs and eyes could no longer be ridden, which shorted the Stewarts valuable work animals. Payments for the horses did not cover the cost of replacing a well-trained mount, but the funds did help the Stewarts develop a better relationship with the AEC.[75] Joe Sanders, one of the investigators who had an eye for horses, handled the Stewarts' claim, reluctantly sending most of the damaged animals to "the chicken or dog food factories." He was actually relieved that one little black filly, three other females, and a gray mare were fine in order to prove the point "that radiation does not affect breeding qualities."[76]

At the same time, Floyd Lamb continued to pursue his claim, but the AEC continued to insist he had not yet filed a formal request with its office or a suit in court. Without the proper paperwork and procedures, the AEC could not compensate him or the office risked setting a problematic precedent for future claims. The agency continued to point to his lease with the air force, arguing that the release clause rendered any claim Lamb might have invalid anyway. But Lamb's cattle in Kawich Valley continued to have problems, remaining more than one hundred pounds smaller than their peers. According to Lamb, after the Upshot-Knothole tests, many of his animals died after drinking water near the test site. But as with the Utah sheep investigation and the Stewarts' cattle investigation, the AEC was not able to experimentally reproduce the damage to his cattle. Senate Bill 3355, proposed in early 1953, would have provided Floyd Lamb with compensation for his losses outside of court through congressional action. However, as the bill set a bad precedent for future claims against the AEC, the measure was never passed. In addition, the bill's sponsor, Nevada senator Pat McCarran, died in 1954 and Lieutenant Governor Clifford Jones left office the following year, leaving Lamb without his political connections.[77]

In 1955, when Lamb finally did file the proper claim forms with the AEC at the Las Vegas Field Office, Seth Woodruff brushed it off, saying, "This office is certain the claim is not a valid one and actually doubts that the claimant has experienced any damage." Lamb tried to get other Nevada ranchers, including the Stewarts, to cooperate with him in a lawsuit against the AEC similar to the one the Utah ranchers had organized. He even contacted Nevada senator Alan Bible, Pat McCarran's successor, for assistance, but it was too late. The law did not cover claims more than two years old, and by this time, and taking its cue from the Las Vegas Field Office, the AEC no longer believed Lamb had at any point actually incurred any damages as a result of the exposure of his cattle to radioactive fallout. The agency accused the embittered Lamb of deliberately agitating the local population against the test site and complained that, if not for his dissatisfaction, "the citizens of Lincoln County, including Alamo, as a whole would accept the tests . . . without complaints." Ironically, the residents of Lincoln County, who had grown wary of nuclear testing despite the AEC's assurances, had elected Lamb to the state senate on the strength of his opposition. In 1957, Lamb finally received approval for one compensation claim made on one horse, a three-year-old stallion damaged in 1957, but Lamb was not home when the appraisers came to review and finalize the claim and he was never paid.[78]

The AEC's final solution to the problem of ranchers running livestock adjacent to the test site was to buy up their herds and conduct fallout studies using their own cattle. By 1958, the AEC had joined the livestock business, and its brand appeared on the Great Basin range. Ken Case, a local cowboy who became a radiation monitor, ran the herds across ground zero after detonations for experimental purposes for the next two decades as the famous Atomic Cowboy. By controlling and monitoring the herds, the AEC only confirmed its findings of the past five years. Since 1951 and the beginning of continental nuclear testing, the commission could confidently assert that only a very small number of livestock had been damaged based on the handful of claims paid, and no person had been damaged by exposure to radioactive fallout. To the AEC, there was no intersection, either geographically or intellectually, between ranching and nuclear testing.[79]

But radioactive fallout did affect livestock in the area downwind of ground zero, and the damage the animals suffered mirrored that which was experienced by many people near the test site. As one rancher wrote, "It is my considered opinion that not only livestock but people in this area have suffered from radioactivity." University of Tennessee veterinarian Bernard F. Trum, who worked for the AEC beginning with the 1953 livestock investigations, ominously stated after the incidents surrounding Operation Upshot-Knothole, "We can certainly anticipate a 'chronic radiation' claim sooner or later from people living near the Proving Ground."[80]

And indeed, people living in that part of the Great Basin were concerned. A resident of Tempiute, near Lincoln Mine, reported that on March 26, two days after the Nancy shot in 1953, a "large feverish place began to raise with [a] blister in [the] center" on their nine-year-old daughter's left cheek. The girl's left eye "became bloodshot and swollen." After a week of treatment, the blister dried up, but her eye remained irritated. Similarly, another Tempiute resident, a thirty-six-year-old woman, reported skin and lung irritation and bloodshot eyes during the Annie and Nancy tests. In mid-April, in conjunction with the Badger and Simon tests, her skin again became irritated and the entire left side of her body turned brown except where her bra straps covered her shoulders. Between the Harry and Grable tests, she again felt skin and lung irritation and suffered from blisters. She stated that if she left Tempiute the evening after a detonation, her skin

Ken Case, the Atomic Cowboy, and the Atomic Energy Commission's brand, pictured circa 1960. Photograph courtesy of the National Nuclear Security Administration/Nevada Field Office.

cleared up, but upon returning the next evening, her skin again became irritated. Others at Lincoln Mine suffered rashes and welts that did not heal, and doctors in Ely and Tonopah had no idea what they were treating. In 1957, the residents of Lincoln Mine, approximately two hundred persons, were permanently relocated after years of continual evacuations every time the AEC conducted a test series. The town's store, gas station, and café all closed at the end of July.[81]

The damage from nuclear testing was everywhere. In 1956, offsite residents filed 638 administrative claims against the AEC, 608 of which were

for "broken windows and cracked walls," "damage to equipment and fur-
nishings such as dishes and mirrors," "loss of operating time," and the "up-
rooting of a palm tree." Of that number, 386 were settled, for a total of
$45,478.18. Residents also filed 16 claims for "biological injury to humans
and livestock," 9 of which were settled for $6,817.16. Most of those claims
had been filed during the first two test series in 1951 and consisted predominantly of claims resulting from blast damage. Of those claims filed for
biological injury, the Stewarts' claim, at $5,900, was the largest, for burn
damage to their Quarter Horses. In addition, seven Utah sheep ranchers
and the Sheahans of Groom Mine filed suit for a combined $750,000, but
the federal courts in Utah and Nevada found in favor of the AEC. This is
what allowed the AEC to declare it had "paid no claims for human biological injures as a result of the tests," and "following full investigation of all
such claims brought to its attention . . . no off-site human injuries have
resulted directly from the tests."[82]

Although radiation monitors had been sent to towns such as Saint
George, Ely, Caliente, and Hiko, very little thought had been given to
reaching ranchers and other residents who lived and worked in the vast
spaces in between. There were no monitoring stations set up at the ranches
and no one tracked the movements of miners and ranchers in the valleys
surrounding the test site until the early 1960s. Neither did the AEC give
consideration to groups whose traditional lifestyles used the region's plant,
animal, and water resources directly. The Western Shoshone hunted deer,
rabbits, and other game, and Basque sheepherders and other ranch hands
out with herds of cattle collected rainwater and melted snow for drinking
water. The deer, rabbits, and precipitation in the region were all contaminated by radioactive fallout. The AEC had difficulty understanding that
in the Great Basin, many residents lived directly off the region's natural
resources. Investigators had found dead and dying rabbits and blind and
burned deer, and of course they knew that precipitation after a test series carried intense amounts of radiation, as this was what the organization
feared most and worked to limit through accurate meteorological data and
weather prediction. But the AEC did not make the direct connection between the environment and the people that lived within it.[83]

The AEC's approach to all those living around the test site was to reas-
sure the ranchers that there was no danger from radioactive fallout, but
it did not explain the details of exposure for fear of alarming them. Alvin
Graves, director of test operations at Los Alamos, wrote that it "might be

exceedingly important to the future of the proving grounds" to establish "positive controls of public utterances" to "insure that the AEC's interests are safeguarded." During the livestock investigations and other inquiries, Graves felt that the dissemination of information about the possible effects of radioactive fallout to ranchers and offsite residents was counterproductive. Telling them about the risk of radiation exposure undermined the AEC's message of safety because from the ranchers' point of view, "any radiation may be considered undesirable, whereas the AEC might consider some radiation necessary." The longevity of test site operations thus depended on maintaining good relations with the general public.[84]

At the advent of the next test series in 1955, the AEC launched an unprecedented public relations campaign designed to educate Americans as to the effects of radiation exposure. The official public guide, titled *Atomic Test Effects in the Nevada Test Site Region*, was one of several publications that grew out of this campaign. Disseminated to offsite communities throughout the late 1950s, the guide opened with a message for local residents: "You are in a very real sense active participants in the Nation's atomic test program. . . . Some of you have been inconvenienced by our test operations. At times some of you have been exposed to potential risks from flash, blast, or fallout. You have accepted the inconvenience or the risk without fuss, without alarm, and without panic." Las Vegas residents seemed pleased with the notoriety the test site brought to the burgeoning town; some residents said it was "a boon to the city" and agreed that Las Vegans had "a reputation for being unconcerned about the effects of radiation fallout." But in the communities surrounding the test site, ranchers knew better. They bore the burden of the risk involved in testing nuclear weapons. The presence of the mushroom cloud on public lands underscored all subsequent debates if for no other reason than ranchers came to distrust most representatives of the federal government. In the years that followed, many of them believed that every new multiple use would cause them some kind of harm.[85]

FOUR

A Threat to Customary Use

At the same time the mushroom cloud from nuclear tests loomed large over the Great Basin, homestead applications inundated the arm of the BLM still responsible for land disposal. Organization of the remaining public domain into grazing range and the establishment of nuclear testing on a sizable piece of real estate had not precluded homesteading in the region. Land disposal was still a viable outcome for public lands, and for many, it was still the best use of those lands. Americans continued to file land applications on the public domain, and by the end of the 1950s, claimants had submitted more applications overall than in any other period since the 1910s. Most of these applications targeted the public lands in the Great Basin. This increase in land applications and a concomitant increase in outdoor recreation caused federal land management agencies to rethink the role public lands played in the nation's cultural and economic framework and to re-create multiple use as a mechanism that would allow these lands to be retained by the federal government.

The rise of land applications corresponded with the postwar suburbanization trend and boom in western migration. But instead of purchasing the detached single-family home, these homesteaders applied for public lands parcels just beyond the edge of town. They sought the same things suburbanites had sought in the postwar era: to avoid city-centered living and to have a house and a higher quality of life. The difference between moving to the suburbs and filing for a homestead was in how some people defined their ideal home and quality of life. Most suburbanites wanted to live in a nice neighborhood that afforded them access to both a job in the city and a yard at home. Land applicants preferred owning acres of property to a manicured yard and were relatively unconcerned with commuting to a job in the city.[1]

The Taylor Grazing Act had not precluded either homesteading or mining claims, though it did make patenting a claim or a land application a little more difficult. Under the temporary withdrawal of the Taylor Grazing Act, public lands continued "to be available for the filing of applications and for disposition under the non-mineral public land laws." Many of these lands had not even been surveyed or classified for their best uses, making them appear available. As a result, during the 1950s, land applications under a variety of disposal authorities increased dramatically. In 1953 alone, Americans filed more than forty thousand land applications, and by the next year, that number increased to sixty thousand. Outside of the Homestead Act in Alaska, the Great Basin and southwestern states offered the best opportunities to acquire public lands under the Desert Land Act. Applications under this land disposal law nearly tripled between the late 1940s and the late 1950s, though the BLM approved less than one-third of them. In addition, beginning in 1938 the Small Tract Act, originally created to facilitate the sale of desert land for health and recreational purposes, allowed Americans to buy or lease five acres or less without any agricultural development requirements. Congress amended the act in 1954 to allow corporations, associations, and local governments, as well as individuals, to buy or lease land for residential, commercial, recreational, and community purposes. These two laws fueled the possibility of owning land and building a home on the outskirts of western cities and in rural towns that abutted public lands.[2]

Edward Woozley, Marion Clawson's successor at the helm of the BLM, described the situation as "unprecedented." Although the number of applications alone was less than during the nineteenth-century land rushes, increased affluence and technological advances had made lands once considered barren potentially productive. In addition, the Eisenhower administration, reacting to the perceived public lands lockdown created by former Secretary of the Interior Harold Ickes during the war, had made a practice of encouraging the sale and privatization of public lands. But the mountain of land applications strained the BLM's ability to properly gauge each land case file. The agency had to research each claim carefully because much of the land under application remained unsurveyed, with the necessary water resources unknown, and multiple applicants often filed for the same lands. The same parcel of land could simultaneously be applied for under Desert Land Act application, Small Tract Act application, and the mining law and was usually also part of a grazing district. The BLM warned potential homesteaders in its informational pamphlet on the subject that although the homesteading laws still existed, "much of the land that would be good for a farm homestead is now already in private ownership." But the desire for land ownership caused many hopeful applicants to ignore the agency's cautions. In this crush of paperwork, the BLM closed on less than half its land applications annually, producing a terrible backlog of paperwork and frustrating land applicants.[3]

To address the overwhelming amount of work generated by the increased number of applications, on February 14, 1961, the Kennedy administration's new secretary of the interior, Stewart L. Udall, announced an eighteen-month moratorium on the filing of nonmineral land applications. Udall stated that "many earnest citizens have manifested the great American ambition to own a piece of land by filing types of applications which the Government could not efficiently handle." He indicated that the "temporary suspension of the privilege of filing applications and petitions under the public land laws" would allow the Department of the Interior "to review the entire land management picture, eliminate work backlogs, and develop long-term land management policies and programs."[4]

This was not an unprecedented decision. During the previous presidential administration, the BLM, at the request of the House Government Operations Committee, had ordered a sixty-day suspension of "all public land sales and transactions" involving land appraisals pending a review of the land appraisal process, which was used to clarify the price of small tract sales and leases. During that time, the agency worked to enact a program that attempted to end land speculation practices under the agricultural settlement acts and all other land acts.[5]

However, Udall's language indicated an important shift in the Kennedy administration's view of land disposal. According to the secretary of the interior, unscrupulous Americans had abused their privilege of acquiring public lands; their unrestricted filing of applications had "seriously impeded both the orderly and expeditious disposal of public lands," wasting taxpayer dollars. The moratorium brought the entire previous land disposal process to a screeching halt. At its termination, the Department of the Interior

Secretary of the Interior Stewart Lee Udall and President John F. Kennedy at the commemoration of the 100th anniversary of the Homestead Act on February 13, 1962. Photograph by Abbie Rowe, courtesy of the Stewart Udall Collection, University of Arizona Libraries, Special Collections.

planned to have a new set of policies in place, putting "public land development on a much more sensible programmed basis." In addition, while the moratorium was in effect, the BLM hoped to "undertake a large-scale land inventory program" to "classify, open and make appropriate lands available for transfer to States, local governments, individuals and business firms."[6]

The same day Udall announced the moratorium on land applications, the new secretary of the interior also explained his public lands conservation policy, which established a "public interest test" for requests to transfer land out of the public domain. The BLM had been defining the public interest as "that which will benefit the most people for the longest period of time, or that which will do the greatest good for the greatest number of people over the long haul." Udall reinterpreted this principle to mean that careful use of the public domain and its natural resources would result in the longest term of use and the most beneficial use monetarily or otherwise. The agency planned to retain lands that could not be properly developed under existing land laws and that were inadequate for agricultural development, requiring "a full return" for its property.[7]

The federal government, only a decade before, had loosely regulated the land disposal process and preferred volume of disposal to quality of disposal. This situation had invited rampant land speculation instead of careful disposition because the basic operating assumption had been that the best use for land was to place it into private hands and onto state and county tax rolls. Under Udall, the BLM would only reluctantly privatize acres in the public domain.

The moratorium solicited an immediate public outcry from four western senators; Wallace F. Bennett from Utah, Henry C. Dworshak of Idaho, Gordon Allott in Colorado, and Barry Goldwater of Arizona protested Udall's unilateral suspension of most of the nation's land disposal laws. They accused the secretary of the interior of usurping Congress's authority to manage public lands and argued he was using a guillotine instead of a scalpel to solve the problem of unethical land disposal. Udall responded that the moratorium would actually prevent the unnecessary rejection of most of the applications and reminded the senators that it had originated from a study conducted by the House Committee on Interior and Insular Affairs under Clair Engle of California and Wayne N. Aspinall of Colorado. Rather than stifle development in the American West, Udall chastised the senators, cleaning up the land application process would create a more appropriate pattern of land use, which, he assured them, would "stabilize tenure status and provide for conservation."[8]

In the Great Basin, Nevada's two senators, Alan Bible and Howard W. Cannon, assured their constituents that the moratorium would speed up the approval process by dealing with the backlog of applications before allowing new ones to be filed. Next to Alaska, the Great Basin had attracted more land applications than anywhere else in the country. In Nevada, the BLM struggled with over 15,000 hopeful land cases in the late 1950s, and by the time the land application moratorium took effect, the agency had already reduced the number of applications to 6,300. Of those, 1,300 were pending Desert Land applications, many of which the state BLM office suspected arose out of ongoing land speculation and promotion activities emanating from Texas. Most of the other land cases consisted of Small Tract filings around Las Vegas and Reno, though a few were entries under the Pittman Underground Water Act, a land law specifically designed in 1919 to encourage settlement in Nevada.[9]

The moratorium did not initially inhibit BLM public land sales in the Great Basin. In rural Nevada counties, the increased land claims generally brought more land onto the tax rolls. In Reno and the burgeoning Las Vegas Valley, applicants facilitated growth of the two economic drivers of the state. In Utah, the State Land Board eagerly sought to take advantage of booming land prices driven by high demand, selling even arid state lands to fund public schools and bring more land onto the county tax rolls. These lands were important to the growing state, though they did not fuel the metropolitan expansion of the Wasatch Front. Rather, the sale of land to private individuals fulfilled the Beehive State's ideological mission of supporting small farmers and privatizing public lands to help fund counties.[10]

But in Lincoln County, Nevada, the Rural Development Committee (RDC) based in Caliente reacted immediately against the Department of the Interior's land application moratorium and the new public lands conservation policy. The RDC, which included local business owners as well as ranchers such as Floyd Lamb, wrote Senator Howard Cannon that the county's severe unemployment as a result of mine closures and railroad reorganizations had decreased the area's population, as many residents had left for Las Vegas to look for work. This had left the county and its remaining residents in dire financial straits. In 1956, the federal government had enrolled the county in its pilot rural development program, which prompted the creation of the RDC, the local group tasked with investigating ways to improve the area's economy. The RDC worked closely with the BLM, Soil Conservation Service, Nevada State Engineer's Office, and the University of Nevada to locate public land parcels that could be developed for agricultural use, which would put residents to work and increase the county's tax base. Several people applied for agricultural acres under the Desert Land and Pittman Acts in Penoyer, Coal, Garden, and Lake Valleys, about seventy-five applications altogether. All of the applicants, mostly land developers from Las Vegas and a handful of local residents, had fronted the funds necessary for locating and acquiring underground water resources that would be used to irrigate hay fields and grow alfalfa, vegetable, and other seed crops. These operations had the potential to double the agricultural income in the county, and the BLM was considering more than half of these applications for approval, but the RDC feared the delay would cause the process to lose momentum and investors to lose interest.[11]

The land moratorium bought time for the BLM to more deeply evaluate these land applications and determine whether releasing grazing range to agricultural or commercial development was the best use of the land. This turned out to be beneficial to several long-time residents in the area. The Whipple family ranched in White River Valley, at the western edge of Lincoln County. John Lytle Whipple had arrived in the central Great Basin in 1898, sent by the Mormon leadership in Salt Lake City to manage the church's White River Land and Livestock Company. In 1904, he and his wife, Rose, purchased the Horton Ranch at Sunnyside to begin their own operation, and fifteen years later, they added the neighboring Lewis Ranch.[12]

Unlike most Mormon families, such as those in Pahranagat Valley to the south who were missionaries sent from Utah to establish settlements in the outlying regions of the Mormon frontier, the Whipples relied on mining as much as ranching for income. In the mid-1860s, Mormon settlers claimed Muddy and Meadow Valleys in the southern Great Basin by cultivating any agricultural lands and filing on the corresponding water rights in order to prevent non-Mormon settlers from filing claims in the area. Their efforts prompted a pattern of settlement replicated throughout the Great Basin in which Mormons used water rights to anchor range access and discourage other settlement. But the ore discoveries on Mount Irish, located above Pahranagat Valley, challenged the Mormon hegemony by drawing outsiders to the area who struck claims and populated the town of Hiko, just sixty miles east of Panaca, the main Mormon settlement in Meadow Valley. By the 1870s, the mining town of Pioche, just twelve miles north of Panaca, was the next big boomtown and drew many more non-Mormons to the area. These population explosions were problematic for the sheltered Mormon communities, but they also proved profitable. The Mormon leadership, which had issued a ban on mining for its members, looked the other way as Mormons guided, supported, and even participated in mining activities. Long after the majority of the claims had played out and most people had moved on to other, more lucrative possibilities, many Mormons took advantage of what ore was left.[13]

John Whipple benefited from the lax enforcement of the mining ban, and by 1905, he had located a large silver vein in the Bristol Range, thirty miles southeast of Sunnyside. Between 1925 and 1933, he owned and operated the Silver King mine. As a result of their lucrative income, the Whipples' ranch operations began growing in 1916, when John's wife, Rose, patented an additional 200 acres to expand the Sunnyside ranch. In 1928, eldest son Murray Whipple patented 642 acres in Cave Valley under the Stock-Raising Homestead Act, purchased the Haggerty Ranch there as his summer range headquarters, and established his own winter range ranch at Hiko. By the early 1930s, John Whipple was the vice president of the Sunnyside Livestock Association, a group of thirty livestock operators in eastern Nevada and western Utah who had organized to oppose nomadic sheepherders grazing flocks in their region. Harsh winter conditions and drought during the early 1930s were hard on the Whipples' livestock operations; in 1933, the ranches of Sunnyside were snowbound for more than a month, and the great drought of 1934 decimated their summer grazing ranges.[14]

John retired from ranching in 1935 and leased the Sunnyside ranch to his youngest son, Clair Whipple. The Whipple family, though they had trepidations about federal oversight, participated in organizing a grazing district, and their area was the only part of Lincoln County organized in 1936. In his retirement, John even served on the local grazing advisory board until 1940. But the Whipples struggled at midcentury. Murray, a dashing and skilled horseman, died prematurely in 1945. His son Keith, a well-respected rancher in his own right, took over the ranch operations in 1950. During the decade of atmospheric nuclear testing, Keith helped decontaminate cars at the local service station in Alamo. By the time land applications spiked in the region, the Whipple family's ranching operations were in a slump.[15]

In Coal Valley, just south of Sunnyside, nine of the Pittman Act proposals, covering nearly six thousand acres, threatened to reduce the Whipples' grazing allotments by 6 percent each. The applicants for the land in Coal Valley actually pressured the Whipples and several other ranchers to sign a form waiving their right to protest the proposals in order to benefit the larger economy of Lincoln County. However, by mid-1961, approval on these and the other applications was delayed as BLM officials reviewed their validity relative to the new conservation policy, which discouraged approval of filings that allowed agriculture on barely productive lands, especially those that relied on unknown or already appropriated water resources. The applicants in Coal, Garden, and Lake Valleys had not received water rights from the State Engineer's Office, nor had they adequately located and developed new underground water resources. Without water rights and with the land unsuited for agriculture, the BLM had no choice but to deny most of the applications. The agency approved only sixteen Desert Land entries and none of the Pittman entries. This decision delighted the Whipples but severely disappointed Lincoln County's RDC; one resident of Caliente complained, "The Udall policy has certainly put a halt to any hope of Western progress."[16]

By the end of 1961, Secretary Udall announced that the BLM had made significant progress in dealing with the backlog of applications. To demonstrate his support of proper land disposal and to alleviate any public frustration, Udall highlighted the thousands of small tracts available in states such as Arizona and California and stated the moratorium would expire as expected in September 1962. However, under this new land conservation policy, Udall explained the BLM would no longer allow agricultural entries that depleted existing water tables in the desert Southwest and the Great Basin in order to "give strong protection for farmers and water users on or near public lands and assure that the programs of the Department of the Interior encourage water conservation, and do not contribute to the unnecessary depletion of underground water reserves."[17]

Arizona was the first state to feel the brunt of the new policy; Udall turned down all of the three hundred homestead applications in the state. The same pattern was repeated in other arid areas, much to the frustration of applicants. In the Great Basin, hundreds of disappointed potential landowners and some existing landowners looking to expand their current livestock or farming operations expressed their frustration to their congressional delegates. Pittman Act applicant Edward E. Willhoyt of Yerrington, Nevada, complained that after he spent $15,000 drilling for water, the BLM denied his land application and those of his brother and partner for an area east of Yerrington because "some big ranchers protested" their use of underground water resources. Desert Land applicant Margaret Barber from Winnemucca believed that the BLM unfairly denied her application for 320 acres to enlarge her original homestead, but approved "real estate promoters and big-money operators." She was not exactly wrong. In keeping with the new conservation policy, the Nevada State Engineer's Office insisted Barber's application was denied because "there was insufficient water available for the irrigation of the land on a sustained basis . . . the available water supply in the Quinn River Valley Basin [was] already allocated to existing agricultural developments."[18]

The vast amount of public lands in the Great Basin and in a few other places in the American West was deceiving, and the number of applications reflected both the demand for land and the perception of its availability. But the BLM warned potential homesteaders that "misuse of the land, wasting it on purposes for which it was never intended, is a luxury of long-dead years when land was our cheapest commodity." Land suited for agriculture under the old laws, the agency told hopeful land applicants, was "severely limited." The BLM worked to redirect applicants' interests, recommending purchase or lease of small tracts in urban or suburban areas for "homes, businesses, or community sites" that abutted public lands away from other federal lands, such as national forests, national parks, and any potential wilderness areas.[19]

As if to drive this point home, on June 4, 1964, the Department of the Interior announced the closure of agricultural land filings in Nevada, particularly Desert Land Act entries, pending groundwater and soil studies that would determine what lands, if any, in the state were suitable for agriculture under the new land conservation policies. In Nevada's seventeen counties, most of the so-called vacant public lands existed within grazing districts; only Esmeralda County, a fifth of Nye County, and a fraction of Washoe, Clark, and Pershing Counties contained public lands outside the grazing system. All of this land was the most marginal desert, with very few water resources. So strict was this new evaluation process that the BLM allowed only one-sixth of the applications examined during the first six months of the ban to even continue toward patent. Secretary of the Interior Stewart Udall warned these applicants that farming unsuitable lands such as these was "futile and destructive."[20]

The root of the problem with most land applications lay with potential landowners trying to bend the old agricultural land laws to new suburban purposes. Most Homestead, Desert Land, and Pittman applicants in Nevada relied on income from a full-time job in urban areas such as Reno or Las Vegas and sought to use these land laws to acquire property at minimal cost farther out from the urban centers in which they worked. But these settlement laws could not facilitate suburban development, as they were specifically designed to encourage agricultural production, mainly farming—an expensive and time-consuming endeavor. The other available land laws, such as the Small Tract Act, offered smaller parcels at fair market value for the land, the price of which steadily increased with rising demand. The BLM and Department of the Interior recognized the importance of releasing public lands into private ownership to meet the growing demand for cheap land and to facilitate growth of the region's tax rolls. This was especially important in Nevada, a state reliant on property taxes and sales tax for income. However, there were only limited ways to accomplish this under the existing land laws. In addition, under the new land conservation policy, the BLM questioned whether these agricultural land laws had ever been good for the Great Basin in the first place. In lieu of changing or repealing them, an endeavor that took an act of Congress, the Department of the Interior and BLM interpreted the agricultural requirements more strictly and worked to clearly classify Great Basin land as unsuitable for agricultural filings, thus eliminating the ability to apply under the old land laws. As a result, most public land transactions thereafter occurred around existing urban areas.[21]

However, the Department of the Interior's deliberate exclusion of most Nevada land for agricultural settlement outraged the state's residents. Alvin May, a potential landowner in Carson Valley, near Reno, served as a very public example of what happened when local residents used the old land disposal laws to acquire cheap land and the BLM was forced to deny their land applications. May had filed for a 160-acre homestead under the 1862 law near Gardnerville in 1957. He built a home for his family of nine children but lacked the funds to develop the irrigation structures necessary to provide water for growing crops for commercial sale on the twenty acres the law required him to bring under cultivation. By 1962, May's five years to make the required improvements on the land had run out, and the BLM faced turning a hard-working man and his family out of their home. The agency struggled to find alternative measures that would allow May to purchase the land on which his home sat under the Small Tract and Public Land Sale Acts, but May lacked the funds to make the purchase. He also lacked the priority for the purchase, since other landowners adjacent to his home had first rights if the public lands came up for sale. Both the BLM and the Mays were caught in an untenable situation. The land management agency could not allow the Mays legal title to the lands under their application because the lands were not suitable for agriculture, the acres already existed in a grazing district anyway, and May did not have water rights and was certainly not farming as his primary source of income. All the Mays had was the sympathy of the region's residents, many of whom felt the "worthless grazing land" was better used in private hands even as a hobbyist's farm and derided the BLM, calling the agency the "tapeworm of the livestock industry."[22]

Worse, the Mays and other denied land applicants believed that they had been unfairly turned away, since earlier applicants had been allowed to patent their land without adequate water for irrigation and suitable crop production. Nevada senator Cannon agreed, stating that "the various laws governing the disposition of public lands were enacted for the explicit purpose of putting these lands insofar as possible into the private ownership and thus on to the state and county tax rolls." Governor Paul Laxalt emphasized that the nation's land laws had conveyed very little land in the Great Basin, especially in Nevada, into public ownership. He said the BLM was obligated to "specifically and energetically" facilitate the movement of "appropriate Federal lands into private ownership at realistic prices." But most ranchers in the state disagreed. Several from around Ely, in the eastern part of the state, wrote Senator Cannon and the state's BLM director, James R. Penny, a well-educated land manager who understood the intricacies of multiple use, that new land entries would entail further underground water pumping, causing the water table to lower and bringing "hardship on the old permanent ranches."[23]

Most of the nation's congressional delegation agreed, although for different reasons. Wayne Aspinall, chairman of the House Interior and Insular Affairs Committee, stated, "We have, subject to isolated exceptions, for all intents and purposes run out of compact areas of 160, 320 and 640 acres of land that can be utilized economically for agricultural purposes. At the same time, we have become an urban-suburban-industrialized country in which the overall need for additional agricultural production has diminished." With the public domain concentrated in the Great Basin and the value of agricultural development and its economic contribution to state and national economies in decline, the land disposal process seemed to be at an end. In 1966, potential homesteaders were warned that "even though there is still plenty of land in the public domain and the Homestead Act of 1862 is still in effect, you'd better think twice before you pull up stakes and rush out to claim your 160 acres . . . although there is roughly 460 million acres of land—about one fifth of the total area of the United States—in the public domain, practically none of it is suitable for homesteading." Even when the moratorium on Desert Land agricultural entries ended seventeen years later, the prohibitive cost of underground water development and the inadequate return on even the most profitable desert crops such as potatoes and alfalfa meant that despite the several thousand applications filed, none could be approved.[24]

All of this, combined with the general reluctance of the Nevada State Engineer's Office to approve new water applications, meant that most of the remaining public lands in Nevada were slated to remain out of private hands. Exceptions to this process were the entries filed by existing ranchers such as the Fallinis and Sharps. Both of these longtime ranching families expanded their water rights and received BLM approval to add several hundred acres to their existing ranches during this time. The Fallinis, whose base of operations was at Twin Springs, expanded deeper into Hot Creek, Reveille, Kawich, and Railroad Valleys, making up ground lost in the 1940s to the bombing range. The Sharps expanded throughout the central portion of Railroad Valley, purchasing the Nyala Ranch in 1950 from Sheldon Lamb. This ranch had once hosted competitors of the 1908 automobile race between New York and Paris as they traveled along the old wagon road straight through Railroad Valley to Twin Springs and Tonopah. The Sharps also secured additional water rights to support their Blue Eagle Ranch.[25]

Despite this apparent benefit, ranchers were unhappy with the new conservation policy. Concomitant with ending homesteading, Udall also announced the reconstruction of the old grazing advisory boards into "Multiple-Use Advisory Boards" whose membership reflected the "many varied interests" of public lands users. This change mirrored the "multiple use interests in the national land reserve," the new name for the nation's public lands. The term "reserve" was meant to redefine the "vacant, un-appropriated, and unreserved public domain," the lands governed by the Taylor Grazing Act of 1934, in the same way as the Forest Reserve Act of 1891 had set aside national forests for their productive use and maintenance for future generations. But the term implied uses beyond just grazing. In addition to involving representatives of livestock and wildlife interests, the multiple-use boards included timber, mining, soil conservation, and recreational interests, urban and suburban planners, and state and county officials.[26]

Federal lands managers had come to think of multiple use as a system in which "no one use and no one user is granted exclusive use of any single area," though a user "may be granted the exclusive practice of one use on an area," such as established by the Taylor Grazing Act. The Forest Service's Multiple-Use Sustained-Yield Act of 1960, a powerful mandate coveted by the BLM, altered the focus of the concept. In this framework, multiple use became "the management of all the variable renewable surface resources . . . so that they are utilized in the combination that will best meet the needs of the American people." Coupled with the idea of sustained yield, the "achievement and maintenance in perpetuity of a high-level annual or regular periodic output of the various renewable resources . . . without impairment of the productivity of the land," multiple use in this new iteration was less focused on the entity using public lands and more focused on the outcome of public lands use. Under this revised version of multiple use, the Forest Service did not presume to equalize uses but instead gave them all equal consideration when making land-use decisions. Depending on the nature of the environment itself, one use or another could predominate. Udall's vision of multiple use essentially incorporated balanced use of natural resources among a broad array of users; his multiple-use boards effectively placed noncommercial and extractive use on par with commercial use.[27]

Without a presumption of hierarchy among users, this philosophy meant restrictions on livestock grazing numbers, lumbering, and mineral development in the finite system of natural resources. Understandably, ranchers in the Great Basin expressed some concern about this transformative policy. John Marvel, chair of the Nevada State Cattlemen's Association Public Lands Committee, noted the "attitude of resource users in the Western States" after a conference on the subject in March 1963. Attendees at the meeting expressed concern about the "increasing threat to the continued enjoyment and use of Federal Lands on a *customary* multiple use basis by all citizens."[28] The end of land disposal protected ranchers in the Great Basin, but the growth of multiple use ensured that grazing would no longer be the dominant use of the public domain.

Though these lands were not deemed suitable for agricultural development, they were ideal for multiple-use classification. To this end, in 1964 the BLM secured passage of the agency's first real mandate, the Classification and Multiple Use Act, which allowed the agency to classify land for either disposal or retention, intensifying multiple-use management on those acres retained in federal possession. This balanced the BLM's attention between putting land into economic production through grazing, agricultural, mineral, timber, or industrial development, and putting land to other uses, including fish and wildlife development, outdoor recreation, watershed protection, and wilderness preservation. The BLM had used land classification, a process of water, soil, vegetation, and wildlife analysis and cadastral surveying, to determine the best purpose for public lands on a piecemeal basis for decades. But this act allowed classification for retention on a permanent basis. The BLM assured concerned citizens that "classifications must be dynamic" and that "the Congress, the Secretary of the Interior, and other responsible officials will continue to exercise their authority in the public interest."[29]

Along with the Forest Service's Multiple-Use Sustained-Yield Act and the Wilderness Act, which passed in the same year but did not apply to BLM lands, the new legislation provided "the first clear congressional directive" for managing the remaining public lands and indicated the permanency of the federal domain. It also marked the BLM's commitment to assisting local development through the sale of public lands that facilitated the growth of communities surrounded by an ocean of public domain. But it was unclear what the results of this classification process would be. Ranchers still hoped the outcome would mean their use of grazing range would remain atop the multiple-use hierarchy as the best and highest economic use of the land. Such was the "customary" vision of multiple use. But the BLM under the new director, Charles H. Stoddard, along with Secretary of the Interior Stewart L. Udall and the Eighty-Eighth Congress, mandated that the classification process and the framing of multiple use result in the proper development and use of public land resources, not necessarily the "combination of uses that will give the greatest dollar return or the greatest unit output." Where ranching might have been the highest economic use of the land, in the 1960s wildlife management and outdoor recreation had achieved equal importance.[30]

The Department of the Interior had three facets of multiple use to take into account. The first was that "all American people of present and future generations be assured adequate outdoor recreation resources" and that "such resources be conserved, developed, and utilized for benefit and enjoyment." But this potentially conflicted with the ways in which public lands provided the "natural resource base for the expansion of our national and regional economies and well-being." A third aspect of multiple use declared that "recognition of the public significance of land endowed with superlative attributes has led to the dedication of land for the preservation of scenic beauty, wilderness, nature wildlife, indigenous plant life, and areas of scientific significance or antiquity." None of these goals was to interfere with the dedication of the public domain to national defense. Put bluntly, the problem for the Department of the Interior and the BLM was that "the present and future needs and objectives of a mature nation [were] complex, ranging from national defense to assuring adequate quality of life to all citizens."[31]

The land classification process left ranchers dependent on public lands grazing in a tough spot. Where the Taylor Grazing Act codified their presence on the public domain and legitimized public lands grazing as the most reasonable economic use of the remaining public lands, the Classification and Multiple Use Act did the same for wildlife management and outdoor recreation. According to the Department of the Interior, there was no requirement that all uses of public lands be "universally intermingled in common." Peter E. Marble, a rancher from Deeth, Nevada, and a member of the state's Public Lands Committee, thought there was room on public lands for both ranchers and outdoor recreationists, especially hunters and anglers. However, Marble preferred that public lands be remanded to the states, which in his mind would "do no violence to the concept of multiple use," since state governments were sensitive to the needs of local communities. The Nevada State Cattle Association wanted the BLM to consider grazing permitees' interests, as users with historical priority, when classifying land for retention or disposal. The Nevada Wool Growers Association agreed. These organizations argued that local interests were best suited to decide which lands were suitable for parks, recreation, wildlife, and grazing. If the federal government transferred any public lands into private hands, ranchers in Nevada wanted the option to purchase those lands they traditionally used as grazing range or, in lieu of purchase, to secure tenure on that range. Ranchers hoped to be compensated monetarily for public lands designated for outdoor recreation and wildlife to the exclusion of grazing.[32]

What had them worried was the issue of water. Ranchers' access to grazing range had been predicated on their water rights, and the value of their ranch was based in part on the relationship those water rights had to that grazing range. The potential allocation of water to other multiple-use purposes threatened to undermine their water and grazing resources, and the value of their entire operation. It certainly did not help that for the first time, federal agencies were allowed under the new BLM law to acquire water rights on public lands to facilitate outdoor recreation and wildlife development. This was not entirely a new problem. The Winters Doctrine, a legal precedent established in 1908, allowed the federal government to control enough water resources on reserved public lands to ensure fulfillment of any federal withdrawal, particularly in supporting the establishment of reservations for American Indian tribes. Federal land management agencies and the military expanded the principle to apply to national forests, national parks, and military bases. If the federal government classified land for other uses that required water resources, the agency reserving the land could also reserve the water rights and deprive existing water users. Besides the land they owned outright, water rights were the only other form of property that ranchers controlled directly. This, more than any other aspect of multiple use, threatened the livelihood of ranchers in the Great Basin.[33]

FIVE

Parks of Lesser Grandeur

At the height of summer 1962, George N. Swallow, a prominent rancher from the Ely area, penned a long letter to Colorado representative Wayne N. Aspinall, chair of the House Committee on Interior and Insular Affairs. His angry missive expressed frustration over the proposed creation of a new national park in the Great Basin and radiated an intense dislike of Secretary of the Interior Stewart L. Udall. Swallow declared he wrote on behalf of the "life long citizens of the area in question" and that the Department of the Interior under Secretary Udall had "ridden over rough shod" the "duly elected park committee," a local body that had recently decided to reduce the proposed park's size to exclude potential mining resources and existing grazing rights. Swallow adamantly insisted, "Nevada needs industry, and to create industry we must to a major extent, encourage the development of mineral resources." The potential beryllium deposits included in the larger version of the park, he said, would "spell death to a new industry for Eastern Nevada plus the loss of payroll for an already shrinking local economy."[1]

Swallow accused Udall of being "no friend of agriculture or business," citing that current Department of the Interior policies were "adverse to the continuity or peace of mind of the livestock operator." Identifying with many Great Basin ranchers who were concerned about Udall's new conservation policy and its impact on their customary use of public lands, the rancher portrayed himself and his fellow livestock operators as an overlooked and underserviced group that would suffer while others benefited. Swallow wrote that Udall's "refusal to consider any compensation" for those ranchers like himself who would lose their grazing rights and be deprived of the "vast amounts of money that will be spent for other purposes in the park" demonstrated Udall's "gross unamerican [*sic*] attitude toward a moral concept of all americans [*sic*]; namely 'look to the welfare of our minorities.'"[2]

Swallow's primary complaint was the importance Udall placed on such "vague and dull subjects as ecological and biological study areas." The rancher challenged Udall to "show the people of Nevada why anyone might be interested in wasting vacation time in this and many other areas of the [proposed] park area." He simply could not understand how anyone would find value in either bristlecone pines or Lexington Arch. The bristlecone pine, he said, had "no peculiar beauty" and was "homely, stunted, [and] gnarled." The limestone arch was not even remotely comparable to those on the Colorado Plateau. He concluded his letter with a warning, writing, "We see a dark cloud rising ominously between ourselves and the public lands offices."[3]

In the early 1960s, most Great Basin ranchers struggled with the transformation of multiple use into an actual public lands policy, and many faulted Secretary of the Interior Stewart Udall and the agency they primarily dealt with—the Bureau of Land Management. Multiple use had once referred to the various roles public lands played in the national economy, but it was swiftly becoming a policy that encompassed the different types of uses Americans desired to make of these lands. Along with improved conservation practices and reprioritized land uses, changing cultural perceptions of nature and the purpose of land had much to do with altering the interpretation and implementation of multiple use in the 1960s. New environmental literature such as Aldo Leopold's *A Sand County Almanac* (1949), biologist Rachel Carson's *Silent Spring* (1962), and the Advisory Board on Wildlife Management's report "Wildlife Management in the National Parks" (1963), known as the Leopold Report, popularized a new vision of public lands management that reconfigured the multiple-use concept relative to the newly embraced belief in the scarcity of public lands and the natural resources and wildlife they contained. Secretary of the Interior Stewart Udall certainly embraced this in his new conservation plan, a vision he expanded on in his publication *The Quiet Crisis* (1963). Rather than value natural resources in terms of economic gain and scenic places merely for their viewshed quality, this literature took a more holistic view of the environment by examining the relationship of humans and nature within ecological systems and the consequences of some of the nation's key innovations. These works frightened many readers, reminding them that processes reliant on pesticides, automobiles, nuclear testing, and modern medicine had associated risks and negative side effects. The authors believed that the environmental and bodily degradation produced by these technologies ought to make Americans think twice about the costs associated with the nation's progress.[4]

Indeed, the tenor of Americans' attitude toward public lands had changed. Conservationist and western historian Bernard DeVoto had spent the better part of the 1950s lambasting the BLM and the Forest Service, agencies he believed deliberately catered to the livestock, mining, and lumbering industries. The acerbic critic penned multiple articles for *Harper's Magazine* detailing the hardship the livestock industry had wreaked on the natural resources of the American West. DeVoto wrote that ranchers would "shovel most of the West into rivers" given half a chance. He argued that their federally subsidized, rampant exploitation of the natural grazing resources of public lands was nothing less than robbery of the American people. He insisted that Americans through the federal government were co-owners of these lands, which ought to be managed for the public's benefit, not the ranchers'. "The reservation of the public lands," he wrote, "was the outcome of the realization that much of our heritage of natural resources had been wasted, that much of what remained was impaired, and that all of it was in grave danger of being exhausted." His general vision of the remaining public domain and the natural resources it contained was that of a great asset held in trust and managed in perpetuity by a federal government dedicated to the values of conservation and preservation. DeVoto fought against freeloaders making a profit on the public domain, whether well regulated or not, and any future privatization of public lands.[5]

DeVoto's emphasis on "our" public lands was adopted by Secretary of the Interior Stewart L. Udall, a native Arizonan who believed the American West needed the federal government to protect it from both outside commercial exploitation and internal abuse. In late 1961, he was scheduled to speak at the first Conference on the History of Western America in Santa Fe on October 13 to an audience that had contributed significantly to his way of thinking. Though his message ended up in the hands of Assistant Secretary of the Interior John A. Carver, who filled in for Udall at the last minute, the sentiment was the same. Carver's speech demonstrated the profound effect DeVoto, and other western historians who criticized the exploitation of the western environment, had on the department's new conservation policies. Carver argued that DeVoto's essays in *Harper's Magazine* profoundly affected his and Udall's vision of public lands management. He embraced historian Walter Prescott Webb's premise in "The American West: Perpetual Mirage" that the heart of the American West was a desert and that the region's aridness created fundamental "deficiencies" that limited its development and required special consideration. So provocative was Webb's essay, he said, that Senator Michael J. Mansfield of Montana read it on the Senate floor.[6]

Senator Mansfield's reading of the essay into the *Congressional Record* outraged several senators, namely Wallace F. Bennett of Utah and Arizona's Barry M. Goldwater, who objected to Webb's use of the word "deficient," which they interpreted as a description of the region's value to the nation. Carver, however, interpreted the concept differently; attempts to conform development in the less desirable areas of the American West, including the Great Basin, to national standards of prosperity had left the region's already minimal water resources depleted and had created second-class, impoverished rural areas. Concluding his speech to the nascent Western History Association, Carver indicated that the customary understanding of multiple use was evolving. He declared that the old pattern of land and natural resource management was driven by a "Neanderthal morality," and "the luxury of frontier wastefulness" was at an end.[7]

Besides these western historians, Carver praised several representatives elected in the late 1950s who were more than happy to help facilitate the shift in multiple use on public lands from locally controlled, client-driven activities to more centralized, regulated oversight that furthered the goals of Udall's new conservation policy. He complimented Senators Clinton P. Anderson of New Mexico, Alan H. Bible and Howard W. Cannon of Nevada, Frank F. Church of Idaho, Michael J. Mansfield and Lee W. Metcalf of Montana, Henry M. Jackson of Washington, John A. Carroll of Colorado, Edward L. Bartlett of Alaska, Clair Engle of California, Gale W. McGee and John J. Hickey of Wyoming, and Frank "Ted" Moss of Utah for demonstrating "fierce devotion to the public interest and the conservation and management of the public's resources."[8]

These elected officials, along with the Department of the Interior and the BLM, worked to implement this new vision of multiple use that focused heavily on accommodating greater numbers of Americans using their public lands. The burgeoning demand for outdoor recreation in the middle of the twentieth century had confounded land management agencies. Throughout the 1950s, greater population in increasingly urban concentrations, a higher standard of living, more leisure time, and better outdoor equipment technology, especially tools and clothing designed to ameliorate inclement weather, strengthened people's ability to participate in outdoor recreation, which became an increasingly important "panacea for the pressures of urban life."[9]

This demand outstripped the recreational infrastructure available to provide for the needs of campers, hikers, hunters, anglers, and other recreationists. In particular, the Forest Service and National Park Service, the federal agencies managing the most popular recreation landscapes, struggled to keep up with the nation's outdoor recreation needs. In 1956, the national parks had over fifty-five million visitors, a 10 percent increase from the previous year. To handle the projected increase over the next several years, the Park Service launched its ten-year Mission 66 program "to put the parks in shape to take care of the 80 million people who are expected to visit them in 1966." The National Park Service constructed new visitor centers and museums and improved campsites to host the dramatically increasing numbers of visitors. Similarly, in 1957 the Forest Service launched its Operation Outdoors program to accommodate the marked increase in national forest visitation. State parks also experienced a significant increase in visitors but could not draw on federal revenues to support the expansion of their infrastructure.[10]

Congress facilitated this growth by funding Mission 66 and Operation Outdoors, and most importantly, by creating the Outdoor Recreation Resources Review Commission (ORRRC), a study group slated to inventory the nation's outdoor recreation resource opportunities. Headed by Conservation Foundation architect Laurance S. Rockefeller, who considered outdoor recreation a "healthy, satisfying, and often creative use of leisure time," the ORRRC submitted its study to President Kennedy and the nation in 1962. The commission reported that "90 per cent of Americans engage in some form of outdoor recreation." The ORRRC recommended developing future recreation resources to "provide recreation for the metropolitan regions which have the biggest population and the least space for it." The greatest problem in developing outdoor recreation options, the ORRRC stated, had little to do with money or infrastructure. It had to do with access. While there was plenty of "land and water acreage for recreation," most of it was not proximate to the population that would use it.[11]

Developing recreation areas was costly, but it could also be profitable; according to the ORRRC's report, federal, state, and local governments spent about $1 billion annually "maintaining and developing outdoor recreation resources," but the economic return on goods and services provided to recreationists amounted to $20 billion per year. The ORRRC recommended five broad courses of action to help facilitate the nation's outdoor recreation development: creation of a recreation bureau in the Department of the Interior, a national recreation plan, expansion and adaptation of existing outdoor recreation programs, federal aid to states for additional development, and most importantly, a classification system for recreation resources. Giving land a recreational identity was a fundamental part of the ORRRC's better planning process, especially near urban areas, in which outdoor recreation development included the expansion of existing recreation systems such as national parks, seashores, and wildlife refuges. All public lands under the multiple-use concept had a recreational capacity, but national parks, monuments, forests, and wildlife refuges had stronger recreational identities since they were protected against commercial extraction of natural resources. To facilitate the growth of this identity, President Kennedy announced in his 1962 conservation message the expansion of the national park and wildlife refuge system, and a program to preserve wilderness.[12]

The remaining public lands in the Great Basin, however, lacked any such recreational identity. The region had some national forest, several wildlife refuges, and a handful of lakes and reservoirs. The Humboldt and Toiyabe National Forests offered camping and hiking in the Great Basin's piñon-juniper sky-islands. Walker and Pyramid Lakes and Lahontan Reservoir provided opportunities to swim, water-ski, and use motorboats, and the Bonneville Salt Flats hosted racing events. The region's few wildlife refuges provided hunting, fishing, and plenty of bird-watching. But the rest of the public lands contained only a few BLM campsites, trails, and several areas for motorized vehicles. There was no equivalent of national parks like Yosemite or Yellowstone, Grand Canyon or Bryce Canyon, Great Smoky Mountains or Mount Rainier to draw visitors and provide an anchor for organized recreational activities in the region.[13]

The BLM managed most of the region's federal domain, and much of the Great Basin's identity was devoted to the economic production of livestock and potential mining opportunities. Cattle, sheep, and open-pit mines were not particularly attractive to outdoor recreationists, and yet some still came to the region to camp, hike, drive, and enjoy the herds of pronghorn, bighorn sheep, mule deer, and other wildlife. To accommodate these recreationists, the BLM worked with state and local authorities to "provide more recreation sites" through the 1926 Recreation and Public Purposes Act, which allowed state, county, and municipal governments to purchase or lease public lands for recreational use. But until the mid-1960s, the BLM did not have the authority to "construct public toilets or even set up a litter barrel on public lands which it found people were using extensively for a recreation area." Gene Peterson, the agency's first recreation specialist, struggled to get the BLM up to speed with even the basics of the other agencies' outdoor recreation programs. BLM state offices in Nevada, Utah, Idaho, Oregon, and three other states devoted one employee each to facilitate outdoor recreation. This meager staff did their best to assess visitation and begin developing the necessary amenities.[14]

Crafting a recreational identity for the Great Basin proved difficult, since the BLM's development program in the 1960s consisted mainly of constructing basic facilities containing garbage cans, toilets, and designated campsites to accommodate the ever-growing numbers of outdoor enthusiasts. These primitive improvements were a far cry from the grandeur of a national park. There were, however, a few parts of the region that, by the 1960s, were known to attract recreational tourists and could potentially secure national park designation. In 1922, Congress had designated the spectacular Lehman Caves a national monument. Located in the Snake Range on the spine of the Great Basin, the caves ranked on par with others such as Timpanogos and Carlsbad. The Forest Service developed the monument as a tourist attraction for outdoor recreationists and it became critically important to the region, especially to the community of Ely, a small town that served as a hub of ranching and mining activity in eastern Nevada. Yet in their muted palette of grays, greens, yellows, and browns, the Lehman Caves and the Snake Range offered no obvious natural beauty or scenic attraction that might warrant designation of a park commensurate with the existing parks. It only afforded visitors the opportunity to enjoy the unique undulating landscape of the Great Basin and its ecosystems.[15]

But in the late 1950s, the Department of the Interior's advisory board on the national parks had recommended that the Park Service create eight new park areas to protect parts of the national coastline and natural environments unrepresented in the system, including the tallgrass prairie and the

Great Basin desert. The 1963 Leopold Report codified the idea that national parks should protect the nation's diverse ecosystems in its famous statement that "a national park should represent a vignette of primitive America." Although preserving the Great Basin's unique natural environment was important, that position actually took a lower priority than the economic needs of its rural residents. Because public lands did not provide property tax income to either the state or the county, to some residents in the Great Basin, growth in the recreational tourist industry promised to be a healthy replacement. This planned expansion in the National Park Service system accomplished three goals at once: new parks provided further outlets for outdoor recreation, protected a greater degree of the nation's ecological diversity, and gave rural communities close to the new parks the opportunity to develop outdoor recreation tourism.[16]

Increasingly in the postwar period, national parks anchored outdoor recreation opportunities and provided the basis for many local tourist economies. The eleven western states contained the nation's most iconic parks: the snowy peaks of Olympic and Rainier and the deep blue waters of Crater Lake in the Pacific Northwest; the incomparable Glacier, Yellowstone, Grand Teton, and Rocky Mountain National Parks in the northern mountain states; Mesa Verde, Bryce Canyon, Zion, and the immense Grand Canyon in the Colorado Plateau region; the stunning Carlsbad Caverns in the desert Southwest; and the wondrous Yosemite, Sequoia, Kings Canyon, and Lassen in California were indelibly stamped in the American mind. Most had lovely scenic drives with attractive names such as Going-to-the-Sun Highway, Trail Ridge Road, Tioga Pass, or Highway by the Sea. Gateway communities at the entry points of these roads benefited economically from the services they provided millions of travelers each year. Though not as colorful or breathtaking as the existing parks, the tall peaks of the Snake Range and the weird beauty of Lehman Caves represented the best chance for the Great Basin province to join the national park system, and the residents of Ely stood to benefit.[17]

Since their discovery, Lehman Caves had been of some interest to travelers before the establishment of the interstate highway system. Prospector and farmer Absalom S. Lehman had stumbled across the cave system, located near his ranch, in 1885. For nearly forty years, several private owners controlled access to the caves, including Charles W. Rowland and P. M. "Doc" Baker, son of former Confederate sympathizer and settler George W. Baker. The Bakers were the largest landowners in Snake Valley, just to the

The tallest peak in the Great Basin at 13,063 feet, Wheeler Peak is located in the Snake Range and was slated to form the heart of Great Basin National Park. Photograph by the author.

east of the Snake Range, where the caves were located. The Lehman Ranch changed hands several times, becoming part of the Rowland Ranch, the Baker Ranch, and the Saval Ranch, and was eventually a key component of the Meek brothers' dude ranch. Like most dude ranches, the Meek Ranch provided visitors a real cowboy experience, but it also offered them a unique chance to explore Lehman Caves. So important had the caves become to the Ely area that when the eastern Nevada portion of Highway 50 opened in 1920, the Forest Service and White Pine County developed a viable road off the main highway to the attraction. Then in 1922, President Warren G. Harding, at the behest of key Nevadans in the area including Vail M. Pittman, the owner of the *Ely Daily Times*, designated the caves a national monument in order to ensure their adequate development and management for outdoor recreation. But the timber-oriented Forest Service, the agency that managed monuments, was not the best choice to oversee Lehman Caves.[18]

Within two years, Governor James G. Scrugham, a former state engineer, began work with the Forest Service to develop the state's outdoor recreation attractions. Top on his list were Lehman Caves. Seeking the best possible designation, Governor Scrugham and Nevada senator Key Pittman introduced a bill to Congress to create Lehman Caves National Park and turn its administration over to the National Park Service. But the Nevada Livestock Association, a powerful political entity in the state, worried that a park designation would restrict ranchers' grazing access. During this time, as many residents of Ely had feared, Forest Service personnel devoted no special time or attention to the caves' care, which placed the entire burden of operation on a local family, who held permits for conducting tours and who alone had constructed a small resort for tourists. In 1928, the family struggled to keep up with the demands of visitation. They wrote Park Service director Stephen Mather for assistance in finding a buyer for their resort. In the six years since its designation as a monument, any meager federal or state funds for improving the caves had never applied to their private property, and their health had deteriorated from the stress of owning the place. But the Park Service had no authority over the matter, and the family's efforts to secure a buyer failed.[19]

Stepping into an administrative vacuum in 1933 to secure local interests, White Pine County, after much trouble issuing bonds for the cause, purchased the private resort and transferred it to the Forest Service. At the same time, Executive Order 6166 gave the National Park Service oversight over all national monuments. Both White Pine County, which had just purchased the resort property for the Forest Service, and the agency itself were unhappy with this designation; they accused the National Park Service of appropriating their efforts to stabilize and improve Lehman Caves. In addition, the Forest Service believed its plans for developing the Snake Range in its entirety were more ambitious and more focused on making the region a major outdoor recreation destination than the Park Service's plans to let it remain a small-scale national monument. Lehman Caves were a fine example of an underground geologic wonder, argued the agency, but they were too small a unit and too far away for the Park Service to pay much attention. Despite public pressure to rectify the situation, Lehman Caves remained under National Park Service administration, lacking the adequate improvements and funding to provide attractive visitor amenities during the 1930s and 1940s.[20]

In the postwar era, the White Pine County Chamber of Commerce, an organization that had never really given up the idea of making Ely a hub of outdoor recreation, once again advocated making the area around Lehman

Caves a national park. The chamber saw an opportunity to diversify the county's economy in the growing numbers of park visitors throughout the country. Mining had dominated the region's economy, with livestock production close behind; further diversification would help abate the often-severe fluctuations in county income, especially after the recent copper mine closures. At the same time, the rediscovery of a glacier in the northern cirque on Wheeler Peak, the tallest peak in the Great Basin, sparked renewed interest in preserving a unique portion of the region as a national park. The White Pine County Chamber of Commerce joined the Sierra Club, Wilderness Society, and the National Parks Association in launching a campaign to bring public and federal attention to the project. In 1956, Nevada's congressional delegation, Senators George Malone and Alan Bible and Representative Clifford Young, requested that the National Park Service conduct a field investigation to evaluate the viability of a Great Basin National Park.[21]

At the end of its examination, the National Park Service concluded that the area was the best example of a Great Basin sky-island, representing the layered biomes rising from the dusty playa below to the rocky peaks above tree line. Besides Wheeler Peak and Lehman Caves, the Snake Range also contained twisted and ancient bristlecone pines, a six-story limestone arch, several small lakes, and a rare desert-bound rock glacier, the Wheeler Glacier. But the Park Service warned that if Lehman Caves and Wheeler Peak were designated a national park, all mining claims, grazing rights, and private property would be subject to acquisition or extinguishment, the same as in other parks throughout the country. Nevertheless, interested parties formed the Great Basin Range National Park Association to pursue the designation, and all three members of Nevada's congressional delegation introduced bills to Congress in 1958 that required the secretary of the interior to investigate the matter. One Nevada newspaper editorial happily stated that this attention proved the Great Basin was more than the "gravel and sagebrush" outsiders thought. State promoters were anxious to overcome Nevada's status as a "bridge state," which visitors traveled through only on their way to other, more engaging recreational experiences.[22]

Yet the Forest Service maintained a vested interest in Lehman Caves and Wheeler Peak. Their designation as a national park would significantly diminish the agency's administration of the surrounding national forest. The Forest Service agreed with the National Park Service as to the unique merits of the Snake Range, from Lehman Caves, Wheeler Peak, and its glacier to the two natural arches, many small alpine lakes, and several of the world's most ancient bristlecone pines and its tallest mountain mahogany tree. But the agency insisted on requiring and participating in a second investigation to allow comparison of the multiple-use capacity provided by existing national forest management with the potential recreational development of the area as a national park. As a counter to the National Park Service's recommendation of the creation of the Wheeler Peak area as a park, the Forest Service had announced its intention to expand recreational development of the range as the Wheeler Peak Scenic Area under Operation Outdoors. This recreation area, to be managed by the Forest Service, would offer protection from mining and grazing for some places, but by and large those activities, as well as hunting and fishing, would not be restricted as they would be in a national park.[23]

The agency left out of this conversation was the BLM and its constituents, which stood to lose acreage that provided grazing range for five livestock operations surrounding the Snake Range. There were also forty-seven outstanding land applications of various types in the area and six mining districts within the proposed boundaries that contained about 20 patented claims and 230 unpatented claims. Yet despite the potential loss of these properties, the excitement surrounding the park idea propelled Great Basin National Park forward. The National Park Service recommended the establishment of a 147,000-acre park that would protect and showcase the region's distinctive ecological communities in addition to the unique geology of Lehman Caves and the soaring Wheeler Peak. No single feature alone provided enough justification for establishing a national park, but taken together, they formed an outstanding example of the Great Basin's environment. The moment was also right for the economic potential a national park would create in terms of outdoor recreation. The former director of Nevada's Department of Economic Development, Peter T. Kelley, headed the Nevada Foundation for a National Park, an organization that was determined to solicit support and funding for a park and that included leading residents such as former governors Vail Pittman and Charles H. Russell as well as casino entrepreneur William Harrah. On September 9, 1959, Representative Walter S. Baring and Senators Alan Bible and Howard W. Cannon introduced legislation to create Great Basin National Park.[24]

The arguments supporting and opposing the creation of a national park in the Great Basin came from a variety of groups and reflected current sentiments toward grazing on the public range and the multiple-use concept. They highlighted the place of and appreciation for the Great Basin environment in the range of the nation's natural wonders, something fairly new in the characterization of the region. And invariably, they also embodied the desperate need of rural White Pine County, like others in the region, to diversify and grow its economy. The question, as posed in newspapers across the nation by Utah journalist Jack Goodman in the *New York Times*, was, "Should Mount Wheeler and its environs continue, under the United States Forest Service [and Bureau of Land Management], to be open to mining, grazing and lumbering, as well as recreation? Or should they be preserved as a national park, under the National Park system, in which case 'multiple use,' in other words, use for commercial purposes, would be banned, leaving recreation as the sole purpose?"[25]

The public controversy surrounding the establishment of the park within the National Park Service and the Forest Service consisted primarily of the agencies territorializing their different land bases. The Forest Service believed the move to make the area a national park represented a "threat toward dismemberment of the national-forest system." In the North Cascades of Washington, the Sawtooth Range of Idaho, and other locations throughout the American West, land management was polarized in a turf war between the Forest Service, with its economically based multiple-use concept, and the National Park Service, with its recreation and preservation mandates.[26] In an infuriating way, the struggle between the two agencies served to confuse the actual issue in the minds of local residents, and land managers seemed to have forgotten that actual people depended on the area under discussion.

New York Times conservation columnist John B. Oakes, who served on the Department of the Interior's advisory board on national parks, pleaded with President John F. Kennedy to bring the competing land management agencies "into line and see to it that bureaucratic rivalries shall not damage the long-range national interest." Oakes argued that "the greatest enemy to the creation of new national parks in the West is the United States Forest Service," because it advocated multiple-use management of public lands to balance organized recreation with extractive uses such as timber, grazing, and mining, instead of giving it priority. The National Park Service promoted outdoor recreation to a much greater degree, permanently guarding the "remnants of the tranquil wilderness" and creating tourist-friendly access. Where the Forest Service, he argued, facilitated "the controlled exploitation of the public lands under its jurisdiction," the National Park Service fostered "the permanent protection and careful preservation *unimpaired* of selected areas of irreplaceable beauty or special significance."[27]

But in the Great Basin, the tension between the Forest Service's multiple use and the Park Service's dual mandate, beyond the territorial fights between agencies, had important economic ramifications for the residents of White Pine County and other rural counties surrounding the proposed park. Both the Forest Service and the National Park Service had dedicated programs to developing recreational amenities that would facilitate outdoor recreation for visitors. The difference was whether recreation in the area should be just one use balanced with others such as grazing and mining, or whether recreation should be a dominant use, supplanting grazing and mining. It was also a question of which interests were to be served and at what scale. A well-preserved national park was certainly commensurate with national interests and would draw attention if not prestige, but multiple-use management for local ranchers, miners, and recreationists offered more benefit on a regional scale. The rhetoric about national parks and the Great Basin environment that different groups used to support their positions divulged where they placed outdoor recreation in the hierarchy of land use and what they believed to be the overall purpose of these public lands.

Beginning in late 1959, Nevada senator Alan Bible conducted hearings in Ely to gauge the local, regional, and national responses to the Great Basin National Park proposal. Opponents of the park generally took the position that Wheeler Peak was "'just another mountain,' far more useful for grazing, mining and hunting, than for 'locking up as a park.'" Floyd Iverson, the forester in charge of the Intermountain Region, based near Salt Lake City, believed that the area was "typical of many other western mountain ranges" and that it did "not have the unique and spectacular features that characterize our national parks." Iverson said this despite his agency's listing of the area's unique features that had warranted a scenic area designation. The Carlin Sportsmen's Club, an affiliate of the larger Nevada Federated Sportsmen organization, argued that it did "not feel that the Wheeler park area in eastern Nevada would do justice to the State of Nevada as a National Park." But not all sportsmen agreed; Roy Torpey, owner of the Silver State Motel in Ely and a member of the Nevada Fish and Game Association who had always gotten his buck every fall, said he would "much rather see these same deer in a park where we could all see and enjoy them."[28]

Arguing against the park on behalf of local miners in the area, Louis D. Gordon of the Nevada Mining Association cautioned that "further land withdrawals, except those vitally necessary to National defense, are . . . inadvisable and not in the best interests of our State, or its economy." He believed that "the economy and welfare of our State can best be served by the orderly and proper development of its natural and basic industries—rather than by withdrawing excessive areas of land within our State Boundaries in order to afford a playground for residents of other States, whose economy is not affected by land withdrawals in Nevada." The mines in the Snake Range had produced about $6 million in gold and $4 million in tungsten, and the recently discovered beryllium ore, a mineral widely used by the defense industry as a hardener, could also be potentially profitable. Joseph Williams of the Nevada Farm Bureau agreed, arguing that creating parks "for the sole purpose of recreation" disregarded "conservation and wise harvesting of the nation's natural resources." His colleague, Fred B. Harris of the Nevada State Cattle Association, concurred and warned that the organization was "seriously concerned about the growing tendency toward the creation of more and more areas for the *sole* purpose of recreation." Reiterating the region's marginal identity, John E. Humphrey of the Nevada Wool Growers Association argued that "the Wheeler Peak Area in Eastern Nevada does not meet National Park qualifications," and that the "area contributes more to the public through regular use of all its resources."[29]

No one in the Ely area, however, had as much to lose as George N. Swallow, whose ranch properties near Shoshone, at the western foot of Mount Washington in the Snake Range, included the Swallow Ranch and the C-B Ranch. Swallow was one of several ranchers set to lose both BLM and Forest Service grazing rights if the park were created. The Swallows were Mormons who had emigrated from England just after the Civil War. The elder George Swallow, the son of an unskilled laborer, had arrived in the United States in 1868 and within two years had migrated to Fillmore, Utah. Swallow worked moving supplies from Fillmore to Milford and the Nevada mining town of Pioche. He also trailed cattle from Pioche to Elko. While working as a cowboy, he met Benjamin Kimball, who had a small farm operation in the tiny mining community of Shoshone. Swallow helped the elderly Kimball work his fields for the next decade. In 1880, he paid Kimball's debt on the farmland in exchange for its title, and this property formed the core of the Swallows' ranching operations. Swallow filed a 120-acre Desert Land Act claim to expand his farming operations, which included grain and hay production, and began ranching both cattle and sheep. Whenever the opportunity presented itself, Swallow also purchased neighboring ranches. He secured essential water rights during the 1920s, an important measure that ensured that when mining boomed at nearby Osceola and demand for water dried up the nearby creek, the Swallows had enough to run their operations.[30]

George and his wife, Anna Day, had seven children, all of whom worked on the ranch, along with several American Indians who provided additional labor. By 1907, the aging George sold his ranch and moved to Salt Lake City with the younger members of his family, where he constructed and operated the Swallow Apartment Building in the early 1910s, just three blocks away from the Salt Lake City Temple. His sons Richard, Alfred, and Ray purchased the highly successful ranch from their father, which included 1,200 cattle and almost 6,000 sheep.[31]

Richard Thomas Swallow, a graduate of the Mormon Church's business college in Salt Lake City, managed the Swallow brothers' ranch throughout the early twentieth century. They added 160 acres to the operation in 1924 under the Desert Land Act and another 440 acres in 1927 under the Desert Land Reclamation Act. The family held water rights along several creeks and springs throughout the south end of the surprisingly verdant Spring Valley. Richard brought the first automobile to the area in 1911 and proudly toured his friends and extensive family around the valley's dirt roads. By 1913, Alfred had grown tired of ranching and sold out his share of the ranch, moving across the Snake Range to Garrison, Utah, where he ran a general store. Three years later, Ray, whose wife was ill, sold his interest in the ranch, which left the whole outfit to Richard. In 1929, just before the Great Depression hit, Swallow diversified the ranch's operations, investing $250,000 in the construction of the new Hotel Nevada in Ely, an establishment that quickly became the town's hub of gambling and bootlegging. The following year, he purchased the Geyser Ranch in Lake Valley, just south of their main ranch. He even served in the Nevada state legislature for several years. But the economic ruin brought on by the stock market crash of 1929 nearly decimated the small town of Ely. By 1931, the Hotel Nevada sold at a terrible loss and the Swallows lost their entire investment, endangering payments on both the new ranch and old debts. In addition, the corresponding drought dramatically decreased haying and livestock production. In 1935, the Swallows sold the Geyser Ranch to recoup some of their financial losses. When the Taylor Grazing Act took effect and the ranch became part of the Ely Grazing District, the Swallows' place on the public rangeland was assured, but the measure did not put money in their pockets. To assuage the problem, Richard's wife, Matilda, began raising chickens to help with the family's finances.[32]

By 1936, Richard Swallow's sons George Neils, an ambitious and serious man, and Richard Mortenson had to make a tough decision about their father's ranch. They decided to finance the family's properties to pay off the remaining debts. The gamble worked, and the following year the Swallows finally obtained a clear title to the ranch. The elder Swallow died in 1943, leaving the two young men to run the outfit: Richard M. looked after the day-to-day ranch operations and George N. continued to evolve as a leader of the region's ranching community throughout the 1940s, serving as spokesperson and secretary of the United Stockmen's Association. In 1949, he organized the famous Operation Haylift during a terrible winter that left thousands of livestock stranded in deep snow across the central Great Basin and became a local hero.[33]

But throughout the next decade, George N. Swallow became increasingly protective of the family's struggling ranching operation. The drought of the early 1950s caused the Swallow Ranch, like many in the region, to lose a significant number of livestock. During the 1953 atomic testing series, Swallow contacted the Atomic Energy Commission about damages to his livestock. His sheep herds on the west side of Wheeler Peak had suffered the same effects as those in Utah exposed to radioactive fallout. When the AEC investigated Swallow's animals, it determined that his herds were not suffering from radiation burns, but from stomatitis, or common mouth ulcers. He lost more than a quarter of his livestock. By the time the proposal for Great Basin National Park reached Congress, Swallow was not supportive. He argued that his grazing allotment on the northwest side of the potential park was the most important annual forage for his livestock. Swallow also worried that a national park would decrease, or at least interfere with, the ranch's water rights. He was not, however, completely averse to recreational development. His C-B Land and Cattle Company owned the area around the Ward Mining District's charcoal ovens, about fifteen miles south of Ely. In 1956, Swallow leased eighty acres of the site and adequate water to Nevada's park commission so it could develop the old mining town as a state park with commensurate outdoor recreation facilities that included campsites and other amenities. In addition, Swallow also supplied deer hunters in Ely with packhorses and wranglers for a fee.[34]

For Swallow, the trouble with a national park had to do with the cultural and legal parameters of park administration and how that kind of focus on outdoor recreation would work. National parks supported camping and hiking but did not support activities such as hunting and fishing. Swallow had a tough time seeing how his family and ranching operation would benefit if a park were created. That they stood to lose important grazing range and water rights so that tourists could have a good recreational experience seemed unreasonable and unfair.

Proponents of the national park, however, viewed the situation differently. Most of them came from urban areas such as Reno and Las Vegas and included the likes of academics, activists, and some supporters from outside the state. They generally believed the public lands involved contained "little commercially viable timber," were "no more nor less pockmarked with dubious mining claims than other Nevada ranges," and had "scanty livestock carrying capacity." Instead, they argued, the value of the Snake Range lay in its unique ecological and geological qualities; within just five miles, Darwin Lambert argued, "it is possible to go from shadscale desert, through the piñon-juniper belt, the aspen-yellow pine belt, the spruce-fir country, and the ancient bristlecones of timberline to vast alpine expanses on the rocky peaks and ridges."[35] The mayor of Ely, N. E. Broadbent, fully agreed with this rationale. He argued that the land withdrawal for the park would take the area out of private use by a very small number of ranchers and miners and allow it "to be used by millions of people as a place to enjoy."[36] The White Pine County Chamber of Commerce concurred, noting that the "establishment of the park is one of great economic importance to the whole State of Nevada." White Pine Tourist Enterprises, a committee comprising fifty members of the county's business community, the Ely Lions Club, and several other chambers of commerce throughout the state, including those in Las Vegas and Tonopah, all supported creation of a national park. They argued that "national parks are just about the greatest tourist magnet in the world." For these groups, a national park would bring in more revenue for their communities and businesses.[37]

Many state organizations were also eager to see Great Basin National Park created. The Nevada Department of Economic Development argued that national park designation would bring national prestige to the state in addition to potential economic benefits. Designating the area a national park, the group hoped, would "launch a new era of respect for Nevada scenery, a new, solid phase of large-scale tourist business founded on the basic attractions of the state." Many state officials believed that Great Basin National Park would attract the same kind of visitation as Zion National Park and the other Utah parks, all of which were within a day's drive of the proposed park, bringing in "tourists by the thousands." The Ely Riding

Cover of the *Proposed Great Basin National Park Nevada* pamphlet, circa 1959. Image courtesy of Howard Cannon Papers, Special Collections, University of Nevada, Las Vegas Libraries.

Club felt that the establishment of Great Basin National Park was critical to creating convenient and attractive places where their clients could ride horses on nice trails and have access to adequate facilities. The pamphlet designed to promote the proposed park provided visual evidence of how central Great Basin National Park was to the development of tourism in eastern Nevada and western Utah. The publication featured colored photos of mountainscapes and visitors enjoying the scenery, and a map placing the park at the center of the region.[38]

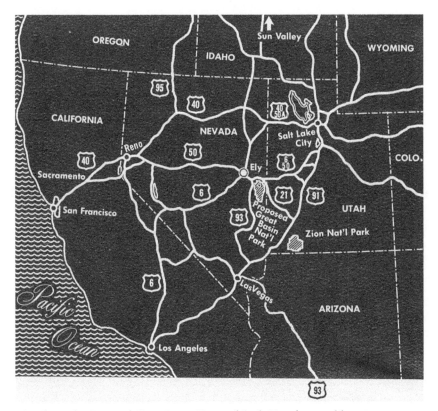

Map from the *Proposed Great Basin National Park Nevada* pamphlet, circa 1959. Image courtesy of Howard Cannon Papers, Special Collections, University of Nevada, Las Vegas Libraries.

The national park, according to the Great Basin Range National Park Association, was not meant to hurt the local economy, but to help it. Most park proponents were aware that its creation would come at a cost—ranchers like the Swallows would be asked to make sacrifices so that the greater Ely community could benefit. Darwin Lambert, a former National Park Service employee and the president of the association as well as the new owner of the *Ely Daily Times*, hoped that "ways might be found to secure the park and hurt no one in the process." Nevada governor Grant Sawyer agreed; he supported the creation of the national park provided satisfactory compensation was given to those holding water and grazing rights.[39]

Between 1960 and 1962, as plans for the park progressed, the debate over creating Great Basin National Park generated intense discussion about the appropriate size of a national park in the region and the role it would play in creating jobs and facilitating local economies. In May 1960, Senators Alan Bible and Howard Cannon introduced a park bill that attempted to "reconcile divergent views of conservationists and local mining and grazing interests." The proposal reduced the area from 147,000 to 124,540 acres and provided that "prospecting and mining as well as grazing [would] be permitted in the area," though both would eventually be eliminated. As the bill worked its way through committee, the Senate even considered adding a hunting provision. The compromises in the bill, however, served only to call the characteristics of national parks into question. George N. Swallow expressed concern that while the legislation allowed for existing grazing rights, the bill made it "impossible for a [grazing] permittee to transfer or dispose of grazing privileges to another party," which would "greatly reduce the value of all base property of any permittee using grazing lands within the boundaries of the proposed Great Basin National Park."[40]

The Nevada Bureau of Mines also opposed the compromise legislation. The group believed the bill did not "protect adequately the development of mineral resources for the economic strength and military security of the United States" because it located decision-making power over mining with the secretary of the interior instead of with the traditionally permissive BLM. In addition, the bureau opposed the Department of the Interior's decision to determine the mining and mineral leasing activities on a restricted basis, as it had done at Glacier Bay National Monument in Alaska, to ensure the "protection of the scenic, scientific, and recreational and other natural values of the lands containing them." The Nevada Federated Sportsmen continued to oppose the park on the basis that it "would have no wildlife management"; whether national parks allowed hunting or not, the group viewed any federal oversight of the matter as restrictive.[41]

But national parks typically did not have provisions for grazing and mining and did not allow hunting activities within park boundaries. Parks had, from their inception, always been natural reserves that provided key service amenities to outdoor recreationists to facilitate their enjoyment of nature. Surprisingly, conservation groups such as the Sierra Club thought the mining, grazing, and hunting concessions were necessary measures in the short term to help secure the park. But, to drive home the very temporary nature of these activities, Richard C. Sill, chair of the organization's Toiyabe Chapter, warned the White Pine County Chamber of Commerce that if the proposed park was "not a true national park because of certain dubious provisions in the law," then mining, grazing, and hunting in Great

Basin National Park would eventually impede the county's ability to secure increased revenue from park visitors. Sill reminded the chamber of commerce that "tourists do not come to a national park to see cattle or sheep or an overgrazed remnant of meadows or forest," or the "highly unsavory destruction of scenic values when big mining concerns get into operation." He thought Great Basin National Park in the fall would draw "a large number of non-hunting tourists during hunting season," which would make "tourists fear their children may be potted [shot] by careless hunters."[42]

In the new wave of national park expansion, the Department of the Interior focused attention on creating new outdoor recreation spaces and preserving key ecosystems representative of those "vignettes of primitive America." But in the absence of iconic landscapes such as those found in the early parks—the "superlative examples of natural beauty, altered as little as possible from their natural state"—new parks were difficult to justify, especially in isolated regions such as the Great Basin. Some national park advocates criticized this expansion program, arguing that several new parks were "below the standards of grandeur and public interest of the national park ideal," including the proposed Great Basin National Park, which was described as a "multiple-use hybrid." Despite this criticism, the National Park Service could not be said to compromise on its recreational ideal for long. At Capitol Reef National Monument, a magnificent geologic swell in central Utah that had a strong Mormon cultural history, the agency was upgrading the area to "more rigid national park standards." This process included eliminating private holdings and off-road vehicle traffic, rerouting roads, and closing trails.[43]

However, by mid-1962, the proposed concessions for Great Basin National Park reached an unacceptable level. The Senate's version of the park, though it included grazing, mining, and hunting, retained the vast majority of the original proposed acreage, but when the bill arrived at the House of Representatives, the size of the park was significantly reduced to about 53,000 acres, a third of its initially proposed size. The reduction was a different kind of compromise for the park—one that removed any potential mining areas and the existing grazing ranges. Secretary of the Interior Stewart Udall wrote Representative Wayne N. Aspinall, chair of the House Committee on Interior and Insular Affairs, of his dissatisfaction with this new iteration. Udall warned that the remaining acreage would not allow the area to qualify as a national park—the new, smaller boundaries excluded Lexington Arch, Mount Washington, and a big forest of bristlecone pines, all of which were essential characteristics and important tourist attractions. Udall accused mining and grazing interests of stripping the park of its essential value.[44]

The House bill was the result of the reluctance of one of the state's congressional representatives. Nevada representative Walter S. Baring had called a meeting in Ely with local ranchers and miners in early June after Senators Alan Bible and Walter Cannon had accused him of "dragging his feet" over supporting the bill in the House. Besides the White Pine County Chamber of Commerce, George N. Swallow, representing the livestock interests; James D. Williams, representing those interested in the beryllium claims; and a representative of the Anaconda Company, a giant mining magnate, met to hash out their differences. Their conference resulted in a recommendation for a smaller park. The group argued that a larger park would hurt the state's industrial development and that a smaller park, though not what the community and chamber of commerce had originally wanted, would nevertheless be "a beautiful start." This seemed to be the central issue blocking the creation of Great Basin National Park. In the minds of those who relied on traditional uses of public lands, national park designation would preclude any industrial development, curtail actual current grazing and mining operations, and prevent any potential future development in those areas.[45]

The creation of Great Basin National Park directly threatened to put the already struggling Swallow family out of business in the early 1960s. In 1959, the Swallow family owned about three thousand acres and once again needed financing to continue their ranch operations. Deeply discouraged and disillusioned with both the economic opportunities available in the central Great Basin and the belief system of the Mormon Church, Swallow felt he was fighting an uphill battle just to make a living. To secure the necessary funds to keep the ranch going, he sold the property and repurchased it under a financing structure that allowed him to pay the debt in small installments. During the next few years, he used the funds from the sale to purchase three more properties and also added another 320 acres under the Desert Land Act. For Swallow, owning more acreage secured more grazing range for his livestock, and in the face of possible reductions if Great Basin National Park were created, this was the best he could do to stave off those losses.[46]

Swallow represented the perspective of most ranchers in the Great Basin, though he was more ambitious, diverse, and entrepreneurial in his endeavors. Between his positions in the livestock industry, as president of the Eastern Nevada Telephone Company, and as a business owner in the White Pine County community, Swallow was very influential and his opinion about the national park carried much weight locally. In 1961, Swallow and twenty other business owners accompanied Nevada governor Grant Sawyer to Detroit to solicit interest in bringing industry to the state. Previous trips for the same purpose to New York, Chicago, Cleveland, and Dallas featured the governor promoting the state's transportation potential, favorable tax structure, amount of land available for industrial development, and the relaxed attitude of Nevadans in general.[47]

That same year, Swallow served on the grazing advisory board as it transitioned to the new Multiple-Use Advisory Board, a step that broadened its membership to include timber, recreation, wilderness, and "other non-livestock groups" and severely decreased the influence of the ranchers in managing public lands. Lamenting the loss of ranchers' priority, Swallow presented a paper at the annual meeting of the state's chapter of the American Society of Range Management entitled "The Place of the Nevada Rancher and His Place on the Public Lands," which outlined the fundamental role and benefits he argued livestock production had on the public domain. Swallow believed that the livestock industry was fundamentally important to Nevada, and that it was a higher use, if not the highest use, of the Great Basin's public lands. The Taylor Grazing Act, he explained, had recognized ranchers' hierarchy within multiple use. Swallow considered outdoor recreation important, but supplementary, especially given its dependence on an influx of outsiders to sustain it. Swallow and other ranchers in the area were not prepared to trade the known income of ranching and mining for the devil's bargain of tourism. Swallow opposed the park if it interfered with Ely's commercial and industrial growth.[48]

This is what prompted Swallow to write his long, caustic letter to Representative Wayne N. Aspinall complaining about Secretary Udall's "socialistic, land grabbing policies." Swallow and his neighbor, a Basque sheepherder named Antonio Omaechevarria, also wrote the entire Nevada congressional delegation that "Udall does not care about the welfare of Western basic industries." Omaechevarria accused the secretary of the interior of sacrificing the "interests of our Nevada working men and their families, as to their homes, job and right to unrestricted recreation." Senator Howard Cannon responded to Omaechevarria, attempting to offer clarity to the rancher's factual understanding, but it did not matter. Omaechevarria was not debating points of fact but expressing frustration over the decline of public lands ranching within multiple use.[49]

The frustration expressed by Swallow and Omaechevarria was echoed in a similar letter to Nevada representative Walter S. Baring, written by James D. Williams of Wheeler Mines, the mining company set to develop the Snake Range's beryllium deposits in conjunction with the Anaconda Company. In his letter, Williams stated that a significant reduction in proposed park acreage was the only way to ensure the protection of mining and grazing interests so that they would not be subjected to the oversight of the Department of the Interior. He complained that "the Secretary [of the Interior] has no basic right to ride roughshod over all private interests in this area, most of which having been established long prior to any thought of a national park." Though the BLM, an agency very much a part of the Department of the Interior, governed both mining and grazing on public lands, it was easier for Williams to target Udall. But the ascendancy of outdoor recreation as a key component of multiple use lay at the core of his real frustration. Even the Nevada Wildlife Federation struggled with the shift. The organization preferred designating the proposed Great Basin National Park a national scenic or national recreation area in order to protect multiple-use practices in the region.[50]

The struggle between Swallow, Omaechevarria, Williams, the White Pine Chamber of Commerce, and Udall's Department of the Interior was part of a larger struggle between private commercial and industrial interests and national environmental and recreational interests conducted within the framework of multiple use. Udall and the National Park Service could not compromise the fundamental principles embedded in the national park ideal in the establishment of Great Basin National Park, and many local interests could not bet on the park replacing the economic income they were certain would be generated from mining, grazing, and even hunting. Udall had no intention of ramming a park "down anybody's throat," and no one locally doubted that outdoor recreation could coexist under the multiple-use concept. The National Park Service was willing to compromise on allowing mining and grazing temporarily and indeed had made similar provisions in other park bills during the same time. The agency could not, however, buy out the grazing privileges as Swallow had suggested because, as Senator Howard Cannon stated, "grazing has always been considered a privilege extended by the Government rather than a right inherent in the permittee." Cannon noted that Congress had "violently opposed" similar suggestions in the past. But most of the interests in White Pine County could not in the end justify elevating outdoor recreation to an equal or higher level with commercial interests. To do so would be "socialistic," serving the greater good of the nation by providing for recreation to the exclusion of local private mining and grazing interests.[51]

Asking ranchers, mining interests, and other local businesses to accommodate the demands of a national park without a guarantee of economic benefit ran counter to their sense of self-preservation, especially since the major supporters of Great Basin National Park were from urban areas inside and outside the region. In Swallow's estimation, Great Basin residents, particularly in Nevada, lived on a vast federal reservation cut off from normal economic progress, unable to reap the economic benefits associated with private property. Representative Walter Baring agreed, declaring that the "people," meaning local residents who lived near the park, not tourists vacationing from major metropolises, comprised the "public" who owned these public lands. He accused Secretary Udall of trying to override the desires of these local residents, who, after all, had to live with whatever national park was created in the area. He reiterated that all the state's Department of Economic Development wanted was some kind of national park, as did the White Pine County Chamber of Commerce. They embraced a broader definition of multiple use for all public lands, including national parks. But the Department of the Interior found the idea abhorrent. National parks did not adhere to multiple use and could not realistically include grazing and mining. As a result, the entire endeavor fell apart at the end of 1966. Succeeding bills to create Great Basin National Park failed in Congress until Representative Walter Baring and Senators Alan Bible and Howard Cannon ceased introducing them.[52]

Great Basin National Park was not the only park proposed in the vast stretch of public lands that occupied most of Nevada and Utah. Canyonlands National Park on Utah's Colorado Plateau had similar issues related to its creation, including opposition from mining and grazing interests, potential elimination of access to natural resources for commercial and private development, and the exploration and discovery of a very profitable oil reserve. But unlike Great Basin National Park, it received the approval of Congress, on September 12, 1964.[53]

The Canyonlands park proposal succeeded in large part because Utahans generally accepted the benefits of outdoor recreation to their state. Between Zion and Bryce Canyon National Parks, as well as Arches and Natural

Bridges National Monuments, residents of the state already benefited from designations that attracted outdoor recreationists to its scenic wonders. Nevada had no such experience in the early 1960s. Some Utahans questioned the qualifications of Canyonlands as a national park, but the scenic value of the Needles and the importance of the confluence of the Green and Colorado Rivers were difficult for critics to deny. Nevadans, however, decried the scenic value and natural worth of Wheeler Peak, Lexington Arch, and even Lehman Caves. In addition, Canyonlands National Park's biggest promoter in Utah, Senator Frank E. Moss, who had pushed the park idea along with mining and grazing protections from the beginning, was willing to make compromises rather than lose the park altogether. Where the Utah congressional delegation was able to hammer out their differences on park boundaries and temporary mining and grazing access, the Nevada delegation was miserably stuck in their polarized positions. When it came down to retaining mining access or losing the park, Senator Moss opted to compromise to retain grazing and secure an important land exchange. The architects of the final Canyonlands National Park were pleased with the outcome and firmly believed they had "done the best thing for Utah and the right thing for the country."[54]

Great Basin National Park proved a failure in the 1960s, and it was not the only category of organized recreation denied the region. The area also received only one very small wilderness designation. The legislation creating wilderness areas was specifically contingent on a bargain struck between Representative Wayne Aspinall and a group of senators who had promoted several wilderness bills in successive congressional sessions in the late 1950s and early 1960s only to have them disappear in the House of Representatives in Aspinall's public lands committee. Cecil Garland, a young hardware and sporting goods store owner in Lincoln, Montana, near the north end of Helena National Forest, helped generate popular pressure for the new bill in the Senate when he learned the Forest Service in that region had plans to build roads and log the beautiful primitive area. He said, "I decided then and there that this was one of the last pieces of beautiful country left intact, and God damn it, they weren't going to tear it up . . . they weren't going to tear up that piece of country with their damn bulldozers."[55]

Garland incited a grassroots movement in Montana that helped propel the wilderness legislation forward. While in Washington, D.C., meeting with the Montana congressional delegation, Garland ran into Aspinall and pressed him about the wilderness proposal. Aspinall, who adamantly opposed restricting possible economic development of public lands, told Garland he would kill the wilderness bill either in committee or on the floor of the House of Representatives. Upset, Garland went to see Montana senator Michael J. Mansfield, who assured him that someday, Aspinall was going to want something very badly and that something would leverage the wilderness legislation. According to Garland, that moment arrived in 1964, when the Senate once again passed wilderness legislation and Aspinall, increasingly concerned about the controversies racking public lands management, wanted support for a public lands investigation—the Public Land Law Review Commission. The compromise wilderness legislation that passed did not include lands managed by the BLM, which, in Aspinall's view, were central to multiple use. Despite the agency's exclusion, however, BLM director Charles Stoddard instructed his staff to identify areas within the public lands system that contained wilderness values. The BLM's report of March 1965 noted sixty-one such areas across the western states, demonstrating the agency's interest in securing some form of greater protection for the land it administered.[56]

Mining and grazing interests in the Great Basin resolutely opposed the Wilderness Act, which was intended to exclude some national forest land from mining, grazing, and other commercial developments. The problem, as stated by the Nevada Mining Association, was that wilderness as created in the legislation ensured that "minerals in these areas will remain unproven and locked up forever." As a result, the Jarbidge Wilderness, a 65,000-acre area in a remote corner of the Humboldt National Forest in the Jarbidge Mountains on the Nevada-Idaho state line, a "hard-to-reach country with peaks more than 10,000 feet high," was the only area designated in 1964. As with the opposition that Great Basin National Park faced in Ely, the residents of Elko, the gateway town to the Jarbidge Wilderness, expressed their disapproval of the wilderness area and its possible future expansion. At a public hearing in 1972, residents indicated their disappointment, arguing that the Forest Service was more concerned about protecting the mountains than "preserving the freedoms of the American people." Wilderness, they believed, embodied restraints and regulations; their vision of multiple use was much broader and still incorporated customary uses of public lands.[57]

Much of the drive to classify some of the Great Basin as wilderness came from the Nevada Outdoor Recreation Association (NORA), a nonprofit group headquartered in Carson City that had conducted its own survey of "scenic, natural, historical, and recreational resources on the public lands in

Nevada." In the mid-1950s, founders of the association, including Charles Watson and Thomas H. Watkins, had examined 350 sites on BLM lands throughout Nevada, many of which, they argued, contained "little-known or previously unknown phenomena" and deserved environmental protection equal with that of national parks and primitive areas in national forests. Originally named the Nevada Public Domain Survey (NPDS), the organization worked diligently to repackage the state's public lands in the popular consciousness. Instead of a wasteland awaiting transfer into private ownership or a potential area for natural resource exploitation, the public domain, the NPDS stated, echoing Bernard DeVoto's sentiment, was a collective ecological commons that belonged to the American public.[58]

Watson, Watkins, and the other members of the NPDS were often at odds with the Sierra Club over whether or not desert, lowland, and wetland areas on public lands deserved preservation. The Toiyabe Chapter in Las Vegas constantly frustrated leading wetlands conservationist Norma Cox, a long-time Las Vegas resident, during this time because "they were primarily interested in mountain issues" and "could see no value of the wetlands." Playas, piñon-juniper forest, sagebrush flats, and sinks held little value for Sierra Club members because they were not part of iconic areas and did not comprise unique scenery, just the average appearance of the Great Basin. The NPDS's "Big Book," the publication resulting from its survey, singled out the Black Rock Desert in the northeastern part of the state and Red Rock Canyon near Las Vegas as places of singular beauty and recreational opportunity. The association's influence on the BLM's public lands management policies throughout the next decade helped create Red Rock Canyon Recreation Lands, an impressive red- and white-banded sandstone cliff the Sierra Club had agreed warranted protection. Red Rocks became the first unit within the BLM system to be devoted to recreational activities. In the mid-1970s, NORA members Watkins and Watson published *The Lands No One Knows*, a study of the evolution of the public domain containing a larger survey of potential wilderness areas throughout the United States.[59]

But the absence of a national park and multiple charismatic wilderness areas was telling. Without a substantial number of public land acres organized into national parks or wilderness areas, the designations most closely associated with outdoor recreation, and only a handful of preserved areas, the Great Basin had only unorganized and vaguely delineated recreation opportunities subsumed in grazing and mining landscapes. But this subordinated outdoor recreation to commercial and industrial interests, which in the Great Basin were subject to the traditional boom and bust trends. Most White Pine County residents had preferred the broader version of multiple use that did not elevate recreation to the level that would attract the same number of visitors as national parks did. Reliant on an economy based on mining and ranching, Ely and the surrounding region suffered economically because the movement to create the national park failed, the Wilderness Act passed them by, and there was no other way to diversify the town's economy. When the major employer in the area, Kennecott Copper Mines, closed within a decade of the park's demise, there was nothing to soften the economic blow. Even ranchers lost out; by the time the park proposal failed, George N. Swallow, who was again deeply in debt, once more tried to sell his ranch in order to repurchase it with new financing. But this time, his resale scheme failed and the Swallows lost their entire operation.[60]

What ranchers, workers, and the White Pine County Chamber of Commerce did not understand was that without a focused place to engage in outdoor recreation, the growing number of outdoor recreationists in the Great Basin would simply go where they wanted and impose themselves on rural residents in other ways. Throughout the 1960s, off-road vehicle (ORV) use had become increasingly popular. Motorcycles, dune buggies, and four-wheel drive vehicles chewed up desert land in large concentrations. They also disrupted existing public land users. But in terms of multiple use, the BLM and the Department of the Interior were obligated to make room for ORVs on public lands. In 1972, President Richard M. Nixon signed Executive Order 11644, which declared that because "an estimated 5 million off-road recreational vehicles—motorcycles, minibikes, trail bikes, snow-mobiles, dune-buggies, all-terrain vehicles, and others—are in use in the United States today, and their popularity continues to increase rapidly," policies and procedures were needed to "ensure that the use of off-road vehicles on public lands will be controlled and directed," "to promote the safety of all users," and "to minimize conflicts among the various uses" on public lands. This attempt to accommodate ORV use and balance it with all the other multiple uses was ambitious, but short-lived.[61]

Nevada governor Donal "Mike" O'Callaghan balked at the restrictions implied by the Nixon administration. He reminded Secretary of the Interior Rogers C. B. Morton that "the people of Nevada have historically enjoyed the great open spaces," and before prescribing any regulations for ORV use, the "needs and desires of the local people" should be given proper consideration. Miners and ranchers feared that ORV regulations

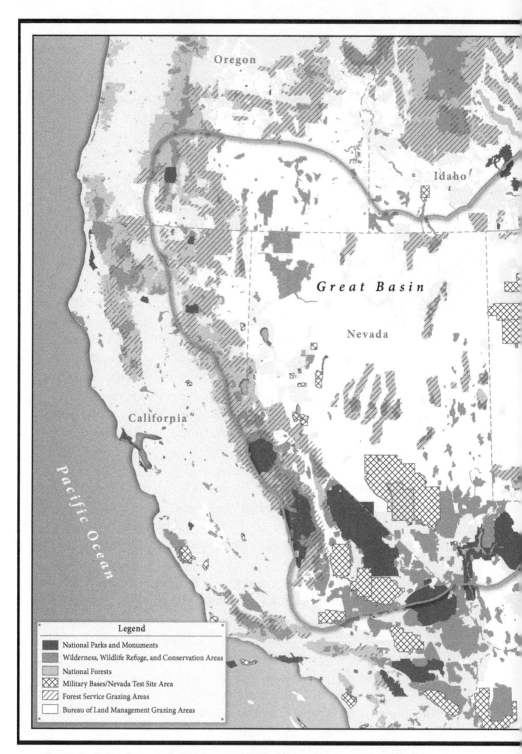

Legend

- ■ National Parks and Monuments
- ■ Wilderness, Wildlife Refuge, and Conservation Areas
- ▨ National Forests
- ⊠ Military Bases/Nevada Test Site Area
- ▨ Forest Service Grazing Areas
- ☐ Bureau of Land Management Grazing Areas

The Great Basin delineating areas in which outdoor recreation and wildlife preservation are organized and focused, including the national forests, national conservation areas, national monuments, national wildlife refuges, wilderness

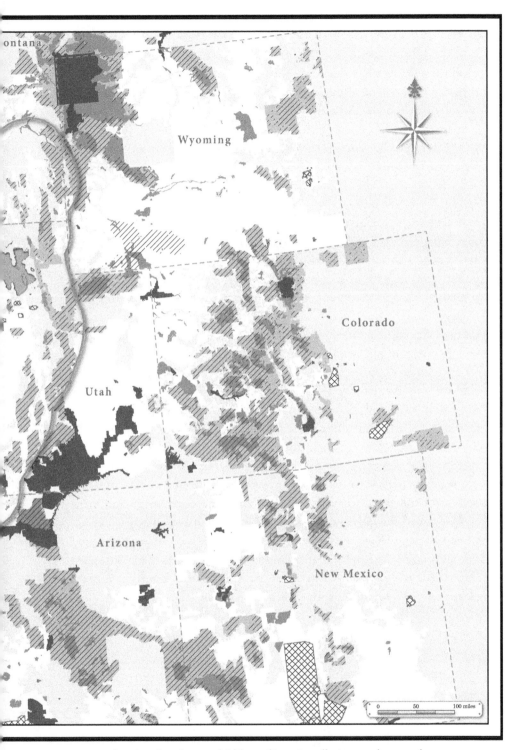

areas, and national parks, overlaid by military installations and areas where
grazing is permitted. Map by Gerry Krieg. *Copyright © 2015 by the University of
Oklahoma Press*

would prohibit them from using their four-wheel drive vehicles to reach their claims and herds. Realistically, much of the Great Basin was accessible only via barely maintained dirt roads. These people did, however, express interest in the BLM creating special areas for snowmobiles, dune buggies, and motorcycles because they could do "a lot of damage by not staying on well traveled roads."[62]

In its response, the BLM notified Governor O'Callaghan that "unless specifically restricted or closed, all BLM land in Nevada is open." Since only Red Rock Canyon near Las Vegas had been closed to ORVs, the entire state remained open to motor vehicles. Further regulations allowed miners and ranchers to use ORVs to prospect and access their livestock. Other public lands management agencies, including the Forest Service, adopted similar regulations that required spark arresters on ORVs and permits for large groups. The noisy, fast-moving vehicles strained the limits of multiple use and directly conflicted with grazing, military activities, other recreational uses of public lands.[63]

But with no designated facilities and no emergency services readily available, ORV users and other recreationists often relied on the nearest residents to provide emergency gas and water, and even to fix the occasional flat tire or provide other forms of assistance. Ranchers, including the Sharps, Fallinis, and Uhaldes, complained about motorists who scared livestock and sped across desert roads in areas still signed as open range. The BLM did not regularly track the numbers of visitors to unregulated public lands, yet with the numbers of recreationists growing in regulated areas, land managers assumed the increase also occurred in unregulated ones, particularly when ORVs cut wide swaths through the sagebrush or left sets of rutted tracks through sandy playas and dunes. As outdoor recreation increased throughout the next several decades, the burden of risk was once again placed on those who lived with the reality of public lands.[64]

SIX

The Last Refuge

Multiple-use management was a hectic and contested proposition by the 1970s. Ranchers coexisted, albeit sometimes uneasily, with outdoor recreationists of various persuasions. Nuclear testing, though by this point conducted underground, and other military activities related to national defense continued to feature prominently on the Great Basin's public lands. None of these activities had precluded wildlife management, though all of them interfered with or in some way altered the habitats of quite a few species, including those valued by hunters. Charismatic fauna such as bighorn sheep, pronghorn, mule deer, mountain goat, Rocky Mountain elk, black bear, and mountain lion had always been present on public lands and had provided the foundation for the region's big game hunting. Wild horses had also roamed the rangeland with them. As multiple use expanded, these species were under increasing threat and required careful oversight to ensure their ongoing health.

In particular, mountain lions required vast stretches of undisturbed habitat to thrive, a condition easily met in the Great Basin, so long as it remained that way. However, with the growth of the livestock industry in the region, fearsome mountain lions became, for many ranchers, unwanted predators. States dependent on the livestock industry often hired big game hunters to suppress mountain lion numbers. In the early 1950s, a particularly charismatic couple, Idahoan Snap Palmer and his wife, Vera, ranged throughout central Nevada eradicating the problematic cats for the state's

Department of Wildlife. The couple received a bounty for every animal they killed. Then in 1965, commensurate with state officials' interpretation of the Leopold Report, Nevada designated mountain lions a valuable big game species and began issuing permits to more closely regulate their populations and reap the benefits of big cat hunting.[1]

The cougar was not the only icon of the American West to have aroused the ire of ranchers. In the nineteenth century, several million wild horses roamed Texas, the Great Plains, California, and the rest of the region, migrating north from New Spain and west from the eastern colonies. When Europeans reintroduced *Equus* to the Americas, the animals underwent a veritable "ecological explosion," proliferating across the continent. By the nineteenth century, horses were fundamentally important to both colonists and Native peoples. But as settlement, farming, and the livestock industry expanded, farmers and ranchers considered the ever-growing wild horse herds a menace. The roaming bands depleted crops and forage, drank up water holes, "raided" ranch herds for mares, and generally threatened legitimate commercial economic interests. The earliest report of trouble over wild horse herds occurred in the 1820s in California when the nascent Mexican government took drastic measures to eradicate the animals, rounding up and slaughtering thousands of horses. Similar efforts took place in succeeding decades in other states, particularly those dependent on livestock production, such as Texas. Wild horses were economically detrimental and were considered unsightly pests, with their short legs, hammerheads, and scruffy coats. Their only redemption was in the entertainment they provided bored and unemployed cowboys in bucking competitions held by early rodeos. The animals also provided extra cash to those willing to round them up and sell them for meat; thus their populations tended to decrease in rough economic times.[2]

The animals had their admirers, though, and developed a fundamental niche in the nation's military during the nineteenth century. Some cavalry officers coveted their attributes, having "never met with any thing of the horse kind that possessed strength, action, and wind equal to the 'mustang' horses, (as they are called by the Spaniards,) or any that could endure fatigue and hunger equal to them, or subsist upon as little, and retain their strength." Their numbers provided a large, profitable pool of animals for the military to draw from for use in wars before the advent of tanks. Some horse breeders even used wild horse herds to supply mares that exhibited good conformation and stamina. They hired professional "mustangers," the slang name given to those who captured wild horses, to shoot the herds' stallions in order to round up the mares and bring them to the breeders. When bred to blooded stallions, particularly Thoroughbreds, these mares produced hardy, long-winded, sensible stock animals that supplied many of the nation's best mounts. Breeders released some of these crossbred animals back into the wild herds in order to continue to improve their conformation at very little expense. The infusion of new genes into the wild horse herd populations, which tended toward inbreeding, was fundamentally important for their survival as it rejuvenated the vitality of the animals. Likewise, domestic horse breeds benefited from the hardiness the arid environment bred into the mustangs. Wild horses were as much important assets in the development of the Quarter Horse as they were undesirable pests, and not surprisingly, they brought out both cruelty and compassion in people.[3]

Beginning in the 1880s, with drought and range degradation well under way in many parts of the country, state and territorial governments across the American West, encouraged by ranchers, began eradicating wild horse herds in earnest, but this time with federal assistance. The nation's newspapers reported a veritable "war" against the wild horses. On the Great Plains, as had already happened in California and Texas, ranchers organized "hunting parties," shot the stallions, and rounded up as many of the animals as they could. The ferocity with which ranchers pursued wild horses mirrored their feelings toward wolves. These were animals that violated property laws; wolves killed livestock and wild horses stole grass, water, and other horses. In some ways, stallions were actually considered worse than wolves because they would take not just one or two animals, but an entire corral filled with horses. But unlike the legendary predators, wild horses did not engender fear. Mustangs could become personal assets and provide monetary gain if they were tamed and "broken" to the saddle. Wild horse hunts were replicated in Wyoming, Arizona, Washington, and other western states beyond the Great Plains. The animals even became an international problem. Australians in Queensland and New South Wales coped with growing numbers of "Brumbies" and took similar measures toward their eradication.[4]

In the Great Basin, the same phenomenon occurred. Wild horse herds in the region had developed in conjunction with the Great Basin's livestock industry. Ranches along the Humboldt River produced horses for freight hauling, in support of the mining industry, and for making hay and working cattle. These equines were turned loose every winter to fend for themselves and then rounded up for work the next spring. In warmer areas and during the spring and summer, ranchers turned their horses out with the cattle when they were not needed for work. Between the constant influx of local horses and general reproduction rates—horses reproduce at a 10 to 20 percent rate of increase annually—the region developed a substantial wild horse population. But the trouble with wild horses, as one Nevadan put it, was that the animals were "eating the grass off, and making it hard picking in places for cattle and sheep."[5]

Ranchers in the central Great Basin, where two hundred thousand or more horses roamed, began a concerted effort to remove what they considered to be the excess. The Nevada state legislature consistently supported this endeavor in the 1890s by allowing anyone to kill "wild, unbranded horses." Wild horse runs, roundups, and shoot-outs became so popular that eager, inexperienced mustangers often mistook branded, shod horses on the range for the wild bands. Similar problems played out in Utah, Idaho, and Oregon. Wild horses regularly fetched reasonable prices for their hides, as an ingredient in chicken feed, and even as canned meat shipped to Europe. In rarer cases they became working animals or breeding stock. Within two decades, Nevada enacted a law that required permits for the destruction of herds in order to slow down and regulate the slaughter. The permitting process identified the mustangers and required them to put up a bond in case they killed privately owned animals. Nevada actually produced some income from the sale of these permits. Permitting became particularly important with the beginning of range regulation under the Forest Service, when wild horse eradication escalated. The agency wanted all feral livestock removed from the national forests and paid mustangers to help. The wild adventure mustanging promised drew the attention of the American public through national newspaper articles, despite the cruel methods used in the capture of wild horses. Earnest eastern greenhorns wrote the Forest Service that they would gladly help.[6]

Will C. Barnes, a native Arizonan, cowboy, and Forest Service employee in the newly designated state, participated in several roundups or captures in the Great Basin and Southwest and wrote about his experiences in *McClure's Magazine* in 1909 to address the increasing public attention on America's wild horses. For those who excitedly offered to participate in the roundup, capture, or shooting of the animals, Barnes wrote, "Forest officers got boundless amusement from these letters. They were all Western men who had lived for years on the open range. They knew from actual experience that these men, with their plans of capture and their certainty of success, knew absolutely nothing, or at best very little, of the subject on which they wrote." Mustangers, he sardonically wrote, used safer, more practical methods than those the greenhorns suggested, and they certainly employed better ones than had been used in the nineteenth century. The old practice of "creasing"—shooting a horse at a dead run just above his shoulder in the fleshy withers—to stun the animal had resulted in one successful capture for every fifty attempts. Most of the time, Barnes noted, as when artist George Catlin attempted to crease a mustang, the cowboy shot the horse and killed it, which defeated the entire purpose of the animal's capture.[7]

Barnes explained that mustangers of his day, the professionals at least, tracked wild horse herds to their water holes and monitored their movements for several days. Three or four riders staged themselves along the horses' regular route to and from their water source and hazed the herd until they broke into a run. Riders ran the herd in a relay until the mustangers could select several desirable animals and cull them out. If the mustangers decided to capture the whole band, the riders would trail the herd and haze them until they tired and could be driven into a corral. Mustanging was fast and dangerous riding; the men rode bareback, without saddles and extra clothing in order to save weight, not something anyone but an exceptional rider could handle. More often than not, the herds would not turn or pass through the gate of the corral and would escape back into the sagebrush, taking any saddle horses that accompanied the mustangers with them. When a roundup was successful, horses and riders alike were often injured or killed. Barnes noted that "more good horses have been killed outright in this work than ever were captured." He challenged those who thought they knew a "sure method" or a better one to present it; the population of wild horses still posed "a difficult and decidedly knotty problem."[8]

Rufus Steele, a popular writer of the American West, echoed Barnes's descriptions of the difficulties inherent in mustanging. His article in *McClure's Magazine* featured another contemporary mustanger, Charles "Pete" Barnum of Nevada, later the same year. Steele called wild horse capturing "the most exciting outdoor trade in the West to-day" and featured a photo of a young, rugged-looking Barnum and a series of pictures that illustrated the intensity of Barnum's work. The mustanger innovated additional methods of capturing wild horse herds, which included constructing hidden corrals with wide brush wings to funnel the animals into the opening and building a portable canvas corral that could be quickly and easily set up in rough terrain. Steele noted that Barnum thought wild horse herds had grown wise to the ways of mustangers and could not be easily outwitted, which made them increasingly difficult to catch. In addition, wild horses were tough to tame. Of the animals successfully captured, about one-quarter died in the process of becoming harness or saddle ready. The act of "breaking" the horses relied on bucking them out until they tired and accepted the rider or driver. This activity became good sport for cowboys and was incorporated into rodeos across the region, which featured authentic wild horses. But the wild horse industry required a lot of effort and investment without much return. Nevertheless, Steele wrote, wild horses made "wonderful saddle-animals, sometimes racehorses." "Many thousands of them," he said, "are to-day drawing farm-wagons, buggies, and delivery-wagons in the States of the Middle West."[9]

Mustangers shipped thousands of animals each year to the Midwest for various purposes, including slaughter. Pete Barnum alone shipped seven thousand animals in six years, a good "two thousand less than he ha[d] caught," if he included losses during breaking and shipping. Those numbers suggest that there had been at least ten thousand animals in Nevada, where Barnum conducted his operations during the first decade of the twentieth century. Steele estimated there were "not less than fifty thousand wild horses" in Nevada in 1909. Even if herds' reproductive rates were low, around 10 percent annually, Barnum's impact on wild horse herds in the state did not actually cut their overall numbers but simply slowed their rate of growth. Nevertheless, beginning with Steele's article, a general sense that wild horse populations were declining crept into the nation's popular consciousness. Steele began his article by writing, "Upon the eastern slope of the Sierra Nevadas, in a harsh region embracing parts of Eureka, Nye, Lander, White Pine, and Elko counties, Nevada, lies the last wild-horse pasture in America. . . . In this barren and nearly inaccessible territory, the wild horse has made his last stand against captivity." No one was certain how many wild horses actually roamed the country, but increasingly, some sympathetic admirers were becoming concerned about their demise.[10]

Only a handful of years after Steele's article, a Reno newspaper commented on the disappearing wild horse herds in an article that praised Nevada's natural resources and natural wonders. The state hoped to attract agricultural and industrial businesses to grow its economic base. Wild horse herds posed a hazard to this growth, especially to the region's expanding

Pete Barnum's portable canvas corral. Photograph courtesy of Anthony Amaral Papers, Special Collections, University of Nevada, Reno Libraries.

livestock industry, which had finally recovered after a series of hard winters in the late nineteenth century. Mustangs roamed the central and eastern sections of the state where broad alluvial fans rose above the ancient La-hontan sinks into high desert and grassy mountain meadows. Near Sunny-side, where the Whipple family owned and operated livestock, employees from the neighboring Riordan Ranch had succeeded in killing two hun-dred horses that competed with cattle in the area for feed. That same year, ranchers near Carson City were relieved to hear reports that the wild horse herds to the east in the Pine Nut Mountains had virtually disappeared and they would be spared the expense and effort of their eradication.[11]

But in the 1920s, the wild horse populations again increased to the point that ranchers actively sought to remove them, especially in the northern and central parts of the Great Basin. The livestock market was booming and the range was crowded with cattle and sheep operations vying for control of the region's forage and water resources. Ranchers and the Forest Service strug-gled to remove wild horses from the national forest ranges. In addition, the increased use of the automobile lessened the need for horses throughout the country. The temporary boom in horse prices created by increased demand during World War I had led to only short-term profits for mustangers. As mounts, the animals were swiftly becoming unnecessary. As hides, chicken feed, and even consumer-grade meat, however, they were increasingly valuable, fetching three times the price they had in previous years. As a result of the animals' improved monetary worth, both legal roundups and hunts to remove wild horses and illegal shootings dramatically increased. Wild horse herds of this era often included privately owned animals that had been turned loose on the range because they were no longer useful. Herd populations soon declined, but within ten years, wild horses were again a menace to the Great Basin range with the economic devastation brought by the drought and Great Depression, and roundups increased.[12]

This was the typical cycle of wild horse herds and the style of herd management, not just in the Great Basin, but also throughout the country. Montana, New Mexico, even Arkansas, Florida, and North Carolina periodically conducted wild horse roundups and hunts. Mustang herds competed with livestock for grass and water, which mattered most in times of drought and when demand for beef and wool was high. When there was also demand for workhorses, chicken feed, canned meat, and hides in conjunction with demand for beef and wool and when forage resources were scarce, mustangers vigorously culled wild horse populations, and drought and hard winters contributed to their losses. When demand for these products decreased and when forage resources were fairly plentiful, wild horse populations were allowed to increase unchecked. When demand for workhorses decreased, as it did after the automobile came into widespread use and ranchers no longer needed or could no longer afford their privately owned animals, massive increases in wild horse populations occurred. Ranchers turned these horses loose on the range, expanding wild horse herds beyond their rate of reproduction.[13]

With the establishment of the Forest Service and the beginnings of federal grazing regulation, wild horses faced yet another pressure, the federal grazing permitting process. Ranchers paid grazing fees for the use of national forest range and resented the Forest Service reducing the size of their grazing permits because wild horses, similar in this case to itinerant sheep herds, had decimated the available forage resources. Efforts at their eradication intensified even further after the implementation of the Taylor Grazing Act in 1934 and the establishment of the public rangeland. By 1943, Secretary of the Interior Harold Ickes, bent on eradicating any lingering disorganization in the grazing districts, ordered the removal of wild horses.[14]

When public rangelands provided free grazing, there was a place for wild horses between the herds of cattle and sheep, especially considering that ranchers ran their own horses on the range in a manner that sustained the mustang herds. Free grass meant free horses. But when the Forest Service and the Grazing Service organized public lands range resources and permitted ranchers certain numbers of livestock such as cattle, sheep, and horses based on range surveys and fee schedules, every wild horse became an unnecessary and threatening mouth to feed. Each blade of grass had an economic value that was translated to every permitted animal. Public lands management agencies were obliged to supress unpermitted livestock in order to legitimately regulate the range. Even wildlife numbers were closely monitored, though deer and pronghorn were also important range animals and produced their own revenues through the sale of hunting licenses. Wild horses generated no such revenue as feral livestock managed by the state agricultural agency. But as Rufus Steele had noted nearly thirty years before, Nevada, and the Great Basin at large, was the last refuge of wild horses. The very act of codifying the entire region as a grazing range, because of the vast expanse of public lands encompassed in grazing districts, still meant there was a place for the animals alongside other livestock.[15]

Ranchers in the Great Basin accepted wild horses as a normal part of the region's environment in the same way they accepted mountain lions. The sons and grandsons of John Uhalde, operating out of Thirty Mile Ranch near Ely and the Uhalde Ranch at Adaven, grew up chasing mustangs. John Uhalde, an immigrant of Basque origin, migrated to Nevada in 1881 after working as a sheepherder in Idaho. In 1917, after losing his brother Gracian to the Spanish flu epidemic, which left him without a partner, he bought the Thirty Mile Ranch with his countryman Bertrand Paris. Both Paris and Uhalde began expanding their sheep herds during the decline of the Adams-McGill Company, the largest operation in the area at the time.[16]

The early 1920s were hard on sheep operations; wool and lamb prices plummeted to less than half their levels of previous years. Despite having to downsize their sheep herds, the Uhalde and Paris families were able to develop ranch properties and water rights adjacent to each other, working cooperatively to secure their range access and using bank loans, with their herds as collateral, to supply the funds. In the mid-1920s, the Uhaldes purchased part of the ranch at Gleason Creek and another ranch at

Adaven, also called Sharp, on Little Cherry Creek in the Quinn Canyon Range. Bertrand Paris bought a ranch at Gleason Creek, just southeast of Thirty Mile, and the adjacent Gibson Ranch several years later. During this same time, Bertrand married Marie, the twin sister of John Uhalde's wife, Marianne, and the widow of John's brother Gracian. The marriage deeply intertwined the Uhalde and Paris families. Together, they filed claims under both the Homestead and Stock-Raising Homestead Acts to acquire greater pasture for their sheep herds and obtained critical water rights in western White Pine County, Coal and Garden Valleys in Nye County, and northern Lincoln County.[17]

The ranchers in those areas, whose operations had folded around the turn of the twentieth century, had just turned their horses loose to run wild. These animals joined the wild herds that comprised other animals that had arrived in the same way. The animals were often well bred and an asset for Basque families who depended on horses for their sheep herding. The Uhaldes turned out their good mares and stallions to reproduce with local wild herds. John's son Gracian Michael chased wild horses in Butte Valley at every opportunity with his brother Alfred and cousins Bertrand and Peter Paris, relaying the animals on a series of mounts until the horses tired and they had the herd turned toward the corrals. The boys made extra money on the horses they sold to the army, but they kept some for their own use. When the Grazing Service issued grazing permits in White Pine County, the Uhaldes and Parises pooled their numbers and continued to raise horses on the range. They, like other ranchers, kept the herds in their area in check and offset their permit costs through sales.[18]

Wild horses provided an important source of income to small ranch operations and American Indian tribes, providing supplemental cash for families each year. As late as the Great Depression and war years, each animal could bring in up to five dollars. At the same time, ranchers continued to use wild horse herds to grow their own remudas. Management of local herds was a customary part of every ranching operation. One rancher from Elko explained, "We turned our saddle horses out on the range. Our horses would mix with the mustangs, and we managed them ourselves. We culled them and sold them like our own horses." Ranchers controlled the herds by bringing in the excess population and selling them for whatever purpose the market demanded at the time. Another rancher from Fallon stated that during the Great Depression, the price of live horses went down, but the price of their hides went up for a while. People ate horse meat, gophers, mud hen eggs, or anything else they could find. He shot and skinned horses to make some extra money but considered it horrible work. Once, the horse population on the Stillwater sink got so bad, the local community opted to "humanely shoot them." "We culled them only once like that," he said, "but it was either that or the alternative—they would all starve to death."[19] Active management of wild horses was critical.

But during the 1930s, two factors emerged that severely impacted wild horse populations throughout the country beyond previous levels and made their eradication imminent. First, the airplane made wild horse gathering much easier than chasing the animals on horseback. In 1925, *Popular Science* ran an article on cowboy-aviator Chance Parry, a Utahan who had worked as a mustanger until World War I. During the war, he joined the army's Air Service and learned to fly. Chasing the animals by plane seemed a better solution than exhausting good saddle horses for very little success. Someone in a plane could spot herds and drive the animals until they became exhausted, steering them toward riders on the ground who could then turn them toward corrals. Parry first used his plane technique to round up a band on the North Rim of the Grand Canyon, and the idea immediately took hold in other parts of the country.[20]

In 1930, pilot W. C. Dibble of Burns, Oregon, chased wild horses deep within the mountainous terrain of Humboldt County, Nevada, with great success. Two years later, North Dakota pilot Dortha Canfield and her husband successfully organized an aerial pursuit business rounding up wild horses and shooting coyotes. Chasing horses by air was tricky, however. Charlie Hahn of Lakeview, Oregon, drove 750 head of wild horses out of the canyons of northwestern Nevada toward a group of cowboys who were entirely unprepared for the vast numbers headed their way. The running horses overwhelmed the cowboys, stampeding past them with the sheer weight of their numbers and uncontrollable speed. All but fifteen of the horses escaped. Moving horses by airplane took time and practice to master and their capture was never certain or perfect. It was also incredibly dangerous for the pilots; some crashed into mountainsides and ravines when their plane's engines failed or the aircraft caught a sudden downdraft. Nevertheless, by 1938 the airplane was an effective means of finding and propelling wild horse herds toward their eventual capture.[21]

The other important shift occurred in the canned meat industry. Besides providing the basis of modern chicken feed, wild horses formed the foundation of the nascent pet food industry. The surplus of horses at the end of the Great War and the advent of the automobile opened the door for alternative uses of horseflesh. Using horse meat in pet food provided a cheap source of protein for an expanding commercial pet food industry. Early pet food manufacturer Ken-L Ration introduced canned horse meat for dogs, a popular item for increasingly convenience-oriented consumers. Rather than feed their favorite pets table scraps, middle-class families fed their canine family members meals of their own. Dog food factories in Los Angeles processed railcar loads of wild horses for pet food. Canned horse meat as dog food became so popular that in 1934, Allan Alexander "Scotty" Allan, the famous Alaskan dog trainer and musher, and the Reno Chamber of Commerce tried to work out a deal to establish a dog food cannery in the area to take advantage of the abundant supply of wild horses in the Great Basin.[22]

Throughout the 1930s, the captured wild horses that did not end up sold as potential saddle or harness animals or as canned meat destined for Europe ended up as canned meat for pets and as chicken feed. The pet food market, however, outstripped even the supply of wild horses. "So extensive has the use of canned cat food and dog food become among the owners of carnivorous pets," stated one newspaper article in 1939, "that every type of cheap meat is being used in their production." So successful had the pet food industry become using "certain types of scrub stock" that wild horses were again becoming scarce on western ranges. In the aggregate, mustangs actually proved a less consistent source and a smaller percentage of meat for America's pets and pet food companies; the main supply of horseflesh came from older or surplus farm animals. Nevertheless, this broadened market for horse meat put continued pressure on wild horse populations, and combined with the increased efficiency of rounding up the animals using airplanes, led to a decline in mustang populations.[23]

Wild herds had a small reprieve during World War II when metal for canned pet food was in short supply and mustangers became soldiers for a while. As in previous wars, some horses were rounded up and sent overseas for military use. Others found their way into butcher shops that specialized in horse flesh at a time when the government rationed other types of meat, and the market price skyrocketed. A butcher from Oakland, California, noted that "in times of meat shortage like this, we're putting that waste [the unwanted wild horses] to some good. We're bringing the meat to the public at half the price of beef, and we're selling the hides to the government to make shoes for soldiers."[24]

After the war, wild horse populations increased and the Forest Service, the newly created Bureau of Land Management, and many ranchers began once again to actively capture herds. The BLM in particular vigorously pursued wild horses as part of director Marion Clawson's efforts to organize and efficiently manage the grazing range. Mustangs were not the only ones who had proliferated after the war; pronghorn and deer herds had also swelled and required several times the number of hunting permits previously issued by wildlife departments to control. But wild horses were not wildlife and had no hunting tag limit, only their price per head. Besides the usual hide, chicken feed, and pet food markets, wild horses also provided meat to the United Nations Relief and Rehabilitation Administration as part of assisting war-torn Europe during the last year of the organization's existence. Americans also sent live animals to help replace lost European stock. In the postwar era, an increasing number of mustangers were not ranchers, but professionals contracted by the BLM or Forest Service who specialized in aerial roundups. Some were also fly-by-night operations looking to make easy money. Pilots became more skilled at hazing wild horses out of their mountains and canyons and placing the corrals in key locations for their final capture. In addition to fixed-wing aircraft, pilots in the northern and central Great Basin began using helicopters, which flew lower and slower and were more maneuverable, to increase each take.[25]

Not everyone in the postwar era accepted wild horse roundups and the animals' fate as pet food, chicken feed, butcher-grade meat, or hides. Since at least the interwar years, concerned people had publicly protested their eradication. Their objections centered on the issue of animal cruelty. In 1931, along with applications for horse hunting positions, Idaho's Bureau of Animal Industry stated it had received letters "protesting the wholesale slaughter [of the horses] as inhumane and unnecessary." The protests continued after World War II and grew in intensity. In 1947, Los Angeles city council member Lloyd G. Davis charged that "wild horses on the plains of western states are being killed from airplanes with machine guns and then used for dog food or for human consumption in foreign countries." While it was doubtful that wild horse herds were being machine-gunned from aircraft, Davis was responding to the wholesale capture of the animals using aircraft and the cruelty often involved with that process.[26]

At the same time, Alexander Tilley, head of the American Society for the Prevention of Cruelty to Animals (ASPCA) in Los Angeles, protested the outright extermination of wild horses, noting that his office had received numerous complaints about the matter. The ASPCA, an organization cre-ated in the late nineteenth century that had cut its teeth on protecting urban cart horses from abusive drivers, had been deeply involved in protest-ing the emerging rodeo industry's use of bucking horses, which in the first two decades of the sport were actually wild horses. No one knew how many of these equines existed throughout the country, but the ASPCA claimed that earlier wild horse gathering had kept up with reproduction rates. The organization insisted that current capture techniques, the increased de-mand of the pet food industry, and the federal contracts for supplying meat to Europe had brought wild horse populations to the brink of extinction.[27] The ASPCA was not alone in its complaints. The American Humane As-sociation also protested the "inhuman treatment in capturing wild horses." By 1952, the organization had written several pieces that showcased the ter-rible conditions wild horse herds faced when water and feed ran short on their home range, and the brutality often involved in rounding them up.[28]

This was the issue that caught the attention of the American public and made saving wild horses an urgent matter of life and death. Capturing wild horses using aircraft, for the purpose of killing them to supply a com-mercial poultry and pet food industry, to the extent that it eradicated their entire existence, was beyond acceptable limits. One Nevadan stated, "I cer-tainly don't mind seeing the scrub stock, the mustangs, the wild horses with bad feet and other deformities, removed from the range, but when it comes to turning good horses into chicken feed, it just makes me sick." More than simply livestock, horses were partners and companions for ranchers. Their eradication in the name of industrialization and human progress engen-dered the same feelings of loss the iconic buffalo had fifty years earlier. As part of the subjugation of the country's American Indian population, the federal government authorized the complete destruction of wild buffalo. Buffalo hunters made fortunes slaughtering entire herds to clear the Great Plains of unwanted animals and the Native peoples who depended on them to make way for settlement and agriculture. Likewise, the federal govern-ment had encouraged the regulation and removal of wild horses from the range to make way for livestock production. The self-indulgence and cru-elty involved in the destruction of the buffalo had prompted George Bird Grinnell to launch a decade-long public campaign to preserve the last of the nation's animals. In the same way, a handful of Nevadans launched a national campaign to save the wild horse.[29]

SEVEN

A Matter of Mustangs

I n the heat of the August sun, a disheartened Joseph Clifford watched as officials from the Bureau of Land Management released seventy captured horses back onto the Stone Cabin Valley range in central Nevada. The lanky, dark-haired cattleman stood by as the corral gate swung open and the animals, in a rush of dust and sweat, left their confinement. In that summer of 1975, the BLM had intended to begin rounding up wild horses to reduce their ever-expanding numbers. Passage of the Wild Free-Roaming Horses and Burros Act several years prior had independently integrated wild horses into the multiple-use schema, and this was the first of several planned roundups to begin reducing the herds. Clifford had hoped the BLM would be able to complete its plans to take four hundred of the estimated one thousand wild horses in the area off the range that his family and several others used to graze their cattle herds. But after the Nevada Agriculture Department impounded the animals and refused to recognize the bureau's authority in the matter, the BLM chose to pull the plug on the roundup.[1]

Frustrated with the entire process, Clifford told the reporter covering the event, "Boy, I didn't want to see them go back out there. There's just too many horses." In contrast, Velma Johnston, the leading advocate for wild horses, was elated. The passionately determined secretary from the Reno area had spent the past twenty-five years fighting to draw the nation's attention to the animals' plight. Appalled at the debilitating and fatal injuries caused by roundups and outraged at the greed of many mustangers, she had

Joseph Clifford, Jr., seated on Mike in 1945. Photograph courtesy of Stone Cabin Valley Collection, University of Nevada Cooperative Extension, Northern Nye and Esmeralda Counties.

launched a campaign in the 1950s to save the wild horses that culminated in the preservation law of 1971. Johnston, who had been present at the roundup in Stone Cabin Valley a week earlier and was closely monitoring events there, argued that any reduction in animals ought to come from the rancher's herds.[2]

As the agency tasked with managing the public lands where most of the wild horses roamed, the BLM was historically sympathetic to ranchers like Clifford, but it needed the good will of Johnston and other wild horse advocates to make the wild horse preservation law a public success. In addition, the bureau had to navigate a tricky jurisdictional topography with states, which normally oversaw wildlife management but which would not be responsible for managing wild horses. The bureau was struggling to reconfigure multiple use to include wild horses as a separate category of animal. Branded neither wildlife nor livestock, wild horses under the new law were declared a national heritage species. However, no one had any real idea what that meant in terms of management. The officials involved in the roundup in Stone Cabin Valley could be certain of only one thing: adjustments to existing public land uses were going to have to be made. The BLM had the nearly impossible task of crafting a multiple-use framework that balanced the new constituents on public lands—wild horses—with grazing herds of cattle and sheep, military test and training activities, outdoor recreationists, and traditional wildlife. No one envied the bureau's position, but everyone expected results.[3]

As with earlier adjustments to multiple use, ranchers stood to lose the most. Their customary activities had already been curtailed several times since passage of the Taylor Grazing Act in 1934. The Cliffords ran a livestock operation west of Railroad Valley along Stone Cabin Creek, a small waterway that emptied into Cactus Flat at the edge of the Nevada Test Site to the south. Edward Clifford, a Scots-Irish immigrant, had arrived in Austin, Nevada, in 1877 with his wife, Esther Hendra. Clifford worked his way south, mining at Ophir Canyon, Belmont, and Tybo. He gained local fame as the second person to stake a claim in the Tonopah region, following the famed Jim Butler. After locating a mine in the Reveille Range at Bellehelen, where the Fallini family also held a claim, in 1883 Clifford purchased the Stone Cabin Ranch, an established property that had been homesteaded in the 1860s. By 1909, the family had a profitable mining operation and was also engaged in cattle ranching. The Clifford mine, discovered by John Peavine four years earlier for the Cliffords, produced a lucrative amount of silver that funded their cattle operation. The family owned water rights at Stone Cabin and Reveille Mill Springs and had developed several wells for stock watering. When Esther fell off a runaway wagon and died not long after, Edward was left to raise five sons and four daughters. Preferring mining to ranching, Clifford continued to locate claims in the vicinity of his ranch,

The Clifford Ranch at Stone Cabin in 1945. Photograph courtesy of Stone Cabin Valley Collection, University of Nevada Cooperative Extension, Northern Nye and Esmeralda Counties.

often finding rich veins of ore in the proximate mountain ranges, and let his livestock operation languish until his death in 1916. Several of Clifford's five sons took over the ranch at Stone Cabin after their father's death and some continued the family tradition of mining in the region.[4]

During the late 1920s and again in the 1930s, overgrazing and drought depleted the range in Stone Cabin Valley; the torrential summer rains and hard winters in the 1940s did similar damage to the family's cattle herds. Joseph H. Clifford, the youngest boy, had married Albina Antoniazzi in 1915 and was the third Clifford brother to marry into that family. These Italian immigrants had been drawn to Ellendale, a boomtown launched by a gold strike found by Joseph's older sister Ellen. Joseph's primary concern was maintaining the health of his ranching operation. Along with the Fallinis, the Cliffords lost access to their southern grazing range and water rights when the military organized the Tonopah Bombing Range. In addition, fledgling pilots training for combat during World War II buzzed their cattle herds. Fighter pilot Chuck Yeager stampeded the Cliffords' herd once in 1943; though he apparently caused serious damage, the charismatic aviator ended up befriending the family. The stout rancher had joined the Sharps and the Fallinis in the Central Nevada Livestock Association, which was created to hold off grazing district organization in 1947. Three years later, along with these families and other stock operators in the area, the Cliffords lodged a final protest against organization under the Taylor Grazing Act.[5]

During atmospheric nuclear testing in the 1950s, the Cliffords experienced the same types of damage from exposure to radioactive fallout as did the Sharp, Fallini, Lamb, Whipple, and Swallow families. Joseph and Albina's children, Marguerite, Joseph Junior, and William (known as Roy), who had families of their own, were appalled to see fallout clouds envelop their cattle herds after detonations. Sometimes the cloud was so thick, they lost sight of their corrals. Anyone working outside, and any animals subjected to the cloud, experienced blisters and burns. In the 1960s and 1970s, the wild horse situation only added to their frustration. The wild horse preservation movement, and the laws that resulted from it, changed their relationship with animals they and other ranchers had always considered feral livestock, subject to the same laws as cattle and sheep. For the first time, wild horses competed with the Cliffords' cattle for range resources without the traditional oversight of and benefit to local ranchers.[6]

The changing role of wild horses in American society came on the heels of the public's shifting attitude toward horses in general. The proliferation of the automobile and mechanized farming equipment and the use of trucks and tanks in warfare had decreased the national demand for equines in the early twentieth century. By the end of World War II, horses had declined in the Census of Agriculture from a height of nearly twenty million in 1910 to just over five million by 1954. Horses became objects of consumption rather than partners in work, no longer necessary to produce goods or facilitate transportation. Rather, by midcentury, most horses were used for riding or in competition and entertainment in the rodeo and racing industries; those that did not fall into that category, including wild horses, supplied the commercial poultry and pet food industries. The growth of affluence and leisure time in the postwar era and the distance most middle-class families had from horses spawned a new political economy for equines. American children, especially little girls, consumed the image of the horse rather than the animal itself. The Breyer Molding Company created its first toy equine model, the Western Horse, in 1950 to adorn a mantle clock sold by the

F. W. Woolworth Company. This twelve-inch replica of a sorrel horse re-
plete with an ornate western saddle changed the entire focus of the plastics
company. The popularity of westerns on television and western-themed
toys spawned a market for realistic model horses, and an untold number of
young horse enthusiasts wanted to pry the miniature off its mount. To meet
the soaring demand for a stand-alone horse, Breyer launched its model
horse line. By the time small-winged aircraft became a prominent part of
wild horse roundups, which often left the animals bloodied and battered,
these captures sparked public outcries of animal cruelty. The distance between the fantasy horses and their reality on public lands was too great for
many Americans to tolerate comfortably.[7]

The day Velma Johnston decided to follow a livestock truck dripping
blood on the dirt road she took into Reno from her Double Lazy Heart
Ranch, she witnessed the worst of the wild horse capture process. Many
interviewers have quoted and paraphrased her descriptions, but they are
nevertheless still difficult to reiterate. According to one recounting, inside
the mustanger's truck she saw "a horrifying tableau of mutilated horses,
some barely alive." Horses had "bloody stumps instead of legs," some had
"sections of their hooves torn off and hides shredded," a foal lay "trampled,
bones crushed and blood-soaked," and a stallion barely stood, "his head
bowed, blood seeping from empty eye sockets." Soon after her encoun-
ter, Johnston and her husband, Charles, ran a clandestine campaign of direct action against wild horse roundups. They sabotaged corrals, gathered
evidence, and released horses back onto the rangeland. Disfigured from
contracting polio in her childhood, Johnston said she took on the wild
horse cause because she adored horses and identified with the unwanted
animals. She served as the historic whistle-blower of mustanging, publiciz-
ing the terrible practices used in wild horse captures including hamstring-
ing and blinding them, sewing their nostrils shut, and denying them food
and water to subdue them. The petite, well-coifed secretary railed against
bounty hunters who cut the ears off the horses, dead or alive, to demonstrate the volume of their cull. She became the focus of many mustangers'
anger, one dubbing her "Wild Horse Annie," a label meant to deride her
unshakable attachment to the animals.[8]

Like others who had become concerned about the brutality that could
be involved in rounding up wild horses, Johnston read through the current literature available on mustangs. J. Frank Dobie's work provided a
sweeping cultural history of the wild horse in North America that detailed

mustanging and different kinds of wild horse capture techniques. But most importantly, she read historian Walker D. Wyman's seminal book *The Wild Horse of the American West.* In 1945, Wyman published an account of the growth and decline of wild horses in the region, which highlighted two important aspects of their history. Wyman began his account with the statement that "the true wild horse, the remote ancestor of the domesticated and feral horse of our era, was indigenous to the American continent." The second was a lament about the demise of the mustang in his final chapter, "Save the Wild Horse!" In Wyman's view, these distinctly western horses, whose blood ranchers had diluted and whose herds mustangers had destroyed, were now only "degenerate estrays" compared to what they once had been. Johnston adamantly disagreed with Wyman on this point; she and other ranchers in the Great Basin owned mustangs and used them as saddle horses. Johnston believed the wild equines were beautiful, sturdy animals with incredible endurance and great intelligence, and in her estimation, the herds left in the region were worth saving.[9]

Johnston helped launch a crusade to create legal protection for wild horses beginning in Storey County, Nevada, where she lived and where a number of herds roamed. She tapped into a growing tide of public discontent over the mechanized methods used in wild horse captures and their commercial sale as meat. The focus of this first effort toward their protection was to ban the use of airplanes, trucks, and other mechanized equipment that she believed had increased the efficiency of wild horse gathers over their reproductive rates. In 1952, a group of concerned citizens around Virginia City, including Velma Johnston; the county's postmaster, Edward "Tex" Gladding; businessman Jack Murray; and the Nevada Humane Society, protested the permitting of an upcoming mechanized roundup in their county. They reasoned that using aircraft and other mechanized equipment, such as trucks, in rounding up wild horses needlessly stressed the animals to the point of extreme panic, which caused them injuries that might otherwise not occur. Horses chased by aircraft and trucks moved faster and exhausted more quickly than those chased by mustangers on horseback. Denying mustangers the use of aircraft, in particular, prevented that severe level of panic that led to injury and also restricted the number of horses mustangers could take in a single gather. The county commissioners denied the permit and a week later banned the use of airplanes, helicopters, and any other aircraft in rounding up wild horse herds. However, the limitation applied only to those animals on county land.[10]

This small victory within Storey County highlighted the contrasting positions Americans took on wild horses. Ranchers continued to believe that unregulated wild horse herds were a menace and reduced range resources for their cattle and sheep. Because they continued to rely on horses for some of their income, they tolerated a number of wild herds, rounding them up and either using them as saddle horses or supplying them to slaughterhouses for some extra income. Others, like Velma Johnston, wanted to ensure that wild horses had a place on the region's public lands separate and apart from the status of other livestock. Johnston, however, did not discount the need for some management; at this point, she just wanted to ban the methods that produced cruel results. Only those living in suburban or urban areas—a small group at first—advocated letting the animals alone completely. Thus in its early stages, the wild horse preservation movement focused primarily on the method of rounding the animals up and not on the roundups themselves. As the influence of this smaller group grew, their numbers swelling as Americans outside the Great Basin learned of the plight of wild horses, the focus of the preservation movement shifted. For the moment, the one truth that all wild horse advocates believed was that the animals' situation was growing desperate.

According to the BLM, there were around four thousand wild horses left in the state, not many considering that their numbers had been three times that only a decade before. To make the ban effective throughout Nevada, the county's state representatives took the issue to the Nevada state legislature. James Slatterly, the state senator from Storey County, and Richard Hardenbrook, the state assembly member from the area, proposed a bill to ban aerial pursuit of wild horses in the 1955 legislative session. Hardenbrook reasoned that wild horse herds should "be preserved as one of the last remnants of the old west," and his colleagues agreed. State legislators approved a ban on the use of aircraft to round up wild horses. This measure had an added benefit for the state's revenue stream; the statewide ban on aerial pursuit also applied to deer and other wildlife since hunters had taken to using aircraft to drive game animals into areas where they would be easier to shoot. The new law went into effect that summer.[11]

Velma Johnston, pleased with the results of their efforts, said the law was designed to "obtain as complete protection as possible for the horses, so that a man—if he wanted to—could ride into the hills and get himself a mustang now and then; and to make it economically impractical to continue the exploitation of the horses to provide the canneries with cheap meat for pet food." However, enforcement of the ban proved problematic because state land made up only one-fifth of the territory wild horses roamed. Most of the herds were scattered around the public lands regulated by the Forest Service and the BLM. Though Colorado, Arizona, and New Mexico followed the precedent set by Nevada, Johnston and her allies believed only a national law would solve the problem of mechanized roundup. Like George Bird Grinnell and the campaign to save the buffalo, she launched a nationwide movement through popular public media in the mid-1950s to save the nation's wild horses.[12]

The drive behind securing a national ban on aerial and mechanized wild horse capture, which advocates widely considered to be the cause of their plummeting numbers and the source of their inhumane treatment, grew out of the widespread publication of a series of photographs that detailed the problem. The photos, combined with the general sentiment that wild horses were nearly gone from the western range, propelled the issue of their protection from a local and regional level to a national level, where it produced a massive public response. Gus Bundy, owner of a guest/divorce ranch near Reno, had snapped images of a wild horse roundup while driving a client, *Life* magazine photographer Bud Gourley, around in 1951. The mustangers took Gourley's camera, but Bundy managed to snap a few pictures, something no one, not even Velma Johnston, had been able to accomplish thus far. Copies of those photographs ended up in the hands of Reno lawyer Charles L. Richards, who passed them on to Johnston in 1953. The photos had played a small role in securing the passage of Nevada's 1955 law, but when she obtained Bundy's permission to use them in *True, The Man's Magazine* to accompany her article on the cruelty of wild horse gathering practices in 1958, they generated national attention. They featured horses running in terror of aerial pursuit down a steep hillside onto a dusty playa where trucks continued to pressure them. On the sandy flats, cowboys hazed the animals from the trucks until ropers tied to the bed lassoed each with a rope attached to a tire. Once roped, the horses dragged the tires across the dry lakebed until exhaustion forced them to stop. The mustangers lassoed and tied down each animal, chained its legs, and dragged it up onto the back of a truck, where they stood it upright again with its companions.[13]

Those photos appeared, often without Bundy's permission, in successive articles published in popular national periodicals such as *Time* and *Sierra* magazines, regional newspapers such as the *Sacramento Bee*, and the academic journal *Geographical Review*. The ASPCA even obtained some

Cowboy roping a wild horse from the back of a speeding truck. Courtesy of Gus
Bundy Collection, Special Collections, University of Nevada–Reno Libraries.

of the Bundy photos for distribution in its own newsletter, accompany-
ing an article entitled "Mustang Murder." These pieces vilified those who
used airplanes and trucks to capture wild horses. They labeled mustangers,
BLM employees, and even ranchers as terrible torturers and murderers. The
flood of support based on those images was overwhelming. The ASPCA,
the American Humane Association, the Humane Society of the United
States, the National Wildlife Federation, and a host of other organizations
all assured Johnston of their support in obtaining protective legislation preventing the use of mechanized methods in capturing wild horses.[14]

Under pressure from a number of their constituents, in 1959 Montana
senator Michael J. Mansfield and Nevada representative Walter S. Baring
and senator Howard W. Cannon introduced bills that extended the ban of

An exhausted wild horse roped to two tires. Courtesy of Gus Bundy Collection, Special Collections, University of Nevada–Reno Libraries.

the use of aircraft and mechanized equipment in rounding up wild horses on the nation's public lands. This set the legislators at odds with the BLM. Supportive of roundups as part of good range management practices, the agency publicly tried to correct the popular perception that its land managers were deliberately cruel to wild horses and wanted to eradicate the animals altogether to make way for larger cattle herds. BLM officials argued that it was not their policy to "eliminate these wild bands, even if that could be done," and that they did not tolerate cruelty toward animals of any kind. Even so, the condemning photographs demonstrated the panic, hurt, and resignation of the animals captured in such a humiliating manner. This sentiment was magnified by the BLM's continued insistence on the necessity of using aircraft and trucks in its roundups. The hearings on the House bill

Mustangers loading a restrained wild horse into a hauling truck. Courtesy of Gus Bundy Collection, Special Collections, University of Nevada–Reno Libraries.

featured a passionate and articulate Velma Johnston and other wild horse advocates from various animal protection and humane associations. Johnston had Representative Baring distribute a report containing the Bundy photographs to many members, who were as shaken by the images as the rest of the country. To their horror, she described a recent legally permitted wild horse capture in which a colt suffered a massive chest wound and never received any veterinary care, pointing to the pictures of the animal in her report. Her testimony and the crush of letters sent to nearly every congressional delegate at the capital by interested parties, most of whom lived outside the Great Basin, was evidence of the strength of public opinion against mechanized roundups.[15]

In fact, the BLM's range management specialist from Nevada, Gerald M. Kerr, was the only voice at the hearings countering that of Johnston and the wild horse advocates. But Kerr, speaking for both the agency and the ranchers with whom it worked, was not as charismatic as Wild Horse Annie. When he argued that neither the BLM nor ranchers condoned cruel methods of wild horse capture, in the face of photographic evidence that could clearly be interpreted otherwise, he sounded insincere. Kerr reminded his audience that the use of chains, tires, and poison for the "indiscriminate slaughter" of the animals was associated only with "operation[s] of 'bootleg' horse runners" that were "not sanctioned or controlled by law enforcement agencies of the states." Aircraft and trucks, if properly used, Kerr stated, were actually the "most humane method," because "the animals are gathered quickly and corralled before they are exhausted from the constant running by relays of riders on horseback." It was impossible, he argued, given the BLM's funding and staff restrictions, for the agency to supervise all wild horse captures on federal land. Because the animals were considered estrays and fell under state jurisdiction, Kerr reminded his listeners that states needed to enforce the proper use of roundup permits. In addition, the BLM argued that with the escape or release of some privately owned animals into the wild and the natural reproduction rates of wild herds, wild horses were not in any danger of extermination.[16]

Throughout the congressional hearings, advocacy groups made an important differentiation between the ranchers who rounded up mustangs on horseback the old-fashioned way and those from out of state who were just out to make a quick dollar. The Humane Affiliates insisted that "the old-time cattlemen, who lived close to the land and understand the true conditions and take the long view," held that "wild horses benefit the range." These ranchers, the organization believed, thought wild horses were an integral part of range management because they grazed only in areas that would not support cattle, reseeding the range with their manure, and even breaking winter ice for cattle at water holes. Profit-driven ranchers and malicious range managers who seemed bent on total wild horse eradication, on the other hand, received the brunt of the organization's blame. There was a great deal of wishful thinking and little actual evidence or study behind these perceptions. The litmus test that divided the good ranchers and the sympathetic officials from the mean and murderous ones seemed to be the mechanized tools used in roundups. Wild horse advocates publicly branded anyone supporting the continued use of airplanes and trucks in wild horse captures propagators of suffering and death. Public pressure and the emotional strength of advocates' testimony made the bill extremely popular. With very little delay, both houses of Congress sent the "Wild Horse Annie Law" to President Dwight D. Eisenhower for signature.[17]

The new law, because it addressed only the method of wild horse capture, spawned a decade of debate as to the place of wild horses on the nation's public lands. Advocates correctly supposed that removing the mechanized aspects of wild horse capture took away the ability of mustangers to make enough money to undergo the effort and expense involved in rounding up entire herds. The despised commercial operations that exploited wild horses and created a market for their removal in large numbers, as well as the amateur mustangers just looking to make a quick dollar, could no longer hope that wild horse roundups would produce a profit. The ranchers who had traditionally culled herds on a smaller scale on horseback, a group Velma Johnston was both familiar with and fond of, were thus not affected. The law presupposed that wild horses would have a place on public lands because its intent was to eliminate the means of their eradication. It did not, however, make the equines' relationship to the range any more understandable or clarify which agency or group was responsible for their management. It also offered no clear definition of what constituted a wild horse.

Johnston presaged this issue in a discussion with Nevada representative Walter S. Baring about the Wild Horse Annie Law. She told Baring she was unhappy with the wording in the bill, especially the use of the term "wild horse." "From past experience," she wrote, "I really feel that there is going to be a lot of controversy over what is and what is not a wild horse, and there will be those who will contend that there are no longer any true wild horses in existence . . . and will try to put the burden of proof upon those trying to protect the mustangs." Johnston preferred the description "wild, unbranded horse, mare, colt or burro running at large on any of the public land or ranges," in order to "avoid future controversy." She was also interested in clarifying which agency was responsible for their management, the BLM or the state within which the animals resided. Typically, states managed wildlife populations and estrays, or feral livestock. Johnston agreed with Mark A. Shipley, a former range manager from northeastern Nevada, that states should strictly control and manage the wild horse populations, culling herds and introducing well-bred horses to improve their bloodlines. Shipley reasoned that wild horses could be raised like timber stands and that in time "a magnificent specimen of horse" would result.

Such a position pushed wild horses closer to the status of wildlife in terms of actively managing them as a part of the ecology rather than treating them as merely estrays.[18]

But this position directly conflicted with the BLM and Forest Service mandates to regulate the public grazing range and conduct range improvements. Federal and state land management agencies generally considered wild horses, and their less charismatic counterparts the wild burros, the most destructive of all grazing and foraging animals. In reality, the consensus on wild horses was that they directly competed against cattle, sheep, and a variety of wildlife for food but provided no significant economic return and caused a great deal of unnecessary erosion. Permitted livestock, wildlife, and unbranded horses all had a place on the federal range under multiple use, but according to Ernest J. Palmer, the BLM's state director in Nevada, "no one interest should be allowed to interfere with the rights of the others." To Palmer, the twenty thousand wild horses ranging throughout the American West, most of which roamed inside his jurisdiction, had a place on the public rangeland so long as they did not exceed the current "reasonable numbers." The Nevada Wool Growers argued that wild horses were "just one class of livestock . . . and usually unlicensed and trespassing animals at that." Limiting the authority of federal land management agencies to control their population preferred horses to other animals on public lands. None of these groups condoned the inhumane treatment of the animals, and they especially condemned the use of trucks, tires, chains, and other methods that caused injury during capture. But all of them believed that aircraft were essential to humanely removing the animals and that federal agencies, particularly the BLM, ought to be responsible for wild horse management as part of their range regulation.[19]

Entwined in the conversation about what constituted a wild horse, which agency should manage them, and how the animals ought to be managed was another dialogue about what they represented historically to the nation. Velma Johnston and many of her supporters maintained that wild horses were not simply "unclaimed and abandoned" livestock. "We who are fighting the big fight," she argued, "are of the opinion that many of the horses are the mustangs and wild ones which are being caught in these indiscriminate commercial roundups." Her differentiation of mustangs within the larger category of wild horses highlighted their historical origin: the moment of European contact and the process of colonization. The term "mustang" evoked a vision of the crested neck and heavy mane of the Andalusian, the most famous Spanish breed. Johnston said their numbers were small, but "the genuine old-time mustang does exist—cross-bred, of course, through the years, with domestic stock that has strayed, but nevertheless retaining the qualities that have made the mustang strain the desirable one that it is." Geographer Tom L. McKnight, using the work of Will C. Barnes, J. F. Dobie, Wyman D. Walker, and Robert M. Denhardt, established that mustangs were the loose horses of Spanish origin that had once formed North America's first feral bands. As settlement grew, more horses escaped and joined these bands, eventually constituting the "native western stock." According to these writers and scholars, "the mustang played an important part in the history of the West."[20]

Where some saw wild horses as one of the last remnants of a bygone era and a symbol of the American West, others viewed them as the shoddy remains of frontier history, a nuisance to ranchers and land managers alike. The BLM, Forest Service, and ranchers generally considered wild horses to be a persistent and recurring problem when their numbers rose above certain levels. George Hardman, assistant director of the Nevada Department of Conservation and Natural Resources, thought that "the wild horse is not a native to our western ranges," and that similar to "many introduced species, the horse found few enemies in the territory he occupied and hence multiplied rapidly." Referring to the mustang, Hardman argued that the "original wild horse was from highly selected Arabian stock," but "over the years inbreeding, introduction of other blood strains, overgrazing of their ranges, and consequent poor nutrition have taken their toll. The present wild horse in Nevada is far from the splendid animal that once roamed the ranges of this State." Johnston astutely observed that what Americans chose to believe about wild horses depended on "which side of the fence the source of the count is obtained." For these equines, it came down to the question of why and for whom the range resources existed.[21]

In the several years after the passage of the Wild Horse Annie Law, these were merely rhetorical positions because the wild horse population had reached what public lands management agencies and most ranchers considered a reasonable low. According to McKnight's research, at the end of the 1950s, there were between 17,330 and 33,660 mustangs left in the American West, more than half of which lived in the Great Basin. But the matter of the wild horses did not disappear from the public forum. In 1961, Arthur Miller's critically acclaimed movie *The Misfits* reiterated the brutal and inhumane aspects of mechanized wild horse capture. Starring Clark Gable and Marilyn Monroe, the film reconstructed in a live-action sequence the Gus Bundy photographs. Based on Miller's 1957 short story published in *Esquire* about three would-be mustangers out to make some quick cash, the plot reflected his perception of wild horse roundups. The money the mustangers in the story figured they earned by rounding up the animals amounted to one hundred dollars, demonstrating how much effort and pain the horses endured for such a small monetary return for the men. The movie ended with a compassionate Monroe begging Gable and the other men to set the horses free. Popular entertainment columnist Hedda Hopper indignantly wondered in her short review of the film, "Where was the humane society when they were stampeding wild horses from an airplane, roping and throwing them?"[22]

Five years later, Marguerite Henry's new novel *Mustang: Wild Spirit of the West*, a children's book telling of Wild Horse Annie's "relentless campaign to save mustangs and other wild horses from capture for an eventual fate as pet food," educated an entire generation of children about the wild horse issue. The story portrayed a fictional heroine, Annie Bronn, as a brave young woman who battled cruel cattlemen to save the noble, but vulnerable, wild horse herds in Nevada. The underdog status of both Bronn and the mustangs captivated little girls across the country who identified with the protagonist's passion for horses and the freedom and power they granted women. The book was so well received that the National Cowboy Hall of Fame in Oklahoma City awarded the novel the Western Heritage Award for juvenile literature in 1967 and created a permanent exhibit featuring the book's original manuscript, illustrations, and the Gus Bundy photographs that had provided visual inspiration.[23]

In addition, two organizations emerged in the Great Basin during these years that broadened and solidified support for the protection of wild horses. The first was John and Helen Reilley's International Mustang Club, later called the International Society for the Protection of Mustangs and Burros (ISPMB), which formed in 1960 and distributed Velma Johnston's advocacy materials. The group's primary goal was to have a refuge set aside in which wild horses would be protected and managed. To this end Secretary of the Interior Stewart L. Udall quietly established a 435,000-acre refuge for wild horses on the north end of the Nellis Bombing and Gunnery Range, an area officially closed to ranching that abutted the Nevada Test Site. The National Wild Horse Refuge, the nation's first dedicated to equines, was not "a showplace for the animals" but rather a "permanent refuge . . . the first step to assure that at least one wild herd will be preserved." Originally, wild horse advocates thought public lands would be set aside in Utah or Wyoming for this purpose, but the concentration of wild horses in Nevada was greater and the seclusion of the military range ensured that contact with the horses would be limited to the BLM and the Nevada Fish and Game Commission. To ensure their protection, the commander of Nellis Air Force Base "agreed not to fire rockets or guns into the refuge."[24]

The refuge on a military base solved the immediate problem of wild horses competing with permitted livestock for grazing forage. In addition, early ranchers had developed much of the region's water resources and some of those structures remained intact for use by the horses. Writing on International Mustang Club letterhead, Johnston thanked one of the refuge's major supporters, Nevada senator Howard W. Cannon, stating, "I am happy that the first step has been taken to establish sanctuaries for them. I am hopeful that it will be continued in other areas of the United States, and that a permanent and workable control and rehabilitation program can be put into operation." So popular was the idea of this first refuge that Australian senator J. A. Mulvihill, from New South Wales, wrote Senator Cannon for advice on how to go about setting aside a large tract of Australia's federal land for wildlife preservation. Senator Mulvihill had the kangaroo and the Brumby in mind when he wrote Cannon, and he wondered how a large refuge could be feasibly created on Australia's western coast. Senator Cannon sent Secretary Udall's description of the process, and after reading that and a copy of *The Quiet Crisis*, the Australian was confident that he would be able to secure "suitable action" from his government.[25]

The second organization to emerge was the National Mustang Association (NMA), formed in Utah by Tom Holland and John McCormack in 1965. The NMA described itself as "organized by a small group of horse-lovers who are also patriotic Americans, and who are interested in keeping the tradition of our American heritage for their children and their children's children." The group's first objective was to "PRESERVE and PROTECT this rapidly disappearing part of early America—the gallant Mustang—the horse that did so much in the making of our country." The NMA was fundamentally disappointed that the first refuge dedicated to wild horses precluded public access. It had hoped to purchase a wild horse refuge near Caliente, Nevada, which would allow the public to "still see Mustangs (born free)." Members of the NMA offered themselves up as a "large force of skilled 'mustangers'" to the BLM and anyone else who needed wild horses rounded up. Besides maintaining an interest in the Old West, the group explained they were also outdoor recreationists who enjoyed trail riding and motorized sports.[26]

The language the NMA used to describe its objectives differed subtly from that of the ISPMB; although both groups sought protection for wild horses, the NMA believed the public should be able to see the horses, whereas the ISPMB was content to know they lived in a highly secluded refuge on a military test and training range. Both groups believed wild horses represented the last remnants of the nation's western heritage, but where the ISPMB avoided participation in wild horse captures, the NMA saw the ban on mechanized roundups as an opportunity to play cowboy. In 1966, Holland, several local residents of Beryl Valley in Utah, and eighty mounted cowboys used an airplane, trucks, and several other off-road vehicles to conduct a sanctioned roundup of a small herd. They were trying to substantiate the existence of a very old mule, the legendary Old Whitey, who was purported to have lived more than fifty years. He had originally been used as a pack mule for the Union Pacific Railroad, and his last known owner had turned him loose in the 1910s. Old Whitey's coat was long and his teeth were worn, but he outran all the horses in the roundup. Holland and his crew eventually caught the mule and verified his Union Pacific brand before letting him loose.[27]

By the late 1960s, the BLM once again began wild horse roundups in the Great Basin. National events of the period overshadowed much of the wild horse issue; concerns over the antiwar protests in Washington, D.C., civil rights protests in the South, the Watts riot in Los Angeles, and the assassinations of Reverend Martin Luther King, Jr., and presidential candidate Robert F. Kennedy far outweighed any public fears that wild horses were being slaughtered. Nevertheless, as part of a burgeoning national consciousness about environmental concerns and animal welfare, regional and national newspapers covered the increasing number of incidents and roundups. Rancher Gordon Zumwalt secured a permit despite some public protest in Nevada to round up forty "unclaimed and unbranded mustangs" for use as brood mares because he did not use mechanized equipment. On the Nevada Test Site, a small herd roamed too far south of the wild horse refuge and the Atomic Energy Commission's Nevada Operation Office planned to remove the horses north, outside its territory. Test site employees had mixed reactions to the presence of the herd. An unsubstantiated rumor circulated that a few men had had some "sport" and a foal had ended up in the trunk of someone's car and died. Upon investigation, Nye County sheriffs did find some evidence of harassment. They also found evidence that test site employees had been developing water resources for the horses in their spare time, which was what had attracted the animals to the area in the first place.[28]

The BLM was careful to improve its public relations image during this time. The agency dutifully registered ranchers' protests against the ban on mechanized roundups and began developing regulations for new wild horse captures without using aircraft or motor vehicles. Under director Karl Landstrom, the BLM also developed a friendlier demeanor with the public. In an agency-wide memo, Landstrom encouraged BLM employees to "be courteous and to give factual, straightforward answers." He said, "Our responsibility is to provide facts and not advice," reminding employees to "avoid advising or influencing any member of the public with respect to applying for any right, use, or title to lands or resources administered by the Bureau." Much of this instruction came about because of the controversy over the land application moratorium, but this, combined with the wild horse issue, had led to a public relations disaster for the BLM. The agency's image, however, only worsened as the wild horse population continued to rise and it struggled to oversee the growing herds.[29]

Matters came to a head when a BLM official in Wyoming made a series of crass statements that inflamed wild horse advocates. For several years, the Tillett family, the community of Lovell, and the agency's district office manager, Dante Solari, had fought over the increasing population of the herd that roamed the Pryor Mountains. The community and the Tillett family, who had run livestock in the region since before the Taylor Grazing Act and who utilized the grazing range the horses roamed, valued the Pryor Mountain herd as a cultural heritage attraction. But the BLM manager, responsible for policing grazing permits, warned the Tilletts that their permits did not include more than twenty horses. Either the Tilletts removed the horses or paid trespass fees for them. Publicly, Solari announced that his preference was to simply have the horses rounded up and slaughtered. Regional newspapers ran inflammatory headlines about the conflict, such as "BLM Ultimatum to Kill Wild Horses" and "Wild Mustangs May End Up as Dog Food." In letters to newspaper editors, Velma Johnston wrote, "It would appear that the BLM, in its slavish service to the monopolistic demands of the cattle barons and sheep moguls for use of the public domain to the exclusion of everything not commercially profitable to themselves, have gone a bit overboard in making an issue of 140 head of horses."[30]

Stepping into the fray, Harold McCracken, director of the Buffalo Bill Historical Center in nearby Cody, stated that the BLM's kill order was "one of the greatest disgraces to conservation and our heritage since the slaughter of the buffalo." But the problem was not that the BLM was held hostage by ranching interests; rather, its general conservation practices only balanced livestock operations with wildlife. The agency still classified wild horses as livestock and thus the animals were subject to permitting restrictions because the Wild Horse Annie Law had never changed the legal status of the animals. This was not an issue if BLM district managers were lenient about requiring ranchers to have permits for wild horses, but as Solari had demonstrated, it was within the agency's jurisdiction to enforce the numbers. To prevent any further embarrassment to the BLM, in April 1966, the agency's Washington office warned Solari to back off and resolve the issue.[31]

During the weeks of controversy, waves of letters from animal protection organizations and children had inundated the offices of Montana governor Tim Babcock and Wyoming governor Cliff Hansen. Solari and the Tilletts agreed to leave the Pryor Mountain herd alone until an official range survey could be completed that would determine whether the range could adequately support the animals without decreasing any livestock grazing permits or causing increased erosion. The following year, BLM director Boyd L. Rasmussen announced a formal BLM policy toward wild horses. "Where it is determined the aesthetic value of wild horses or burros on bureau-administered land is a public asset," he stated, "a planned management program shall be initiated to accommodate a reasonable number of animals." In other situations "where wild horses or burros compete with livestock or wildlife for limited forage or water," Rasmussen stated, "BLM will work with interested groups, livestock men and wildlife agencies to assure good management of all." The BLM director's statements implied removal of wild horses when deemed necessary, a position borne out by the final verdict on the Pryor Mountain herd, which after the range study was slated to drop to one-sixth its original size. But after a damaging ABC documentary on the wild horses that generated further protest, Secretary of the Interior Stewart L. Udall established a second wild horse refuge at the end of 1968 in the Pryor Mountains and created a committee to decide how to manage the animals.[32]

The crisis over the Pryor Mountain herd, combined with increased wild horse numbers in the late 1960s, highlighted a shift in public thinking about the equines. Whereas previous rhetoric focused on the inhumane treatment of the animals during mechanized roundups, the new language indicated dissatisfaction with removing and killing wild horses in general. This concern gave rise to a growing desire to create an explicit place for wild horses on public lands. Compounding this desire were an increasing number of problems with the 1959 law itself. The Wild Horse Annie Law prohibited mechanized roundup of wild horses, but if the herd contained branded horses, then privately owned animals could be captured using any means available. Some unscrupulous mustangers and ranchers had been deliberately releasing branded animals into wild herds throughout the Great Basin and then applying for and securing permits to round up the horses, branded and wild alike.

One such individual was Julian Goicoechea, a rancher of Basque descent, who ran cattle and sheep in Newark Valley in White Pine County, Nevada. Goicoechea had filed for several hundred acres in the mid-1960s, despite the land application moratorium, to establish a land base, but he failed to secure water rights in the area. Without a land base, Goicoechea relied on access to grazing range via other ranchers' permits and made extra money harvesting wild horses. In 1967, Nevada Bureau of Livestock Identification supervisor Stanley F. Routson charged Goicoechea and two other men, Art Cook and Ted Barber, with violating the law against mechanized roundup. In federal court, Goicoechea argued that the horses he captured were branded and therefore could be taken in such a manner. Goicoechea's position reflected a common attitude that wild horses were not actually wild per se, but domestic strays turned feral. Velma Johnston, who testified at the trial, countered that feral horses were all wild. But there was no physical way, except through the presence of brands, to tell the difference. All she could do was portray Goicoechea as "one of Nevada's wealthiest cattlemen" out to eradicate the animals for his own greedy purposes. As a result, the jury failed to convict Goicoechea because the prosecution could not prove the horses were in fact wild.[33]

The outcome of the trial motivated wild horse advocates to launch a campaign for a federal law that clearly established the definition of a wild horse and delineated an explicit place for them on public lands. Johnston and other wild horse advocates believed that without adequate standing under federal law, wild horses would consistently remain subject to other aspects of multiple use. The problem, as she put it, was the difference between the terms "preserve" and "permit to exist." Where the permitting concept allowed a certain number of horses relative to other livestock, preservation elevated wild horses above the commercial production of cattle and sheep and placed them on par with wildlife—native animals within the ecosystem. In writing Secretary of the Interior Stewart L. Udall and Ernest F. Swift of the National Wildlife Federation, Johnston suggested that the BLM and other public lands management agencies had examined only possibilities that balanced wild horse numbers on a sliding scale against livestock and wildlife such as deer, pronghorn, and bighorn sheep. Her hope was that wild horse preservation would be rated higher than that of livestock and that the horse herds, like wildlife populations, would be prioritized in terms of water and range resources within multiple use. Ranchers, particularly those who fought against Great Basin National Park, did not oppose the presence of wild horses on public lands; rather, they opposed prioritizing them as wildlife. This was why Johnston and other wild horse advocates increasingly emphasized the creation of limited-use landscapes specifically for wild horses. While the National Wild Horse Refuge had sufficed in the early 1960s, wild horse advocates hoped to secure more refuges along the lines of the Pryor Mountain model, which created "a showplace for the wild horse heritage." Johnston believed wild horses would be safe from "poachers" only in specially designated areas on public lands. The best option, to her, was to have the animals classified as an endangered species.[34]

To launch her offensive, Johnston enlisted the help of the nascent American Horse Protection Association (AHPA)—organized in 1966 on a wave of animal welfare protection codified in that year's Animal Welfare Act—and the Great Basin organizations ISPMB and NMA to mount a campaign to reclassify wild horses as endangered wildlife, such that the animals would fall under the nation's emerging endangered species program and be managed by the federal government. Johnston even asked the advice of Starker A. Leopold of the National Park Service, author of the 1963 report on wildlife management in the national parks, "on the matter of semantics insofar as the status of the wild horses and burros." To Johnston's disappointment, however, Leopold carefully replied that not much was known about the ecological value of *Equus* and he refused to offer the animals an official classification. Undeterred, Johnston argued that "over the years, the wild horses have become important to the American people as a symbol outranked only by Old Glory and the American Eagle"; to her, they represented "the very symbol of the freedom that is our heritage." Johnston and her allies

sent out provocative mailers to raise public support for a federal law proposed by Senator Frank E. Moss that would give the horses protected status
based on their ecological and historic value.[35]

The AHPA was particularly suited to this task. Pearl Twyne and Joan
Blue, the women involved in its genesis in Washington, D.C., had been
working diligently to secure passage of the Horse Protection Act, which
banned the practice of "soring" horses' feet, making them painful to force
them step to higher in the show ring. They already had the attention of an
army of equestrians, most of whom were white, middle- and upper-class
women. Letters from constituents poured into congressional offices with
statements that echoed the emotionally charged mailers. "I feel this bill
will put the matter of protection of wild mustangs and burros where it
can be adequately enforced," wrote one Las Vegas resident. She continued,
writing that "the wanton slaughter for personal profit of these wild species
by poachers must be stopped now if they are to be saved from extinction."
The daughter of a military serviceman opined that "the mustang, like the
Indian, could be called 'the first American,'" and "wouldn't it be wonderful if these courageous animals could be preserved for our future children
and ancestors to admire?" Letters sent by schoolchildren became the most
powerful symbols of support. One child wrote, "I like horses alot especially
mustangs and colts are my favorite. I wish there were some way that they
could be saved."[36]

Reaffirming this view, journalist Hope Ryden, who had worked closely
with the Tillett family on behalf of the Pryor Mountain horses while film-
ing the 1968 ABC documentary on the subject, published an exposé on
wild horses in October 1970. Entitled *America's Last Wild Horses*, it portrayed the animals as "victims," "scapegoats," the "prey of profiteers" who
were "tormented," "trapped," and "stalked" by poachers, and generally had
become "the object of widespread prejudice." Ryden opened her book with
a chapter that asserted that because *Equus* had originally evolved on the
North American continent and fossils at every stage of the species' development could be found there, the horse must be "a native of North America,"
emphasizing the innate place she believed wild horses had once had and
continued to have in the ecosystem. Ryden also emphasized the Spanish
heritage of the animals, placing importance on the term "mustang." She argued that "since the public-domain lands where wild horses are still found
had little economic value, and since this land in any case belongs to all of
us equally, whether stockmen, hunter, or city dweller, it was the plea of

the horse lovers that more refuges be quickly established for the wild horse whose long centuries of service to man had earned it the right and the privilege to return to the wild."[37]

Ryden's work publicized the most provocative aspects of wild horse advocates' argument for their place on public lands. Rather than relegating the equines to refuges, where as feral animals they would continue to be regarded as "interloper[s] and illegitimate," Ryden supported Congress "granting permanent status and place to the last bands of horses living like hunted fugitives in the West they helped build." Her book was widely popular, informing the perceptions of the American public and, most importantly, the nation's congressional leaders.[38]

The villains in Hope Ryden's work and Velma Johnston's rhetoric were ranchers. Those in the Great Basin, especially, often fulfilled the negative role in which advocates portrayed them. Joseph Fallini, Jr., son of the elder Joseph Fallini and a neighbor of the Clifford family, had a rough time grappling with his wild horse problem in the late 1960s. The family had always run horses on the grazing range with their cattle, a common practice especially in drier areas such as the Kawich and Railroad Valleys. Beginning in 1951, the BLM required the family to keep their livestock to the permitted numbers, and thereafter, there was a much clearer line between the Fallini horses and the wild herds. But each season, when the Fallinis transferred their cattle and horses from the summer to winter ranges and shut off their stock watering systems, wild horse herds migrated with them. In addition, herds from the Nellis refuge drifted north onto the Fallinis' grazing district to follow the water and grass. The family had customarily rounded up what they considered excess animals and sold them to slaughterhouses, but this was never really to their liking. With the creation of the NMA in the mid-1960s, Fallini saw an alternative and offered to sell them the excess horses. Despite his best intentions, NMA members were outraged. Kent Gregersen, the organization's secretary, completely misinterpreted Fallini's intentions and accused the rancher of graft. He wrote Velma Johnston that "the ranchers pay no grazing fees on these horses in almost all cases. Now they hear of a bill in Congress which may stop their operations in Nevada [and] they are going all out to get all the horses they can, while they can, before a law can prohibit them."[39]

Compounding matters, the distasteful figure of the mustanger lingered in the public consciousness. One case in particular confirmed advocates' fears that mechanized roundups still occurred, that they were terribly cruel, and that wild horses were still being sold and slaughtered. John Casey and his son-in-law James A. Williams of Gerlach, north of Pyramid Lake in Nevada, were ranchers only in the loosest sense of the term. Casey owned a slaughterhouse and was known to have rustled cattle. In July 1969, he and mustanger pilot Jerry "Chug" Utter rounded up 150 horses using an airplane and shotguns. State brand inspector Stanley Routson and local law enforcement secured arrest warrants for the men, but the state did not file a criminal complaint and the horses went to the slaughterhouse anyway. The following year, one of Johnston's informants caught Utter illegally constructing a trap for capturing wild horses near Virginia City and introducing branded horses into the wild herds. When Utter disappeared, Johnston and University of Nevada biology professor Michael Pontrelli, who along with his graduate student Steven Pelligrini had worked to help the Pryor Mountain horses, planned to dismantle the trap for the media to illustrate the problem of poaching practices. But, before they could arrange the event, a group of concerned Virginia City residents dismantled the trap in angry protest. Utter filed a civil suit for property damage against those "responsible," specifically Dr. Pontrelli, who was then notified by the university that his contract would not be renewed. The media attention the incident received more than confirmed to the American public that the wild horse was indeed still in danger of extinction.[40]

The final blow to resistance to a federal law granting wild horses special status on public lands came when California enacted a ban on using "Nevada mustang flesh" or "free-roaming wild horses" in pet food at the end of 1970. Along with alligator shoes and leopard- or tiger-skin coats, wild horse meat could no longer be processed or sold in the state. Advocates hoped the new law would save "a number of dwindling species from extinction at the hands of professional hunters and poachers." Riding on a tidal wave of public support and feeling pressure from his young son who had read Marguerite Henry's book, Representative Gilbert Gude of Maryland took up the wild horse cause and proposed placing the equines under the protection of the Department of the Interior, with the BLM acting as custodian, and potentially setting aside more special ranges for their preservation. On public lands, the BLM intended to manage wild horses under the multiple-use concept; on their designated preserves they would have a higher level of priority. This was no different than the way the agency handled other additional uses. The BLM was making a similar arrangement for the designation of special off-road vehicle areas, managing them under multiple use on most public lands and prohibiting them from special protected areas. Besides Gude's bill, other members of Congress rushed to introduce their own version of the new law. So many bills appeared on Capitol Hill in the first few months of 1971 that Velma Johnston declared she was unsure "which ones we should support."[41]

At the same time national legislation was under way, a parallel proposal surfaced in Nevada over whether or not the state, home to the majority of the nation's wild horse herds, should take over the protection and care of the animals. The debate on the Nevada measure highlighted the tensions at the national level. The conversation centered on the issue of whether the wild horses slated for protection were in fact remnants of the Spanish horses of the sixteenth century, a justification the NMA used to confirm their place in the nation's heritage. Kent Gregerson had gone even a step further in advocating Hope Ryden's position that the horse was once native to North America. Yet the general feeling among ranchers, because many of them had once actively managed these herds and because the early literature on the disappearing mustang suggested it, was that the current wild horses bore little resemblance to the legendary Spanish Andalusians. Floyd Lamb, now a state senator from Las Vegas, caustically argued, "You're barking up the wrong tree when you try to protect this type of an animal." Lamb accused Velma Johnston and his fellow state senator Cliff Young from Reno of "brain-washing the children." Lander County rancher and sheriff George Schwin agreed, stating that the horses around his area were just plain old wild horses. But biology professor and wild horse expert Michael Pontrelli said the amount of so-called mustang blood did not matter and all wild horses symbolically represented a part of the nation's heritage. This was the same argument Velma Johnston made. To many critics and supporters alike, the connection of contemporary wild horses with those of the Spanish explorers legitimized the animals' place in the American West and on public lands.[42]

A secondary issue had to do with cost, both that which would be required to adequately manage the animals and that which would be incurred if wild horses were allowed to displace livestock. Most Nevadans, like Pontrelli, Johnston, and Utter, agreed that wild horse numbers ought to be actively managed since the animals did proliferate over time if left unchecked, and they did do damage to the public rangelands. But no one knew exactly what that rate of proliferation was, nor did anyone understand the impact wild horses actually had on the range as a separate species. In addition, no single group had the funding available to create and staff a management program for their preservation.[43]

Under Nevada's proposed law, the Nevada Fish and Game Department would manage the horses if the state accepted responsibility for them, but the agency required increased staff and funding to carry out any protective measures enacted by the state. Nevada lacked a state income tax and relied on the volatile fluctuations of sales tax to fund its programs. The Fish and Game Department sold hunting and fishing licenses to help fund its wildlife mandates, but horses were unlikely to provide that kind of revenue except through the roundup permitting process, the very situation advocates sought to avoid. Without an income, the state could not bear the financial burden of wild horse management, and the proposed measure went nowhere. In contrast, Utah announced that it would rather its Division of Fish and Game manage the animals and not have the federal government "stepping in and telling it what to do where wild horses are concerned." Ranchers remained fundamentally convinced that the animals would wreck decades of range improvements as they had in earlier decades. Floyd Lamb reminded Nevadans that "we should consider the ranchers a people who have to endure these animals . . . they developed the land and dug the wells." As Chug Utter so crassly put it, "there's only one end to being a horse, whether he's a champion race horse or a plug: dog food."[44]

Congress, motivated by a massive letter-writing crusade by schoolchildren and excellent television coverage, seemed willing to place wild horses under federal administration. In early 1971, Nevada representative Walter S. Baring and Washington senator Henry M. Jackson introduced identical bills in their two respective chambers to accomplish this. Colorado representative Wayne Aspinall, who opposed the measure along with Arizona representative Sam Steiger, and Idaho senator Frank Church, conducted hearings on the Baring and Jackson bills. Supporters included nearly the entire Great Basin delegation, particularly Nevada senators Alan Bible and Howard W. Cannon, Oregon senator Mark Hatfield, and Utah senator Frank E. Moss and representative Gunn McKay. Both measures essentially supported creating a new categorical description of wild horses: neither domestic strays nor wildlife, wild horses were to be a "national heritage species" and an "esthetic resource," based on their cultural meaning to the country as the last remnants of the American West. In large part, this was done to avoid the problematic terms "feral" and "wildlife," as such language was already established in state and federal laws in ways that clearly did not appeal to either wild horse advocates or their opponents. Instead, the bills used the term "free-roaming" to describe the animals' state of being.[45]

These congressional hearings proved no less emotionally charged than those held a decade before. Proponents of the wild horse legislation asserted the animals' place in the nation's history and the importance of their preservation on public lands. Velma Johnston again testified, declaring that ranchers "must realize that their years of dominant use of the public lands are over." She argued, "We, the people, recognize we have a right, too, to this rapidly diminishing resource for purposes other than to provide forage for privately owned cattle and sheep, or to provide forage for target animals to oblige the hunters." Michael Pontrelli reiterated that "wild horses have been extremely important to our American heritage, as there is account after account of using a wild horse as breeding stock with a more popular breed to instill ruggedness, stamina and a better ability to perform in the harsh western environment." Hope Ryden testified to the amount of public support for wild horse protection, evidenced by the popularity of her documentary, book, and recent article in *National Geographic*. Even a fourth-grade teacher, sponsored by the AHPA, pleaded with the representatives to save the wild horses because they served as a "symbol of that tenacious will to survive in the face of encroaching civilization and man's rapacious greed."[46]

In contrast, Karl Weikel of Searchlight, Nevada, who represented both the National Cattlemen's Association and the National Wool Growers Association at the hearings and spoke for the majority of ranchers in the country, argued that from the beginning, the wild horse issue had been "clouded by controversy, accusations, counteraccusations and recriminations based mostly upon misunderstanding of, and impatience with, past mistakes, abuses, misuses and poor management decisions resulting from mistaken policy and too little factual information." Commending wild horse advocates on their efforts to protect the animals from human-induced suffering, he reminded them that "we of the western range livestock industry live with and respect these animals and have done so for many years." No one knew the horses better, Weikel argued, but he stated that "we take a more practical and less emotional approach to the very same objective." That pragmatism included active management of herd sizes, culling excess animals, the humane destruction of aged or sick horses, and the sale of viable stock. Weikel also reminded Congress that it was not so long ago that Americans condoned eating horse meat and that "we have gotten pretty finicky in this country in the last several years."[47]

Weikel's commonsense approach, echoed by the BLM's range managers, did not help either group's position. Their language made them sound old and out of touch with the nation's shifting environmental values. By October, the two bills had been passed by both congressional houses and were in the process of being reconciled. Both measures made harassing, killing, and selling the remnants of wild horses a federal offense and both recognized the cultural importance of the wild horse to the American public. In the process of reconciliation, the compromise bill did not mention creating any refuges or offer protection to herds on state lands. Instead, it mandated that the secretary of the interior and secretary of agriculture protect them wherever they roamed on public lands, though without providing any direction as to how, except to ban the use of aircraft in wild horse roundups.[48]

This vague but symbolic gesture provided a place for wild horses on public lands but did not make clear any of the specific details as to how, where, and at what level wild horses would be managed. The Wild Free-Roaming Horses and Burros Act of 1971 satisfied advocates' most important criterion: it protected wild horses from being rounded up and then sold for commercial uses such as pet food. As the primary agency designated to implement the new law, the BLM had only a short time to decide how to proceed. Between passage of the law and its enforcement in 1974, the bureau required ranchers to remove any privately owned animals in order to sort out which horses qualified for federal protection. For ranchers and the land management agency, this loomed as an onerous task. Never one to abandon the job to others, to help oversee this process and work with the BLM in enforcing the new law, Velma Johnston founded Wild Horse Organized Assistance (WHOA) and served on the Department of the Interior's national advisory committee on wild horses.[49]

Johnston and the BLM, however, faced an uphill battle with Great Basin ranchers, who had been nationally vilified and embarrassed in the national campaign for the preservation law. Leslie Stewart, a rancher from Paradise Valley, Nevada, who served as chair of the state's Multiple-Use Advisory Board, complained that unregulated horse herds threatened his family's livelihood and that "if the people want the wild horses as a national heritage, they [the wild horses] should be where they could see them." Stewart suggested that if Americans wanted to see the animals on display, maybe they should be placed in city zoos. He called the public's perception of wild horses a distorted emotional image. Johnston furthered this public polarization and continued to shame ranchers by accusing them of creating an "unfavorable image of the wild horses" in order to downplay their importance and acting as though they were being robbed of valuable resources.[50]

In the first few years, the BLM, as the agency charged with managing most of the existing herds, seemed unsure how to proceed and uneasy with moving forward. The BLM did not even allocate any funds or dedicate any staff specifically for managing the wild herds until 1975. Between the passage of the new law and 1974, ranchers were supposed to remove their animals, presumably those that could be claimed by the brands they wore, from public lands. The bureau's slow, even reluctant, approach to the wild horses and burros act left a vacuum that placed the animals at even greater risk than before. Some ranchers took advantage of the situation to clear entire herds off the public rangeland, claiming the animals were privately owned. In one such instance, near Howe, Idaho, in 1973, a roundup gone horribly wrong ended with the bloody death of multiple horses. Between eight and ten animals were found shattered at the base of a two-hundred-foot cliff, including one pregnant mare that had aborted her foal. Many of the horses had been mutilated, with their noses stapled shut to restrict their breathing. None of the animals had brands or were shod—indicators of most privately owned horses. Velma Johnston, aging though ever vigilant, brought the matter to the attention of the regional Forest Service office in Ogden, Utah, which sent investigators to the site along with the BLM.[51]

The incident near Howe was even more complicated than either Johnston or the federal agencies knew. According to the district BLM office, ranchers in the area did claim ownership of those horses but had left them unbranded to cheat the grazing permit system. The roundup, the agency said, occurred because it had advised ranchers in the area to pull their horses off the grazing ranges. But the BLM's field and state office personnel disagreed as to whether a permit or some other type of permission was needed for the ranchers to proceed. Velma Johnston, WHOA, and the Humane Society were not convinced this roundup was about collecting private property. Why would ranchers cause the destruction of their own animals? As the story unfolded, the reality of the new law set in. Johnston helped locate the live animals collected during the roundup, which had been shipped through Winnemucca, Nevada, and Ogden, Utah, with only cursory brand inspections, at a slaughterhouse in North Platte, Nebraska. The ranchers in Howe insisted they had hired a mustanger to capture the animals to sell to "horse lovers," but Johnston, the Humane Society, and the AHPA, which had now gotten involved, doubted their motives. To them, it seemed more likely the ranchers wanted the horses off their grazing ranges before they could be declared "wild." A full investigation found that those involved had used snowmobiles and a helicopter to capture the animals and had cut the animal's throats to weaken them. Some of the horses had broken their legs and those pursuing them had used chain saws to remove their shattered limbs. Outraged, the AHPA and Humane Society filed a civil suit against the Department of the Interior and the BLM that also implicated ranchers and Idaho state officials in violating the Wild Horse Annie Law, the Wild Free-Roaming Horses and Burros Act, and a number of other animal protection acts.[52]

The roundup at Howe, one of the first to be conducted under the new law, had been so badly botched that wild horse advocates lost faith in the BLM right from the beginning. It was clear the agency had no idea how to conceptualize and manage horses as "wild." Proponents of the animals had assumed that the "free-roaming" aspect of the law, which defined their status, was enough to clarify the difference between domestic horses and their feral counterparts. But in the Howe incident, their free-roaming status was not enough to keep the animals from being claimed by ranchers in the area who did not want to give up a single blade of grass to wild horse preservation. By the following year, when the BLM once again began rounding up excess wild horse populations, Velma Johnston, WHOA, the AHPA, the Humane Society, and other advocacy groups began staunchly opposing any roundups without reductions in livestock numbers occurring first.[53]

The Howe massacre also highlighted another looming issue. Neither BLM officials nor wild horse advocates knew exactly what to do with the excess wild population once they were captured if the animals were not sent to slaughter. Ranchers, the BLM, and even Velma Johnston knew that at some point, herd sizes grew too big for their range. Adjustments would have to be made eventually. But once the BLM captured them, no one was quite sure who was responsible for their welfare. The BLM's adoption program, created in 1973, made horses available for private ownership, but wild horse advocates contested purchasers' ability to actually secure title to the animals, fearing slaughterhouses and commercial processors would use the program to continue purchasing horseflesh. Most adopters lived in Reno, the closest population center to the BLM's primary holding pens in Palomino Valley. There, the animals lived in close quarters under conditions that ruined their feet and spread equine illnesses. Would-be adopters were wretched at the sight of manure-filled corrals and had a hard time imagining bringing home one of the filthy, frightened animals. One California woman came to Palomino Valley with her children to see the wild horses only to watch an employee shoot one in the head and drag the carcass, pouring red blood, through the snow and mud.[54]

During this time, Great Basin ranchers struggled to adapt to the new law. Families like the Cliffords had a rough time navigating the difficult terrain of public opinion and their own self-interest. When Joseph Clifford watched the agency release those horses from his corral in Stone Cabin Valley, he could not help but feel disheartened. It had taken so long to get the roundup properly approved and conducted that when it resulted in the successful capture of nearly a fifth of the number of animals slated for removal, it was wrenching to see them released as if nothing had even been accomplished. In this case, the BLM's jurisdictional battle with the state of Nevada was to blame, but this was becoming the norm. Every wild horse roundup was contested and resulted in public outcry, if not outright failure.

To make matters worse, the agency began looking for options that directly infringed on ranchers' property rights. Joseph Fallini, who along with Floyd Lamb served on Nevada's wild horse committee, had once toured Velma Johnston around the area near Tonopah, trying to explain their problem with increased wild horse numbers, though Johnston proved unsympathetic. Fallini had, at the time, suggested using a land bequest to the state from a notable Nevadan for another wild horse refuge. But unknown to the Fallinis, and the Cliffords as well, Nevada senator Paul Laxalt was working with Governor Mike O'Callaghan and the BLM to solve the state's wild horse problem from another angle by expanding the National Wild Horse Refuge, located on the Nellis range, north into the Stone Cabin and Reveille Valleys, making it into a recreation area. BLM state director Edgar I. Rowland believed that "establishment of wild horse and burro ranges and removal of the animals from the balance of the State" was "the only practical solution to the horse problem." Both families owned property and held water and grazing rights in the area and stood to have their livestock operations seriously reduced, if not eliminated altogether. This particularly affected the Fallinis, who had not kept up their property at Eden Creek or used all their water rights since so little had been available in the past decade. This gave the impression that the southern portion of their grazing range was unused.[55]

At a meeting with bureau officials and the Fallini family, in which they discussed the development of this park and wild horse refuge, the BLM rolled out a map of the recreation area that clearly included the Fallinis' Eden Creek property. Unpleasantly surprised, Helen Fallini said, "We jumped up and told them like hell." The agency attempted to persuade the Fallinis of the soundness of its plan by offering to allocate them some other land in exchange. "We had quite a battle over that that night," said Helen Fallini, "and they were telling all the other people around who were sitting in there how they were going to take it over and it was going to be a historical site and all that." The Fallinis were deeply offended and strongly opposed the BLM's efforts to create what would have been a one-million-acre wild horse refuge and recreation area. Both families struggled with the BLM's indecision and the headaches involved in conducting a roundup; it took until the summer of 1976 for the agency to finally cull the four hundred wild horses out of Stone Cabin Valley and the surrounding area.[56]

The wild horse herds on military ranges, however, were not as safe as wild horse advocates hoped. The same year the BLM thinned the Stone Cabin herd, a strange mass death of wild horses occurred at Dugway in July. In 1968, a number of sheep deaths caused by exposure to chemical agents had occurred in the same area, leading residents to believe that a similar incident had transpired. A pilot had spotted nearly one hundred animals from the air, many of which were dead, their carcasses contaminating the water hole around Orr Springs near the Cedar Mountains. Military and BLM officials carefully examined the situation with veterinarians, who determined that "elevated environmental temperatures, forced exertion and increased water consumption, leading to heat exhaustion, associated with water intoxication" had caused the fatalities. The Humane Society of Utah thought otherwise, however, and conducted its own investigation, determining that increased military activities had agitated the animals and kept them from using the water hole. The uncertainy surrounding the animals' deaths left room for speculation; the AHPA believed the horses exhibited signs of the rare African horse sickness, a respiratory disease transmitted by insects that was nearly always fatal and had decimated horse populations in sub-Saharan Africa. Before releasing their final report, the military and BLM entertained the idea that the toxic rat poison 1080 might have contaminated the water. When investigators released their findings, the deaths of twenty horses seemed to have resulted from a combination of heat exhaustion and inadequate access to regular water sources. Though increased military activities the previous year did not necessarily result directly in the animals' deaths, residents of the base had complained frequently about the wild horses causing sanitation problems in the area and had advocated their removal.[57] It was possible they had dealt with the animals themselves.

Wild horses occupied an important cultural place in the nation's heritage and a cherished romantic space in the American psyche, but they struggled for traction in the actual environment. The animals still did not really have a physical place outside their designated refuges in the Great Basin except through the sheer presence of their numbers. When herds reached the point they became noticeable, the BLM reduced their size. But wild horse advocates wanted them to be noticeable and resented any reductions, pointing to ranchers' livestock, which were many times more numerous, saying that they should be reduced instead. In the Pryor Mountains on the Wyoming-Montana state line and in the Book Cliffs of Colorado, where a refuge was established in 1973, wild horses had designated spaces. But in the Great Basin, the animals had only the refuge on the military range, which naturally spilled out onto the grazing ranges in Reveille, Stone Cabin, and Railroad Valleys where ranchers resented their presence. Wild horse advocates spoke about the right of the animals to be on public lands at the same time ranchers defended their right to the same. Discussions of their management brought out the less cooperative side of all groups involved, each working to protect its stake in public lands. It did not help that much of the rhetoric had a gendered quality. Most news articles featured ranchers and mustangers, like the Cliffords, the Fallinis, and those in the Gus Bundy photographs, who were primarily male and took a hard line against the growth of horse herds. The wild horse advocates were in large part women like Velma Johnston, Helen Reilly, Hope Ryden, Pearl Twyne, and Joan Blue, giving the movement a gendered appearance; hence ranchers' criticism of the "emotional" nature of preserving wild horses.[58]

However, these women were far from similar in their backgrounds, which informed their views on how wild horses ought to be managed. They really agreed on only one thing—that the federal government ought to take responsibility for wild horses. But the AHPA argued for minimal management, allowing "cyclical population trends to which all wild animals are subject" to apply to wild horses. The organization believed the 1971 law gave the animals "a preferred status in the multiple use policy for the public lands" and complained the BLM did not ascribe them an equitable position or work to equal out the numbers of horses and other livestock. The AHPA and other groups actively opposed roundups, sterilization procedures, or any direct management program. Their desire was to manage wild herds

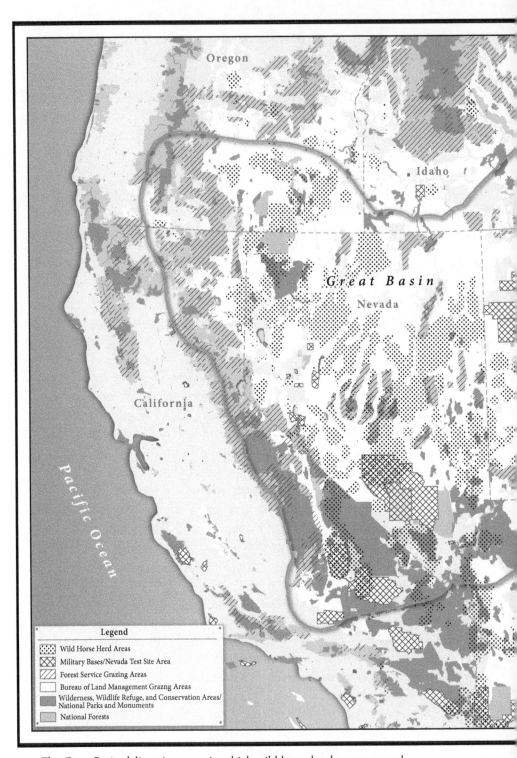

Legend

- ⣿ Wild Horse Herd Areas
- ⊠ Military Bases/Nevada Test Site Area
- ⧄ Forest Service Grazing Areas
- ☐ Bureau of Land Management Grazng Areas
- ■ Wilderness, Wildlife Refuge, and Conservation Areas/ National Parks and Monuments
- ▨ National Forests

The Great Basin delineating areas in which wild horse herds are managed, overlaid by military installations, areas designated for outdoor recreation, and

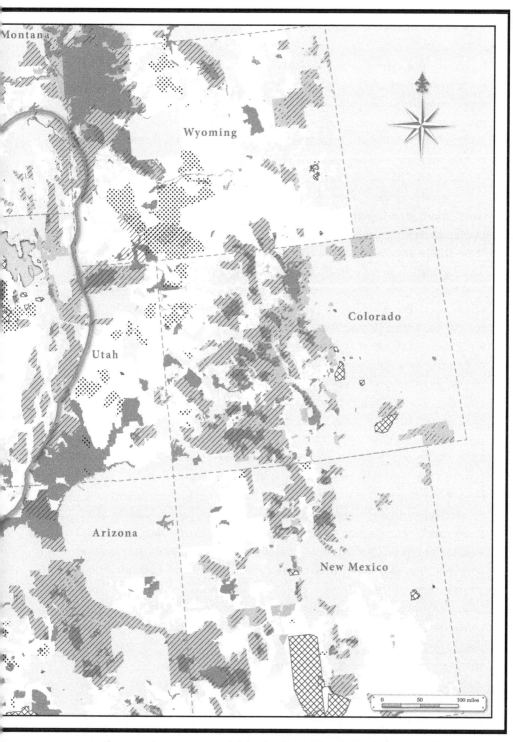

areas where grazing is permitted. Map by Gerry Krieg. *Copyright © 2015 by the University of Oklahoma Press*

humanely and carefully, even anthropomorphically, keeping herd families together and letting the animals self-regulate their own populations. Their single-minded contempt for the BLM and ranchers ground to a halt any dialogue about and participation in wild horse management.[59]

Ranchers, wildlife advocates, and BLM officials took a different perspective on wild horse management. A very small number of them wanted the animals off the land altogether, but most really did enjoy seeing free-roaming horses on the range. Robert Wright, president of the Nevada Cattlemen's Association, maintained that "the wild horse is part of our American heritage and certainly needs to be preserved for future generations." Instead, these groups advocated a more active approach to wild horse management. The Toiyabe Chapter of the Sierra Club in Nevada supported "retention of wild horses . . . in such numbers that are consistent with the importance of the Great Basin habitat to their continued wild and free-roaming existence." The group also supported cooperation with ranchers in developing water resources for both wild horses and wildlife. Tina Nappe, the daughter of Gus Bundy and a key member of the organization, argued that retaining ranching as a way of life was key to the survival of wild horses, wildlife, and ranchers alike. But as much as Nappe supported ranching as a way to retain open space, she resented the "continued intransigence" of some ranchers in the region, which "prevented any meaningful resolution" on the wild horse issue. She argued that these ranchers demonstrated "Nevada's hostility" and provided "grist for the mill for the wild horse organizations" to oppose every BLM activity.[60]

By the late 1970s, Nappe noticed an increasing intractability in Great Basin ranchers. As a key wildlife conservationist in the state, she found herself turning more often, though reluctantly, to wild horse advocates as potential allies against the livestock industry. She wrote, "Traditional conservation groups can no longer afford to ride the fence on the wild horse issue. Feelings about the present wild horse law are spilling over into other conservation issues and are definitely contributing to the 'sagebrush rebellion.'" But wild horse advocates were not exactly receptive to partnering with a group that essentially considered horses, wild or not, an introduced species, secondary to key charismatic fauna such as mule deer, bighorn sheep, and mountain lions. In this fractured and contested landscape of public lands management, the BLM had to find a way to stitch all multiple uses together just as each faction increasingly hardened its position. Caught in the middle of ballooning numbers of public lands interests, the BLM had to serve as mediator and was losing the confidence of its various constituents, most of whom had very personal investments in their positions. As Helen Fallini complained, voicing the concerns of many public lands users, "the Bureau of Land Management has been nothing but a pain in the butt. No matter what you do, it's wrong to them . . . you can get everything to where you think you're pretty well settled, and all of a sudden, here they come with some other daggone thing."[61]

Conclusion

By the mid-1970s, those who relied on public lands in the Great Basin to make their living struggled to navigate the cluttered collection of legal structures that governed the landscape. Besides the Wild Free-Roaming Horses and Burros Act, the National Environmental Protection Act and the Endangered Species Act incorporated additional aspects of multiple use by prioritizing the health of the environment itself and the wildlife it supported above other uses. For the most part, these things had always been aspects of multiple use, but only insofar as they supported the ecological health needed to contribute to productivity. Now the BLM and other federal agencies grappled with environmental assessments, impact statements, and a multitude of new considerations that directly affected ranchers, the military, and outdoor recreationists. And because wild horses were not considered wildlife, endangered species preservation took priority over them as well. In this context, Helen Fallini's complaint that the BLM made it increasingly difficult to conduct "normal" business had much to do with these new regulations she and her family now had to navigate.[1]

To portray the tension as merely a political conflict between commercial users of public lands and environmentalists obfuscates the increasing complexity of multiple use as it developed throughout the twentieth century and the inherent tension the concept contained. Multiple use could not exclude any reasonable use of public lands. Its function was to put the Great Basin wasteland to use and, once used, to make sure that public lands were not going to waste by returning the maximum benefit, the definition of which evolved to incorporate both commercial and environmental interests. The early land economists had believed all land required some kind of identity; if not private property, they argued, land should be reserved for its important resource quality as national forests or for its scenic quality as national parks. But the Great Basin, where the majority of the remaining public lands were located, posed a particular problem. In this region, most lands could not be disposed of under the existing land laws, but neither did they qualify for reservation as park or forest. Multiple use, crafted at first to legitimize the prior use of public lands as grazing range by local residents without precluding land disposal or wildlife management, evolved to fill this vacuum. Additional legal structures codified other prior uses in the same space, such as military testing, outdoor recreation, and wild horse preservation, as national interests changed. The laws that codified these activities were manifestations of how important it was to give these lands identity, and their intersections evidenced how increasingly difficult it was to accommodate all the possible uses.

Great Basin residents played a central role in developing multiple use, but they also had to cope with the consequences of these conflicting and intersecting landscapes. Sometimes they demonstrated remarkable resilience. Other times, they sat at the losing end of legal battles that subverted their interests to national priorities. Such was the case with grazing fees. In 1934, the Taylor Grazing Act had instituted grazing fees for the purpose of funding range management and improvement. Great Basin ranchers contested grazing fees from the very beginning. In 1936, at the first hearings discussing the act, one Great Basin rancher argued that "we feel that we have a legitimate basis for asking that the fees in Nevada be not set at the same rate as those set in the better grazing areas of some other states. It takes two years to raise one lamb and twelve pounds of wool in our state. We feel that we have a legitimate argument and that these fees should be set up by states, rather than by the country as a whole." Nevertheless, the Grazing Service settled on fees of five cents per head of cattle and one cent per sheep, regardless of the local environment in which they were raised.[2]

While not disputing the ability of the Grazing Service to collect fees, Great Basin ranchers believed they should be charged only enough to cover a long-term permit and range administration and improvement in their locality. They argued that fees set too high would bankrupt their operations and that a uniform grazing fee was simply unfair because not all range

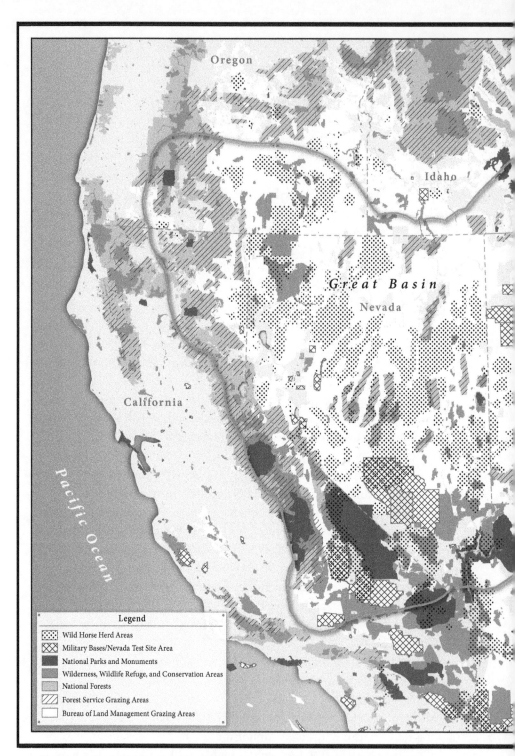

Legend

- Wild Horse Herd Areas
- Military Bases/Nevada Test Site Area
- National Parks and Monuments
- Wilderness, Wildlife Refuge, and Conservation Areas
- National Forests
- Forest Service Grazing Areas
- Bureau of Land Management Grazing Areas

The Great Basin delineating the various uses of public lands, including grazing, military activities, outdoor recreation, wildlife preservation, and wild horse

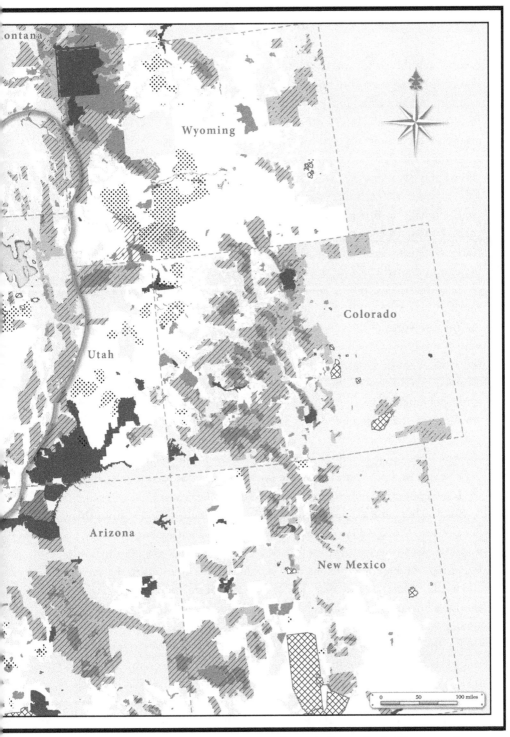

herd management. Map by Gerry Krieg. *Copyright © 2015 by the University of Oklahoma Press*

quality on public lands was the same. As many stockmen in the Great Basin had constructed their entire operation on free access, any alteration to their economic system could indeed financially ruin them. In order to block collection of fees on grazing allotments, these Great Basin ranchers took their argument for a more targeted fee structure to court and lost.[3]

In 1945, the BLM attempted to raise grazing fees several times and continued to meet with stiff opposition by ranchers in the Great Basin. In 1948, fees increased on cattle from five cents to eight (fees on sheep increased proportionally to one and a half cents); in 1951, they increased to twelve cents; by 1962, they were nineteen cents. Then in 1963, new BLM director Karl Landstrom shocked ranchers by announcing both a 50 percent fee increase and a reduction in the numbers of permitted livestock in response to the criticism that public lands ranchers were not paying their fair share for their use of the public grazing range. Landstrom explained, "We believe . . . the full worth of the valuable resources on public lands may be realized with a minimum expense to the taxpayer." During the 1950s and 1960s, the Izaak Walton League, a conservation and outdoor recreation group founded in Chicago in the 1920s, consistently complained that ranchers using public lands received special privileges, which gave them an unfair advantage in the livestock industry and allowed them inequitable use of the public's land. Writer Bernard DeVoto on several occasions suggested that the American taxpayer require livestock operators to "get their hands out of your pocket and pay the market rate for grazing," or at least require them to "bid competitively for the privilege of using your ranges."[4]

But ranchers in the Great Basin did not understand the issue from this perspective. The Sharp family in Nye County, who had "made all necessary improvements on the range" before being "forced into a grazing district," stated that the increased grazing fees "would be very injurious to the sheep and cattle industry," and that "the livestock industry has been trying to survive without subsidies and therefore feel that we cannot pay any larger grazing fees." Clair Whipple in Lincoln County declared that a fee increase would "ruin our economy." George Swallow of White Pine County challenged that "any increase in grazing fees would amount to confiscation" of their property. In general, they felt that making a living off the livestock industry was becoming more and more difficult because of "increasing competition for the use of the land, as a result of population growth and industrial demands, and frequent withdrawal of large tracts with public use," "cancelled or restricted grazing," and increased grazing fees. More than others who used public lands, ranchers were wholly dependent on them for a living.[5]

The region's congressional delegation understood the importance of the issue to their constituents and asked the Department of the Interior to make a much smaller series of adjustments to thirty cents and then forty-four throughout the 1960s until the Public Land Law Review Commission (PLLRC), the fourth and final federal review of public lands, could deliver its report. But when the committee published its recommendations, it deliberately framed natural resources, including "traditional resources of minerals, timber, forage, intensive agriculture, water, and fish and wildlife" and "various spatial uses such as for residential, commercial, and industrial purposes," as commodities. This oriented public lands and the resources they contained around consumption. Consonant with this determination, the PLLRC recommended basing grazing fees on a fair market system. Ranchers in the Great Basin felt betrayed.[6]

The PLLRC did recognize that while the public lands were "relatively unimportant to the national livestock economy," they were "often crucial to individual ranch operations." It recommended clarifying the parameters and procedures of administering grazing permits to include precise conditions under which livestock reductions, changes in improvement responsibilities, and cancellations might occur. It even suggested that some grazing ranges might be better managed in private ownership. Nevertheless, the PLLRC insisted that fair market value, "the value that ordinarily would be established by operation of the open market," protected the "interest of the public as landlord." Though it recognized that ranchers deserved some consideration as to the "variances in operating and economic situations or differences in the quality of public range land and forage yield," the PLLRC accepted a uniform base fee for all lands, allowing for only minor adjustments relative to the quality of the forage. After the committee's report, grazing fees increased from the previous decade's $0.44 to $1.89, the highest fee in the BLM's history, which set the agency on par with the Forest Service.[7]

Not only were grazing fees much higher than Great Basin ranchers were prepared to tolerate, but the PLLRC also placed the burden on ranchers to accommodate other public lands users. Because "pressures on public lands for non-grazing use have inevitably led to conflicts between permittees and other users," the PLLRC sought "a balance between competing uses of public lands which is fair to all users." The commission noted that "resolution of the conflict between grazing and other uses will be largely dependent upon public understanding and acceptance of reasonable ground rules governing use." This gave ranchers little consolation since the power for making balanced use work resided exclusively with the very public that offered their industry so much criticism.[8]

This situation was further codified in the Federal Land Policy and Management Act (FLPMA) of 1976, which officially mandated what the BLM had already been doing throughout the previous decade. The agency adopted multiple use as its management framework, defining it as "the management of public lands and their various resource values so that they are utilized in the combination that will best meet the present and future needs of the American people." The resource values listed included, but were not limited to, "recreation, range, timber, minerals, watershed, wildlife and fish, and natural scenic, scientific, and historical values." Phrases such as "the most judicious use of the land," "a combination of balanced and diverse resource uses," and "harmonious and coordinated management" indicated a very real attempt to accommodate all the different public land uses, with the qualifier that this would occur "without permanent impairment of the productivity of the land and the quality of the environment with consideration being given to the relative values of the resources and not necessarily to the combination of uses that will give the greatest economic return or the greatest unit output." The law provided the BLM with a directive akin to the 1916 Organic Act of the National Park Service, but instead of a dual mandate it authorized a multiple one.[9]

The outcry against FLPMA in the Great Basin could be heard across the region. Ranchers still believed that the Taylor Grazing Act "established grazing as the *highest use* of certain lands and gave to permittees, an *exclusive* right as to all other users (excepting hunters and fishermen)." Their frustration boiled over in a tumultuous protest called the Sagebrush Rebellion. This was not the larger national political movement to turn public lands over to the states or that begun by sisters Mary and Carrie Dann to assert Western Shoshone treaty rights and Native sovereignty a few years earlier. This Sagebrush Rebellion was a smaller remonstration originating in the region that sought to curb the negative impact national interests and pressures had on their ranching operations. Seen from the perspective of ranchers in the Great Basin, constantly increasing grazing fees did not stabilize their livestock operations, nor did reductions or cancellations in their grazing permits facilitate security. While all of these activities seemed logical and appropriately efficient in terms of public lands management practices, Great Basin ranchers lived on the very margins, and most could not survive without cheap forage resources in light of the rising costs of other necessities such as fuel, electricity, and food. This situation was not directly reflected in the BLM's reports, but it was one with which the region's ranchers constantly struggled. In addition, livestock owners could not comprehend why they paid fees to use the resources of public lands while outdoor recreationists, wild horse advocates, and the military did not.[10]

Not long after the passage of FLPMA, Great Basin ranchers found political allies with the region's conservative politicians who sought to privatize the nation's natural resources, particularly in Nevada. Floyd Lamb, who had his grazing permits cancelled for "continued failure to live up to the permit conditions and requirements," was one of those politicians. In 1979, Lamb and others who served in the state's legislature conducted hearings on proposals to transfer administration of the public domain to the state and asked residents what they thought should be done to better manage Nevada's public lands. Joseph Fallini explained that since its organization in 1946, the BLM had "acquired 1/3 of the land mass of Europe," yet it had been formed for "the purpose of being a disposal agency." Fallini, in alluding to the agency's original mission, emphasized the priority once given public lands ranching because it fulfilled the general purpose of disposal by putting the land to use. The Sierra Club weighed in to support "the continuance of family-based ranching as an integral and desirable component of public lands." The group hoped to ward off any land transfer to the state since Nevada historically promoted privatization. Nevertheless, those who relied on public lands for their livelihood were unrelenting; as one Idaho rancher put it, "there's no way we can control our destiny while Washington controls the land."[11]

Increasing grazing fees were not the only ongoing hardship Great Basin residents faced. The consequences of radioactive fallout in the region had been surfacing in horrifying ways. Helen Fallini complained that the radiation monitors the Atomic Energy Commission (AEC) sent to their Twin Springs ranch in the 1950s had lied to her. She remembered they told her that radioactive fallout "wasn't supposed to hurt us in any way, shape or form and yet we got that fallout so heavily that it was unbelievable." Helen suffered from eye trouble she attributed to radiation exposure and wondered, "Why is fallout harmful if it goes over Las Vegas and not harmful if it comes over here?" Her husband, Joe, described fallout clouds completely engulfing everything, burning people and animals, and killing birds. They watched one of their neighbors, Minnie Sharp at Nyala, lose her hair after being exposed, and their nephew, Martin Bordoli, succumb to leukemia.[12]

Across the Grant Range at Adaven, Gracian Michael Uhalde bought a Geiger counter and scintillator to measure the radioactive fallout himself. While the AEC monitors told him there was nothing to worry about, the measurements on his Geiger counter indicated that often after tests, his hay was heavily irradiated. His son Gracian was ten when the cloud from the Sedan test in 1962 passed over his home; the fallout rained like snow and his mother refused to let him play outside for three or four days afterward, though the half-life of many radioactive isotopes lasted a week or more. Even after the 1963 Limited Test Ban Treaty, which restricted nuclear testing to underground venues, radioactive fallout still blanketed the area north and east of the test site. These incidents with families, and especially children, made ranchers want the testing stopped.[13]

Nuclear testing did not end until 1992, though over time, Great Basin residents, as the AEC had hoped, came to accept testing as a routine part of their lives. This was not, however, because they stopped hating its effects. Beginning in 1964, the AEC contracted with the Public Health Service (PHS) to set up permanent monitoring stations staffed by full-time personnel throughout the region. This was a significant improvement over the previous decade's monitoring program, which had employed young men who had no background in ranching or any love for the Great Basin. Lina Sharp at Blue Eagle Ranch had always thought monitors were snotty young kids who looked down on ranchers. She said, "We didn't want to cooperate with them because we didn't like their attitudes and we weren't going to do anything with them . . . they were just young kids who were not very smart, intelligent, or anything." The younger Gracian Uhalde joked that most monitors were "barely able to get around," often getting lost in the network of dirt roads that connected the ranches and small communities.[14]

That changed with the permanently hired radiation monitors who arrived in the 1960s. The PHS assigned monitoring personnel "fixed routes," and most were "personally acquainted with every man, woman, and child in their area, as well as every cowpath." The agency expected monitors to maintain "personal contact with everyone in the off-site areas who might be affected by a nuclear mischance." The consistent presence of monitors reassured residents more than any other previous effort. These young men established personal relationships with Great Basin residents that transcended individual views of the contested effects of radiation exposure. Regardless of whether the monitors thought radioactive fallout was damaging, many managed to convey sympathy and understanding to residents simply by being there and providing what information they could.[15]

Lina Sharp and her family established a particularly good relationship with Charles Costa, a dark-haired college graduate from Massachusetts. "He had such an easy manner and such a friendly way that we talked to him," she said. "He spent lots of time in this area as a field man. . . . He was easygoing and we liked him, so we cooperated with the government then." Costa was an unlikely addition to the monitoring staff. Trained as a civil engineer, he enlisted in the PHS in lieu of serving in the military to fulfill his draft obligations. Not long after Costa arrived at the Nevada Test Site for orientation in 1962, the AEC sent him out to Currant, at the north end of Railroad Valley. At the sight of the huge, empty expanse, he had serious misgivings about negotiating the vast, open territory he was supposed to monitor. He stopped at the one-room schoolhouse in Currant where Lina taught and ended up reading stories to the children in his East Coast accent. Costa got lost a lot in the first few years driving the route between Mercury and Ely. Once he got turned around at the south end of Garden Valley and nearly ran out of gas. He happened to run into Helen Uhalde, who had a flat tire. He changed her tire and she fueled his vehicle and gave him directions to Mercury. Costa became a fixture in the lives of the Sharps, Fallinis, and Uhaldes. The ranchers fed him, talked with him, and let him drive their children around in the government truck for fun. He said the families "had their concerns about the test site, but as long as they saw you out there, as long as they believed that we were sincere, they accepted everything that we did at the test site."[16]

Gracian Uhalde, though he was just a kid at the time, remembered seeing a variety of different radiation monitors, but to him, Donald James stood out more than most. He said, "Everybody liked Don James because . . . he didn't have all the answers and he didn't really care. He was just here basically to have a good time and to do whatever he could do. He was a real human being, you know. These other guys that came around in these monkey suits and stuff, you'd just as well shoot them as look at them." Residents adopted a handful of radiation monitors and through consistent contact established good working relationships, which relaxed tensions over nuclear testing and its impact on the communities surrounding the test site. James, a Coloradan who had grown up on a farm and worked at Rocky

Flats producing detonators, moved to Nevada in 1961. James developed relationships with the Fallinis, Sharps, Uhaldes, and many other ranching families north of the test site and knew every mountain and valley between Las Vegas and the Idaho border. He found that many of the ranchers were bitter about the way the AEC had treated them in the past. James believed that "you can't fool those people, they're pretty smart." He said, "We'd tell them everything, we never held back on anything. You know, of course, the DOE [Department of Energy] says you don't say this, don't say that, or anything. When we were asked, we'd tell them . . . that's what they liked . . . they didn't appreciate [the previous] people . . . because they wouldn't say anything, and then when they did answer the people, they'd lie to them, and that just doesn't work." On the days he had to pick up milk samples, James bought gallon containers of milk in Las Vegas or Ely and exchanged that milk for the samples so that the children would not have to drink contaminated milk.[17]

But none of the early radiation monitors and very few of the permanent ones came to the Western Shoshone Duckwater Reservation, just north of Currant in Railroad Valley. Bennie Reilly grew up there and used to listen for the AEC to announce the tests on the radio. He and other children at Duckwater got up before dawn to watch the denotation, "because we could see the big orange flame go up and later on you could see the big old white cloud just go straight up in the air, then watch it break up." Reilly, similar to members of other ranching families in the area, grew up eating rabbit, deer, pronghorn, and pine nuts harvested from the nearby mountains and valleys, vegetables grown in their garden, and beef and milk from their cattle herds. Exposure to radioactive fallout caused many Duckwater residents to suffer from thyroid problems and cancers that manifested as they grew up. Like Minnie Sharp, Doug George, who worked at the state highway station at Currant Summit off Highway 6 on the way to Ely, lost his hair during the atmospheric testing period. Reilly developed esophageal cancer and his uncle, who worked at Twin Springs for Joseph Fallini, developed prostate and stomach cancer. But as bad as living under the cloud was, the testing program provided jobs for many Great Basin residents, especially those in Nye, Lincoln, and Clark Counties who did not ranch. Reilly worked for the AEC as a security guard at the sites for the Shoal test near Fallon and the Faultless test near Warm Springs.[18]

By 1979, the American public expressed deep concern as to the effects of exposure to radioactive fallout. On March 28, a new nuclear power plant on Three Mile Island in southeastern Pennsylvania underwent a reactor crisis. Just twelve days earlier, the new film *The China Syndrome*, starring Michael Douglas, Jane Fonda, and Jack Lemmon, about a near accident at a nuclear power plant, debuted in the nation's theaters. In a bizarre parallel to fiction, nuclear power plant officials at Three Mile Island struggled to control the increasing temperatures within one of the plant's two nuclear cores and the system suffered a partial meltdown. Within several days, officials had the problem contained, but the safety systems at the plant had released an unclear amount of radioactive material into the environment. Radiation monitors from the test site, including Donald James and Charles Costa, who since 1970 had worked under the Environmental Protection Agency (EPA), arrived to mitigate the radioactive materials. Residents of Harrisburg and Middleton, Pennsylvania, experienced a phenomenon that Great Basin residents had already learned to live with: decontamination.[19]

Concomitant with the Three Mile Island accident, Congress conducted hearings on the effects of low-level radiation exposure. The mother of Martin Bordoli, who believed her son developed leukemia as a result of exposure to radioactive fallout, testified that more than seventy residents in Railroad Valley and the area north and east of the Nevada Test Site had petitioned their congressional delegation to stop the nuclear tests in 1957. The document declared it "both undemocratic and un-American to subject one group of citizens to hazards which others are not called upon to face." AEC commissioner Lewis L. Strauss responded by stating, "I believe the conclusion one must inevitably reach after balancing all factors is this— we have the choice of running a very small risk from testing . . . which has been, we believe, the deterrent to aggression since 1945." But the four hundred persons who lived with the size of the risk were unwilling to live in continual peril. The proposal of a high-level nuclear waste repository on the test site at Yucca Mountain in the subsequent decade only widened the gap between local residents and national interests. Furious, and thinking of his childhood exposure, Gracian Uhalde declared, "Right down here at the Nevada Test Site, they created Frankenstein and now they want to bring the son of Frankenstein home."[20]

Increasing grazing fees and the Sagebrush Rebellion, the ongoing militarization of the region and the establishment of Yucca Mountain provide continued evidence that multiple use is highly contested and deeply fraught with risk to those who live with the reality of public lands. However, these are not the only costs of multiple use in the region. In 1986, Great Basin

National Park finally received its designation, but it has never achieved the importance White Pine County had hoped. It is the smallest of the national parks and has no major highways connecting it with any metropolitan centers. As a result, it is a forgotten gem in the Park Service pantheon and offers few amenities to visitors; its economic promise never materialized. Wild horse herds still roam the Great Basin, but their management has become so paralyzing that the BLM cannot conduct a roundup without incurring a lawsuit and a tidal wave of bad press. The underfunded agency relies on private contractors to house the ever-increasing excess populations, and its small adoption program offers the only other alternative. Despite our desires to the contrary, multiple use requires the Great Basin to be all these things—a place to graze livestock, conduct tests for national defense, recreate in the outdoors, and provide room for wild horses to roam—regardless of their incompatibility. It was difficult to understand how this was possible, and that seemed to be the point of my conversation with Gracian Uhalde and his allusion to loss and hope.

Driving toward the highway that would eventually take me to Alamo and back to my home under the glittering lights of Las Vegas, I thought about Uhalde's final statement, the one that had brought our interview to a close. He said, "We're at a crossroads where, you know, this way of life, I guess I see it fading out, to a certain extent. I think if you want to and you're hungry enough to hang on to it, there may be a chance."[21] In light of our conversation, he meant that we can no longer afford to rationalize the size of the risk. Despite the contradiction, multiple use has made the Great Basin public lands a grazing range, test site, recreational venue, and wild horse territory. Because it is predicated on the interplay between local needs and national interests, we are all complicit in its construction and responsible for its consequences. We as a nation bear the collective responsibility for designing multiple use. Uhalde's point is that we must craft it better, and we must act with empathy toward those who bear the burden of public lands for us, both locals and land managers alike.

At its best, multiple use is a dialogue between local residents who rely on public lands, the federal agencies that maintain those lands, and the American public for whom the lands are managed. It is a framework that can be particularly sensitive to both local needs and national interests and pressures. But since the late 1970s, those positions have become increasingly misaligned. Multiple use can be a pragmatic solution to land going to waste, and it has often been an accommodating one. Most of the nation has benefited from the efforts to improve meat production and ranchers' economic well-being, as well as national security, outdoor recreation, animal welfare, and protection of the environment in which all of this takes place. However, we cannot forget that these decisions have occurred at the expense of certain groups; ranchers and other local residents, wild horses and wildlife, and the entire region have been vilified or ignored because we still portray the Great Basin as a wasteland, and these lands are distant from most Americans' physical reality. But the true measure of the efficacy of multiple use is the health of the region's residents and the environment in which they live. Fermi's four hundred persons have navigated the conflicts that created and were created by multiple use, and their persistence in living in a place that few even think about should encourage us to think differently about our public lands and to include them in our thought processes. If we fail to recognize our collective responsibility, we will callously continue to casually sacrifice the region's population and its environment for the greater good of the nation.

The designation of the National System of Public Lands (NSPL) in 2008 by the Department of the Interior provides a glimmer of hope. Established to promote "understanding of the public lands' many uses, resources, and characteristics," the department constructed NSPL such that it "accurately characterizes the interconnectedness of the public lands and their multiple uses." The Department of the Interior argued that "lack of identity" had made it "difficult for the public to readily understand the diversity of the public lands that BLM manages under its multiple-use missions." Giving public lands a distinct identity and a corresponding utility is critical to making multiple use work—it organizes and informs our behavior toward these lands. It reverses our relationship to them by ascribing their value directly instead of by default. It limits our expectations of them, invites our participation with them, and tacitly acknowledges the need to properly fund, manage, and use them. Instead of persisting as the perceptive hole on the nation's mental map, the Great Basin must become an organized, legible landscape. And in embracing its people and its incredibly diverse environment, we can take a step toward recalculating the size of the risk.[22]

Notes

1. Gracian N. Uhalde, interview by the author, December 1, 2006, Nevada Test Site Oral History Project (NTSOHP). For a description of the experience interviewing Gracian N. Uhalde, see Carr Childers, "Every Mine, Every Cow Camp, Every Ranch: Oral History as Fieldwork," in Embry, *Oral History, Community and Work*, 291–93.

2. Frémont, *Report of the Exploring Expedition*, 139, 175–76, 275–77; White, "*It's Your Misfortune and None of My Own*," 123–24; Francaviglia, *Mapping and Imagination*, 83–95.

3. Twain, *Roughing It*, 126–28, 136, 145–46, 175. The Nevada State Historic Preservation Office states that the hostile Forty-Mile Desert claimed 1,061 mules, 5,000 horses, and 3,750 cattle between 1843 and 1850. During this same time, surveyors counted 953 graves.

4. Robert Ridgeway, "Ornithology," in King, *Report of the Geological Exploration*, 353, 357–60; Bartlett, *Great Surveys*, 167–68; Francaviglia, *Mapping and Imagination*, 126–30.

5. Hazen, "Great Middle Region," 18–20; Cleveland Abbe, "Obituary: William Babcock Hazen," *Nature*, April 17, 1887, 541–43. See also William B. Hazen, "Barren Lands in the Interior of the United States," *New York Tribune*, February 27, 1874; Israel C. Russell, "The Great Basin," *Overland Monthly and Out West Magazine*, April 1888, 421–26; Moehring, *Urbanism and Empire*, 83–166. Russell's statement about the larger expanse of land designated as "desert" on earlier maps can be interpreted as a reference to unexplored territory. In this context, the descriptive term "desert" on the map indicates areas that are unknown and assumed to be unpopulated as well as places that are arid.

6. Brewer, "Great Basin," 197, 205, 215–19, 224–27; Chittenden, "Biographical Memoir," 302–304.

7. "Senators Emerge from Great Desert," *New York Times*, September 19, 1925; White, "*It's Your Misfortune and None of My Own*," 405–406.

8. Geographer Donald Meinig described Nevada and Utah as the Mormon Cultural Region, an area dominated by the Mormon religion and noted for its highly successful communal irrigation projects. Meinig argued that Mormonism left an indelible mark on the development of the Intermountain West, visible through the verdant farming

oases in the brown desert. Meinig, "Mormon Culture Region," 199, 213–20. In Nevada, the region between Las Vegas and Ely, Lincoln County in particular, contains a high concentration of Mormons. However, despite the seeming homogeneity of the Mormon religion to outsiders, there are in fact distinct differences between Mormons in urban Las Vegas and those in the rural communities of Alamo and Lund.

9. Totoricaguena, *Identity, Culture, and Politics,* 19–54, 66, 71, 126; Douglass, *Basque Sheepherders,* 16–33. The communities of Ely, Elko, and Reno all contain significant concentrations of Basques. According to William Douglass, Basque sheepherders were "the indispensible backbone of the sheep industry," though most of the livestock industry only latently recognized their economic contribution. So closely identified were Basques with sheepherding that "to say 'sheepherder' was to mean 'Basque.'"

10. Corbin Harney, interview by Suzanne Becker and Mary Palevsky, August 4, 2005, NTSOHP, Special Collections, UNLV; Virginia Sanchez and Kim Townsend, interview with the author, December 4, 2008, personal collection; Crum, *Road on Which We Came,* 25–26, 59, 163–83; Blackhawk, *Violence over the Land,* 272–74; Solnit, *Savage Dreams.* Nevada still contains some of the smallest reservations in the Bureau of Indian Affairs system. The primary land bases for the Western Shoshones are in the northeastern and central portions of the state. They include the Duck Valley, South Fork, Yomba, Battle Mountain, Duckwater, and Goshute Reservations. In addition, the Western Shoshones also have colonies established in towns such as Elko, Ely, Wells, and Sparks. The primary reservations for the Paiutes are in the western and southern portions of the state. They include Pyramid Lake, Walker River, and Moapa River. Collectively, the Nevada land held in trust for Native tribes by the Bureau of Indian Affairs amounts to just over one million acres. It is important to note that the Western Shoshones never ceded any of their ancestral territory, Newe Sogobia, via treaty and thus still have claim to the vast majority of Nevada. In comparison, Native lands held in trust in New Mexico comprise nearly four million acres, those in Utah comprise nearly six million acres, and Arizona contains more than eighty-five million acres of tribal land.

11. Hibbard, *History of the Public Land,* 383–471, 529–37; Scott, *Seeing Like a State,* 37–44. The 1862 Homestead Act, the 1912 and 1916 alterations that emphasized livestock production, the Timber Culture Act of 1873, the 1877 Desert Land Act, the 1878 Timber and Stone Act, and the 1894 Carey Act all promoted settlement through farming, livestock production, and irrigation projects that were impossible to conduct on a large scale in the Great Basin. The region contained only a small number of surface water resources. Even the Forest Reserve Act of 1891 could protect only a limited number of forested areas, and the National Park Service Act of 1916 simply did not apply.

12. Richard White, "Trashing the Trails," in Limerick, Milner, and Rankin, *Trails Toward a New Western History,* 37.

13. "Discussion of Radiological Hazards Associated with a Continental Test Site for Atomic Bombs," Los Alamos Scientific Laboratory, September 1, 1950, National Nuclear Security Administration/Nevada Field Office (NNSA/NFO); AEC memorandum, "Desirability of an Area in the Las Vegas Bombing Range to Be Used as a Continental Proving Ground for Atomic Weapons," November 22, 1950, NNSA/NFO; Mythen, *Ulrich Beck,* 12–15.

14. John B. Wright, "Land Tenure: The Spatial Musculature of the American West," in Hausladen, *Western Places, American Myths,* 33, 85; Cronon, *Changes in the Land,* 6–13; G. Nash, *Federal Landscape.*

15. Gracian Uhalde, interview by the author, December 1, 2006, NTSOHP, 46.

Chapter 1

1. White Pine County Farm Bureau to Senator Key Pittman, letter, March 3, 1936, Richard Kirman Papers (RKP), Box 92, Folder 4.

2. Ibid.

3. Ibid.

4. Steen, *U.S. Forest Service*, 26–28, 71–81, 104–13, 152–67, 202–204.

5. General Land Office (GLO) records 006391 (February 3, 1889) and 006695 (May 3, 1900); Nevada State Water Rights (NSWR) vested rights V01705 (May 29, 1920), V01354 (June 25, 1922), and V01789 (June 25, 1922); NSWR certificate 932 (December 21, 1923); Lina Sharp, interview by Robert D. McCracken, August 14, 1992, Nye County Town History Project (NCTHP); McCracken and Howerton, *History of Railroad Valley*, 161–67; Stewart, *History of Pahranagat Valley*, 8–9, 14, 35; Hulse, *Lincoln County, Nevada*, 51–53.

6. Angel, *History of Nevada*, 516, 526; NSWR certificates 1790–93 (March 31, 1932) and 1927 (March 17, 1933); "Body of Missing Rancher Found," *Nevada State Journal* (Carson City, NV), July 24, 1934; McCracken and Howerton, *History of Railroad Valley*, 162–73; Stewart, *History of Pahranagat Valley*, 8–9; Lina Sharp, interview by Robert D. McCracken, August 14, 1992, NCTHP. In 1881, Henry's brother Lewis had purchased Blue Eagle Ranch in Railroad Valley from Jewett Adams, a cattle rancher and former Nevada governor. Adams had originally purchased the property from Alex Beatty, the first Railroad Valley resident. Beatty had started the mining boom nearby in Troy Canyon with a silver strike in 1867. Alexander Beatty's original homestead entry is GLO record 001432 (March 30, 1880). After running livestock in the valley for twenty years, Lewis Sharp sold out to Martin Horton in 1901 and moved to Elko County with his sons to take advantage of the higher-quality grazing there. Also in 1881, George Sharp registered his "21" cattle brand with the state to commemorate his birthday and made plans to construct a livestock operation of his own in the area; it was mere coincidence that George ended up buying out Martin Horton for his uncle's former ranch.

7. Milton A. Pearl, "Public Land Commissions," *Our Public Lands*, Summer 1967, 14; Public Land Commission, *Public Domain*, 25–27; Donaldson, "Public Lands," 204–10. While not as familiar as John Wesley Powell's *Report on the Lands of the Arid Region of the United States*, the first land commission's report proved more compelling to Congress.

8. "Roosevelt Declares Himself on the Public Land Question," *Ogden (Utah) Standard-Examiner*, February 13, 1907; "Stockmen Are Not Unanimous," *Salt Lake Herald*, February 14, 1907; Milton A. Pearl, "Public Land Commissions," *Our Public Lands*, Summer 1967, 16–17; Hibbard, *History of the Public Land*, 479–83.

9. Frederick Jackson Turner, "The Significance of the Frontier in American History," in Faragher, *Rereading Frederick Jackson Turner*, 49, 55; Ely, *Outlines of Economics*, 56–57; Ely, Adams, et al., *Outlines of Economics*, 68–70; Wrobel, *End of American Exceptionalism*, 38–39.

10. Ely, Hess, et al., *Foundations of National Prosperity*, 3–10, 27–46; Ely, *Land Economics*, 48–73, 222–70; Rader, *Academic Mind and Reform*, 29–53; Ely, *Ground under Our Feet*, 234–41, 279–82.

11. Rader, *Academic Mind and Reform*, 41–53; Hibbard, *History of the Public Land*, 552–53. For a history of the concept of efficiency in public lands and natural resource management, see Hays, *Conservation and the Gospel of Efficiency*, and Hays, *Beauty*,

Health, and Permanence. For a defense of the place of public lands in the market system and a justification for efficient management, see R. Nelson, *Public Land and Private Rights.*

12. Young and Sparks, *Cattle in the Cold Desert,* 35–36, 48–49, 239–40; Starrs, *Let the Cowboy Ride,* 9–18. Jim Fox, former district manager of the Bureau of Land Management Battle Mountain District, used the phrase "unallotted commons" to describe the range in central Nevada that ranchers used free of charge until the 1950s.

13. Young and Sparks, *Cattle in the Cold Desert,* 137–51, 160–79.

14. Shamberger, *Evolution of Nevada's Water Laws;* "Nevada Water Law," State of Nevada Division of Water Resources, http://water.nv.gov/waterrights/waterlaw/.

15. GLO homestead entry survey numbers 117 (March 1, 1919), 118 (September 16, 1919), and 153 (March 10, 1919); GLO records 762229 (July 16, 1920), 674359 (April 16, 1919), and 769857 (August 26, 1920); NSWR certificates 447 (May 5, 1919), 1860 (November 16, 1932), and 1906 (January 17, 1933); NSWR applications for permit 4348 and 4349 (March 9, 1917), 7615 (January 8, 1926), 8058 (March 28, 1927), and 10053 (November 19, 1936); McCracken and Howerton, *History of Railroad Valley,* 196–98.

16. Office of the State Engineer, *Water Law of Nevada Embracing All Amendments to the Present Time and the Stock Watering Act of April 1, 1925* (Carson City, Nev.: State Printing Office, 1927), 33–34; Shamberger, *Evolution of Nevada's Water Laws,* 48.

17. Office of the State Engineer, *Water Law of Nevada,* 13; "Nevada Livestock Growers Will Discuss Range Problems," *Reno (Nev.) Evening Gazette,* December 9, 1926; "Eureka Water Case Is Heard," *Reno Evening Gazette,* September 10, 1927; "Stockmen Hear State Engineer," *Reno Evening Gazette,* October 31, 1927; *In Re Calvo,* 50 Nev. 125 (1927); "Nevada Stockmen Gather in Elko for Important Convention Next Friday," *Reno Evening Gazette,* November 16, 1927; Clel Georgetta, *Golden Fleece in Nevada,* 129–47.

18. "Water Rights on the Open Range," *Tonopah (Nev.) Daily Times and Bonanza,* December 10, 1929.

19. "Stock Water Law Test Is Filed before High Court," *Reno Evening Gazette,* October 31, 1929; "State Livestock Association to Join in Effort to Have Stock Water Law Sustained," *Reno Evening Gazette,* December 6, 1929.

20. For a list of the Sharps' vested water rights, see note 5. "State Range Map Work Started at Carson," *Reno Evening Gazette,* January 11, 1928; "Development of Water for Stock Holds Importance," *Ely (Nev.) Daily Times,* February 6, 1930; Shamberger, *Evolution of Nevada's Water Laws,* 49.

21. Inter-Tribal Council of Nevada, *Newe,* 82–100; Knack, "Saga of Tim Hooper's Homestead," 125–51; Crum, *Road on Which We Came,* 59–117; Blackhawk, *Violence over the Land,* 280–93.

22. Hibbard, *History of the Public Land,* 562–69; Rader, *Academic Mind and Reform,* 200–201.

23. Hibbard, *History of the Public Land,* 565–70.

24. "Letter Clearly States His Policies on Public Domain," *Los Angeles Times,* August 27, 1929; "Hoover Land Proposal Taken Up by Stockmen," *Reno Evening Gazette,* October 11, 1929; Thomson, *In Nevada,* 127–28. For a brief history of agricultural prices, see Holecheck, Hawkes, and Darden, "Macro Economics and Cattle Ranching," 118–23. For a further discussion of Hoover's decision, see Merrill, *Public Lands and Political Meaning,* 105–107.

25. "Governors Back Plan," *Ely Daily Times,* August 27, 1929; "New Public Lands Policy," *Los Angeles Times,* August 28, 1929; "Public Lands Control Will Be Referred,"

Tonopah Daily Times, August 28, 1929; "Western Senators Protest Hoover's Public Land Plan," *Ely Daily Times*, August 28, 1929; "Need Federal Aid for Nevada Roads," *Ely Daily Times*, August 28, 1929; "Balzar Visits in Ely; Tells about Governor's Meet," *Ely Daily Times*, August 29, 1929; "Hoover Proposal Looked Upon as Basis for New Policy," *Reno Evening Gazette*, August 30, 1929; Georgetta, *Golden Fleece in Nevada*, 201. Although many representatives agreed with Hoover that the administration of the public lands was an unnecessary financial burden, western states such as Nevada relied on federal funds for basic services such as road construction. An article in the Ely newspaper declared, "Nevada don't want that government land if federal aid for highways is to cease." The article indicated that there was no possible way the state could realize the same kind of financial benefit from the public lands. Newspapers in Utah also indicated that residents of that state were equally concerned about losing federal highway funds.

26. "New Lands Idea Urged," *Los Angeles Times*, August 27, 1929; "Government Should Keep Public Land," *Garfield County (Utah) News*, October 4, 1929; "Public Land Plan Discussed by Mining Men at Meet," *Reno Evening Gazette*, October 2, 1929.

27. "Garfield to Head Public Domain Board of Hoover," *Reno Evening Gazette*, October 16, 1929; "President Names Garfield to Be Public Lands Chairman," *Reno Evening Gazette*, October 17, 1929; "Malone Is Named as Member of Public Land Board," *Reno Evening Gazette*, October 18, 1929; "Ely Plans Meet of Stockmen Tuesday," *Reno Evening Gazette*, October 24, 1929; "Range Livestock Program Adopted," *Tonopah Daily Times and Bonanza*, December 6, 1929.

28. "Permanent Grazing Rights on Nevada's Public Lands Advocated by Stockmen," *Reno Evening Gazette*, October 29, 1929. Many stock operators ranched in Nevada whether they owned base property in the state or not. Ranch operations in eastern Oregon, southern Idaho, and western Utah could easily access the northern Nevada ranges. As a result, any livestock association in Nevada included ranchers from other states.

29. "Stockmen's Meeting Considered a Success as Progress Is Made," *Ely Daily Times*, October 30, 1929; "Stockmen of Ely Discuss Land Proposal," *Reno Evening Gazette*, November 1, 1929.

30. "Fears Federal Lands under State Control Will Not Be Handled for Benefit of Small Settler," *Tonopah Daily Times*, November 8, 1929; Merrill, *Public Lands and Political Meaning*, 103–34.

31. "Fears Federal Lands under State Control Will Not Be Handled for Benefit of Small Settler," *Tonopah Daily Times*, November 8, 1929; "Rancher Voices Objection to Land Plan," *Reno Evening Gazette*, November 9, 1929.

32. For more information on the Garfield Commission and Hoover's proposal, see "Permanent Grazing Rights on Nevada's Public Lands Advocated by Stockmen," *Reno Evening Gazette*, October 29, 1929; "Stockmen Voice Opinions on Acceptance by Nevada of Unappropriated Lands," *Reno Evening Gazette*, December 7, 1929; "Grazing Lands Profits Grow, Report Shows," *Los Angeles Times*, December 12, 1929; O. A. Fitzgerald, "Do You Want 'Free' Land?" *Los Angeles Times*, January 5, 1930; "Development of Water for Stock Holds Importance," *Ely Daily Times*, February 6, 1930; "Stockmen Bring Parley to Close with Smoker Given by Businessmen," *Ely Daily Times*, October 29, 1930.

33. "Stockmen Voice Opinions on Acceptance by Nevada of Unappropriated Lands," *Reno Evening Gazette*, December 7, 1929; "Against Proposal to Dispose of Public Domain," *Tonopah Daily Times and Bonanza*, December 9, 1929; "Gift of Domain May

Be Incubus," *Los Angeles Times*, January 5, 1930; George H. Cecil, "Public Lands," *Los Angeles Times*, November 6, 1930; William Peterson, "Public Land Should Be Ceded Back to States, Hoover Board Reports," *Salt Lake Telegram*, March 9, 1931.

34. "Land Problem Compromised," *Los Angeles Times*, November 28, 1930; "Land Report Given Hoover," *Los Angeles Times*, February 15, 1931; "Public Lands Row Flares," *Los Angeles Times*, January 13, 1931. At the Western States Governor's Conference in October 1931, the executives of the eleven western states, despite lingering support for the surface transfer of the public domain, were unable to construct any unifying legislation that would have requested that the federal government grant western states the surface rights to the remaining public domain. "Public Lands Change Urged," *Los Angeles Times*, March 9, 1931; Milton A. Pearl, "Public Land Commissions," *Our Public Lands*, Summer 1967, 17.

35. Clawson, *Western Range Livestock Industry*, 179–90. Despite their small numbers, ranches in the Great Basin, especially in northern Nevada, were reasonably profitable. According to the 1930 Census of Agriculture, only 67,000 ranches (distinguished from a farm by the sale of livestock as a chief source of income and by the use of native forage as feed for the animals) existed in the range livestock region comprising the seventeen states on or west of the 100th meridian. Of that number, Idaho, Nevada, Oregon, and Utah contained a total of 11 percent of the ranches in the region, while Texas alone contained one-quarter.

36. "Reveille Valley under Water of the Bottom Land," *Tonopah Daily Times*, August 17, 1929; "Cattle Outlook Good, Declared in Local Meeting," *Ely Daily Times*, August 28, 1929; "Range Revival Bound to Come with Rich Feed," *Tonopah Daily Times*, August 28, 1929; James A. Young and R. A. Evans, "Silver State Rangelands: Historical Perspective," *Rangelands*, October 1989, 202; White, "*It's Your Misfortune and None of My Own*," 464–65, 477–80; Holecheck, Hawkes, and Darden, "Macro Economics and Cattle Ranching," 118; Merrill, *Public Lands and Political Meaning*, 137–38. For a brief discussion of the effects of drought, overgrazing, and severe winter weather in the 1880s Great Basin, see Hulse, *Silver State*, 133–42.

37. For more information on the history of Utah counties, see the Utah Historical Society's Centennial Series by county. Bradley, *History of Beaver County*, 221–97; Blanton, *History of Tooele County*, 226–46; Young and Evans, "Silver State Rangelands," 202; "Ely First in Cattle Purchase," *Ely Daily Times*, June 25, 1934. Initially, ranchers had rejected an Agricultural Adjustment Act assistance program in 1933 because in exchange for income supplements, ranchers had to accept federally mandated reductions in production. But, historian Donald Worster has argued, "as the droughts grew worse and the laissez-faire noose tightened, they began to repent." Worster, *Dust Bowl*, 112–14; White, "*It's Your Misfortune and None of My Own*," 478–79.

38. "Stock Raisers Hail Proposed Change in Land," *Salt Lake Telegram*, January 22, 1934; "West Battles Grazing Bill," *Los Angeles Times*, April 29, 1934; Merrill, *Public Lands and Political Meaning*, 138. Utah Representative Donald B. Colton introduced a grazing bill in 1928 that would have set up locally governed grazing districts throughout the public domain. Secretary of the Interior Hubert Work supported the bill, stating that grazing district organization was "the best use of the remaining public lands for the benefit of the whole people." However, Colton's colleagues from Utah voted down the measure in Congress. "Colton Bill May Be Restricted," *Salt Lake Telegram*, March 13, 1928; "Colton Sees New Public Land Bill," *Salt Lake Telegram*, March 10, 1931; "Colton Grazing Measure Okehed," *Salt Lake Telegram*, June 22, 1932; "Grazing Land Measure

Favored by Stockmen," *Salt Lake Telegram*, October 26, 1932; "Colton Grazing Plan Memorial Is Killed in House," *Garfield County (Utah) News*, February 10, 1933.

39. "Range Measure Discussed," *Reno Evening Gazette*, May 1, 1934; "Elko Stockmen Ask Places on Board," *Reno Evening Gazette*, May 2, 1934; "Nevada Governor Is Opposed to Taylor Bill," *Reno Evening Gazette*, May 4, 1934; "State Range Group Condemns Taylor Control Bill," *Ely Daily Times*, May 5, 1934; "Livestock Value in State Shows Increase," *Reno Evening Gazette*, May 7, 1934; "Forestry Service Transfer to Be Made Part of Bill," *Reno Evening Gazette*, May 19, 1934; Peffer, *Closing of the Public Domain*, 214–22; Lee Sharp, "Overview of the Taylor Grazing Act," in *Taylor Grazing Act*, 9. Nevada reported a loss in cattle and sheep numbers but a gain in value for 1933, providing negotiators a false sense of security and leverage.

40. "Grazing Measure Is Considered by Senate Group," *Reno Evening Gazette*, May 23, 1934; state engineer George W. Malone, "Meeting of Livestock Men," September 26, 1934, RKP, Box 92, Folder 4; Peffer, *Closing of the Public Domain*, 247–78. Senator Pat McCarran has been credited with fighting to include grazing range in the value of ranch property in order to ensure greater access to credit for ranchers. However, it was state engineer George W. Malone who presented the "unit earning power" amendment to McCarran, who then offered to present it to the Senate and "filibuster the entire bill if the amendment were not accepted."

41. "Clause in Taylor Bill Will Protect Vested Water Rights, Says Pittman," *Ely Daily Times*, May 7, 1934.

42. "Dust Storms Due to Soil Erosion," *New York Times*, May 14, 1934; "Stock Industry in State Badly Hit by Dry Season," *Ely Daily Times*, May 21, 1934; "Nevada Drought May Drop Prices on State Livestock," *Ely Daily Times*, May 31, 1934; "West Will Ask Drouth Funds," *Salt Lake Telegram*, June 15, 1934.

43. "Taylor Range Control Bill on Must List," *Ely Daily Times*, May 23, 1934; "Range Control Bill Passes Senate," *Ely Daily Times*, June 13, 1934; Hugh Hammond Bennett, "Soil Loss through Erosion Threatens 'Our Basic Asset,'" *New York Times*, June 17, 1934; "Taylor Range Bill Opposition Eases," *Ely Daily Times*, June 26, 1934. President Roosevelt and several senators believed the public rangelands ought to be administered by the Forest Service. However, a deep-seated animosity already existed between the timber agency and western ranchers. As a result, the Taylor Bill left it to the secretary of the interior to create a management system for the rangelands. In addition, not all ranchers considered the drought and its effects on securing the passage of the Taylor Grazing Act the same way. Some believed the bill was introduced in Congress in a manner that overemphasized the drought-stricken range environment and the need for range controls. McCracken and Howerton, *History of Railroad Valley Nevada*, 174–75.

44. Emphasis added. Taylor Grazing Act of 1934, Public Law 482, 73rd Cong., 2nd sess. (June 28, 1934); Bureau of Land Management, "Taylor Grazing Act of June 28, 1934"; "Grazing Measure Signed by President; Aim Called to Conserve Public Lands," *Reno Evening Gazette*, June 28, 1934; "Public Domain Question Settled," *Los Angeles Times*, June 29, 1934; Merrill, *Public Lands and Political Meaning*, 135–56.

45. Taylor Grazing Act of 1934, Public Law 482, 73rd Cong., 2nd sess. (June 28, 1934); "Executive Order 6910 on Withdrawal of Public Lands for Conservation," November 26, 1934, The American Presidency Project, http://www.presidency.ucsb.edu/index. php; "Grazing Act Affects a Large Number," *Kane County (Utah) Standard*, August 10, 1934; "Department of the Interior Memorandum for the Press," August 26, 1934, Folder 76–06, Public Lands Foundation Archives (PLFA). Similar to the Reclamation Act of

1902, the Taylor Grazing Act of 1934 applied to the arid unallocated and unreserved lands west of the 100th meridian. Pending their official classification, a total of no more than eighty million acres of public lands was eligible for organization into grazing districts. However, within the first two years, 142 million acres required organization.

46. William G. Leavell's summary of Virgil Starr's notes, April 1996, Folder 76–06, PLFA; Carpenter, *Confessions of a Maverick*, 1–72; Gale Chambers, "Ferry Carpenter," in *Taylor Grazing Act*, 7–8; Farrington R. Carpenter, interview by Jerry A. O'Callaghan, October 17, 1971, PLFA. Farrington Carpenter ranched in the Yampa Valley between 1912 and 1933. Also during that time, he worked for the Colorado district attorney's office, assisting with the prosecution of cattle thieves. Carpenter felt it essential that ranchers be involved in administering the Taylor Grazing Act instead of "people mainly interested in something else besides livestock."

47. William B. Wright to Richard Kirman, letter, December 21, 1934, RKP, Box 92, Folder 4; "Public Domain Question Settled," *Los Angeles Times*, June 29, 1934; "Taylor Grazing Bill Discussed by Legislators," *Tonopah Daily Times and Bonanza*, January 24, 1935; "Cattle, Sheepmen Shortsighted Charges Ickes," *Tonopah Daily Times and Bonanza*, February 12, 1935; Carpenter, *Confessions of a Maverick*, 151–74; Shane, *Taylor Grazing Act*, 2–4.

48. George W. Malone to F. R. Carpenter, letter, December 21, 1934; RKP, Box 92, Folder 4; George W. Malone, "Range Control," February 11, 1935, RKP, Box 92, Folder 4; George W. Malone, "Statement by Nevada Representatives before the Secretary of the Interior," February 12, 1935, RKP, Box 92, Folder 4; "Nevada Officials Attend Denver Meeting Today," *Tonopah Daily Times and Bonanza*, February 12, 1935; John S. Sinai to Richard Kirman, letter, January 26, 1935, RKP, Box 92, Folder 4; Richard Kirman to F. R. Carpenter, letter, February 9, 1935, RKP, Box 92, Folder 4; Farrington R. Carpenter, interview by Jerry A. O'Callaghan, October 17, 1971, PLFA.

49. George W. Malone to F. R. Carpenter, letter, December 21, 1934; RKP, Box 92, Folder 4; George W. Malone, "Range Control," February 11, 1935, RKP, Box 92, Folder 4; George W. Malone, "Statement by Nevada Representatives before the Secretary of the Interior," February 12, 1935, RKP, Box 92, Folder 4.

50. Georgetta, *Golden Fleece in Nevada*, 231–35; "Sheepmen Map Definite Public Domain Program," *Salt Lake Tribune*, December 7, 1929; "Growers Sell Clip of Wool," *Reno Evening Gazette*, April 24, 1930.

51. Georgetta, *Golden Fleece in Nevada*, 231–35; "Ickes Blasts Stock Raisers," *Ely Daily Times*, February 12, 1935; "Cattle, Sheepmen Shortsighted Charges Ickes," *Tonopah Daily Times and Bonanza*, February 12, 1935. Clel Georgetta remembers that during the conference in Denver, "the local press made some mention of the livestock opposition to the proposed rules, but from then on little was said in the papers about the 'livestock rebellion,'" and that the later transcript of the meeting contained no mention of the ranchers' vote of no confidence in Secretary of Interior Harold Ickes.

52. George W. Malone to F. R. Carpenter, letter, December 21, 1934; RKP, Box 92, Folder 4; George W. Malone to Richard Kirman, letter, February 12, 1935, RKP, Box 92, Folder 4; George W. Malone to Richard Kirman, letter, February 16, 1935, RKP, Box 92, Folder 4.

53. Division of Grazing, "Proposed Rules for the Guidance of District Advisors in Recommending the Issuance of Grazing Licenses," circa February 1935, RKP, Box 92, Folder 4; Grazing Service, "Second Annual District Advisors' Conference, Division of Grazing, Salt Lake City, Utah," December 9–11, 1936, RKP, Box 92, Folder 4, 23;

Farrington Carpenter, "Beginnings of the Division of Grazing: Reminiscences of Ferry Carpenter Part I," *Our Public Lands*, April 1963, 11.

54. "Range Safeguards Promised Ranchers under Taylor Bill," *Ely Daily Times*, January 24, 1935; "Taylor Grazing Bill Discussed by Legislators," *Tonopah Daily Times and Bonanza*, January 24, 1935; Division of Grazing, "Proposed Rules for the Guidance of District Advisors in Recommending the Issuance of Grazing Licenses," circa February 1935, RKP, Box 92, Folder 4; "Livestock Owners to Benefit from Taylor Graze Act," *Tonopah Daily Times and Bonanza*, February 22, 1935.

55. "Rancher Aid Summarized," *Ely Daily Times*, January 11, 1935; "Livestock Men Urged to Attend Conference," *Tonopah Daily Times and Bonanza*, January 18, 1935; "Taylor Range Meet in Reno Thursday," *Ely Daily Times*, January 21, 1935.

56. "Stockmen Ask East Central Grazing Area Be Established," *Ely Daily Times*, January 19, 1935; "Taylor Range Act Explained to Lions," *Ely Daily Times*, March 28, 1935; "Taylor Bill Brings Lincoln Group Here," *Ely Daily Times*, April 8, 1935; "Stockmen Hold Large Meeting Here Yesterday," *Tonopah Daily Times and Bonanza*, April 16, 1935; "Stockmen Set Meeting in Ely," *Ely Daily Times*, April 22, 1935; "Producers Group Seek Interest of Nevada Stockmen," *Ely Daily Times*, April 26, 1935.

57. "White Pine County Not in Taylor Grazing Bracket," *Ely Daily Times*, May 2, 1935; "Nevada Allotted Only 2 Districts under Taylor Act," *Tonopah Daily Times and Bonanza*, May 2, 1935; "2nd Taylor Area Created in State," *Ely Daily Times*, October 11, 1935; Thomas E. Buckman, circular letter no. 10, October 12, 1935, RKP, Box 92, Folder 4; "First Grazing Area Formed," *Salt Lake Telegram*, May 29, 1935; Thomas E. Buckman, circular letter no. 11, November 1, 1935, RKP, Box 92, Folder 4; Division of Grazing, grazing bulletin, March 1936, RKP, Box 92, Folder 4.

58. "Grazing Limit to Be Lifted," *Ely Daily Times*, May 9, 1935; "Letup on Taylor Restriction to Grazing Sought," *Ely Daily Times*, May 13, 1935; "Livestock Men Hold Meet in Elko Today," *Tonopah Daily Times and Bonanza*, May 13, 1935; Harold L. Ickes, memorandum, August 26, 1935, RKP, Box 92, Folder 4; Franklin D. Roosevelt, memorandum, September 5, 1935, RKP, Box 92, Folder 4; Peffer, *Closing of the Public Domain*, 222–31.

59. "Cattle Grazing Permits Go to Small Owners," *Tonopah Daily Times Bonanza*, October 11, 1935; Division of Grazing, grazing bulletin, March 1936, RKP, Box 92, Folder 4; "Utah's Grazing Records Lead Western Area," *Garfield County News*, July 10, 1939; Farrington R. Carpenter, interview with Jerry A. O'Callaghan, October 17, 1971, PLFA. At this point, the Department of the Interior considered the range organization process a success and reported at the end of 1935 that 52 percent of the 10,458 cattle-grazing permits went to cattle ranchers operating with less than 50 head of stock, and 93 percent of the total permits went to those operating with less than 500 head of stock. Only four permits had been issued to livestock operators with over 10,000 head, which seemed to demonstrate that the Taylor Grazing Act had curtailed large cattle operations taking advantage of public lands grazing. Of the 1,738 sheep permits, nearly 39 percent went to sheep ranchers with less than 500 head, 5 percent went to those with less than 3,000 head, and less than 1 percent were issued to livestock operators with over 10,000 head. More than half the sheep permits went to those with herds between 3,000 and 10,000 head. In total, 1,576,976 cattle, 145,753 horses, 6,515,825 sheep, and 172,481 goats legitimately grazed the eighty million acres of organized range. Utah claimed the most permits and livestock, followed by Colorado, New Mexico, and Oregon. Ferry Carpenter said he received the friendliest reception in Utah because "the Utah people

through their religion are taught to cooperate, and they were willing to cooperate with the government." However, Carpenter stated that ranchers in Wyoming and Nevada were particularly hostile. He remembered the "big operators felt it [control] should be put into the hands of their state public land people whom they controlled politically."

60. "White Pine County Not in Taylor Grazing Bracket," *Ely Daily Times*, May 2, 1935; "Nevada Allotted Only 2 Districts under Taylor Act," *Tonopah Daily Times and Bonanza*, May 2, 1935; White Pine County Farm Bureau to Senator Key Pittman, letter, March 3, 1936, RKP, Box 92, Folder 4; Shane, *Taylor Grazing Act*, 1–2.

61. "Grazing Control Discussion at Pioche Oct. 23," *Tonopah Daily Times and Bonanza*, October 19, 1935; "Grazing Control to Be Considered at Meeting in Ely," *Ely Daily Times*, October 21, 1935; Thomas E. Buckman, circular letter no. 10, October 12, 1935, RKP, Box 92, Folder 4; "Cattlemen Select Winnemucca as Convention City," *Tonopah Daily Times and Bonanza*, November 9, 1935; "Grazing Control Fight Looms at Coming Session," *Garfield County News*, November 29, 1935.

62. Key Pittman to Richard Kirman, letter, February 26, 1936, RKP, Box 92, Folder 4; White Pine County Farm Bureau to Key Pittman, letter, March 3, 1936, RKP, Box 92, Folder 4; "Utah's Grazing Records Lead Western Area," *Garfield County News*, July 10, 1936; Archie D. Ryan to Richard Kirman, July 17, 1936, RKP, Box 92, Folder 4; Thomas E. Buckman, circular letter no. 12, August 3, 1936, RKP, Box 92, Folder 4; "Nye Ranchers to Discuss Taylor District at Austin Meet Dec. 11," *Tonopah Daily Times and Bonanza*, November 17, 1937; Farrington Carpenter, "Beginnings of the Division of Grazing: Part II," *Our Public Lands*, July 1963, 16; Shane, *Taylor Grazing Act in Nevada*, 1–2.

63. "Nevada Livestock Growers Will Discuss Range Problems," *Reno Evening Gazette*, December 9, 1926; "National Forest Policies Alleged to Be Unsuited to Conditions in Nevada," *Reno Evening Gazette*, July 9, 1927; "Nevada Livestock Owners to Talk on Problems," *Reno Evening Gazette*, October 10, 1927; "Nevada Stockmen Gather in Elko for Important Convention Next Friday," *Reno Evening Gazette*, November 16, 1927; "Forest Grazing Fee Fight to Continue," *Reno Evening Gazette*, November 21, 1927; "Stock Grazing Fees Increase," *Ely Daily Times*, February 26, 1935; "Grazing Permits Said Good for Only One Year," *Tonopah Daily Times and Bonanza*, March 13, 1935; "Livestock Men Hold Meet in Elko Today," *Tonopah Daily Times and Bonanza*, May 13, 1935; Merrill, *Public Lands and Political Meaning*, 141–42. Most of the national forests surrounding the Great Basin had been established as forest reserves under the General Land Office in the 1890s and then consolidated into national forests soon after the establishment of the Forest Service. However, Nevada's national forests were not created until the late 1910s at the behest of local ranchers in the Ruby Mountains and other ranges overrun by an increasing number of new ranchers. Surrounded by the new grazing districts in Nevada, the Forest Service worried about the health of the range and the Department of the Interior's ability to actually implement new conservation practices. Forest Service permits were contingent on the forage resources, and they set the number of livestock that ranchers could operate on the range and determined when they could operate. Even the fees the two agencies charged for grazing permits were different. Opposed to the Taylor Grazing Act for these reasons, chief forester Ferdinand A. Silcox canceled all long-term grazing permits in 1935 pending reevaluation of the national forest ranges. Ranchers in the Great Basin at large looked to the new Division of Grazing as a less restrictive model for range regulation. The major point of contention for most ranchers was the Forest Service's grazing fees and focus on watershed and

timber management above grazing. For more information on the Forest Service and its grazing policy, see Rowley, *U.S. Forest Service Grazing*. For more information on Nevada's national forests, see Wilson, *Privies, Pastures, and Portables*.

64. Richard Kirman to Key Pittman, letter, March 12, 1936, RKP, Box 92, Folder 4; "National Forest Policies Alleged to Be Unsuited to Conditions in Nevada," *Reno Evening Gazette*, July 9, 1927.

65. "Nye Ranchers to Discuss Taylor District at Austin Meet Dec. 11," *Tonopah Daily Times and Bonanza*, November 17, 1937; "New Federal Grazing District Seen for Nevada," *Tonopah Daily Times and Bonanza*, March 21, 1940.

66. Lina Sharp, interview by Robert D. McCracken, August 14, 1992, NCTHP; McCracken and Howerton, *History of Railroad Valley*, 174–78.

67. Oscar L. Chapman, "Public Notice, May 18, 1943," Folder 468, PLFA; "Grazing District Hearings in State Ordered Postponed," *Tonopah Times Bonanza*, June 19, 1943; Senate Committee on Interior and Insular Affairs, *Administration and Use of Public Lands: Hearings on S. 241*, 79th Cong., 1st sess. (May 23–25, 1945), 5028–30; Knudsten, *Here Is Our Valley*, 29–31; Skillen, *Nation's Largest Landlord*, 17.

68. Taylor Grazing Act of 1934, Public Law 482, 73rd Cong., 2nd sess. (June 28, 1934); Foss, *Politics and Grass*, 180–81; Muhn and Stuart, *Opportunity and Challenge*, 41; Skillen, *Nation's Largest Landlord*, 15–16.

69. Norman Waddell to Byron Mock, letter, May 2, 1947, Folder 76–06, PLFA; Skillen, *Nation's Largest Landlord*, 18–19.

70. "Central Nevada Stockmen Study Grazing Ruling," *Reno Evening Gazette*, October 12, 1947; Skillen, *Nation's Largest Landlord*, 17.

71. Sue Locke Holloway, interview by Robert D. McCracken, June 8, 1988, NCTHP, 9, 13; "Stockmen Oppose Federal Control," *Reno Evening Gazette*, September 16, 1947; "Central Nevada Stockmen Study Grazing Ruling," *Reno Evening Gazette*, October 12, 1947; "60 Ranchers Attend Meet," *Nevada State Journal*, March 5, 1948; Skillen, *Nation's Largest Landlord*, 17.

72. "Stockmen Vote to Organize Grazing District at 4-County Meeting Held in Tonopah," *Tonopah Times Bonanza*, December 10, 1948; "Nevada's Livestock Men Are Facing Losses of Millions," *Nevada State Journal*, January 21, 1949; "State Stockmen Lose Fight," *Reno Evening Gazette*, February 10, 1951; Paris, *Beltran*, 157–69.

73. "Cattlemen Take New Steps toward Staving Off Federal Control," *Tonopah Times Bonanza*, November 21, 1947; "Formation Taylor District at Tonopah Meeting Ends in Postponement," *Tonopah Times Bonanza*, March 3, 1950; "United Stockmen Select Officers," *Reno Evening Gazette*, March 17, 1950.

74. "Secretary Chapman Announces Nevada Public Hearing on Grazing District," Bureau of Land Management news release, February 13, 1950, file folder 468, PLFA; "Interior Dept. Ready to Organize District Six Taylor Grazing," *Tonopah Times Bonanza*, February 17, 1950; "State Stockmen Lose Fight," *Reno Evening Gazette*, February 10, 1951; Clawson, *Western Range Livestock Industry*, 104–106; Clawson, *Bureau of Land Management*, 52–53, 76–78; Roger A. Sedjo, "Marion Clawson and America's Forests: A Lifetime of Commitment," in Sedjo, *Vision for the U.S. Forest Service*, 2–3; Merrill, *Public Lands and Political Meaning*, 7–8; Skillen, *Nation's Largest Landlord*, 23.

75. "Secretary Chapman Announces Formation of New Nevada Grazing District," Bureau of Land Management news release, February 9, 1951, Folder 371, PLFA; "State Stockmen Lose Fight," *Reno Evening Gazette*, February 10, 1951; "New Grazing District Set Up in Nevada," *Reno (Nev.) Gazette-Journal*, February 11, 1951; "Nye, Lander, Eureka

are Organized into Taylor Grazing District No. 6," *Tonopah Times Bonanza*, February 16, 1951; "Delay in Grazing District Is Urged," *Reno Evening Gazette*, February 23, 1951; "New Grazing District Is Not Wanted," *Nevada State Journal*, February 24, 1951.

76. "Nye Importance as Stock Region Given by Figures," *Tonopah Daily Times and Bonanza*, June 18, 1936; "Nye, Esmeralda, Lander, Eureka Ranch Owners Protest New Grazing District," *Tonopah Times Bonanza*, March 2, 1951; "Postponing Taylor Grazing Act Turned Down by Chapman," *Tonopah Times Bonanza*, March 23, 1951; "Election Planned in Grazing District," *Reno Evening Gazette*, May 1, 1951; Sawyer, *Nevada Nomads*, 78; Clawson, *Western Range Livestock Industry*, 121. According to Marion Clawson, the range livestock region consisted of North and South Dakota, Nebraska, Kansas, Montana, Wyoming, Colorado, Oklahoma, Texas, New Mexico, Arizona, Idaho, Utah, Nevada, Washington, Oregon, and California.

77. "Nye, Esmeralda, Lander, Eureka Ranch Owners Protest New Grazing District," *Tonopah Times Bonanza*, March 2, 1951; "Request to Delay Formation of New Grazing District Is Turned Down in Washington," *Nevada State Journal*, March 18, 1951.

78. "Warns of Danger in Using All Roads on Big Bombing Range," *Tonopah Times Bonanza*, December 15, 1950; "Tonopah Base Still on Unactive List," *Tonopah Times Bonanza*, January 15, 1951; "AEC Will Improve Atomic Test Grounds," *Tonopah Times Bonanza*, February 23, 1951; "Nye Land Owners Urged File Claims," *Tonopah Times Bonanza*, April 27, 1951; Fehner and Gosling, *Origins of the Nevada Test Site*, 20–21, 44–48.

79. The first atomic test conducted at the Nevada Test Site occurred on January 27, 1951. "AEC Will Control All Air Flights over Bombing Range," *Tonopah Times Bonanza*, January 26, 1951; "Atomic Energy Commission Warns of Trespassing on Bombing Range," *Tonopah Times Bonanza*, January 26, 1951; "Postponing Taylor Grazing Act Turned Down by Chapman," *Tonopah Times Bonanza*, March 23, 1951; "Taylor Grazing Meeting Set for Tonopah Next Thursday," *Tonopah Times Bonanza*, May 4, 1951; "New Graze District Organized," *Tonopah Times Bonanza*, May 18, 1951.

80. "Warns of Danger Using All Roads on Big Bombing Range," *Tonopah Times Bonanza*, December 15, 1950; C. P. Trussell, "Atom Bomb Testing Ground Will Be Created in Nevada," *New York Times*, January 12, 1951; "Nevada's Bomb Range," *New York Times*, January 14, 1951; "Good Deal Secrecy Surrounds AEC Nye Development," *Tonopah Times Bonanza*, January 19, 1951; "No Public Announcement Planned of Atom Blasts at Vegas Range," *Reno Evening Gazette*, January 25, 1951; "AEC Will Control All Air Flights over Bombing Range," *Tonopah Times Bonanza*, January 26, 1951; "Atomic Energy Commission Warns of Trespassing on Bombing Range," *Tonopah Times Bonanza*, January 26, 1951; Fehner and Gosling, *Atmospheric Nuclear Weapons Testing*, 46.

81. "Chapman Turns Down Plea to Delay Grazing District," *Reno Evening Gazette*, March 16, 1951; "More Atomic Tests Planned," *Reno Evening Gazette*, March 16, 1951; *United States Nuclear Tests*, 2–3.

82. "Taylor Grazing District Formed at Nye Session," *Reno Evening Gazette*, May 24, 1951; "Nevada's New Grazing District in Operation," *Nevada State Journal*, September 22, 1951.

83. Marion Clawson, "A Tentative Draft of Report on Administrative Policy on Federal Range Lands," circa 1950, Folder 646, PLFA; Penny and Clawson, "Administration of Grazing Districts," 29; Clawson, *Western Range Livestock Industry*, 11, 104–106; Roger A. Sedjo, "Marion Clawson and America's Forests," in Sedjo, *Vision for the U.S. Forest Service*, 2–3. Marion Clawson served as BLM director until 1953, when the Eisenhower administration replaced him with another political appointee. Clawson took his

expertise in the western range livestock industry and put it to work for the Forest Service. He spent the rest of his career working on problems of public lands management.

84. Lina Sharp, interview by Robert D. McCracken, August 14, 1992, NCTHP, 40; Paul Herndon, "History of Grazing on the Public Lands," in *Taylor Grazing Act*, 3; Paul F. Starrs, "An Inescapable Range, or the Ranch as Everywhere," in Hausladen, *Western Places, American Myths*, 66, 72.

CHAPTER 2

1. "Choosing of Utah Site for Bombing Range Said Blow to Local Chances," *Tonopah Daily Times and Bonanza*, April 4, 1940; "Utah Agrees to Land Exchange for Bombing Range," *Tonopah Daily Times and Bonanza*, April 5, 1940; "Desolation Pays for Utah," *Salt Lake Telegram*, April 8, 1940; "Air Corps May Expand Plans at Tonopah Field," *Tonopah Daily Times and Bonanza*, June 7, 1940; "Bomb Range Acquired Near Tonopah," *Reno Evening Gazette*, June 7, 1940; "Army Acquires Bombing Land," *Salt Lake Telegram*, June 7, 1940; "U.S. Starts Action on Bombing Tract," *Salt Lake Tribune*, June 8, 1940; "Tonopah Range Is Official Name," *Tonopah Daily Times and Bonanza*, July 22, 1941; G. Nash, *American West Transformed*, 17–36; White, "*It's Your Misfortune and None of My Own*," 497; Maria E. Montoya, "Landscapes of the Cold War West," in Fernlund, *Cold War American West*, 14, 24.

2. "Drive for Bombing Range in Nye Area Goes to Congress," *Tonopah Daily Times and Bonanza*, January 13, 1940; "Nye Residents Seek Bombing Practice Area," *Nevada State Journal*, January 19, 1940; "Bomber Range Given Backing," *Nevada State Journal*, February 2, 1940; "Army Officer Opens Study of Nye Bombing Site," *Tonopah Daily Times and Bonanza*, February 27, 1940; "Bomb Range Land Acquired near Tonopah," *Reno Evening Gazette*, June 7, 1940; "Scrugham Holds Bombing Range as Important Project," *Tonopah Daily Times and Bonanza*, June 27, 1940; "Scrugham Reveals Bomb Range Plans Are Being Pushed," *Nevada State Journal*, July 1, 1940.

3. "McCarran Says Utah Bombing Range Site Is Not Definite," *Tonopah Daily Times and Bonanza*, April 9, 1940; "Army Board Said Impressed by Nye Site for Bomb Range," *Tonopah Daily Times and Bonanza*, April 24, 1940; "Highway Department to Spend 4 Million in State in 1940," *Tonopah Daily Times and Bonanza*, April 15, 1940; "National Convention of U.S. Highway 6 May Be Held Here," *Tonopah Daily Times and Bonanza*, April 29, 1940; "Tonopah Seen as Major Tourist Center of State," *Tonopah Daily Times and Bonanza*, May 3, 1940; "Bombing Gunnery Range Drive Is Renewed by Group," *Tonopah Daily Times and Bonanza*, May 17, 1940; "Tonopah Township Population Set at 2449, County at 3562," *Tonopah Daily Times and Bonanza*, May 22, 1940; "Bombing Range Site Uncertain," *Tonopah Daily Times and Bonanza*, May 23, 1940; "Nye Bomb Range Said Approved by Army," *Reno Evening Gazette*, May 27, 1940; "Army Officers Select Local Bombing Site, Says McCarran," *Tonopah Daily Times and Bonanza*, May 27, 1940; "Southern Nye County Scenic Attraction Described Today," *Tonopah Daily Times and Bonanza*, June 3, 1940; "Air of Mystery Covers U.S. Action on West Bombing Range," *Tonopah Daily Times and Bonanza*, June 5, 1940; "War Department Says Nye Bomb Range Chosen," *Tonopah Daily Times and Bonanza*, June 6, 1940; "Air Corps May Expand Plans at Tonopah Field," *Tonopah Daily Times and Bonanza*, June 7, 1940; "Air Corps Chief Outlines Program for Bombing Range," *Tonopah Daily Times and Bonanza*, June 26, 1940; "$185,000 Airport Project Slated

for Tonopah," *Tonopah Daily Times and Bonanza*, August 21, 1940; "No Conflict Seen for Air Corps on West Bomb Range," *Tonopah Daily Times and Bonanza*, August 23, 1940; "McCarran Seeks Early Activity on Bombing Range," *Tonopah Daily Times and Bonanza*, February 6, 1941; "Bombing Range Funds Set Aside," *Tonopah Daily Times and Bonanza*, March 15, 1941; *A Concise History of Nellis Air Force Base, Nevada* (Office of History, Headquarters, U.S. Air Force Warfare Center, March 15, 1997), 9–12.

4. "Army, Grazers in Agreement," *Ogden Standard-Examiner*, September 19, 1940; "Army Seeks Bids on Air Bomb Range," *Salt Lake Tribune*, October 2, 1940; "New Obstacle Holds Up Bombing Range," *Salt Lake Tribune*, October 13, 1940; "Comparison of Grazing District Acreages, Attachment 2: Miscellaneous Acreages of Withdrawn or Reserved Public Lands in Grazing Districts as of June 30, 1944," file folder 468, PLFA.

5. "Grazers Get Delay Blame," *Ogden Standard-Examiner*, September 18, 1940; "Army Chief Bemoans Delay," *Salt Lake Tribune*, October 7, 1940; "New Obstacle Holds Up Bombing Range," *Salt Lake Tribune*, October 13, 1940; "Robinson Sees Early Start on Bomb Field," *Salt Lake Tribune*, October 15, 1940.

6. "Ranchers Ask Utah to Oppose 'Rocket Range,'" *Salt Lake Telegram*, August 5, 1941; "Krug Plans Study of Grazing Land Withdrawals," *Salt Lake Telegram*, August 7, 1941; Senate Committee on Interior and Insular Affairs, *Administration and Use of Public Lands: Hearings on S. 241*, 77th Cong., 1st sess. (October 2–4 and October 8–10, 1941), 924–29.

7. "Army Takes Over Vast Testing Area," *Salt Lake Tribune*, February 28, 1942; National Archives and Records Administration, "Executive Order 8579 on Withdrawal of Public Land for Use of the War Department as an Aerial Bombing and Gunnery Range; Utah," *Federal Register* 5 (October 29, 1940); National Archives and Records Administration, "Executive Order 9053 on Withdrawal of Public Land for Use of the War Department as a Chemical Warfare Range; Utah," *Federal Register* 7 (February 6, 1942); Bureau of Land Management, "Taylor Grazing Act of June 28, 1934;" O. N. Malmquist, "More Than $52,000,000 Spent on Tooele County War Plants," *Salt Lake Tribune*, July 11, 1943; "Hill Aerospace Museum," Hill Air Force Base, http://www .hill.af.mil/library/museum/index.asp; "Dugway Proving Ground History," Dugway Proving Ground, http://www.dugway.army.mil/History.aspx; Edgington, *Range Wars*, 150–53.

8. "Pittman to Seek Roosevelt's Aid in Bombing Action," *Tonopah Daily Times and Bonanza*, July 25, 1940; "McCarran Sees Early Action by Air Corps on Local Range," *Tonopah Daily Times and Bonanza*, July 26, 1940; "Withdrawal of Bombing Site from Public Domain, Nearing," *Tonopah Daily Times and Bonanza*, August 26, 1940; "Tonopah Seen as Becoming Major Defense Sector," *Tonopah Daily Times and Bonanza*, October 15, 1940; "Bombing Range Land Withdrawal Approved," *Tonopah Daily Times and Bonanza*, October 12, 1940; "Roosevelt Signs Bombing Range Order," *Tonopah Daily Times and Bonanza*, October 31, 1940; "Tonopah Airport Project Is Given Approval by FDR," *Tonopah Daily Times and Bonanza*, November 30, 1940; "Details of New Airport Project Here Described," *Tonopah Daily Times and Bonanza*, December 4, 1940; "Tonopah Airport Work Will Start on Monday, Revealed," *Tonopah Daily Times and Bonanza*, December 7, 1940; "McCarran Seeks Early Activity on Bombing Range," *Tonopah Daily Times and Bonanza*, February 6, 1941; "Bombing Range Given Support," *Nevada State Journal*, February 22, 1941; "Scrugham Sees Early Start on Tonopah Project," *Tonopah Daily Times and Bonanza*, March 1, 1941; "Bombing Range Is Given Title," *Reno Evening Gazette*, July 22, 1941; "Nevada's Participation in National

Crisis Listed by Bunker," *Nevada State Journal*, August 22, 1941; G. Nash, *American West Transformed*, 7, 22–23.

9. "Nye Bomb Range Said Approved by Army," *Reno Evening Gazette*, May 27, 1940; "Interior Depart. Holding Up Bomb Range Work," *Tonopah Daily Times and Bonanza*, July 24, 1940; "Army Construction Work Near," *Tonopah Daily Times and Bonanza*, March 1, 1941; "Bombing Range Funds Set Aside," *Tonopah Daily Times and Bonanza*, March 15, 1941; "Quarters for Two Thousand Soldiers Slated at Tonopah," *Tonopah Daily Times and Bonanza*, March 19, 1941; "Grazing Details on Bombing Range to be Clarified," *Tonopah Daily Times and Bonanza*, April 5, 1941; "Tonopah Airport Program to be Outlined Early Next Week," *Tonopah Daily Times and Bonanza*, April 17, 1941; "Bombing Range to Cover Some Mining Claims," *Nevada State Journal*, May 19, 1941; "Appraisers Hired to Sift Protests on Bombing Range," *Tonopah Daily Times and Bonanza*, May 19, 1941; "U.S. to Probe Title to Area," *Nevada State Journal*, June 4, 1941; "'Active' Mining Claim Owner to Report Holdings," *Tonopah Daily Times and Bonanza*, June 6, 1941; "Statement Made on Bomb Range by McCarran," *Reno Evening Gazette*, June 23, 1941; "Assessment Work to Be Required on Mine Claims within Bomb Range," *Nevada State Journal*, June 24, 1941; "Bombing Range Ruling Is Made," *Tonopah Daily Times and Bonanza*, July 24, 1941; "Construction Work at Airport Starts Shortly," *Tonopah Daily Times and Bonanza*, August 1, 1941; "Largest Type Warplane Slated for Local Field," *Tonopah Daily Times and Bonanza*, August 2, 1941; "Government Granted Right for Bombing Range Acreage," *Tonopah Daily Times and Bonanza*, August 26, 1941; "Bombing Range to Be Cleared," *Nevada State Journal*, November 16, 1941; "Speedy Action on Tonopah Range Is Ordered by Army," *Tonopah Daily Times and Bonanza*, December 12, 1941; "Tonopah Bombing Range Now in Use by Army Gunners," *Tonopah Daily Times and Bonanza*, December 20, 1941; "Bombing Range Halts Mining of Tungsten," *Reno Evening Gazette*, February 18, 1942; Senate Committee on Interior and Insular Affairs, *Administration and Use of Public Lands: Hearings on S. 241*, 77th Cong., 1st sess. (October 2–4, October 8–10, November 25–26, 28, and December 1–2, 1941), 930, 1664–66, 1671–72.

10. "Crews Survey Bombing Range," *Nevada State Journal*, September 26, 1941; Senate Committee on Interior and Insular Affairs, *Administration and Use of Public Lands: Hearings on S. 241*, 77th Cong., 2nd sess. (October 28 and November 19–20, 1942), 1826–35.

11. Helen L. Fallini, interview by Robert D. McCracken, October 25 and 26, 1987, NCTHP; McCracken and Howerton, *History of Railroad Valley Nevada*, 195, 281–85. The *Las Vegas (Nev.) Review-Journal* celebrated the 150th anniversary of Nevada's statehood in 2014 and selected the Fallini family as one that was present in the state at the time of its founding (Jennifer Robinson, "Hard Work and Worries Dog a Nevada Ranch Family," June 15, 2015). Although the Fallini family was not yet present in Nevada in 1864, they are one of the oldest families to have consistently ranched in the state.

12. GLO records 833630 (November 21, 1921) and 919004 (October 2, 1923); NSWR certificates 318 (December 23, 1916), 388 (December 16, 1918), 521 (March 7, 1921), 665 and 666 (November 12, 1922), 949 (December 26, 1923), 1077–1079 (December 5, 1924), 1110 (March 13, 1925), 1235 (September 10, 1926), 1393 (May 4, 1928), 1937 (March 22, 1933), 2155 (November 19, 1935), 2533 (May 7, 1940), 2892 (August 29, 1945), 2909–2912 (October 24, 1945), NSWR vested rights V01936, V02681–84, V03762–69, V04558–60, V04667–88, and V04743–64, secured between October 7, 1970, and April

4, 1989; Helen L. Fallini, interview by Robert D. McCracken, October 25 and 26, 1987, NCTHP; McCracken and Howerton, *History of Railroad Valley*, 148–50, 195, 281–85. The Fallinis purchased many of their water rights from the United Cattle and Packing Company and relatives such as Gustaf Peterson, who had homesteaded 320 acres near the Bellehelen mine and whose wife, Minnie, was an aunt to the Fallinis.

13. Helen L. Fallini, interview by Robert D. McCracken, October 25 and 26, 1987, NCTHP; Iverson, *When Indians Became Cowboys*.

14. Senate Committee on Interior and Insular Affairs, *Administration and Use of Public Lands: Hearings on S. 241*, 77th Cong., 2nd sess. (October 28 and November 19–20, 1942), 1829.

15. National Archives and Records Administration, "Executive Order 8578 on Withdrawal of Public Land for Use of the War Department as an Aerial Bombing and Gunnery Range; Nevada," *Federal Register* 5 (October 29, 1940); "Army Prepared Bombing Site for Early Use," *Nevada State Journal*, December 22, 1941; "Huge Acreage in Nevada Now Held by Government," *Nevada State Journal*, June 4, 1942; Senate Committee on Interior and Insular Affairs, *Administration and Use of Public Lands: Hearings on S. 241*, 77th Cong., 2nd sess. (October 28 and November 19–20, 1942), 1826–35; Nickel, "Dollars, Defense, and the Desert," 306–307.

16. "Tonopah Bombing Land Suit Is Drawn," *Reno Evening Gazette*, August 25, 1941; "Grazing Region to Be Protected," *Nevada State Journal*, September 23, 1941; "TAAF to Be Reduced Temporary Inactive Status by War Dept.," *Tonopah Times-Bonanza*, August 24, 1945; "Fate of TAAF Not Definitely Decided," *Tonopah Times-Bonanza*, August 31, 1945; "Fate of TAAF Not Yet Determined," *Tonopah Times-Bonanza*, September 7, 1945; "Status TAAF Unchanged," *Tonopah Times-Bonanza*, September 14, 1945; "Hammer Field to Use Tonopah Army Air Field as Sub-Base," *Tonopah Times-Bonanza*, September 28, 1945; "Miners Advised to Keep Off Lands in Local Bombing Range," *Tonopah Times-Bonanza*, September 28, 1945.

17. "Wendover Range to Be Expanded," *Reno Evening Gazette*, August 16, 1946; "Westerners Battling Army on Rocket Range Proposal Involving Wendover Land," *Nevada State Journal*, September 29, 1946; "War Department Asks Retention of Tonopah Air Field," *Tonopah Times-Bonanza*, October 19, 1945; "Future TAAF Still Rests with War Officials," *Tonopah Times-Bonanza*, October 26, 1945; "TAAF Largest Base Acreage in United States," *Tonopah Times-Bonanza*, November 9, 1945; "McCarran in Talk Here Tells of Outlook for Silver, Believes Tonopah Air Base Will Be Retained by War Department," *Tonopah Times-Bonanza*, November 16, 1945; "U.S. Continues Suit for Land," *Reno Evening Gazette*, December 30, 1946; "Hill Air Force Base," http://www.hill.af.mil/index.asp.

18. "Construction Work at Airport Starts Shortly," *Tonopah Daily Times and Bonanza*, August 1, 1941; "Tonopah Base Still on Unactive List," *Tonopah Times-Bonanza*, January 19, 1951; "Nellis Air Force Base Library," Nellis Air Force Base, http://www.nellis.af.mil/library/index.asp. The relationship between the Tonopah range and the Las Vegas range was a close one from its inception. The military used the Las Vegas base as a training facility and devoted the more remote Tonopah range to bombing practice. After the war, the Tonopah facilities became less active and the military transferred administrative personnel to Las Vegas.

19. Atomic Energy Act of 1946, Public Law 79–585 (August 1, 1946); Sumner T. Pike to Robert LeBaron, letter, March 8, 1949, National Nuclear Security Administration/ Nevada Field Office (NNSA/NFO); Titus, *Bombs in the Backyard*, 26–28; Fehner and Gosling, *Atmospheric Nuclear Weapons Testing*, 30–36; Hacker, *Elements of Controversy*,

40. In late 1946, Congress authorized four oversight bodies to handle the nation's new nuclear industry: the AEC, comprising five civilians to manage research, production, and application of atomic energy; the General Advisory Committee, comprising nine atomic scientists to advise the commission, many of whom worked for Los Alamos Scientific Laboratory, the builders of the first bomb; the Joint Committee on Atomic Energy, comprising nine members of each house of Congress to handle legislative matters; and the Military Liaison Committee to oversee weapons development of atomic technology.

20. David Lilienthal to Robert LeBaron, memorandum, September 24, 1948, NNSA/NFO.

21. Howard B. Hutchinson, "Project Nutmeg Report," 1947, NNSA/NFO; "Discussion of Radiological Hazards Associated with a Continental Test Site for Atomic Bombs," Los Alamos Scientific Laboratory, September 1, 1950, NNSA/NFO; Fehner and Gosling, *Atmospheric Nuclear Weapons Testing*, 36–37.

22. "Discussion of Radiological Hazards Associated with a Continental Test Site for Atomic Bombs," Los Alamos Scientific Laboratory, September 1, 1950, NNSA/NFO. The equation used was surprisingly simple: $H = \sum p(r_i)/(r_i)^2$, where $p(r_i)$ is the population at distance r_i from ground zero.

23. "Discussion of Radiological Hazards Associated with a Continental Test Site for Atomic Bombs," Los Alamos Scientific Laboratory, September 1, 1950, NNSA/NFO; "Desirability of an Area in the Las Vegas Bombing Range to Be Used as a Continental Proving Ground for Atomic Weapons," November 22, 1950, NNSA/NFO; Ryan Edgington, "Fragmented Histories: Science, Environment and Monument Building at the Trinity Site, 1945–1995," in Pearson, Coates, and Cole, *Militarized Landscapes*, 192–97.

24. "Discussion of Radiological Hazards Associated with a Continental Test Site for Atomic Bombs," Los Alamos Scientific Laboratory, September 1, 1950, NNSA/NFO; "Desirability of an Area in the Las Vegas Bombing Range to Be Used as a Continental Proving Ground for Atomic Weapons," November 22, 1950, NNSA/NFO.

25. "Discussion of Radiological Hazards Associated with a Continental Test Site for Atomic Bombs," Los Alamos Scientific Laboratory, September 1, 1950, NNSA/NFO; "Desirability of an Area in the Las Vegas Bombing Range to Be Used as a Continental Proving Ground for Atomic Weapons," November 22, 1950, NNSA/NFO. The 1 percent probability reflected the likelihood of unpredicted rain. At most, Fermi thought, only 1 percent of the area would be rained on if that occurred.

26. "Desirability of an Area in the Las Vegas Bombing Range to Be Used as a Continental Proving Ground for Atomic Weapons," November 22, 1950, NNSA/NFO; Carroll Tyler to James McCormack, memorandum, December 1, 1950, NNSA/NFO; Marion W. Boyer to Frederick J. Lawton, letter, June 14, 1951, NNSA/NFO; Fehner and Gosling, *Atmospheric Nuclear Weapons Testing*, 38–44; Palevsky, *Atomic Fragments*, 113; Hacker, *Elements of Controversy*, 40–43.

27. "Atomic Blast Shakes Las Vegas Fifty Miles Away," *New York Times*, January 28, 1951; Gladwin Hill, "Flash Seen in Four States," *New York Times*, January 28, 1951; Gladwin Hill, "2D Atomic Blast in 24 Hours Jolts Wide Nevada Area," *New York Times*, January 29, 1951; Gladwin Hill, "3D Atom Test Lights Nevada Dawn; Peaks Stand Out in Weird Glare," *New York Times*, February 2, 1951; *United States Nuclear Tests*, xvii–xviii; Fehner and Gosling, *Atmospheric Nuclear Weapons Testing*, 45–46, 58–65; Miller, *Under the Cloud*, 83–106; Hacker, *Elements of Controversy*, 48–53.

28. Chester Smith to Robert Tumbleson, letter, January 22, 1951, Charles Russell Papers (CRP), Box 174, Folder 1; Shelby Thompson to Chester Smith, letter, January

22, 1951, CRP, Box 174, Folder 1; Chester Smith to Shelby Thompson, letter, January 25, 1952, CRP, Box 174, Folder 1; Fehner and Gosling, *Atmospheric Nuclear Weapons Testing*, 46–58; Hacker, *Elements of Controversy*, 44–48. The AEC made a concerted effort to allow Nevada governor Charles Russell access to information about the tests that was not distributed to the general public. Charles Russell's assistant, Chester Smith, and Shelby Thompson and Robert Tumbleson of the AEC's Public Information Service had a close relationship, which included time at the roulette tables in Reno and Carson City.

29. Jeannette and Walter Theile to Charles H. Russell, letter, January 27, 1951, CRP, Box 174, Folder 1; Chester Smith to Shelby Thompson, letter, January 31, 1951, CRP, Box 174, Folder 1.

30. "Vegas Calm under 'Bombs,'" *Nevada State Journal*, January 30, 1951; Gladwin Hill, "3D Atom Test Lights Nevada Dawn; Peaks Stand Out in Weird Glare," *New York Times*, February 2, 1951; Robert K. Plumb, "Increased Radiation Levels Found in East; Laid to Atom Tests, Held Harmless," *New York Times*, February 3, 1951; "Gen. Collins Looks for Atomic Shells," *New York Times*, February 6, 1951; "Great Blast Ends Atom Test Series," *New York Times*, February 7, 1951; Thomas L. Shipman to Officer-In-Charge, Station Hospital, Mather Air Force Base, letter, March 9, 1951, NNSA/NFO; "A-Radiated Rain Shower Burns 2," March 4, 1951, NNSA/NFO; Thomas L. Shipman to Francis M. Pottenger, letter, May 5, 1951, NNSA/NFO; Fehner and Gosling, *Atmospheric Nuclear Weapons Testing*, 64–65; Hacker, *Elements of Controversy*, 50–53.

31. "Atomic Test Blast Shakes Las Vegas, Fifty Miles Away," *New York Times*, January 28, 1951; "A Kind of Flash," *Time*, February 5, 1951; J. Keith Glermean to Brien McMahon, letter, July 3, 1951, NNSA/NFO; James McCormack to Roscoe C. Wilson, letter, July 8, 1951, NNSA/NFO; "Average Citizen Still Endorses All-Out Defense," *Nevada State Journal*, August 8, 1951; Gordon Dean to Oscar Chapman, letter, October 25, 1951, NNSA/NFO; Sumner T. Pike to Oscar Chapman, letter, November 2, 1951, NNSA/NFO; Carroll L. Tyler to Charles H. Russell, letter, March 13, 1951, CRP, Box 174, Folder 1; Charles H. Russell to Carroll L. Tyler, letter, March 17, 1951, CRP, Box 174, Folder 5; "More Atomic Tests Planned," *Reno Evening Gazette*, March 16, 1951.

32. "More Atomic Tests Planned," *Reno Evening Gazette*, March 16, 1951; J. Keith Glermean to Senator Brien McMahon, letter, June 3, 1951, NNSA/NFO; Marion W. Boyer to Frederick J. Lawton, letter, June 14, 1951, NNSA/NFO; Gaelen Felt to Alvin C. Graves, memorandum, "Jangle Fallout Problems," June 28, 1951, NNSA/NFO; "New Atomic Tests Slated in Nevada," *New York Times*, August 29, 1951; "5000 U.S. Fighting Men in Nevada for Instruction in Atomic Warfare," *Reno Evening Gazette*, September 18, 1951; Hanson W. Baldwin, "The Nevada Atom Tests," *New York Times*, September 21, 1951; "Secrecy to Blanket Coming Atom Games," *New York Times*, October 4, 1951; AEC press release, October 5, 1951, NNSA/NFO; "New Atomic Tests Near," *New York Times*, October 9, 1951; "Little A-Bombs," *New York Times*, October 14, 1951; "Atomic Arms Set for G.I.'s in Nevada," *New York Times*, October 15, 1951; "Troops Arriving for Atomic Tests in Nevada," *New York Times*, October 17, 1951; Gladwin Hill, "Tactical Bomb Test 'Secrets' Open to Thousands but Not to Newsmen," *New York Times*, October 18, 1951; "Desert Atom Test Will Use Animals," *New York Times*, October 19, 1951; "U.S. Touches Off Tiny Atom Charge," *Nevada State Journal*, October 23, 1951; "Desert Officials Report Only Flicker of Light—Officials Satisfied," *New York Times*, October 23, 1951; "The Nevada Atomic Tests," *New York Times*, October 28, 1951; Robert Bennyhoff, "A-Bomb Explodes; Tests Near Climax," *Nevada State Journal*, October 30, 1951; "Atom Observers Gather," *New York Times*, October 30, 1951; "Scientists Study

Dual Action Blast," *Reno Evening Gazette*, October 31, 1951; Robert Bennyhoff, "First Atomic Combat Maneuvers Set to Go," *Nevada State Journal*, November 1, 1951; Gladwin Hill, "Huge Blast Marks First Atom Games Involving Troops," *New York Times*, November 2, 1951; "Evaluation of Blast Effects Year-Long Job at Test Site," *Nevada State Journal*, November 2, 1951; "Radiation Detected on Coast," *New York Times*, November 1, 1951; "Radioactivity in Upstate Snow," *New York Times*, November 3, 1951; "New Atomic Tests to Sift Bomb's Effect on Weapons," *New York Times*, November 3, 1951; Bill Becker, "Assorted Bombs Included in U.S. War Kit," *Reno Evening Gazette*, November 6, 1951; "Mighty Blast Ends Atom Test Series," *New York Times*, November 6, 1951; "Las Vegas Feels Blast," *New York Times*, November 14, 1951; "New Atom Tests Started in Nevada," *New York Times*, November 20, 1951; "Top Army Leaders Watch Atomic Test," *New York Times*, November 30, 1951; Fehner and Gosling, *Atmospheric Nuclear Weapons Testing*, 66–72; Miller, *Under the Cloud*, 119–34; Hacker, *Elements of Controversy*, 60–72.

33. Mary Palevsky, interview with the author, October 6, 2010; Marion W. Boyer to Frederick J. Lawton, letter, June 14, 1951, NNSA/NFO; Gordon Dean to Oscar L. Chapman, letter, October 25, 1951, NNSA/NFO; Sumner T. Pike to Oscar L. Chapman, letter, November 2, 1951, NNSA/NFO; "Atom Chief Confirms Nevada Tests 'Vital,'" *Reno Evening Gazette*, December 11, 1951; "Nevada A-Bomb Tests Produce 'Vital' Data," *Nevada State Journal*, December 12, 1951; excerpts from remarks by Carroll L. Tyler in meeting with the press at Las Vegas, March 31, 1952, CRP, Box 175, Folder 2; Hacker, *Elements of Controversy*, 53, 71–72.

CHAPTER 3

1. The letter Floyd Lamb wrote to the AEC, dated October 15, 1951, was not itself available but was summarized in Milton Rex's note to his files. Milton A. Rex to files, "Letter from Floyd Lamb," October 18, 1951, National Nuclear Security Administration/Nevada Field Office (NNSA/NFO); lease between Willard Cattle Company and United States of America, April 18, 1949, NNSA/NFO.

2. Milton A. Rex to files, "Letter from Floyd Lamb," October 18, 1951, NNSA/NFO.

3. "Home on the Range—But a Bombing Range," *Reno Evening Gazette*, January 3, 1945; "G.I. Cowboys Herd Cattle on Bombing Range," *Reno Evening Gazette*, May 25, 1945.

4. "More Atom Blast Tests Indicated," *Nevada State Journal*, March 1, 1951; "Evaluation of Blast Effects Year-Long Job at Test Site," *Nevada State Journal*, November 2, 1951; "A-Bomb Test Claims Processed," *Reno Evening Gazette*, May 8, 1951; James McCormack to Roscoe C. Wilson, letter, July 9, 1951, NNSA/NFO; "Damage Claims in Bomb Tests Are Summarized," *Reno Evening Gazette*, November 30, 1951.

5. Shields Warren to James McCormack, memorandum, July 17, 1951, NNSA/NFO; "Radiation Detected on Coast," *New York Times*, November 1, 1951; "Radioactivity in Upstate Snow," *New York Times*, November 3, 1951; Merril Eisenbud to Julian Webb, letter, July 22, 1952, NNSA/NFO; Miller, *Under the Cloud*, 90–91; Hacker, *Elements of Controversy*, 50–51.

6. Stafford L. Warren to Fred A. Bryan, letter, November 23, 1951, NNSA/NFO.

7. "Corn Freaks Grow from Atomic Tests," *New York Times*, December 16, 1951; "Atom Bomb Tests Verify UCLA Research Finds," *Los Angeles Times*, March 2, 1952.

8. Titus, *Bombs in the Backyard*, 36–54. The damage suffered by the Japanese in Hiroshima and Nagasaki and by the Marshallese in the Pacific was far greater than anything that occurred within the continental United States. For detailed personal accounts from two scientists who studied both groups, see the oral histories with James Yamazaki and Roger Ray in the Nevada Test Site Oral History Project archive at http://digital.library.unlv.edu/ntsohp/.

9. Nevada State Water Rights (NSWR) certificates 208 (July 22, 1914), 350 (July 23, 1914), and 468 (December 3, 1919); NSWR vested water rights V01505 (May 17, 1917), V01506 (May 17, 1917), V01507 (May 17, 1917), and V01798 (June 25, 1922); General Land Office record 935763 (April 4, 1924) and 940203 (June 18, 1924); "Obituary: William G. Lamb," *Nevada State Journal*, July 16, 1939.

10. "Obituary: William G. Lamb," *Nevada State Journal*, July 16, 1939; NSWR certificates 2778 (March 9, 1944) and 2830 (January 5, 1945); "Alamo Ranchers Ask More Water," *Reno Evening Gazette*, April 9, 1947; lease between Willard Cattle Company and United States of America, April 18, 1949, NNSA/NFO; Ed Koch, Mary Manning, et al., "Lamb, Longtime Nevada Politician, Rancher, Dies," *Las Vegas Sun*, June 3, 2002; Stewart, *History of Pahranagat Valley*, 16–17, 32, 38–39, 42.

11. Milton A. Rex to files, "Letter from Floyd Lamb," October 18, 1951, NNSA/NFO.

12. Carroll L. Tyler to John C. Burgher, TWX, January 31, 1952, NNSA/NFO. These tests also included military troops.

13. Hacker, *Elements of Controversy*, 70. It is worth noting that the Camp Desert Rock exercises, eight in total, exposed more than a quarter of a million troops to radioactive fallout. For more information on the experiences of these people, see the oral histories of Atomic Veterans in the Nevada Test Site Oral History Project archive at http://digital.library.unlv.edu/ntsohp/.

14. Kenneth E. Fields to Carroll L. Tyler, letter, February 27, 1952, NNSA/NFO; press release, circa March 1952, Charles Russell Papers (CRP), Box 175, Folder 2; Hacker, *Elements of Controversy*, 74.

15. Hacker, *Elements of Controversy*, 77–78. Most press personnel and civilians had sought views of the test site from the road that wound across the ridge separating Kyle Canyon from Lee Canyon, the two major watersheds east of Mount Charleston.

16. Gene Sherman, "Atomic Gains Told as New Test Nears," *Los Angeles Times*, April 1, 1952; Gene Sherman, "GIs Four Miles from Biggest A-Bomb Blast," *Los Angeles Times*, April 23, 1952; "Mushroom Clearly Seen at Mt. Wilson," *Los Angeles Times*, April 23, 1952; "Viewing the Atom Explosions," *New York Times*, April 27, 1952; Walter Millis, "Public Peek at A-Bomb Desired in Nevada Blast," *Los Angeles Times*, May 2, 1952; Gene Sherman, "Every Atom Blast Signifies a Tremendous Scientific Labor," *Los Angeles Times*, May 4, 1952; Miller, *Under the Cloud*, 137–56.

17. Draft press release, May 8, 1952, NNSA/NFO.

18. "Atomic Bomb Lights Desert," *Reno Evening Gazette*, May 7, 1952; Robert Bennyhoff, "Atom Blast Brightest Ever Fired in Nevada," *Nevada State Journal*, May 8, 1952; "Mine Camp, Population 11, Evacuated for A-Bomb Test," *Nevada State Journal*, May 18, 1952; William R. Kennedy to Jerome Dummer, memorandum, April 26, 1882, NNSA/NFO. This document contains photocopies of radiation monitor Thomas N. White's notebook.

19. Dan Sheahan to Seth Woodruff, letter with attachments, April 6, 1953, NNSA/NFO; Hacker, *Elements of Controversy*, 78–80.

20. "Winds Cover State with Atomic Dust," *Salt Lake Tribune*, May 8, 1952; "A-Blast's Dust 'Dying Out,'" *Salt Lake Tribune*, May 9, 1952; "We Don't Know Enough," *Salt Lake Tribune*, May 9, 1952; Corbin Allardice, "Controls Make Atomic Tests Harmless," *Salt Lake Tribune*, May 29, 1952.

21. James E. Reeves to George P. Kraker, TWX, July 31, 1952, NNSA/NFO; Carroll L. Tyler to Kenneth E. Fields, TWX, July 31, 1952, NNSA/NFO.

22. Thomas L. Shipman to Alvin C. Graves, letter, August 6, 1952, NNSA/NFO.

23. "Foot and Mouth Outbreak Alerts U.S. Stockmen," *Reno Evening Gazette*, April 10, 1952; "Heavy Livestock at Lund Is Investigated," *Reno Evening Gazette*, July 8, 1952; "Strange Death of 14 Cattle Believed Caused by Allergy," *Nevada State Journal*, July 8, 1952; Walter D. Claus to Carroll L. Tyler, TWX, August 6, 1952, NNSA/NFO; John C. Burgher to Carroll L. Tyler, TWX, August 14, 1952, NNSA/NFO.

24. Carroll L. Tyler to John C. Burgher, TWX, January 31, 1952, NNSA/NFO; Thomas L. Shipman to Alvin C. Graves, letter, August 8, 1952, NNSA/NFO.

25. Thomas L. Shipman to Alvin C. Graves, letter, August 8, 1952, NNSA/NFO; Cyril L. Comar, report, November 11, 1952, NNSA/NFO.

26. Richard G. Elliott to Kenneth E. Fields, TWX, August 12, 1952, NNSA/NFO.

27. Robert E. Thompsett, Harry O. Whipple, and Thomas N. White to Carroll L. Tyler, letter, August 18, 1952, NNSA/NFO.

28. Thomas L. Shipman to Alvin C. Graves, memorandum, August 23, 1952, NNSA/NFO.

29. Press release, August 28, 1952, NNSA/NFO; "Cattle Survive Radiation from Atomic Blasts," *Nevada State Journal*, August 29, 1952.

30. Leonard A. Jacobvitz to Chester G. Brinck, letter, August 22, 1952, NNSA/NFO.

31. John I. Munson to Seth R. Woodruff, TWX, September 10, 1952, NNSA/NFO; Seth R. Woodruff to John I. Munson, TWX, September 18, 1952, NNSA/NFO; Seth R. Woodruff to John I. Munson, memorandum with lease and supplemental agreement, September 24, 1952, NNSA/NFO.

32. Seth R. Woodruff to Carroll L. Tyler, memorandum, September 9, 1952, NNSA/NFO; Carroll L. Tyler to Seth R. Woodruff, memorandum, September 12, 1952, NNSA/NFO.

33. Seth R. Woodruff to Floyd Lamb, letter, September 17, 1952, NNSA/NFO; Floyd Lamb to AEC, letter, October 10, 1952, NNSA/NFO; William U. Schofield, Jr., affidavit, October 9, 1952, NNSA/NFO; J. A. Hail, affidavit, October 10, 1952, NNSA/NFO; Wilson Stewart, affidavit, October 20, 1952, NNSA/NFO. Seth R. Woodruff forwarded these affidavits to Chester G. Brinck at the general counsel's office. See Seth R. Woodruff to Chester G. Brinck, memorandum, October 28, 1952, NNSA/NFO.

34. Joe B. Sanders to Carroll L. Tyler, memorandum, October 13, 1952, NNSA/NFO.

35. Chester G. Brinck to Miles N. Pike, letter, October 17, 1952, NNSA/NFO.

36. Seth R. Woodruff to Floyd Lamb, letter, October 20, 1952, NNSA/NFO.

37. George P. Kraker to Frank C. DiLuzio, memorandum, October 21, 1952, NNSA/NFO; Chester G. Brinck to Miles N. Pike, letter, November 3, 1952, NNSA/NFO.

38. Robert E. Thompsett to Frank C. DiLuzio, letter, November 18, 1952, NNSA/NFO.

39. Chester G. Brinck to Miles N. Pike, letter, November 3, 1952, NNSA/NFO; Miles N. Pike to Floyd Lamb, letter, November 17, 1952, NNSA/NFO; Miles N. Pike to Chester G. Brinck, letter, November 17, 1952, NNSA/NFO.

40. Chester G. Brinck to Miles N. Pike, letter, January 16, 1953, NNSA/NFO; Hacker, *Elements of Controversy*, 80–81.

41. Chester G. Brinck to Seth R. Woodruff, memorandum, January 15, 1953, NNSA/ NFO; Chester G. Brinck to Miles N. Pike, letter, January 16, 1953, NNSA/NFO; Seth R. Woodruff to David Goldwater, letter, January 20, 1953, NNSA/NFO; Seth R. Woodruff to James W. Johnson, letter, January 20, 1953, NNSA/NFO; Hacker, *Elements of Controversy*, 80–81.

42. Joe B. Sanders to Seth R. Woodruff, memorandum, March 3, 1953, NNSA/ NFO; Robert E. Cole to files, memorandum, June 24, 1953, NNSA/NFO.

43. "Fact Sheet on Nevada Proving Ground," March 31, 1952, CRP, Box 175, Folder 2; Norris Bradbury to Carroll L. Tyler, letter, January 5, 1953, NNSA/NFO; Darol K. Froman to Reuben E. Cole, memorandum, February 3, 1953, NNSA/NFO; Hacker, *Elements of Controversy*, 90–91. In 1952, the AEC changed the name of the test site to Nevada Proving Ground, which, according to the agency, conformed to the federal government's standard terminology for similar installations such as the Dugway Proving Ground in Utah where military technologies, especially weapons, were tested. In late 1954, the leadership at Los Alamos Scientific Laboratory pushed to officially designate the place the Nevada Test Site.

44. Jack L. Armstrong to Carroll L. Tyler, memorandum, September 2, 1952, NNSA/NFO; Thomas L. Shipman to Carroll L. Tyler, memorandum, September 5, 1952, NNSA/NFO; Alvin C. Graves to Thomas L. Shipman, memorandum, September 6, 1952, NNSA/NFO; Carroll L. Tyler to Kenneth E. Fields, memorandum, September 12, 1952, NNSA/NFO; Jack L. Armstrong to Carroll L. Tyler, memorandum, September 24, 1952, NNSA/NFO; William Gorvine to files, December 19, 1952, NNSA/NFO; Carroll L. Tyler to Kenneth E. Fields, memorandum, December 23, 1952, NNSA/ NFO; Jack L. Armstrong to Carroll L. Tyler, memorandum, January 8, 1953, NNSA/ NFO; Richard Elliott to distribution, October 30, 1952, NNSA/NFO. Several months later, when the AEC's general counsel had worked out a way to legally word a purchase agreement with Floyd Lamb that did not locate any liability for damages with the AEC, the Division of Biology and Medicine, believing the window of opportunity had closed to view the radiation effects, chose to rescind its request because of "the extended lapse of time involved since the cattle were exposed to radiation."

45. Raymond P. Campbell to Kenneth E. Fields, memorandum, September 15, 1952, NNSA/NFO; William S. Johnson to Alvin Graves, memorandum, September 29, 1952, NNSA/NFO; John C. Clark to William S. Johnson, memorandum, October 4, 1952, NNSA/NFO; Carroll L. Tyler to Kenneth E. Fields, memorandum, October 14, 1952, NNSA/NFO; William S. Johnson to John C. Clark, memorandum, October 21, 1952, NNSA/NFO; Thomas N. White to David M. Stearns, memorandum, November 10, 1952, NNSA/NFO; John C. Clark to distribution, memorandum, November 29, 1952, NNSA/NFO; Carroll L. Tyler to Kenneth E. Fields, memorandum, December 5, 1953, NNSA/NFO; Carroll L. Tyler to Kenneth E. Fields, memorandum, December 31, 1952, NNSA/NFO; W. P. Dearing to Marion W. Boyer, letter, January 7, 1953, NNSA/NFO; Deputy Chief, Bureau of State Services to Duncan A. Holaday, memorandum, January 19, 1953, NNSA/NFO; Thomas Shipman to John Burgher, letter, February 5, 1953, NNSA/NFO; Merril Eisenbud to Potter Campbell, memorandum, February 13, 1953, NNSA/NFO. In addition to the more intensive participation by the Public Health Service, the AEC's Division of Biology and Medicine collected the individual exposure records of the 1951 and 1952 tests from various groups at Los Alamos and the Armed

Force Special Weapons Project (AFSWP) for processing and storage in one location. To continue to improve its relationship with the general public, the AEC arranged for three hundred Federal Civil Defense Administration observers, two hundred reporters, and two scientists from the Eastman Kodak Company to observe the tests scheduled for the spring of 1953.

46. R. N. Isbell to chief, Armed Forces Special Weapons Project, memorandum, February 17, 1953, NNSA/NFO. Scientists calculated the standard level for the ionizing radiation dose for test personnel at 3.9 roentgens per test operation, thermal radiation at 1 calorie per cm^2, and blast or force tolerance at 2 pounds per in^2.

47. Atomic Energy Commission, "AEC Continental Weapons Tests . . . Public Safety," March 31, 1953, NNSA/NFO.

48. Sidney Lohman, "News and Notes from the Studios," *New York Times*, March 15, 1953; William L. Laurence, "Millions on TV See Explosion That Rocks Desert Like Quake," *New York Times*, March 18, 1953; Robert Bennyhoff, "Bennyhoff Sees Blast, Finds It Disappointing," *Reno Evening Gazette*, March 18, 1953; Fehner and Gosling, *Atmospheric Nuclear Weapons Testing*, 93–98; Miller, *Under the Cloud*, 159–66; Hacker, *Elements of Controversy*, 101–102. Not all Americans were impressed with the power of this particular detonation. Veteran bomb reporter Robert Bennyhoff expressed disappointment in the blast, writing, "It felt more like the gentle but determined roll of an earthquake than the jolt of nuclear fission. Nor was the atomic cloud anywhere near as beautiful as many other previous tests had been."

49. AEC press release, March 24, 1953, NNSA/NFO; AEC press release, March 31, 1953, NNSA/NFO; AEC press release, April 11, 1953, NNSA/NFO; James C. Watson to Robert G. Lindberg, letter, April 23, 1953, NNSA/NFO; Robert E. Cole to files, memorandum, June 24, 1953, NNSA/NFO.

50. "Powerful Blast Lights Up Sky at Las Vegas," *Reno Evening Gazette*, April 25, 1953; AEC press release, April 25, 1953 (there are three from this date), NNSA/NFO; Richard Elliott to distribution, memorandum, April 25, 1953, NNSA/NFO; Fehner and Gosling, *Atmospheric Nuclear Weapons Testing*, 103–104; Miller, *Under the Cloud*, 169–71; Hacker, *Elements of Controversy*, 102–103.

51. Radiation monitor Otto Paganini mentioned to his supervisor William S. Johnson that he had encountered some difficulties in conducting contamination procedures. While the public was generally very cooperative and seemed satisfied with the small amount of information Paganini was authorized to give them, the physical infrastructure needed to decontaminate people and equipment in the field was not in place. For instance, Paganini noted that car wash facilities were generally not available in towns such as Alamo, and neither were handheld vacuum cleaners. Paganini recommended that mobile radiation monitoring units bring water, roadblock signs, record books, and the right kind of vacuum cleaners. He also recommended further study in developing procedures for decontaminating personal effects and clothing. Otto Paganini to William S. Johnson, memorandum, April 28, 1953, NNSA/NFO.

52. Radiation monitor Richard Fetz reported to his supervisor William S. Johnson that the roadblock in Saint George proved busier than anticipated. Fetz enlisted the help of three service stations to provide free car washes to the public and three Utah state troopers to manage the roadblock, check vehicles for radiation levels, and record vehicle owners' information. In order to ensure that every car got washed, Fetz relieved the drivers of their license until they returned from the car wash. Of the nearly three hundred vehicles that passed through the roadblock, Fetz noted one that they were

unable to clean, belonging to a Mr. Prisbey, who was told to take his car to Las Vegas for further decontamination. Fetz made recommendations to Johnson similar to those of his colleague Paganini in Alamo because rural towns had few if any car washing facilities or vacuum cleaners. Fetz also suggested that highways be shut down right after test detonation until the radioactive cloud passed over and that vehicle occupants remain in their cars until they passed the contaminated area. Richard H. Fetz to William S. Johnson, memorandum, April 30, 1953, NNSA/NFO.

53. "Radioactive Matter Falls on Nevada Roads," *Los Angeles Times*, April 26, 1953; "Atom Dust Falls on Autos, Bus," *Ogden Standard-Examiner*, April 26, 1953; "Atom Blast Downs Drone Plane," *Provo (Utah) Sunday Herald*, April 26, 1953; "Final Atomic Tests Planned," *Reno Evening Gazette*, April 27, 1953.

54. John C. Burgher to Kenneth E. Fields, letter, April 15, 1953, NNSA/NFO.

55. Carroll L. Tyler to George P. Kraker, TWX, May 8, 1953, NNSA/NFO; Raymond P. Campbell to Kenneth E. Fields, memorandum, May 8, 1953, NNSA/NFO; Thomas L. Shipman to Darol Froman, memorandum, June 2, 1953, NNSA/NFO; Alvin C. Graves to James E. Reeves, memorandum, July 13, 1953, NNSA/NFO; Raymond P. Campbell to William L. Guthrie, memorandum, July 27, 1953, NNSA/NFO; Gaelen Felt to Alvin C. Graves, memorandum, August 31, 1953, NNSA/NFO. Carroll Tyler recommended that the exposure limit, at that time set at 3.9 roentgens over thirteen weeks, be raised and extended over a broader time period of twelve months, which would allow more flexibility in the testing process. Both the AEC and Los Alamos hoped that over time and with further scientific study, the testing organization would be able to knowledgeably set the range of acceptable radiation dosages, accurately predict test yields, safely increase test size, and better understand the effects of radiation exposure in a manner that would not be too expensive, compromise the testing process, or cause the population adjacent to the test site to oppose its activities.

56. AEC press release, May 8, 1953, NNSA/NFO; Robert Bennyhoff, "Atomic Blast Equals 300,000 Tons of TNT," *Nevada State Journal*, May 9, 1953; AEC press release, June 4, 1953, CRP, Box 175, Folder 3; Gene Sherman, "Atom Blast, Greatest of All, Set Off," *Los Angeles Times*, June 5, 1953; Fehner and Gosling, *Atmospheric Nuclear Weapons Testing*, 106–108; Miller, *Under the Cloud*, 171–73, 180–81; Hacker, *Elements of Controversy*, 103–104.

57. "Plan to Move Cannon," *Reno Evening Gazette*, April 25, 1953; "Assemble Cannon for Atomic Test," *Reno Evening Gazette*, May 4, 1953; "Atomic Cannon in Nevada for Tests," *Reno Evening Gazette*, May 6, 1953; "Atomic Cannon Firing Planned," *Reno Evening Gazette*, May 9, 1953; "Atomic Cannon Moved to Nevada Test Site," *Los Angeles Times*, May 11, 1953; Marvin Miles, "Big Cannon Set Up for Atomic Test," *Los Angeles Times*, May 25, 1953; "Shot Ends Series of Nevada Tests," *Reno Evening Gazette*, May 25, 1953; AEC press release, May 25, 1953, CRP, Box 175, Folder 3; Gladwin Hill, "Cannon Fires Atomic Shell," *New York Times*, May 26, 1953; "Atomic Cannon 'Shot Heard around the World,'" *Nevada State Journal*, May 26, 1953; Fehner and Gosling, *Atmospheric Nuclear Weapons Testing*, 102; Miller, *Under the Cloud*, 177–80; Hacker, *Elements of Controversy*, 105.

58. AEC press release, May 19, 1953 (there are three for this date); NNSA/NFO; Richard G. Elliott to distribution, May 19, 1953, NNSA/NFO; John C. Clark to Kenneth E. Fields, TWX, May 20, 1953, NNSA/NFO; Fehner and Gosling, *Atmospheric Nuclear Weapons Testing*, 105–106; Miller, *Under the Cloud*, 173–77; Hacker, *Elements of Controversy*, 103–105; Fradkin, *Fallout*, 1–4. Radiation monitors scrambled to establish checkpoints near Alamo on Highway 93, in North Las Vegas and Glendale on Highway

91, and in Saint George, and to warn residents to stay inside their homes. The AEC issued a public warning that fallout could occur, but that it would not "exceed the non-hazardous levels experienced after the April 25 shot." By midday, monitors recorded problematic levels of radioactive fallout near Alamo and Saint George and ordered vehicles to car washes for decontamination.

59. "Robot Plane Survives 9th Atomic Blast," *Provo Daily Herald*, May 19, 1953; "Nevada Atom Test Affects Utah Area," *New York Times*, May 20, 1953; "A-Blast Cloud Brings Closing of Utah Town," *Chicago Daily Tribune*, May 20, 1953; "Utah Clear of Harmful Cloud," *Ogden Standard-Examiner*, May 20, 1953; "Atom Fallout Blocks Two Nevada Highways," *Nevada State Journal*, May 20, 1953; "AEC Checks Utah Atomic Area, Denies Harm Done," *Ogden Standard-Examiner*, May 21, 1953; "Nevada, Utah People Given Added Assurance They Will Not Be Injured by Fallout," *Nevada State Journal*, May 21, 1953.

60. Douglas R. Stringfellow to Gordon Dean, letter, May 20, 1953, NNSA/NFO; AEC press release, May 20, 1953, NNSA/NFO; "The Public Forum," *Salt Lake Tribune*, May 28, 1953; Lewis L. Strauss to Douglas R. Stringfellow, letters: August 5, September 16, and September 25, 1953; January 11, March 9, April 20, and May 4, 1954, NNSA/NFO. Representative Stringfellow sent several letters to the AEC throughout 1953 and 1954 supporting the investigations into the exposures, particularly the sheep deaths, that resulted from the Upshot-Knothole series.

61. Fehner and Gosling, *Atmospheric Nuclear Weapons Testing*, 106–107; Miller, *Under the Cloud*, 177; Hacker, *Elements of Controversy*, 104–105.

62. Daniel Sheahan to Seth R. Woodruff, letter, April 6, 1953, NNSA/NFO; William W. Allaire, note, circa June 1953, NNSA/NFO; Daniel Sheahan to Pat McCarran, letter, June 16, 1953, NNSA/NFO; Daniel Sheahan to Pat McCarran, letter, January 30, 1954, NNSA/NFO; Daniel Sheahan to Charles H. Russell, letter, July 7, 1954, CRP, Box 175, Folder 5; Charles H. Russell to Daniel Sheahan, letter, July 20, 1954, CRP, Box 175, Folder 5; Daniel Sheahan to James E. Roberts, letter, August 18, 1954, CRP, Box 175, Folder 5; Joe B. Sanders to files, memorandum, June 24, 1953, NNSA/NFO; Carroll L. Tyler to Kenneth E. Fields, memorandum, June 29, 1953, NNSA/NFO; Thomas L. Shipman to distribution, TWX, July 8, 1953, NNSA/NFO; Kenneth E. Fields to Thomas E. Murray, memorandum, July 15, 1953, NNSA/NFO; Gerard C. Smith to Thomas E. Murray, memorandum, July 16, 1953, NNSA/NFO; William L. Guthrie to Joe B. Sanders, memorandum, July 29, 1953, NNSA/NFO; A. L. Scott to Carroll L. Tyler, letter, August 4, 1953, NNSA/NFO; Carroll L. Tyler to A. L. Scott, letter, August 10, 1953, NNSA/NFO; John C. Burgher to Carroll L. Tyler, memorandum, August 7, 1953, NNSA/NFO; Kenneth E. Fields to Carroll L. Tyler, TWX, August 18, 1953, NNSA/NFO; James E. Reeves to Kenneth E. Fields, memorandum, August 24, 1953, NNSA/NFO; Joe B. Sanders to Bernard T. Trum, letter, September 23, 1953, NNSA/NFO; Seth R. Woodruff to Daniel Sheahan, draft letter, circa October 1953, NNSA/NFO; Carroll L. Tyler to A. L. Scott, letter, October 13, 1953, NNSA/NFO; A. L. Scott to Carroll L. Tyler, letter, October 19, 1953, NNSA/NFO; Joe B. Sanders to files, January 6, 1954, NNSA/NFO; George P. Kraker to N. D. Greenberg, memorandum, April 5, 1954, NNSA/NFO; James E. Roberts to Charles H. Russell, letter, July 28, 1954, CRP, Box 175, Folder 5; Lewis L. Strauss to Charles H. Russell, letter, August 16, 1954, CRP, Box 175, Folder 5; Donald J. Leehey to Kenneth E. Fields, memorandum, August 20, 1954, NNSA/NFO; Seth R. Woodruff to Donald J. Leehey, memorandum, April 23, 1955, NNSA/NFO; Daniel Sheahan to Seth R. Woodruff, letter, July 6, 1955, CRP, Box 175, Folder 5; Daniel Sheahan to James E. Robert, letter, July 6, 1955, CRP,

Box 175, Folder 5; Daniel Sheahan to Charles H. Russell, letter, July 8, 1955, CRP, Box 175, Folder 5; Charles H. Russell to Daniel Sheahan, letter, July 11, 1955, CRP, Box 175, Folder 5; Daniel Sheahan to James E. Reeves, letter, August 5, 1955, NNSA/NFO; Donald J. Leehey to Alfred D. Starbird, memorandum, September 9, 1955, NNSA/NFO; Kenner F. Hertford to Alfred D. Starbird, TWX, March 4, 1958, NNSA/NFO; Chalmers C. King to Charles F. Eason, memorandum, July 3, 1958, NNSA/NFO; Henry G. Vermillion to Rodney L. Southwick, memorandum, January 30, 1956, NNSA/NFO; Solnit, *Savage Dreams*, 33–35. Dan Sheahan, a resident of Groom Mine, protested the regular evacuations and damage that occurred every time a nuclear test was conducted. He filed a claim with the AEC in 1952, but the dollar amount was in excess of the limit allowed under administrative claims. After the Upshot-Knothole series, he wrote Nevada senator Pat McCarran and Governor Charles Russell of the current damage to his property, his horses, and himself. When Sheahan tried to sell his operation at Groom Mine to the AEC or the air force and threatened a very public court battle, the AEC would not set a precedent by paying the Sheahans for their property. Besides the AEC's tests, Sheahan was concerned about wayward air force pilots that often strafed his structures with fifty-caliber guns. Ironically, Kenneth E. Fields of the AEC's Division of Military Applications believed that Groom Mine was constantly in danger because of "inaccuracies in air-to-ground firing," but he did not think that the Sheahans were in any danger from fallout. The only compensation the Sheahans received from the AEC was $1,000 on a 1952 claim for losses incurred when it shut down Groom Mine during the Tumbler-Snapper series and a $100 payment on his sixteen-year-old "nag" that had lesions caused by exposure to fallout.

63. Notes on alleged radiation effects on cattle and sheep in Nevada area, December 31, 1953, NNSA/NFO; Joe B. Sanders to files, memorandum, December 31, 1953, NNSA/NFO; "Sheepmen Await Word on Atomic Blasts and Malady," *Ogden Standard-Examiner*, June 7, 1953; "Mystery Disease Killing Ewes, Lambs in Utah," *Provo Sunday Herald*, June 7, 1953; F. H. Melvin to Bennett T. Simms, letter, June 8, 1953, NNSA/NFO; Richard G. Elliott to files, memorandum, June 9, 1953, NNSA/NFO; Gordon Dunning to files, June 12, 1953, NNSA/NFO; data on sheep losses, preliminary investigation, June 17, 1953, NNSA/NFO; Fehner and Gosling, *Atmospheric Nuclear Weapons Testing*, 109–10, 112; Miller, *Under the Cloud*, 182–86; Hacker, *Elements of Controversy*, 106–30; Fradkin, *Fallout*, 147–62; Fox, *Downwind*, 53–63. The veterinarians included Robert E. Thompsett (Los Alamos Scientific Laboratory), Robert H. Veenstra (Naval Radiological Defense Laboratory), Arthur H. Wolff (Public Health Service), Monroe A. Holmes (Utah Department of Health Division of Disease Control), and A. C. Johnson (Cedar City). The other investigators were William J. Hadlow (Public Health Service pathologist), Joe Sanders (Las Vegas Operations Office deputy manager), and Steve Brower (Iron County agricultural agent). Paul B. Pearson headed all the livestock investigations for the AEC's Division of Biology and Medicine. F. H. Melvin, from the Utah Department of Agriculture's Bureau of Animal Industry, and John I. Curtis, from the Utah State Veterinarian's Office, had examined the sheep two weeks earlier and noted that the afflicted sheep exhibited blisters on their faces and in their noses, carried high temperatures, shed wool in clumps, and aborted full-term stillborn lambs. The state veterinarians were concerned this was a full-scale epidemic, as no sheep rancher in the area had ever seen these problems before. Curtis had notified George Spendlove at the Utah Department of Health of a possible epidemic, but the ranchers themselves contacted the AEC.

64. Kenneth E. Fields to Carroll L. Tyler, TWX, June 16, 1953, NNSA/NFO; Richard G. Elliott to distribution, memorandum, July 15, 1953, NNSA/NFO; Stafford L. Warren to John C. Burgher, letter, July 17, 1952, NNSA/NFO; B. M. Brundage to Stafford L. Warren, memorandum, June 16, 1953, NNSA/NFO. Apparently this news segment developed out of Roger E. Sprague, NBC's Western Division director of news and special events, and his personal interest in the effects of exposure to radioactive fallout. Sprague's sister had suffered from what he believed to be symptoms of radiation exposure. Sprague had contacted the AEC in 1952 for answers regarding the matter but had not been satisfied with its response.

65. B. C. Lyon to Seth R. Woodruff, letter, June 17, 1953, NNSA/NFO; "Sheep-Killing Weed," *Life*, January 15, 1951, 55–56; data on sheep losses, second preliminary investigation, June 17, 1953, NNSA/NFO; W. T. Huffman to H. W. Schoening, letter, June 23, 1953; NNSA/NFO; Howard C. Brown, note on TWX, July 8, 1953, NNSA/NFO; Richard G. Elliott to Kenneth E. Fields, memorandum, July 16, 1953, NNSA/NFO; "Southeast Nevada Cattle Crisis Worsens; 1400 Animals Dead," *Las Vegas (NV) Review-Journal*, July 16, 1953; "Report of Committee Investigating Drought Conditions—State of Nevada," July 21, 1953, NNSA/NFO; John L. O'Harra to Joe B. Sanders, letter, July 25, 1953, NNSA/NFO; W. T. Huffman to H. W. Schoening, letter, August 26, 1953, NNSA/NFO; Karl E. Herde to Lauren R. Donaldson, letter, November 18, 1953, NNSA/NFO; Bernard F. Trum, report, March 31–April 20, 1953, NNSA/NFO; Fox, *Downwind*, 63–77.

66. "Cooperative Battle against Weeds Is Being Worked Out," *Nevada State Journal*, February 19, 1950; "Spread of Weed Worries Ranchers," *Nevada State Journal*, February 24, 1950; "Stock Toll Feared as Poison Weed Spreading in Utah," *Ogden Standard-Examiner*, March 17, 1950; "Halogeton Livestock Threat Mounts in Western States," *Salt Lake Tribune*, November 26, 1950; "Russian Weed Threatening Livestock, Says Welling," *Ogden Standard-Examiner*, November 27, 1950; Murray Moler, "Russian Weed Is Threat to Western U.S.," *Nevada State Journal*, November 29, 1950; John Brosnan, "Farm Letter," *Salt Lake Tribune*, December 31, 1950; "Halogeton on the Western Range," circa 1950, Folder 236, Public Lands Foundation Archive (PLFA); "Halogeton," circa 1950, Folder 236, PLFA; "Sheep-Killing Weed," *Life*, January 15, 1951, 55–56; "Improved Ranges to Halt Halogeton," *Reno Evening Gazette*, January 20, 1951; "Poison Weed Battle Asked by McCarran," *Nevada State Journal*, January 21, 1951; "Discussion Held on Rainmaking," *Nevada State Journal*, March 7, 1951; Kenneth B. Platt, "Halogeton: Recognize It! Fight It!," *Our Public Lands*, April 1951, 6; "Public Land Aid Draws Halogeton Battle Line," *Salt Lake Telegram*, July 26, 1951; "The Halogeton Problem in Utah," circa 1951, Folder 236, PLFA; Fred Othman, "Weed Warfare," *Washington (D.C.) Daily News*, February 13, 1952; Halogeton Glomeratus Control Act of 1952, Public Law 529, 82nd Cong., 2nd sess. (July 14, 1952); Fenley et al., "With the Sections," 430–32; "Halogeton in Nevada—Animal Poisoning and Control Studies," December 1952, Folder 236, PLFA; L. A. Stoddart, report on livestock conditions, June 23, 1953, NNSA/NFO; C. Wayne Cook and L. A. Stoddart, "The Halogeton Problem in Utah," November 1953, Folder 236, PLFA; Ernest J. Palmer, "Can We Control Halogeton?," *Our Public Lands*, January 1955, 4–5, 18–19, 22–23; "Killing Halogeton with Chemicals," March 1955, Folder 236, PLFA; Stoddart and Smith, *Range Management*, 234–57; Young and Clements, *Cheatgrass*, 73–76, 153–60.

67. Crawford Houston, "Writer Portrays Need for Control of Public Lands," *Garfield County News*, February 10, 1933; "$525,000,000 Asked for Quick Relief in Drought

Areas," *New York Times*, June 5, 1934; "Wallace to Buy Cattle in Drought-Ridden Areas; Federal Control Planned," *New York Times*, July 3, 1936; "Ranges in South Hit by Drought," *Reno Evening Gazette*, April 3, 1946; "Drought Conditions Prevail in State, Report Reveals," *Nevada State Journal*, June 30, 1946; "Clear and Bright Weather Holds On," *Reno Evening Gazette*, February 21, 1947; "July Was Driest Month since 1903," *Nevada State Journal*, August 13, 1947; "Shortage of Livestock Feed Forecast Because of Drought," *Nevada State Journal*, January 29, 1948; "Rain Benefits West," *Nevada State Journal*, June 25, 1948; "Drought Disaster Proclaimed by Ike," *Nevada State Journal*, July 2, 1953; "Cattlemen Split over Value of Government Aid," *Reno Evening Gazette*, July 2, 1953; minutes of the annual meeting of the Central Nevada Livestock Association, July 18, 1953, CRP, Box 187, Folder 37; "President Pledges Quick Drought Aid," *New York Times*, July 11, 1953; "Southeast Nevada Cattle Crisis Worsens; 1400 Animals Dead," *Las Vegas Review-Journal*, July 16, 1953; R. E. Lytle to Monroe A. Holmes, letter, July 20, 1953, NNSA/NFO; Ellis J. Folsom and Thomas Buckman to Charles Russell, report, July 20, 1953, CRP, Box 187, Folder 38; "Livestock Toll Mounts in State during Drought," *Reno Evening Gazette*, July 20, 1953; "Report of Committee Investigating Drought Conditions—State of Nevada," July 21, 1953, CRP, Box 187, Folder 38; "Governor Pursues Drought Aid Plea," *Nevada State Journal*, July 21, 1953; "Effort to Get Drought Fund Will Continue," *Reno Evening Gazette*, July 24, 1953; "Nevada Will Get No Drought Aid," *Nevada State Journal*, July 24, 1953; "Nevada Farm Bureau Joins Move to Secure Drought Relief Funds," *Reno Evening Gazette*, July 25, 1953; "Drought Area Ranchers Eligible for U.S. Aid," *Reno Evening Gazette*, July 29, 1953; "Drought Relief Loans Available," *Nevada State Journal*, July 30, 1953; "Nevada's Drought Conditions Worsen," *Reno Evening Gazette*, July 31, 1953; Clifford Young to Charles Russell, telegram, August 3, 1953, CRP, Box 187, Folder 41; "Drouth Emergency Declared in State," *Reno Evening Gazette*, August 3, 1953; "President Keeps Feed Moving to Drought Areas," *Nevada State Journal*, November 19, 1953; "Report on Drought Situation in Lincoln County Nevada," November 22–23, 1954, CRP, Box 187, Folder 50.

68. Paul B. Pearson to John C. Burgher, memorandum, August 13, 1953, NNSA/NFO; Robert H. Veenstra to Paul B. Pearson, letter, December 23, 1953, NNSA/NFO; Robert E. Thompsett to Reuben E. Cole, letter, circa August 1953, NNSA/NFO; Monroe A. Holmes to S. C. Ingrahan, letter, April 14, 1954, NNSA/NFO.

69. Atomic Energy Commission, *Fourteenth Semiannual Report of the Atomic Energy Commission—January 1953–June 1953* (Washington, D.C.: Government Printing Office, 1953); Carroll L. Tyler to Kenneth E. Fields, TWX, August 19, 1953, NNSA/NFO; M. A. Holmes, "Compiled Report on Cooperative Field Survey of Sheep Deaths in Southwest Utah," August 31, 1953, NNSA/NFO; Atomic Energy Commission, *Progress Report to the Joint Committee on Atomic Energy, June–November 1953* (Washington, D.C.: Government Printing Office, 1953); "Report on Sheep Losses Adjacent to the Nevada Proving Grounds," January 6, 1954, NNSA/NFO, also in CRP, Box 175, Folder 5; AEC press release, January 8, 1954, NNSA/NFO; "Atomic Blasts Didn't Kill Utah Sheep—AEC," *Ogden Standard-Examiner*, January 12, 1954; "AEC Tests in Nevada Not Responsible for Mysterious Sheep Deaths in Utah," *Provo Daily Herald*, January 12, 1954; "What Caused Sheep to Die Still Unsolved," *Ogden Standard-Examiner*, January 14, 1954; "AEC Denies Rays Killed Utah Sheep," *New York Times*, January 17, 1954; Monroe A. Holmes to Stephen Brower, letter, April 15, 1954, NNSA/NFO. The initial findings appeared in the AEC's fourteenth semiannual report to Congress, which stated that about five thousand sheep grazing on the Nevada-Utah border directly east of the test site suffered burns, blindness, and death—a 30 percent loss of lambs and 20

percent loss of mature sheep—during the same period as the 1953 tests. AEC personnel had investigated the causes of the burns and the sheep deaths but concluded that the timing of their injury and death was only coincidental with the test series. They said the sheep suffered from malnutrition because their grazing areas were particularly lean in the drought of that year. The AEC recommended further investigation. The resulting final report on the sheep deaths in Utah stated that "the peculiar lesions observed in the sheep around Cedar City in the spring of 1953 and the abnormal losses suffered by the several sheepmen cannot be accounted for by radiation or attributed to the atomic tests conducted at the Nevada Proving Grounds."

70. Monroe A. Holmes, report, August 31, 1953, NNSA/NFO; meeting of livestock men and AEC officials, January 13, 1954, NNSA/NFO; Seth R. Woodruff to Donald J. Leehey, memorandum, January 18, 1955, NNSA/NFO; Warren E. Burger to AEC general counsel, letter, June 20, 1955, NNSA/NFO; Fradkin, *Fallout*, 161–62; Fox, *Downwind*, 89.

71. Joe B. Sanders to files, memorandum, June 1, 1953, NNSA/NFO; August T. Rossano, report, June 6, 1953, NNSA/NFO; Joe B. Sanders to files, memorandum, June 6, 1953, NNSA/NFO; Bernard F. Trum to Paul B. Pearson, letter, January 14, 1953, NNSA/NFO; Seth R. Woodruff to Paul B. Pearson, memorandum, January 25, 1954, NNSA/NFO; Bernard F. Trum to Paul B. Pearson, letter, January 14, 1953, NNSA/NFO.

72. Gordon M. Dunning to V. G. Huston, memorandum, June 11, 1953, NNSA/NFO; Chester G. Brinck to files, June 11, 1953, NNSA/NFO; J. H. Rust, B. F. Trum, and C. L. Comar, report of farm animal survey at Nevada Test Site, June 16, 1953, NNSA/NFO; Paul B. Pearson to John C. Burgher, memorandum, June 21, 1953, NNSA/NFO; John C. Burgher to Carroll L. Tyler, memorandum, August 7, 1953, NNSA/NFO; W. L. Guthrie to Kenneth E. Fields, memorandum, August 11, 1953, NNSA/NFO; Sterling F. Black to files, August 12, 1953, NNSA/NFO; James E. Reeves to Seth R. Woodruff, memorandum, August 19, 1953, NNSA/NFO; Kenneth E. Fields to Carroll L. Tyler, TWX, August 18, 1953, NNSA/NFO; Paul B. Pearson to Carroll L. Tyler, memorandum, August 18, 1953, NNSA/NFO; Carroll L. Tyler to Kenneth E. Fields, TWX, August 19, 1953, NNSA/NFO; Kenneth E. Fields to Carroll L. Tyler, TWX, August 24, 1953, NNSA/NFO; "Horses Found Injured in Nevada Atom Tests," *Los Angeles Times*, August 25, 1953; John C. Burgher to Marion W. Boyer, memorandum, August 26, 1953, NNSA/NFO; photos of sample damaged horses and cattle, NNSA/NFO; Joe B. Sanders to files, memorandum, August 27, 1953, NNSA/NFO; Bernard F. Trum to Stewart brothers, letter, November 30, 1953, NNSA/NFO; Hacker, *Elements of Controversy*, 106–107. Virtually the same personnel investigated all the incidents of livestock damage in 1953. In particular, Robert E. Thompsett, contract veterinarian with the Los Alamos Scientific Laboratory, and Joe B. Sanders, assistant field manager of the Las Vegas Operations Office, worked most of the cases. The investigation also included Bernard F. Trum, a veterinarian with the University of Tennessee's AEC program; Seth R. Woodruff, field manager of the Las Vegas Operations Office; Gordon Dunning of the Division of Biology and Medicine; Dee Broadbent of the Agricultural Experiment Station; L. A. Stoddart, professor of range management and botany at Utah State Agricultural College; John L. O'Harra, Nevada State Department of Agriculture veterinary inspector; Robert H. Clark, a Las Vegas veterinarian; William A. Allaire, of the AEC's Santa Fe Operations Office; and several others.

73. John C. Burgher to Marion W. Boyer, memorandum, August 26, 1953, NNSA/NFO; Joe B. Sanders to files, memorandum, October 30, 1953, NNSA/NFO; Seth R. Woodruff to Carroll L. Tyler, memorandum, December 10, 1953, NNSA/NFO; John H.

Rust, pathology report on special AEC problem, December 31, 1953, NNSA/NFO; Bernard F. Trum to Paul B. Pearson, letter, January 14, 1954, NNSA/NFO; Seth R. Woodruff to Paul B. Pearson, memorandum, January 25, 1954, NNSA/NFO; Paul B. Pearson to Seth R. Woodruff, memorandum, January 29, 1954, NNSA/NFO; Seth R. Woodruff to Carroll L. Tyler, memorandum, February 11, 1954, NNSA/NFO; Donald J. Leehey to John C. Burgher, TWX, February 13, 1954, NNSA/NFO; William W. Allaire to files, February 24, 1954, NNSA/NFO; Paul B. Pearson to Donald J. Leehey, TWX, February 24, 1954, NNSA/NFO; Chester G. Brinck to Seth R. Woodruff, memorandum, February 26, 1954, NNSA/NFO; Seth R. Woodruff to Donald J. Leehey, February 26, 1954, NNSA/NFO; Bernard F. Trum to Joe B. Sanders, letter, February 27, 1954, NNSA/NFO; William W. Allaire to files, March 2, 1954, NNSA/NFO; Joe B. Sanders to Bernard F. Trum, letter, March 22, 1954, NNSA/NFO; Roy B. Snapp to distribution, memorandum, May 6, 1954, NNSA/NFO; James E. Reeves to Seth R. Woodruff, memorandum, August 11, 1954, NNSA/NFO; Bernard F. Trum to Seth R. Woodruff, letter, December 30, 1954, NNSA/NFO; Bernard F. Trum to Joe B. Sanders, letter, December 30, 1954, NNSA/NFO; R. K. Somers to Bernard F. Trum, letter, December 31, 1954, NNSA/NFO; G. R. Farmer to P. Stewart, letter, October 18, 1958, NNSA/NFO; G. R. Farmer to files, memorandum, May 11, 1959, NNSA/NFO. Epithelioma is a condition in which the tissue that covers the surface of all the body's organs and other structures grows abnormally. *Anaplasma marginale* is a pathogen that causes the common tick-borne anaplasmosis disease, which leads to severe anemia. Grass tetany is a metabolic disorder characterized by low magnesium levels that causes cattle to stagger, thrash around, and die suddenly. The bacterium *Clostridium hemolyticum*, which can be found in poorly drained irrigated areas with alkaline soil, produces bacillary hemoglobinuria, or red water disease. The bacteria colonize the liver and destroy the red blood cells.

74. Gordon M. Dunning to V. G. Huston, memorandum, June 11, 1953, NNSA/NFO; Chester G. Brinck to files, June 11, 1953, NNSA/NFO; J. H. Rust, B. F. Trum, and C. L. Comar, report of farm animal survey at Nevada Test Site, June 16, 1953, NNSA/NFO; Paul B. Pearson to John C. Burgher, memorandum, June 21, 1953, NNSA/NFO; John C. Burgher to Carroll L. Tyler, memorandum, August 7, 1953, NNSA/NFO; W. L. Guthrie to Kenneth E. Fields, memorandum, August 11, 1953, NNSA/NFO; Sterling F. Black to files, August 12, 1953, NNSA/NFO; James E. Reeves to Seth R. Woodruff, memorandum, August 19, 1953, NNSA/NFO; Kenneth E. Fields to Carroll L. Tyler, TWX, August 18, 1953, NNSA/NFO; Paul B. Pearson to Carroll L. Tyler, memorandum, August 18, 1953, NNSA/NFO; Carroll L. Tyler to Kenneth E. Fields, TWX, August 19, 1953, NNSA/NFO; Kenneth E. Fields to Carroll L. Tyler, TWX, August 24, 1953, NNSA/NFO; "Horses Found Injured in Nevada Atom Tests," *Los Angeles Times*, August 25, 1953; John C. Burgher to Marion W. Boyer, memorandum, August 26, 1953, NNSA/NFO; photos of sample damaged horses and cattle, NNSA/NFO; Joe B. Sanders to files, memorandum, August 27, 1953, NNSA/NFO; Bernard F. Trum to Stewart brothers, letter, November 30, 1953, NNSA/NFO; Hacker, *Elements of Controversy*, 106–107.

75. Joe B. Sanders to files, memorandum, August 28, 1953, NNSA/NFO; Carroll L. Tyler to Seth R. Woodruff, memorandum, September 4, 1953, NNSA/NFO; Joe B. Sanders to Richard G. Elliott, memorandum, October 9, 1953, NNSA/NFO; Jack Wollenzien, horse appraisal, October 13, 1953, NNSA/NFO; Stanley Wells, horse appraisal, October 13, 1953, NNSA/NFO; Seth R. Woodruff to Chester G. Brinck, memorandum,

October 16, 1953, NNSA/NFO; Chester G. Brinck to Seth R. Woodruff, memorandum, October 23, 1953, NNSA/NFO; George P. Kraker to Seth R. Woodruff, letter, December 29, 1953, NNSA/NFO. The Stewarts filed six claims for eighteen horses at $300 each and one claim for two horses at $250 each.

76. Joe B. Sanders and Bernard Trum shared an enjoyment of horses, as evidenced by their periodic exchanges about racetracks, jockeys, and fine animals. Bernard Trum had actually met Eddie Arco, the jockey for Native Dancer, in 1953, the year the horse nearly won the Triple Crown. Bernard F. Trum to Joe B. Sanders, letter, August 28, 1953, NNSA/NFO; Joe B. Sanders to Bernard F. Trum, letter, September 23, 1953, NNSA/NFO; Bernard F. Trum to Joe B. Sanders, letter, October 14, 1953, NNSA/NFO.

77. Chester G. Brinck to James L. Morrison, memorandum, May 13, 1954, NNSA/NFO; Lewis L. Strauss to William Langer, letter, July 9, 1954, NNSA/NFO; Joe B. Sanders to Clifford A. Jones, letter, October 21, 1953, NNSA/NFO; Madison B. Graves to Chester G. Brinck, letter, February 9, 1954, NNSA/NFO; Chester G. Brinck to James L. Morrison, memorandum, May 14, 1954, NNSA/NFO; Lewis L. Strauss to William Langer, letter, July 9, 1954, NNSA/NFO; Atomic Energy Act of 1954, Public Law 703, 83rd Cong., 2nd sess. (August 30, 1954); Joe B. Sanders to files, memorandum, December 9, 1954, NNSA/NFO; Donald J. Leehey to Kenneth E. Fields, memorandum, December 23, 1954, NNSA/NFO; Paul B. Pearson to V. R. Bohman, letter, December 30, 1954, NNSA/NFO; Bernard F. Trum to Seth R. Woodruff, letter, December 30, 1954, NNSA/NFO.

78. Seth R. Woodruff to Floyd Lamb, letter, January 29, 1955, NNSA/NFO; Joe B. Sanders to files, memorandum, April 2, 1955; Clifford A. Jones to AEC, letter, April 4, 1955, NNSA/NFO; Seth R. Woodruff to Floyd Lamb, letter, April 12, 1955, NNSA/NFO; Donald J. Leehey to John C. Burgher, memorandum, April 13, 1955, NNSA/NFO; Seth R. Woodruff to Donald J. Leehey, memorandum, April 14, 1955, NNSA/NFO; Joe B. Sanders to files, memorandum, June 10, 1955, NNSA/NFO; Ralph P. Johnson to Seth R. Woodruff, memorandum, June 13, 1955, NNSA/NFO; Alan Bible to Lewis L. Strauss, letter, October 11, 1953, NNSA/NFO; Joe B. Sanders and Chalmers C. King to files, memorandum, October 6, 1955, NNSA/NFO; Chalmers C. King to Floyd Lamb, letter, November 23, 1955, NNSA/NFO; Chalmers C. King to Carleton P. Lamb, letter, November 23, 1955, NNSA/NFO; Joe B. Sanders to files, April 13, 1956, NNSA/NFO; Joe B. Sanders to Chalmers C. King, memorandum, July 9, 1956, NNSA/NFO; Herbert E. Hoffman to Chalmers C. King, TWX, August 1, 1956, NNSA/NFO; William W. Allaire to Rulon A. Earl, letter, August 30, 1956, NNSA/NFO; Edward L. Johnson to Max E. Smith, memorandum, August 5, 1957, NNSA/NFO; Sherman H. Sullivan to files, memorandum, September 9, 1957, NNSA/NFO; Gallagher, *American Ground Zero*, 5–9.

79. Donald J. Leehey to John C. Burgher, memorandum, February 11, 1955, NNSA/NFO; James E. Reeves to Charles L. Dunham, memorandum, December 21, 1956, NNSA/NFO; Edward L. Johnson to Kermit H. Larson, letter, August 10, 1956, NNSA/NFO; Robert L. Corsbie to Kermit H. Larson, letter, August 24, 1956, NNSA/NFO; Max E. Smith to Floyd Lamb, letter, May 29, 1957, NNSA/NFO; James E. Reeves to Alfred D. Starbird, memorandum, June 4, 1957, NNSA/NFO; Max E. Smith to L. J. Cotton, memorandum, July 25, 1957, NNSA/NFO; Alfred D. Starbird to James E. Reeves, TWX, July 11, 1957, NNSA/NFO; redacted to C. L. Weaver, memorandum, January 8, 1959, NNSA/NFO; Alvin C. Graves to James E. Reeves, letter, March 2, 1961, NNSA/NFO.

80. Monroe A. Holmes to Sir, form letters with responses, July 16, 1953, NNSA/NFO; notes taken at meeting of Atomic Energy Commission, State Health Department, Public Health Department, livestock men, and others, August 9, 1953, NNSA/NFO; statements by Webster, Corry, Adams, Clark, Seegmiller, and Higbee, September 3–October 31, 1953, NNSA/NFO; statement by Adams, September 16, 1953, NNSA/NFO; Bernard F. Trum to Joe B. Sanders, letter, December 30, 1954, NNSA/NFO; Commoner, *Closing Circle*, 21–23, 49–65; Fradkin, *Fallout*, 147; Fox, *Downwind*, 125–26.

81. Handwritten note (redacted), May 25, 1953, NNSA/NFO; handwritten chronology (redacted), circa May 25, 1953, NNSA/NFO; additional information on the skin burns at Lincoln Mine, June 6, 1953, NNSA/NFO; Gordon Dunning to files, memorandum, June 12, 1953, NNSA/NFO; E. Van der Smissen to Roscoe Goeke, letter, December 12, 1957, NNSA/NFO; William W. Allaire to James E. Reeves, memorandum, July 23, 1957, NNSA/NFO.

82. Henry G. Vermillion to Rodney L. Southwick, memorandum, January 30, 1956, NNSA/NFO.

83. James C. Watson to Robert G. Lindberg, letter, April 23, 1953, NNSA/NFO; Robert E. Cole to files, memorandum, NNSA/NFO; Edward L. Johnson to Joe B. Sanders, memorandum, January 10, 1956, NNSA/NFO.

84. Norris E. Bradbury to Carroll L. Tyler, letter, January 5, 1953, NNSA/NFO; "Report of Committee on Operational Future of Nevada Proving Grounds," May 11, 1953, NNSA/NFO; Marcus F. Cooper to Carroll L. Tyler, memorandum, July 7, 1953, NNSA/NFO; "Importance of the Nevada Proving Grounds to the Department of Defense," August 25, 1953, NNSA/NFO; Carroll L. Tyler to Kenneth E. Fields, memorandum, September 23, 1953, NNSA/NFO; "The Public Relations of Continental Tests," September 23, 1953, NNSA/NFO; Alvin L. Graves to William Allaire, letter, November 30, 1953, NNSA/NFO; "Report of Committee on Operational Future of Nevada Proving Grounds," December 31, 1953, NNSA/NFO; Hacker, *Elements of Controversy*, 115–22, 129–30.

85. The AEC published this booklet in 1955 and again in 1957 under the title *Atomic Tests in Nevada*. "Atomic Test Effects in the Nevada Test Site Region," February 1955, NNSA/NFO; Ralli, *Viva Las Vegas*, 28; Best and Hillyer, *Las Vegas*, 162–64; Richard G. Elliott to Kenneth E. Fields, memorandum, December 10, 1954, NNSA/NFO; "Official Calms Utah Fears on '55 A-Blasts," *Salt Lake Tribune*, January 21, 1955; "West Reassured on Atomic Tests," *New York Times*, January 23, 1955; Morse Salisbury to Paul F. Foster, memorandum, March 22, 1955, NNSA/NFO; "Bomb Tests Seek to Stress Safety," *New York Times*, May 12, 1957; "AEC Sets New Precautions for Nevada Tests," *Los Angeles Times*, May 14, 1957; Gladwin Hill, "Atomic-Test Area Calm on Fallout," *New York Times*, June 9, 1957.

Chapter 4

1. For a discussion of continued homesteading in the postwar era, see Cannon, *Reopening the Frontier*; Jackson, *Crabgrass Frontier*; Muhn and Stuart, *Opportunity and Challenge*, 90–91; Clapson, *Suburban Century*, 51–78.

2. For a history of the Small Tract Act, see Stringfellow, *Jackrabbit Homestead*. Bureau of Land Management, "Homesteading Past and Present," Department of the Interior, 1960, Folder 271, Public Lands Foundation Archive (PLFA); Landstrom,

"Reclamation," 629–38; Lou Bellesi, "BLM and the Small Tract Act in the Southern California Desert—A Brief History," circa 2000, Folder 1306, PLFA; Muhn and Stuart, *Opportunity and Challenge*, 87–92.

3. Bureau of Land Management, "Homesteading Past and Present," Department of the Interior, 1960, Folder 271, PLFA; "Unsurveyed Areas of the U.S. Reduced to 100 Million Acres," *Our Public Lands* 5 (July–August–September 1955): back cover; Muhn and Stuart, *Opportunity and Challenge*, 72–74, 87–92.

4. Department of the Interior Information Service, press release, February 14, 1961, Howard Cannon Papers (HCP), 87th Cong., Box 18, Folder 228; "Nonmineral Applications on Public Lands Halted by Udall for 18 Months," *Provo Daily Herald*, February 14, 1961; "Udall Orders Land Sale Moratorium," *Salt Lake Tribune*, February 15, 1961; "Moratorium Ordered on Land Filings," *Reno Evening Gazette*, February 16, 1961.

5. Department of the Interior Information Service, press release, December 10, 1959, HCP, 87th Cong., Box 18, Folder 228; Department of the Interior Information Service, press release, February 23, 1960, HCP, 87th Cong., Box 19, Folder 233.

6. Department of the Interior Information Service, press release, February 14, 1961, HCP, 87th Cong., Box 18, Folder 228; "Moratorium Not Handicap, Land Bureau Aid Avers," *Salt Lake Tribune*, February 17, 1961; "Moratorium on Public Land Sale Should Help, Is Claim," *Reno Evening Gazette*, February 23, 1961.

7. Robert A. Jones, "Land Classification—Key to Land Use," *Our Public Lands*, July 1960, 4; Department of the Interior Information Service, press release, February 14, 1961, HCP, 87th Cong., Box 18, Folder 228; "Udall Says Public Power 'Necessary Good.' Not Evil," *Ogden Standard-Examiner*, February 15, 1961.

8. "4 Solons Rap Udall over Land Order," *Salt Lake Tribune*, February 26, 1961; "4 Western Senators Rap Udall," *Ogden Standard-Examiner*, March 2, 1961; "Udall Hope High for West," *Salt Lake Tribune*, March 17, 1961; Department of the Interior Information Service, press release, February 28, 1961, Folder 453, PLFA.

9. W. Reed Roberts to Howard Cannon, letter, March 24, 1959, HCP, 87th Cong., Box 19, Folder 235; report, "BLM in Nevada," circa January 1961, HCP, 87th Cong., Box 18, Folder 228; joint press release, March 22, 1961, HCP, 87th Cong., Box 18, Folder 228; "Land Application Speed Up Slated," *Reno Evening Gazette*, March 23, 1961.

10. "State Rides on Boom of Arid Land Sales," *Salt Lake Tribune*, March 30, 1961; "Public Land Sales Move on Schedule," *Reno Evening Gazette*, April 14, 1961.

11. James H. Gottfredson to Howard Cannon, letters, March 30 and November 17, 1960, HCP, 87th Cong., Box 18, Folder 231.

12. Hall, *Preserving the Glory Days*, 110–11.

13. "Opens Silver Mine at Bristol," *Reno Evening Gazette*, December 7, 1915; "Option Taken on Silver King," *Reno Evening Gazette*, December 26, 1936; Hulse, *Lincoln County, Nevada*, 6–10, 13–15, 40; Townley, *Conquered Provinces*, 7, 10–12, 30–31, 53.

14. General Land Office (GLO) patent numbers 543095 (August 19, 1916) and 1011813 (February 3, 1928); "Livestock Group Holds Session at Ely," *Reno Evening Gazette*, November 9, 1932; "Ely Planes Drop Supplies to Cave Valley Ranchers," *Reno Evening Gazette*, February 23, 1933; "Ranges in Worst Shape on Record," *Nevada State Journal*, August 25, 1934.

15. Hall, *Preserving the Glory Days*, 111; Fradkin, *Fallout*, 8–9.

16. Form letter to Coal Valley range users, circa January 1961, HCP, 87th Cong., Box 18, Folder 231; E. J. Palmer to Howard Cannon, letter, April 18, 1961, HCP, 87th Cong., Box 18, Folder 231; Lloyd Rooke to Howard Cannon, letter, May 2, 1961, HCP, 87th Cong., Box 18, Folder 233; Howard Cannon to Lloyd Rooke, letter, May 17, 1961, HCP,

87th Cong., Box 18, Folder 233; Lloyd Rooke to Howard Cannon, May 22, 1961, letter, HCP, 87th Cong., Box 18, Folder 233; Howard Cannon to Lloyd Rooke, letter, May 31, 1961, HCP, 87th Cong., Box 18, Folder 233; Lester C. Mathews to Howard Cannon, letter, September 27, 1961, HCP, 87th Cong., Box 18, Folder 231; J. R. Penny to Howard Cannon, letter, October 12, 1961, HCP, 87th Cong., Box 18, Folder 231; Jack Conlon to Lester C. Mathews, letter, October 17, 1961, HCP, 87th Cong., Box 18, Folder 231; GLO records NVN0056333 and NV0056334 (November 1, 1963); Nevada State Water Rights (NSWR) applications 19676 (October 10, 1961) and 19677 (April 18, 1962); NSWR certificate 7247 (January 5, 1970).

17. Department of the Interior Information Service, press release, September 24, 1961, Folder 453, PLFA; Department of the Interior Information Service, press release, December 26, 1961, Folder 472, PLFA; "Claim Backlog of Public Land Pleas Reduced," *Reno Evening Gazette*, December 26, 1961; "Udall Reports Progress in Western Land Freeze," *Salt Lake Tribune*, December 26, 1961; "Land Ban to End," *Salt Lake Tribune*, June 21, 1962; "Public Lands Moratorium to Be Lifted," *Reno Evening Gazette*, June 23, 1962.

18. NSWR application, 14936 (March 23, 1953); GLO record NVN0010843 (September 10, 1956); E. E. Willhoyt to Howard Cannon, letter, February 9, 1961, HCP, 87th Cong., Box 18, Folder 227; Margaret Barber to Stewart L. Udall, letter, March 1, 1961, HCP, 87th Cong., Box 18, Folder 230; Margaret Barber to Howard Cannon, letter, circa April 1961, HCP, 87th Cong., Box 18, Folder 230; E. J. Palmer to Howard Cannon, letter, April 25, 1961, HCP, 87th Cong., Box 18, Folder 230; Howard Cannon to Margaret Barber, May 2, 1961, HCP, 87th Cong., Box 18, Folder 230; E. E. Willhoyt to Bureau of Land Management, letter, February 8, 1962, HCP, 87th Cong., Box 18, Folder 227.

19. Irving Senzel, "New Facts about Our Agricultural Land Laws," *Our Public Lands*, July 1962, 8–11; Bureau of Land Management, "Bureau of Land Management in Nevada," January 1963, HCP, 88th Cong., Box 35, Folder 448.

20. Charles H. Stoddard to Howard Cannon, letter, January 24, 1964, HCP, 88th Cong., Box 18, Folder 202; Stewart L. Udall, "Nevada's Future and Uncle Sam," *Reno Evening Gazette*, February 1, 1964; Stewart L. Udall to Howard Cannon, letter, June 2, 1964, HCP, 88th Cong., Box 18, Folder 204; Department of the Interior Information Service, press release, June 4, 1964, HCP, 88th Cong., Box 18, Folder 204; "Homestead Land Applications Unaffected—Bible," *Reno Evening Gazette*, June 8, 1964; J. R. Penny to Howard Cannon, letter, June 29, 1964, HCP, 88th Cong., Box 18, Folder 202; "Land Entries Win Approval," *Nevada State Journal*, October 21, 1964.

21. Joe Midmore, "Nevada Land Management; Vast and Complex Problem," *Reno Evening Gazette*, May 28, 1964; Howard Cannon to Stewart L. Udall, letter, April 14, 1964, HCP, 88th Cong., Box 17, Folder 201; J. R. Penny to Howard Cannon, letter, May 14, 1964, HCP, 88th Cong., Box 17, Folder 201; Charles H. Stoddard to Alan Bible, letter, June 12, 1964, HCP, 88th Cong., Box 17, Folder 201; Robert E. Wolf to Charles H. Stoddard, report, June 12, 1964, HCP, 88th Cong., Box 17, Folder 201; Charles H. Stoddard to Howard Cannon, letter, June 17, 1965, HCP, 88th Cong., Box 17, Folder 201; Tom Nolan, "Homestead? Better Think Twice before Claiming Your 160 Acres," *Reno Evening Gazette*, June 9, 1966.

22. GLO record NVN0043628 (June 4, 1970); NSWR applications 17174 (August 26, 1959) and 20388 (June 15, 1971); Robert E. Wolf to Charles H. Stoddard, report, June 12, 1964, HCP, 88th Cong., Box 17, Folder 201; "Nevada's Enemy the BLM Hasn't Changed Its Colors," *Las Vegas Review-Journal*, June 24, 1964.

23. Paul Laxalt to Howard W. Cannon, letter, circa 1964, HCP, 90th Cong., Box 18, Folder 303; "Statement of Howard W. Cannon before the Public Lands Subcommittee of the Senate Committee on Interior," circa June 1964, HCP, 88th Cong., Box 29, Folder 339; White Pine County ranchers to Howard Cannon, letter, October 15, 1964, HCP, 89th Cong., Box 27, Folder 263.

24. Joe Midmore, "People Have to Get Along as Best They Can with Outdated Laws," *Reno Evening Gazette*, June 1, 1964; Tom Nolan, "Homestead? Better Think Twice before Claiming Your 160 Acres," *Reno Evening Gazette*, June 9, 1966; J. Nelson, *Summary of Agricultural Potential*; Skillen, *Nation's Largest Landlord*, 106.

25. The Fallinis' postwar water rights include NSWR certificates 3103–3106 (April 9, 1948), 3123 (June 21, 1948), 3253 (April 21, 1949), 3297 (October 28, 1949), 3325 (December 14, 1949), 3383–3386 (January 9, 1950), 3430 (March 22, 1950), 3512 (September 21, 1950), 3521 and 3522 (November 17, 1950), 3536 (November 28, 1950), 3571–3573 (February 5, 1951), 3515 and 3615 (May 1, 1951), 3618–3621 (May 23, 1951), 3659 and 3660 (July 12, 1951), 3696 (September 24, 1951), 3797 (June 24, 1952), 3844 (September 22, 1952), 3902 (November 10, 1952), 3932 (February 25, 1953), 4213 (February 14, 1955), 4624 (December 30, 1957), 4798 and 4800 (September 8, 1958), 5048 (November 23, 1960), 5209 (September 27, 1961), 5506–5508 (September 12, 1963), 5615 and 5616 (September 19, 1963), 5739 (June 24, 1964), 5763 (October 6, 1964), 6872 and 6873 (December 6, 1968), and 6979 (April 10, 1969). The Sharps' water rights at Nyala include NSWR certificates 2207 and 2208 (February 24, 1936), 2842 (January 16, 1945), 3011 (November 25, 1946), 3039 (March 20, 1947), 3429 (March 22, 1950), 4104 (July 21, 1954), 4050 (January 25, 1954), 4254 and 4255 (December 1, 1955), and 4623 (December 30, 1957); NSWR vested water rights Vo2340 and Vo2341 (February 10, 1947), and Vo2353 (September 20, 1948). The Sharps also secured several other water rights, including those once held by the United Cattle and Packing Company. See NSWR certificates 0200, 3085, 3348, 3893, 0261, 2243, 2244, 0048, 2207, 2208, 2373, 3046, 3047, 5836, 0287, 0288, 2220, 0324, 2533, 2841, 4104, 4329, 3011, 5040, 4255, 4254, and 4623 and NSWR vested water rights Vo0736, Vo2203, Vo2248, Vo2340, Vo2341, Vo2353, and Vo2878. Expanded water rights at Blue Eagle Ranch included NSWR certificates 3902 (November 10, 1952), 4162–4166 (January 24, 1955), 4798 (September 8, 1958), 4800 (September 8, 1958), and 5506–5508 (September 12, 1963). McCracken and Howerton, *History of Railroad Valley*, 148–50.

26. Department of the Interior Information Service, press release, December 13, 1961, Folder 453, PLFA; "What Is the National Land Reserve?," *Our Public Lands*, April 1962, 21; Karl Landstrom, remarks at the meeting of the National Advisory Board Council for Public Lands, November 15, 1962, Folder 453, PLFA.

27. Kelso, "Current Issues," 1300–1301; "'Multiple Use,'" *New York Times*, June 27, 1960; Karl S. Landstrom to Robert Sykes, letter, March 29, 1962, Folder 453, PLFA; Karl S. Landstrom to legislative counsel, memorandum, August 3, 1962, Folder 453, PLFA; Multiple-Use Sustained-Yield Act of 1960, Public Law 517, 86th Cong., 2nd sess. (June 12, 1960); Wilderness Act, Public Law 577, 88th Cong., 2nd sess. (September 3, 1964); Skillen, *Nation's Largest Landlord*, 42–43.

28. Emphasis on the term "customary" appears in the original letter. John Marvel to Howard Cannon, letter, March 27, 1963, HCP, 88th Cong., Box 18, Folder 206; Public Lands Council, "The Western Livestock Industry and the Public Lands," 1968, Paul Laxalt Papers (PLP), Box 355, Folder 14.

29. John Kamps, "A Big Batch of Land Bills!," *Reno Evening Gazette*, August 3, 1964; "Bills Promise Federal Land Opening: Bible," *Reno Evening Gazette*, August 22, 1964;

Classification and Multiple Use Act of 1964, U.S. Code, vol. 43, secs. 1411–18 (September 19, 1964); "Bills Bring Horse, Buggy Land Laws into Line," *Reno Evening Gazette*, September 23, 1964; Boyd L. Rasmussen to Howard W. Cannon, letter, November 6, 1967, HCP, 90th Cong., Box 18, Folder 303.

30. Charles H. Stoddard, "What the New Legislation Means to You," *Our Public Lands*, Fall 1964, 4–6; "Public Land Responsibility Defined," *Reno Evening Gazette*, November 21, 1964; Robert H. Woody, "BLM Effect Tantalizing to Land Board Chief," *Salt Lake Tribune*, December 15, 1964.

31. "Statements on Maximum Public Benefits Condensed from Sources in the Department of the Interior," circa 1970, Guidelines for Retention or Disposition of Public Lands, PLFA; Smith, "John Kennedy," 329–62.

32. John A. Carver to Howard W. Cannon, letter, May 14, 1963, HCP, 88th Cong., Box 18, Folder 207; Peter E. Marble to Grant Sawyer, letter, February 23, 1966, Grant Sawyer Papers (GSP), Box 328, Folder 18; "Statement of Nevada State Cattle Association to Public Land Law Review Commission," November 11, 1967, HCP, 90th Cong., Box 18, Folder 303.

33. "Cattlemen Need Stable Policy, Rancher Claims," *Reno Evening Gazette*, February 11, 1965; "U.S. Discretion Asked in Public Land Decisions," *Reno Evening Gazette*, April 13, 1965; Public Lands Council, "The Western Livestock Industry and the Public Lands," 1968, 11–12, PLP, Box 355, Folder 14.

CHAPTER 5

1. George N. Swallow with Shirley G. Robison to Wayne N. Aspinall, letter, August 15, 1962, Howard Cannon Papers (HCP), 86th Cong., Box 34, Folder 535. Robison was Swallow's uncle's brother's son and a game warden.

2. Ibid.

3. Ibid.

4. These three publications, along with Paul R. Ehrlich's *The Population Bomb* (1968), Roderick Nash's *Wilderness and the American Mind* (1967), Barry Commoner's *The Closing Circle: Nature, Man, and Technology* (1971), and Peter Singer's *Animal Liberation* (1975), form the basis for late-twentieth-century environmental thought. Leopold et al., *Wildlife Management*; Department of the Interior Information Service, press release, February 14, 1961, HCP, 87th Cong., Box 18, Folder 228; "Udall Says Public Power 'Necessary Good.' Not Evil," *Ogden Standard-Examiner*, February 15, 1961; Worster, *Nature's Economy*, 284–90, 340–87; Rothman, *Saving the Planet*, 112–20; Smith, "John Kennedy," 329–62.

5. Bernard DeVoto (all citations in Brinkley and Limerick, *Western Paradox*), "The West against Itself" (January 1947), 69–70; "Sacred Cows and Public Lands" (July 1948), 77; "Two-Gun Desmond Is Back" (March 1951), 120–21; "Billion Dollar Jackpot" (February 1953), 130; "To the Traveler's Eye" (1955), 200.

6. Bernard DeVoto, "The West: A Plundered Province" (August 1934), 3–21; Bernard DeVoto, "The West against Itself" (January 1947), 45–73; Webb, "American West," 25–31; also see Webb, *Great Plains*; address by Assistant Secretary of the Interior John A. Carver, Jr., October 13, 1961, HCP, 87th Cong., Box 17, Folder 225; Smith, "John Kennedy," 329–62. The Conference on the History of Western America in 1961 became the Western History Association the following year. This organization represents historians who study the American West.

7. Address by Assistant Secretary of the Interior John A. Carver, Jr., October 13, 1961, HCP, 87th Cong., Box 17, Folder 225.

8. Ibid.

9. Sylvia Porter, "Your Money's Worth," *Reno Evening Gazette*, July 23, 1958; Emerson Chapin, "Satisfactions of an Out-of-Doors Vacation," *New York Times*, May 3, 1959; B. Olson, "Paper Trails," 4.

10. "Public Lands Program Urged at Coast Meet," *Reno Evening Gazette*, March 22, 1955; "Reno Pushes Public Land Development," *Reno Evening Gazette*, March 22, 1955; Clawson and Held, *Federal Lands*, 341; "Forest Plans Are Developed," *Reno Evening Gazette*, February 21, 1958; Sylvia Porter, "Your Money's Worth," *Reno Evening Gazette*, July 23, 1958; Edward Woozley, "Intensified Public Resource Management," *Our Public Lands*, October 1958, 6–7, 14; Conrad L. Wirth, "Conservation: The Future," *New York Times*, October 4, 1959; Runte, *National Parks*, 173–76; Hirt, *Conspiracy of Optimism*, 151–70; Rothman, *Devil's Bargains*, 23–25.

11. House Committee on Interior and Insular Affairs, *Establishment of a National Outdoor Recreation Resources Review Commission: Hearings on HR4819, 3592, 3593, 3594, 3596, 4819, 4822, 5238, 6884, 7230*, 85th Cong., 1st sess. (May 13–14, 1957); Senate Committee on Interior and Insular Affairs, *Outdoor Recreation and Resources Commission: Hearings on S846*, 85th Cong., 1st sess. (May 15, 1957); "Recreation Unit Backed," *New York Times*, January 30, 1958; "Resources Job Goes to L. S. Rockefeller," *New York Times*, September 16, 1958; John C. Devlin, "Mass Recreation Called a Necessity," *New York Times*, March 5, 1959; "25 Named to Advise Recreation Board," *New York Times*, April 6, 1959; "The Recreation Report," *New York Times*, February 2, 1962; Vale, *American Wilderness*, 41–58. The ORRRC also comprised members of the University of Michigan Forestry School, the American Forestry Association, the Weyerhaeuser Lumber Corporation, the Izaak Walton League, the vice president of the Prudential Life Insurance Company, and a former Minnesota conservation commissioner. Later members of the ORRRC included Senator Clinton P. Anderson of New Mexico, Senator Henry C. Dworshak and Representative Gracie Pfost of Idaho, Senator Henry M. Jackson of Washington, Senator Jack Miller and Representative John H. Kyl of Iowa, Representative John P. Saylor of Pennsylvania, and Representative Ralph J. Rivers of Alaska. Of the twenty-five members on the advisory council who were considered ordinary citizens, only one person was from a Great Basin state—Mrs. Harold Christensen of Springville, Utah, just south of Salt Lake City. The majority of the council members were from urban areas on the east coast, Chicago, and Sacramento. Several others were from the Midwest and the South.

12. "Outdoor Recreation Study Offers 40-Year Program," *New York Times*, February 1, 1962; "The Recreation Report," *New York Times*, February 2, 1962; Robert Berkvist, "Playroom for Tomorrow," *New York Times*, February 4, 1962; "Text of Kennedy's Conservation Message Asking an Expanded 8-Year Program," *New York Times*, March 2, 1962; "The Conservation Message," *New York Times*, March 3, 1962; Vale, *American Wilderness*, 41–58.

13. "Lake Lahontan Enjoying Busiest Season in History," *Reno Evening Gazette*, August 9, 1958; "Outdoor Recreation Resources," *Our Public Lands*, April 1962, 22–25; Glenn A. Carpenter, "The U.S. Bureau of Land Management's Role in Resource Management of the Bonneville Salt Flats," in Gwynn, *Great Salt Lake*, 500–501.

14. Peterson, *Pioneering Outdoor Recreation*, 24–31. Outdoor recreation activities increased across the federal domain, mostly in national forests and national parks, but also on the public lands managed by the BLM. Evidence of this increase is anecdotal,

but as one former BLM employee remarked, the public lands were "being found" because of "a greater desire for the out-of-doors experience."

15. Joe Midmore, "Efforts Made to Develop Nevada Land for Citizens," *Reno Evening Gazette*, June 4, 1964; "Lehman Caves in Nevada Established as Monument," *Salt Lake Tribune*, February 1, 1922; Unrau, *Basin and Range*, 329.

16. Richard L. Neuberger, "The West Puts Its Brand on Congress," *New York Times*, February 1, 1959; "Eight Additions Urged to National Parks," *New York Times*, April 29, 1959; "Vast Addition of Park Land Urged," *New York Times*, December 4, 1959; "Parks for the Future," *New York Times*, December 5, 1959; John B. Oakes, "Conservation: Keeping the Score," *New York Times*, January 3, 1960; Leopold et al., *Wildlife Management*, 3.

17. Jack Westeyn, "A Road by Any Other Name Is Still a Route," *New York Times*, June 21, 1959; E. Carr, *Wilderness by Design*; Zinser, *Outdoor Recreation*.

18. "Jarbidge Road Will Be Built," *Ogden Standard-Examiner*, January 9, 1922; "Lehman Caves in Nevada Established as Monument," *Salt Lake Tribune*, February 1, 1922; "Lehman Caves to Be Dedicated August 6," *Nevada State Journal*, July 25, 1922; "New Auto Road across Nevada," *Ogden Standard-Examiner*, August 1, 1922; "More Nevada Parks," *Nevada State Journal*, August 4, 1922; "Lehman Caves Are Public Property," *Nevada State Journal*, August 7, 1922; C. C. Boak, "Lehman Caves—The Wonder-Under-World of Nevada," *Nevada State Journal*, June 22, 1924; "Beauties of Lehman Caves Repay Reno Traveler," September 28, 1924; "Lehman Cave in Nevada to Be Given Publicity," *Salt Lake Tribune*, May 8, 1927; "Fantastic Lehman Caves Now Opened to Motorists," *Salt Lake Tribune*, July 17, 1927; Trexler, *Lehman Caves*, 26–30; Unrau, *Basin and Range*, 178–94, 321–30; Gutfreund, *20th Century Sprawl*, 7–60.

19. C. C. Boak, "Lehman Caves—The Wonder-Under-World of Nevada," *Nevada State Journal*, June 22, 1924; "Beauties of Lehman Caves Repay Reno Traveler," September 28, 1924; "New Finds in Lehman Caves," *Provo Daily Herald*, October 12, 1924; Unrau, *Basin and Range*, 330–76.

20. "New Development of Lehman Caves Sought by White Pine County Business Organizations," *Nevada State Journal*, February 2, 1931; "Lehman Caves Bill Passed," *Reno Evening Gazette*, March 5, 1931; "Lehman Caves Will Be Used as Dude Ranch," *Reno Evening Gazette*, March 23, 1933; "Camp Is Moved to Moapa Site," *Reno Evening Gazette*, October 12, 1933; "Work Continuing on Lehman Caves," *Reno Evening Gazette*, October 17, 1934; "Lehman Caves Work Is Done," *Reno Evening Gazette*, March 8, 1935; "Lehman Highway Survey Is Made," *Reno Evening Gazette*, February 25, 1937; "New Entrance in Lehman Is Opened," *Reno Evening Gazette*, July 28, 1938; Unrau, *Basin and Range*, 330–76.

21. "Lee, Pittman Talk Good Will, Roads at Lehman Caves," *Salt Lake Tribune*, August 15, 1949; "Ely Tourist Travel Gains," *Nevada State Journal*, December 12, 1952; "Famed Lehman Caves Featured in Article," *Nevada State Journal*, April 6, 1952; "Lehman Cave Return Hit by McCarran," *Reno Evening Gazette*, February 16, 1954; "Lehman Caves, Nevada's National Monument, Attracts Wide Notice," *Nevada State Journal*, February 19, 1954; "Lehman Caves Transfer Fight Ends Abruptly," *Reno Evening Gazette*, April 15, 1954; "Mount Wheeler Is Center of Great Primitive Area in Eastern Nevada," *Nevada State Journal*, June 20, 1954; "Lehman Promotion Unit Is Organized," *Reno Evening Gazette*, August 17, 1955; "Young Invites National Park Director to Look at Lehman Caves in White Pine County," *Nevada State Journal*, February 26, 1956; "Park Designation of Caves Fought," *Reno Evening Gazette*, April 5, 1956; "Lehman

Caves-Mount Wheeler Area Survey Scheduled to Decide Park Possibility," *Reno Evening Gazette*, August 13, 1956; Murray M. Moler, "Park Service Studies Lehman Cave Area for National Park Use," *Ogden Standard-Examiner*, October 11, 1956; Unrau, *Basin and Range*, 376–83.

22. "Portion of Nevada Urged as National Park Site," *Nevada State Journal*, June 29, 1958; "National Park Bill Approved," *Reno Evening Gazette*, July 10, 1958; "Great Basin Park Tour Is Conducted," *Nevada State Journal*, July 15, 1958; "National Park Bill Approved," *Reno Evening Gazette*, July 19, 1958; Darwin Lambert, "Great Basin," circa 1958, HCP, 86th Cong., Box 34, Folder 535; "Field Study of Proposed Park Opened," *Nevada State Journal*, October 24, 1958; "Nevada Looks Ahead to Its Own National Park," *Reno Evening Gazette*, January 6, 1959; Darwin Lambert, "Wheeler Area's Qualifications as Park," *Salt Lake Tribune*, May 9, 1959; Darwin Lambert, "Wheeler Peak Park Endorsed," *Nevada State Journal*, May 10, 1959; "Cooperation Assured to Get Parks," *Nevada State Journal*, July 30, 1959; "Sawyer Aid Testifies at Park Hearing," *Reno Evening Gazette*, December 2, 1959; Unrau, *Basin and Range*, 376–83.

23. "Back Wheeler Peak-Lehman Cave Park," *Reno Evening Gazette*, April 29, 1959; "Wheeler Area Expansion Is Scheduled," *Reno Evening Gazette*, April 29, 1959; "Ex-Governors Join Forces," *Reno Evening Gazette*, May 7, 1959; "Nevada Park Foundation in First Meeting," *Nevada State Journal*, June 20, 1959; "Urge Early Action on Ely Area Park," *Nevada State Journal*, June 26, 1959; Ivan Sack to Louis D. Gordon, letter, November 23, 1959, HCP, 86th Cong., Box 34, Folder 536; "Management of the Wheeler Peak Scenic Area," HCP, 89th Cong., Box 29, Folder 283; Unrau, *Basin and Range*, 383–88; Rothman, "'Regular Ding Dong Fight,'" 141–61.

24. True D. Morse to James E. Murray, letter, July 3, 1958, HCP, 86th Cong., Box 34, Folder 536; "Three Named to Foundation," *Reno Evening Gazette*, July 9, 1959; "Wilbur Clark, Las Vegas, Joins Foundation for National Park," *Reno Evening Gazette*, August 27, 1959; "Nevada National Park Bill Introduced in Congress," *Nevada State Journal*, September 11, 1959; "Lehman Caves National Park Bill Offered," *Reno Evening Gazette*, September 12, 1959; "Statement by Ernest J. Palmer, State Supervisor for Nevada, Bureau of Land Management, on Proposed National Park Withdrawal," circa September 1959, HCP, 86th Cong., Box 34, Folder 536; Ivan Sack to Louis D. Gordon, letter, November 23, 1959, HCP, 86th Cong., Box 34, Folder 536; Unrau, *Basin and Range*, 383–88.

25. Jack Goodman, "Another Summit," *New York Times*, December 29, 1959; "Obituary: Jack Goodman," *Deseret News*, June 7, 2003.

26. E. L. Peterson to Kenneth B. Pomeroy, letter, September 3, 1959, HCP, 86th Cong., Box 34, Folder 536; "Park-Forest Feud Has Wide Implications," *Salt Lake Tribune*, December 8, 1959; "Park Hearing Is Underway," *Reno Evening Gazette*, December 5, 1959; "Park-Forest Conflict Moves to Idaho," *Salt Lake Tribune*, February 15, 1960.

27. Emphasis on the term "unimpaired" appears in the original article. John B. Oakes, "Conservation: Fight for Parks," *New York Times*, October 2, 1960.

28. E. W. McElhiney to Howard W. Cannon, letter, November 21, 1959, HCP, 86th Cong., Box 34, Folder 536; "Forester Opposes Nevada Park Plea," *Salt Lake Tribune*, December 6, 1959; "Statement of Floyd Iverson, Regional Forester, Forest Service, U.S. Department of Agriculture, before the Public Lands Subcommittee of the Senate Interior and Insular Affairs Committee at Ely, Nevada, December 5, 7, and 8, on S.2664," circa December 1959, HCP, 86th Cong., Box 34, Folder 536; "Observers Expect Cut in

Park," *Salt Lake Tribune*, December 9, 1959; Roy Torpey to Alan Bible, letter, December 16, 1959, HCP, 86th Cong., Box 34, Folder 53; Jack Goodman, "Another Summit," *New York Times*, December 29, 1959; Unrau, *Basin and Range*, 389–93.

29. Emphasis on the term "sole" appears in the original statement. Robert W. Bernick, "S.L. Concerns Bare Vast Metals Deal," *Salt Lake Tribune*, September 20, 1959; "National Park Value Seen as Both Positive, Negative," *Nevada State Journal*, October 24, 1959; "Resolution by Board of Directors of Nevada Mining Association," November 16, 1959, HCP, 86th Cong., Box 34, Folder 535; Ivan Sack to Louis D. Gordon, letter, November 23, 1959, HCP, 86th Cong., Box 34, Folder 536; John E. Humphrey to Alan Bible, letter, November 23, 1959, HCP, 86th Cong., Box 34, Folder 536; Louis D. Gordon to Alan Bible, December 1, 1959, HCP, 86th Cong., Box 34, Folder 536; Fred B. Harris, "Statement of Fred B. Harris, Secretary of the Nevada State Cattle Association, filed with the Senate Committee holding hearings in Ely, Nevada, December 5, 7, and 8, 1959," HCP, 86th Cong., Box 34, Folder 536; "Mine Group against Park," *Nevada State Journal*, December 6, 1959; "Proposed Park 'Promising' for Mining," *Salt Lake Tribune*, December 8, 1959; "Farm Bureau Set against Eastern Nevada Park," *Reno Evening Gazette*, December 12, 1959; Unrau, *Basin and Range*, 388.

30. Nevada State Water Right (NSWR) vested water right V01026 (February 23, 1911); General Land Office (GLO) record 668067 (February 28, 1919); Robison, *Our Swallow Heritage*, vol. 1, 44–87, vol. 2, 7–8; Read, *White Pine Lang Syne*, 182–83.

31. Robison, *Our Swallow Heritage*, vol. 2, 8–11, 21–23.

32. GLO records 938903 (May 24, 1924), 999993 (April 12, 1927), 1001918 and 1001919 (May 21, 1927), and 1003370 (June 1, 1927); NSWR vested water rights V01970–V02027 (December 19, 1925), V02111–V02125 (October 11, 1927), V02198 (December 17, 1928), V02199 (December 17, 1928), and V02201 (December 17, 1928), NSWR certificate 2410 (August 8, 1929); Robison, *Our Swallow Heritage*, vol. 2, 24–25.

33. "Stockmen Face Heavy Losses as Winter Storms Continue," *Reno Evening Gazette*, January 21, 1949; "Airplanes Start Food Lift to Supply Starving Stock," *Reno Evening Gazette*, January 24, 1949; "Air Force Orders Reinforcements for Nevada's 'Operation Haylift,'" *Reno Evening Gazette*, January 29, 1949; "Haylift Crews Speed Up Tempo of Operations," *Reno Evening Gazette*, February 2, 1949; "Operation Haylift Burns Gasoline to Feed Livestock," *Reno Evening Gazette*, February 5, 1949; "Haylift Helped by Mild Weather," *Reno Evening Gazette*, February 10, 1949; Robison, *Our Swallow Heritage*, vol. 2, 83–84.

34. Joe B. Sanders to Paul H. Pearson, memorandum, August 24, 1953, National Nuclear Security Administration/Nevada Field Office (NNSA/NFO); report on examination of sheep in vicinity of Ely, Nevada, August 1953, NNSA/NFO; John O'Harra to Bernard F. Trum, letter, September 5, 1953, NNSA/NFO; Bernard F. Trum to John L. O'Harra, letter, August 28, 1953, NNSA/NFO; report on examination of sheep, August 31, 1953, NNSA/NFO; "First Nevada Ram Sale Set at Ely Aug. 3–4," *Reno Evening Gazette*, July 17, 1956; "First Ram Sale in White Pine Called Success," *Reno Evening Gazette*, August 11, 1956; "State Park Officers Visit in White Pine," *Reno Evening Gazette*, August 27, 1956; Glenn Spuller, "Outdoor Fun," *Reno Evening Gazette*, October 18, 1957; George N. Swallow to Alan Bible, letter, November 30, 1959, HCP, 86th Cong., Box 34, Folder 536.

35. "Background Told on Work for Nevada National Park," *Nevada State Journal*, May 3, 1959; "National Park at Wheeler Peak Has Top Backers," *Reno Evening Gazette*, May 6, 1959; Darwin Lambert, "Wheeler Peak Park Endorsed," *Nevada State Journal*,

May 10, 1959; "Park Area Feature," *Nevada State Journal*, September 5, 1959; Jack Goodman, "Another Summit," *New York Times*, December 29, 1959.

36. "Silver Strike, Olympiad Feted," *Nevada State Journal*, January 6, 1959; "Color Films Depict Nevada Native Beauty," *Nevada State Journal*, January 6, 1959; "Magazine Features State's Park Drive," *Nevada State Journal*, September 9, 1959; "Statement by N. E. Broadbent, Mayor of Ely, Nevada, Member of the Board of Regents of the University of Nevada for the Establishment of Great Basin National Park," circa December 1959, HCP, 86th Cong., Box 34, Folder 536.

37. "Silver Strike, Olympiad Feted," *Nevada State Journal*, January 6, 1959; "Wheeler Peak Park Boosted," *Nevada State Journal*, April 29, 1959; "National Park at Wheeler Peak Has Top Backers," *Reno Evening Gazette*, May 6, 1959; "National Park in Nevada Viewed as Tourist Magnet," *Nevada State Journal*, May 13, 1959; "Support Park Idea," *Nevada State Journal*, June 14, 1959; "Ely Area Pushes 'Great Basin Park,'" *Salt Lake Tribune*, June 16, 1959; Lyle Reade to Howard W. Cannon, letter, August 31, 1959, HCP, 86th Cong., Box 34, Folder 535; Betty C. Whitehurst to Howard W. Cannon, letter, September 16, 1959, HCP, 86th Cong., Box 34, Folder 535; "National Park Value Seen as Both Positive, Negative," *Nevada State Journal*, October 24, 1959; "State Has a Stake," *Las Vegas Review-Journal*, December 6, 1959; Dan Oxborrow to Howard W. Cannon, letter, December 10, 1959, HCP, 86th Cong., Box 34, Folder 535; Leo L. Curto to Howard W. Cannon, letter, December 10, 1959, HCP, 86th Cong., Box 34, Folder 535; Alan P. Gruer to Howard W. Cannon, letter, April 15, 1960, HCP, 86th Cong., Box 34, Folder 535.

38. "Nevada Looks Ahead to Its Own National Park," *Reno Evening Gazette*, January 6, 1959; "State Board Reaffirms Park Effort," *Nevada State Journal*, March 1, 1959; "State Board Works for First Park," *Reno Evening Gazette*, March 2, 1959; "Outdoor Beat," *Nevada State Journal*, May 3, 1959; "Outdoor Beat," *Nevada State Journal*, May 5, 1959; "National Park in Nevada? Official Hearings Open," *Nevada State Journal*, December 5, 1959; Mrs. Grant Oxborrow to Roy Whiteacre, letter, December 17, 1959, HCP, 86th Cong., Box 34, Folder 535; "Proposed Great Basin National Park Nevada," circa 1959, HCP, 86th Cong., Box 34, Folder 535; Jack Lehman to Howard W. Cannon, letter, February 4, 1960, HCP, 86th Cong., Box 34, Folder 535; "White Pine Region Seeks Official U.S. Designation," *Reno Evening Gazette*, February 13, 1960; "Nevada Plans Park Expansion under New Policy," *Reno Evening Gazette*, June 7, 1961.

39. Hugh A. Shamberger to Grant Sawyer, memorandum, June 25, 1959, Grant Sawyer Papers (GSP), Box 246, Folder 15; Darwin Lambert to Howard W. Cannon, letter, September 19, 1959, HCP, 86th Cong., Box 34, Folder 535; Grant Sawyer to Darwin Lambert, letter, October 28, 1959, GSP, Box 246, Folder 15; "Statement of the Honorable Grant Sawyer, Governor of Nevada, on Hearing before Subcommittee of Senate Interior Committee on S. 2664 regarding Establishment of Great Basin National Park, December 5, 7, and 8, Ely, Nevada," circa 1959, GSP, Box 246, Folder 15. For more information on the "devil's bargains" small towns make when they turn to tourism to boost local economies, see Rothman, *Devil's Bargains*.

40. Office of Alan Bible, press release, May 3, 1961, HCP, 87th Cong., Box 35, Folder 447; George N. Swallow to Howard W. Cannon, letter, May 9, 1961, HCP, 87th Cong., Box 35, Folder 447; Howard W. Cannon to George N. Swallow, letter, May 18, 1961, HCP, 87th Cong., Box 35, Folder 447; "Statement of Howard W. Cannon before the Public Lands Subcommittee of the Senate Committee on Interior and Insular Affairs on S. 1760—Great Basin National Park," August 3, 1961, HCP, 87th Cong., Box 35,

Folder 447; "Parks Future Uncertain," *Salt Lake Tribune*, January 28, 1962; "'No Tie,' Senator Avers, in Park Bill, Speech," *Salt Lake Tribune*, February 9, 1962; Unrau, *Basin and Range*, 393–98; Elliott, *Senator Alan Bible*, 101–104; Vernetti, *Senator Howard Cannon*, 75.

41. "Sportsmen Oppose Park," *Reno Evening Gazette*, June 24, 1961; Vernon E. Scheid to Howard W. Cannon, letter, August 1, 1961, HCP, 87th Cong., Box 35, Folder 447; "Statement of the Secretary of the Interior Stewart L. Udall before the Public Lands Subcommittee of the Senate Interior and Insular Affairs Committee on S. 1760, a Bill to Establish the Great Basin National Park," August 3, 1961, HCP, 87th Cong., Box 35, Folder 447; James D. Williams to Walter S. Baring, letter, July 28, 1962, HCP, 87th Cong., Box 35, Folder 447.

42. Richard C. Sill to William Grant, letter, June 7, 1962, HCP, 87th Cong., Box 35, Folder 447; Carola Hutcherson to Grant Sawyer, letter, December 20, 1963, GSP, Box 301, Folder 26; Richard C. Sill, "Report on Great Basin National Park," April 18, 1966, HCP, 89th Cong., Box 30, Folder 300.

43. "National Park Program Puzzle to Many," *Salt Lake Tribune*, November 24, 1961.

44. "Udall Opposes Proposed Cut in Park Area," *Reno Evening Gazette*, July 16, 1962; "Baring Introduces in House National Park Bill Providing for 51,300 Acres," *Ely Daily Times*, June 25, 1963; M. Burrell Bybee to Stewart L. Udall, letter, August 21, 1963, HCP, 88th Cong., Box 20, Folder 222; Stewart L. Udall to Bruce R. Theissen, letter, October 14, 1963, HCP, 88th Cong., Box 20, Folder 222; "Baring, Udall Views Clash in Park Issue," *Ely Daily Times*, December 9, 1963; Unrau, *Basin and Range*, 397–99.

45. "Great Basin Meet Today; Reduction Plan Possible," *Nevada State Journal*, June 6, 1962; "Great Basin Park's Eventual Boundaries May Be Pared Down," *Nevada State Journal*, June 7, 1962; "Baring Introduces in House National Park Bill Providing for 51,300 Acres," *Ely Daily Times*, June 25, 1963; "Baring, Udall Views Clash in Park Issue," *Ely Daily Times*, December 9, 1963; Unrau, *Basin and Range*, 397–99.

46. General Land Office Record (GLO) 1207591, April 13, 1960; Robison, *Our Swallow Heritage*, vol. 2, 72–79.

47. "Trip to Lure Industry Slated by Nevada Group," *Reno Evening Gazette*, November 1, 1960; "Plan Would Broaden Board Duties," *Reno Evening Gazette*, September 10, 1961.

48. "Ranges Topic for Meeting at Winnemucca," *Reno Evening Gazette*, January 13, 1962; "Range Policy Talks Slated," *Nevada State Journal*, January 14, 1962; Rothman, *Devil's Bargains*, 10.

49. George N. Swallow and Shirley G. Robison to Wayne N. Aspinall, letter, August 15, 1962, HCP, 86th Cong., Box 34, Folder 535; George N. Swallow to Robert Warren, letter, May 19, 1965, HCP, 89th Cong., Box 29, Folder 280; Antonio Omaechevarria to Alan Bible and Howard W. Cannon, letter, June 7, 1965, HCP, 89th Cong., Box 29, Folder 282; Howard W. Cannon to Antonio Omaechevarria, letter, June 11, 1965, HCP, 89th Cong., Box 29, Folder 282.

50. Richard P. Hronck, "Proposed Park 'Promising' for Mining," *Salt Lake Tribune*, December 8, 1959; "Park Site Covers Mining Area," *Salt Lake Tribune*, May 20, 1961; James D. Williams to Walter S. Baring, letter, July 28, 1962, HCP, 87th Cong., Box 35, Folder 447; James D. Williams to Walter S. Baring, January 6, 1966, HCP, 89th Cong., Box 29, Folder 280; "Federation Favors National Scenic Area," *Reno Evening Gazette*, June 14, 1965.

51. Howard W. Cannon to M. Burrell Bybee, letter, August 23, 1963, HCP, 88th Cong., Box 20, Folder 222; "Federal Land Holdings Hurt Nevada's Industrial Drive,"

Reno Evening Gazette, November 12, 1963; John Osborne to Howard W. Cannon, letter, February 23, 1965, HCP, 89th Cong., Box 29, Folder 282; Lee Dearden to Grant Sawyer, letter, May 3, 1965, GSP, Box 314, Folder 6; Stewart L. Udall to Wayne N. Aspinall, letter, May 14, 1965, HCP, 89th Cong., Box 29, Folder 280; "Udall Criticized on Park Move," *Reno Evening Gazette*, June 4, 1965; "Charges Fly from All Directions on Nevada's Park Issue," *Reno Evening Gazette*, June 5, 1965; "Remarks by Robert Warren, Director, Nevada Department of Economic Development, Panel Discussion on Proposed Great Basin National Park," June 12, 1965, GSP, Box 314, Folder 4; Thomas L. Lake to Grant Sawyer, letter, June 18, 1965, GSP, Box 314, Folder 4; Albert A. Stone to Grant Sawyer, letter, June 17, 1965, GSP, Box 314, Folder 4; M. Burrell Bybee to Alan Bible, letter, July 17, 1965, HCP, 89th Cong., Box 29, Folder 283; Walter S. Baring to M. Burrell Bybee, letter, August 6, 1965, HCP, 89th Cong., Box 29, Folder 280; R. E. Llewellyn to Grant Sawyer, letter, August 16, 1965, GSP, Box 314, Folder 2; Walter S. Baring to Alan Bible, letter, August 31, 1965, HCP, 89th Cong., Box 29, Folder 280; "Rep. Baring Blames Udall for Basin Park Stalemate," *Nevada State Journal*, September 8, 1965.

52. Bill Stall, "Charges Fly from All Directions on Park Issue," *Reno Evening Gazette*, June 5, 1965; "Warren: Baring Should Not Withdraw Park Bill," *Reno Evening Gazette*, June 10, 1965; "Bible Calls Basin Park Issue 'Basic,'" *Reno Evening Gazette*, June 18, 1965; "Baring Urges Park Backing," *Nevada State Journal*, August 10, 1965; Walter S. Baring to Alan Bible, letter, August 31, 1965, HCP, 89th Cong., Box 29, Folder 280; "Rep. Baring Blames Udall for Basin Park Stalemate," *Nevada State Journal*, September 8, 1965; Virlis L. Fischer, "Formula for Mediocrity," *American Forests*, January 1966, HCP, 89th Cong., Box 30, Folder 300; Walter S. Baring to Stewart L. Udall, letter, January 24, 1966, HCP, 89th Cong., Box 29, Folder 280; Stewart L. Udall to Walter S. Baring, letter, February 5, 1966, HCP, 89th Cong., Box 29, Folder 280; Charles J. Armstrong to Howard W. Cannon, letter, March 22, 1966, HCP, 89th Cong., Box 30, Folder 300; Alan Bible to Walter S. Baring, letter, March 26, 1966, HCP, 89th Cong., Box 30, Folder 300; Vernon E. Scheid to Howard W. Cannon, letter, April 15, 1966, HCP, 89th Cong., Box 46, Folder 456; Bill Stall, "Here's a Rundown on Park Controversy," *Reno Evening Gazette*, April 18, 1966; Bill Stall, "Great Basin Stalled," *Las Vegas Review-Journal*, April 18, 1966; "Meeting of the Nevada Congressional Delegation to Discuss S. 499 Pertaining to the Proposed Great Basin National Park, Nevada," April 19, 1966, HCP, 89th Cong., Box 30, Folder 300; Vern E. Jeppson to Stewart L. Udall, letter, April 25, 1966, HCP, 89th Cong., Box 30, Folder 300; "Udall Hopes Baring Doesn't Kill Nevada Park Plan," *Reno Evening Gazette*, April 26, 1966; Unrau, *Basin and Range*, 399–403; Elliott, *Senator Alan Bible*, 161–67.

53. Western Historical Studies, Inc., *Canyonlands National Park*, 184–87.

54. "Recreation Should Not Bar Other Uses," *Salt Lake Tribune*, March 9, 1961; "Parks Future Uncertain," *Salt Lake Tribune*, January 28, 1962; "Hearings to Review Canyonlands Bill," *Salt Lake Tribune*, February 8, 1962; "Moss Criticizes Canyonlands Foes," *Salt Lake Tribune*, February 13, 1962; "Canyonlands Urged—But Is It a Park?" *Salt Lake Tribune*, March 3, 1962; "Clyde Sees Support for Smaller Park," *Salt Lake Tribune*, March 9, 1962; "Canyonlands Oil," *Salt Lake Tribune*, March 16, 1962; "Praises Board," *Salt Lake Tribune*, March 18, 1962; "House to Ponder Canyonlands," *Salt Lake Tribune*, May 6, 1962; "Canyonlands Confab Planned," *Salt Lake Tribune*, May 17, 1962; "Broaden Park Use Moss Asks," *Salt Lake Tribune*, June 7, 1962; "Important Milestone for Canyonlands," *Salt Lake Tribune*, August 5, 1964; "Burton Sees Delay on Canyonlands," *Ogden Standard-Examiner*, August 8, 1963; Frank Hewlett, "Hopes Fade

for Utah Park Okeh," *Salt Lake Tribune*, January 12, 1964; "Canyonlands Hearings in Spring, Moss Hears," *Salt Lake Tribune*, February 11, 1964; "South Utahns 'Approve' Park Plans," *Salt Lake Tribune*, June 21, 1964; "Utah's Feud to End on Canyonlands," *Ogden Standard-Examiner*, June 30, 1964; "Canyonlands Bill Wins House OK," *Ogden Standard-Examiner*, August 20, 1964; "Utah Vitally Affected by New Programs," *Salt Lake Tribune*, August 21, 1964; Frank Hewlett, "Economic Benefits Roll into S. Utah," *Salt Lake Tribune*, August 23, 1964; "Canyonlands Moves to Joint Parley," *Salt Lake Tribune*, September 2, 1964; Frank Hewlett, "Canyonland Park Bill Passes Test," *Salt Lake Tribune*, September 3, 1964; "Utah's Third Park," *Salt Lake Tribune*, September 5, 1964; "Udall Applauds Beauty of Utah Canyonlands," *Salt Lake Tribune*, September 5, 1964; "Benefits of Tourism Noted by State Bureau," *Provo Daily Herald*, November 10, 1964; Abbey, *Desert Solitaire*; Western Historical Studies, Inc., "Canyonlands National Park," 184–87.

55. Harvey, *Wilderness Forever*, 226–44; Cecil Garland, interview by the author, July 20, 2006, Nevada Test Site Oral History Project (NTSOHP); Dant, "Making Wilderness Work," 237–72.

56. Harvey, *Wilderness Forever*, 226–44; Cecil Garland, interview by the author, July 20, 2006, NTSOHP; Dant, "Making Wilderness Work," 237–72; Skillen, *Nation's Largest Landlord*, 48–49; Peterson, *Pioneering Outdoor Recreation*, 47.

57. "Assembly Joint Resolution 11," *Statutes of the State of Nevada* (Carson City, Nev.: State Printing Office, 1958), 938; "Wilderness Bill under Attack by Reno Man," *Reno Evening Gazette*, September 17, 1959; Nevada Mining Association to Howard W. Cannon, letter, March 12, 1963, HCP, 88th Cong., Box 29, Folder 323; "Nevada's Only Wilderness Area near Jarbidge, Part of Picturesque, Interesting Vacation Land," *Nevada State Journal*, January 29, 1964.

58. Weatherly, "Transforming Space into Place," 8; Kirk, *Counterculture Green*, 137–39.

59. Norma Cox, interview by the author, April 27, 2010, Las Vegas Wash Project Oral History Program at the Southern Nevada Water Authority, Las Vegas, Nev.; "Red Rock Canyon Recreation Lands," *Our Public Lands*, Winter 1968, 12–13; Watkins and Watson, *Lands No One Knows*; Weatherly, "Transforming Space into Place."

60. Swallow Ranches, Inc., v. Leonard Bidart and Bidart Brothers, 525 F.2d 995; Robison, *Our Swallow Heritage*, vol. 2, 79; Elliott, *Senator Alan Bible*, 167.

61. Other terms for the machines include all-terrain vehicles and off-highway vehicles. Arthur E. Tower, "Desert Rallies," *Our Public Lands*, Spring 1969, 5–7; Walter Troy Spencer, "Dune Buggies: We're Even Sending One to the Moon," *New York Times*, July 11, 1971; "Executive Order 11644 on Use of Off-Road Vehicles on the Public Lands," *Federal Register* 37 (February 8, 1972); Darlington, *Mojave*, 234–39.

62. Norman Hall to Mike O'Callaghan, memorandum, June 30, 1972, Donal "Mike" O'Callaghan Papers (MOP), Box 570, Folder 22; Mike O'Callaghan to Rogers C. B. Morton, letter, July 3, 1972, MOP, Box 570, Folder 22; J. M. Reynolds to Rogers C. B. Morton, letter, July 5, 1972, MOP, Box 570, Folder 22.

63. Norman Hall to Mike O'Callaghan, memorandum, June 30, 1972, MOP, Box 570, Folder 22; Edgar I. Rowland to Mike O'Callaghan, letter, July 6, 1972, MOP, Box 570, Folder 22; Norman Hall to Mike O'Callaghan, memorandum, January 22, 1973, MOP, Box 584, Folder 9; Edgar I. Rowland to Elmo J. DeRicco, letter, April 22, 1974, MOP, Box 623, Folder 29; Webb and Wilshire, *Environmental Effects of Off-Road Vehicles*, 409–10.

64. Helen Fallini, interview by Robert McCracken, October 25–26, 1987, Nye County Town History Project (NCTHP); Lina Sharp, interview by Robert D. Mc-Cracken, August 14, 1992, NCTHP; Gracian Uhalde, interview by the author, December 1, 2006, NTSOHP; Webb and Wilshire, *Environmental Effects of Off-Road Vehicles*, 403–408.

Chapter 6

1. "Lion Hunting Couple Kills Large Cats," *Reno Evening Gazette*, July 7, 1949; "Snap Palmer, Official Lion Hunter Has One of Nevada's Biggest Jobs," *Nevada State Journal*, January 22, 1950; "Reno Men Bag Mountain Lions in White Pine County Junket," *Nevada State Journal*, April 25, 1951; "Mountain Lion," Nevada Department of Wildlife, http://www.ndow.org/Species/Furbearer/Mountain_Lion/.

2. Denhardt, "Role of the Horse," 13–22; Wyman, *Wild Horse of the West*, 47–88, 91–109; Dobie, *Mustangs*, 33–58; Young and Sparks, *Cattle in the Cold Desert*, 216–32; White, "*It's Your Misfortune and None of My Own*," 18–26; Clutton-Brock, *Horse Power*, 141–48; S. Olson, *Horses through Time*, 99–100; Flores, *Horizontal Yellow*, 97–100; Clark, *They Sang for Horses*; Her Many Horses and Horse Capture, *Song for the Horse Nation*; Hamalainen, *Comanche Empire*. There is currently no archaeological evidence that an *Equus* population of any kind has been continuously maintained in the Americas.

3. Henry C. Brisch, "On the Wild Horses of the Far South-West," *American Turf Register and Sporting Magazine*, May 1834, 463–64; James B. Bailey, "The Wild Horses of America," *Forest and Stream*, May 25, 1876; "Western Range Horses," *Massachusetts Ploughman and New England Journal of Agriculture*, June 30, 1900; Young and Sparks, *Cattle in the Cold Desert*, 216–32; Wyman, *Wild Horse of the West*, 91–109; Denhardt, *Quarter Horses*, 3–6.

4. "Australia Overrun with Wild Horses," *Reno Evening Gazette*, March 4, 1881; "Round About," *Reno Evening Gazette*, June 4, 1881; "War against Wild Horses," *Chicago Daily Tribune*, December 29, 1884; "California Wild Horses," *Los Angeles Times*, May 27, 1890; Honda, "The Last Wild Horse of the Kanab Desert," *Outing*, October 1891, 68–69; "Wild Horses a Pest," *Chicago Daily Tribune*, October 24, 1897; "Wild Horse Bands," *Los Angeles Times*, April 1, 1899; "Extermination of Wild Horses: *San Francisco Chronicle*," *Current Literature*, November 1899; Baker, "Great Southwest," 535–45; "Ranchmen Will Round Up Herd Wild Horses," *Reno Evening Gazette*, July 9, 1903; Symanski, "Contested Realities," 251–69; Coleman, *Vicious*. Known as Brumbies, Australia's wild horses share a similar history. There are, however, important differences in the laws governing the animals' removal, and in the fact that *Equus* was never present on the Australian continent.

5. "A News Item Which Will Astonish Our Stockmen," *Reno Evening Gazette*, February 27, 1888; "Brevities," *Reno Evening Gazette*, April 23, 1888; "The Wild Horses of Nevada," *Daily Nevada State Journal*, December 28, 1890; Nevada Statute 3957, "Stallion Running at Large," February 17, 1893, in Hillyer, *Nevada Compiled Laws 1929*, 1170; "A Good Law," *Weekly Gazette and Stockman*, February 23, 1893; "Nevada Surprises Them All," *Reno Evening Gazette*, September 2, 1893; "The Mustang Nuisance," *Daily Nevada State Journal*, September 11, 1893; "The Wild Horses of Nevada," *New York Times*, November 30, 1894; "Brevities," *Nevada State Journal*, December 9, 1896.

6. "The Legislature," *Weekly Gazette and Stockman*, February 25, 1897; "Legislative Enactments," *Nevada State Journal*, March 16, 1897; "Hunting Wild Horses," *Nevada State Journal*, April 29, 1897; "Illegal Shooting of Wild Horses," *Nevada State Journal*, April 7, 1900; "All around the State," *Nevada State Journal*, October 10, 1901; "Wild Horse Hunt Begins," *Chicago Daily Tribune*, October 11, 1901; "All around the State," *Nevada State Journal*, October 22, 1901; "All around the State," *Nevada State Journal*, February 14, 1902; "All around the State," *Nevada State Journal*, February 22, 1902; "All around the State," *Nevada State Journal*, April 26, 1902; "State News," *Nevada State Journal*, August 19, 1902; "Wild Horses," *Reno Evening Gazette*, August 27, 1902; "Fleet Little Broomtails, Wild Horses of the Breaks," *New York Times*, April 17, 1904; "May Shoot Wild Horses," *Reno Evening Gazette*, January 10, 1906; "Horse Hunter Has Confessed," *Reno Evening Gazette*, January 31, 1906; "Starving Band of Wild Horses," *Reno Evening Gazette*, February 6, 1906; "Will Slaughter Wild Horses," *Reno Evening Gazette*, March 6, 1906; "The Horse," *Massachusetts Ploughman and New England Journal of Agriculture*, June 16, 1906; "Gossip Heard around Town," *Reno Evening Gazette*, July 26, 1906; "To Slaughter Wild Horses," *Reno Evening Gazette*, February 8, 1908; "Capture Many Wild Horses," *Reno Evening Gazette*, July 6, 1909; "Capturing Wild Horses," *Reno Evening Gazette*, August 30, 1909; "Wild Horses Doomed," *Reno Evening Gazette*, March 18, 1911; Nevada Statutes 3958–3961, "Destruction of Wild Horses and Burros," March 13, 1913, in Hillyer, *Nevada Compiled Laws 1929*, 1170–171; "Killing Many Wild Horses," *Reno Evening Gazette*, June 6, 1913.

7. Will C. Barnes, "Wild Horses," *McClure's Magazine*, January 1909, 285–94; Wyman, *Wild Horse of the West*, 219–43; Amaral, *Mustang*, 25–54.

8. Will C. Barnes, "Wild Horses," *McClure's Magazine*, January 1909, 285–94; Wyman, *Wild Horse of the West*, 142–42.

9. Rufus Steele taught writing at the University of Miami, Florida. His most popular work on horses was the posthumously published *Mustangs of the Mesas: A Saga of the Wild Horse*. Rufus Steele, "Trapping Wild Horses in Nevada," *McClure's Magazine*, December 1909, 198–209; Wyman, *Wild Horse of the West*, 237–38; Amaral, *Mustang*, 34–54.

10. Rufus Steele, "Trapping Wild Horses in Nevada," *McClure's Magazine*, December 1909, 198–209; "Capturing Wild Horses," *Reno Evening Gazette*, August 30, 1909.

11. "Nevada Is One of Best States," *Nevada State Journal*, January 19, 1914; "Wild Horses Hurt Ranges of Nevada," *Reno Evening Gazette*, April 16, 1915; "Killing Wild Horses," *Reno Evening Gazette*, June 2, 1915; "Editorial Page," *Reno Evening Gazette*, September 30, 1915.

12. "Roundup Wild Horses on Forest Reserve," *Reno Evening Gazette*, June 10, 1920; "Slay Wild Horses in Newark Valley," *Nevada State Journal*, June 24, 1920; "Hunters Seek Wild Horses for Skins," *Reno Evening Gazette*, August 17, 1920; "Range Menaced by Wild Horses," *Reno Evening Gazette*, November 28, 1923; Will C. Barnes, "The Passing of the Wild Horse," *American Forests* 30 (November 1924): 643–48; "Wild Horses Used for Chicken Feed," *Reno Evening Gazette*, September 23, 1925; "500 Wild Horses to Be Rounded Up near Elko," *Reno Evening Gazette*, February 10, 1926; "Wild Horse Men Kill Tame Ones Is Claimed," *Reno Evening Gazette*, August 19, 1926; "Killing Mustangs," *Nevada State Journal*, September 3, 1926; "Wild West Horses to Furnish Meat for Europe Diners," *Reno Evening Gazette*, September 9, 1926; "Ridding Range of Wild Horses," *Reno Evening Gazette*, December 4, 1926; "Wild Horses Are Destroyed," *Reno Evening Gazette*, February 4, 1927; "Wild Horses," *Salt Lake Tribune*, February 10, 1927;

"To Renew Drive against Wild Horses," *Reno Evening Gazette*, April 1, 1927; "Wild Mustangs Will Be Killed," *Reno Evening Gazette*, July 9, 1927; "Nye Wild Horses to Be Wiped Out," *Reno Evening Gazette*, July 11, 1927; "Mustangs Given Attention by Assembly," *Reno Evening Gazette*, January 30, 1929; "Bootlegging Wild Horses Charged," *Nevada State Journal*, April 6, 1930; "Elko Ranchers Are Rounding Up Horses," *Nevada State Journal*, May 22, 1930; "Oregon's Last Wild Horse Drive Is Held," *Ogden Standard-Examiner*, August 8, 1930; "Hunter Slays 300 Horses on Nevada Ranges," *Reno Evening Gazette*, August 27, 1930; "Oregon Holds Last Drive of Wild Horses," *Salt Lake Tribune*, August 17, 1930; "Cowboys Capture Many Wild Horses," *Nevada State Journal*, September 6, 1930; "Many Watch Wild Horses," *Reno Evening Gazette*, September 8, 1930; "Nevada Horses to Be Canned," *Nevada State Journal*, October 24, 1930; "Desert Horses Sent to Coast," *Reno Evening Gazette*, October 24, 1930; "Wild Mustangs Being Tamed," *Reno Evening Gazette*, October 25, 1930; "Not a Heroic Figure," *Reno Evening Gazette*, April 30, 1931; "Wild Horse Industry Picking Up," *Reno Evening Gazette*, November 17, 1931; "Rounding Up Wild Horses Seems to Be Up to Nevada," *Reno Evening Gazette*, February 2, 1932; "Number of Wild Horses Reduced by Hard Winter," *Nevada State Journal*, June 23, 1932; "Wild Horses Still Form Problem to Farmers of Elko and Humboldt," *Nevada State Journal*, September 4, 1932; "Still Wild Horses," *Reno Evening Gazette*, January 4, 1933; James F. Taggart, "An Elusive Crop," *Los Angeles Times*, August 13, 1933; "Wild Mustangs Disappearing Rapidly from Nevada Ranges Commission Report Shows," *Reno Evening Gazette*, November 15, 1933; "Big Thrills of the Wild Horse Hunt," *Ogden Standard-Examiner*, February 25, 1934.

13. "Wild Horse Died," *Nevada State Journal*, March 11, 1922; "Cayuses Hunted for Their Lives," *Reno Evening Gazette*, March 22, 1924; Owen P. White, "Montana Seals Fate of 400,000 Wild Horses," *New York Times*, June 7, 1925; "Wild Horses," *Los Angeles Times*, March 1, 1926; "The New Range War," *Los Angeles Times*, July 16, 1926; "Wild Horses Rounded Up," *Reno Evening Gazette*, March 28, 1928; "Wild Horses Take Their Last Trail," *New York Times*, September 23, 1928; "Horse Meat on Sale for Use of Oregon Folk," *Reno Evening Gazette*, October 27, 1928; "Slaughtering Wild Horses," *Reno Evening Gazette*, November 2, 1928; "Cowboys Are Riding after Wild Horses," *Nevada State Journal*, May 20, 1930; "Arkansas Again Competes," *Reno Evening Gazette*, February 9, 1932; "Burro Meat Good Says Hunter of Horses," *Reno Evening Gazette*, March 5, 1932; "Oregon's Last Wild Horse Drive Is Held," *Ogden Standard-Examiner*, August 8, 1930; "Wild Mustangs Disappearing Rapidly from Nevada Ranges Commission Report Shows," *Reno Evening Gazette*, November 15, 1933; "Ranges of West Being Cleared of Mustangs," *Reno Evening Gazette*, December 4, 1933; "Wild Horses in Florida," *Reno Evening Gazette*, November 6, 1934; Richard L. Neuberger, "Wild Horses of the West Are Vanishing," *New York Times*, February 10, 1935; "Wild Horses Rounded Up," *Reno Evening Gazette*, December 23, 1935; "Outlaw Horses Cause Problem," *Reno Evening Gazette*, February 21, 1936; "New Snow Hits Eureka Region," *Reno Evening Gazette*, March 11, 1952.

14. "Starving Band of Wild Horses," *Reno Evening Gazette*, February 6, 1906; "Capturing Wild Horses," *Reno Evening Gazette*, August 30, 1909; "Roundup Wild Horses on Forest Reserve," *Reno Evening Gazette*, June 10, 1920; "Killing Mustangs," *Reno Evening Gazette*, September 3, 1926; "U.S. Hunters Kill Mustangs," *Nevada State Journal*, September 2, 1926; "To Renew Drive against Wild Horses," *Reno Evening Gazette*, April 1, 1927; "Twenty-Five Years Ago," *Reno Evening Gazette*, February 8, 1933; "Horses Provide Range Problem in Idaho," *Reno Evening Gazette*, November 17, 1939;

"Use of Game and Wild Horses Suggested by Grazing Service," *Reno Evening Gazette*, March 20, 1943; "Grazing Officer Sets New Goals," *Reno Evening Gazette*, June 5, 1944; "Wild Mustangs Disappearing from Rangelands," *Ogden Standard-Examiner*, May 29, 1945; "Oregon Rancher Rounding Up Mustangs," *Ogden Standard-Examiner*, October 26, 1945; "Wild Horse Herds Said Diminishing," *Reno Evening Gazette*, November 27, 1947; Robert M. Hyatt, "Vanishing Horses," *Salt Lake Tribune*, March 4, 1951; Mc-Knight, "Feral Horse," 506–25; Wolfe, "Wild Horse and Burro Issue," 179–92.

15. Rufus Steele, "Trapping Wild Horses in Nevada," *McClure's Magazine*, December 1909, 198–209.

16. Paris, *Beltran*, 37–54, 63–67, 87–88, 108–109; Gracian N. Uhalde, interview by the author, December 1, 2006, Nevada Test Site Oral History Project (NTSOHP).

17. The Paris family's water rights include Nevada State Water Right (NSWR) certificates 14550 (May 21, 1911), 30 (June 25, 1912), 119–120 (May 14, 1913), 549–550 (March 15, 1921), 838 (October 30, 1923), 1708–1710 (June 8, 1931), 1711–1717 (June 12, 1931), 1822 (June 16, 1932), 2071 (April 4, 1934), 2471 and 2472 (June 21, 1939), 4503 (March 26, 1957); NSWR vested water rights V01508–V01510 (May 7, 1917). Their land records include General Land Office (GLO) records 1024072 and 1024073 (February 20, 1929). The Uhalde family's water rights include NSWR certificates 392 (December 16, 1918), 529 and 530 (March 10, 1921), 546 (March 15, 1921), 578, 610–617 (February 8, 1922), 734 and 785 (August 31, 1923), 904, 906, 907, and 909 (December 11, 1923), 930 (December 21, 1923), 941–944 (December 26, 1923), 1000 (March 3, 1924), 1019 (March 31, 1924), 1026 (April 4, 1924), 1047 and 1048 (August 14, 1924), 1061 (September 24, 1925), 1208 (September 10, 1926), 1254–1258 (October 18, 1926), 1355 (April 13, 1928), 1450 and 1451 (September 29, 1928), 1516 and 1517 (February 21, 1929), 1544 and 1545 (March 6, 1929), 1553 (March 21, 1929), 1567 (April 8, 1929), 1698 (June 1, 1931), 1810 (April 27, 1932), 1920 (February 18, 1933), 1953, 1959, and 1960 (May 10, 1933), 2234 (March 24, 1936), 2329 and 2330 (March 9, 1937), 4454 and 4456 (October 23, 1956), 4871 (March 3, 1959), 6129 (January 18, 1967), and 7177 (October 10, 1969); NSWR vested water rights V00794, V00795, V00800, V01035, V01139–V01141, V01143–V01145 (October 26, 1912), V01152 and V01153 (July 22, 1912), V01266 (November 12, 1913), V01539–V01541 (January 22, 1918), V01542–V01544 (February 18, 1918), V01636 (September 6, 1919), V01804 and V01805 (October 9, 1922), and V01947 and V01848 (May 15, 1924). Their land records include GLO records 0589376 (June 26, 1917), 1220440 (June 13, 1961), and 1221568 (July 28, 1961). Sawyer, *Nevada Nomads*, 81–83, 87–99; Totoricaguena, *Identity, Culture, and Politics*, 63–68, 70–72.

18. Gracian N. Uhalde, interview by the author, December 1, 2006, NTSOHP, 29–33; "Nevada Trio Busy Roping Wild Horses," *Salt Lake Tribune*, August 12, 1935; Morin, *Honest Horses*, 129–34, 207–11.

19. "To Spend $40,000 on Roundup and Night Show," *Reno Evening Gazette*, June 11, 1919; Rollins, *Cowboy*, 287–317; "Winnemucca Opens Big Rodeo Today," *Nevada State Journal*, September 3, 1932; "Baker's Stampede Postponed a Week Due to Storm," *Nevada State Journal*, November 3, 1936; "Little-Known Industry of Nye County Results in Income for Ranchers," *Nevada State Journal*, December 8, 1939; "Pyramid Mission Given Approval," *Reno Evening Gazette*, June 9, 1949; "The Iron Mustanger," *Reno Evening Gazette*, July 13, 1954; Westermeier, *Man, Beast, Dust*, 165–68, 189–90; Morin, *Honest Horses*, 87–91, 101–109.

20. Arthur Chapman, "How a Cowboy-Aviator Hunts Wild Horses," *Popular Science Monthly*, November 1925, 16–17, 163–65.

21. "Plane Is Used to Round Up Horses," *Reno Evening Gazette*, August 12, 1930; "An Aerial Cowgirl Who Is Fighting the Wild Horse Menace," *Ogden Standard-Examiner*, December 11, 1932; "'The Plainsman' with Hosses, Is Week's Topliner," *Nevada State Journal*, January 16, 1937; "An Aerial Cowboy Herds Wild Horses," *Life*, July 4, 1938, 2–3; "Wild Horse Run Planned at Pyramid," *Reno Evening Gazette*, September 22, 1938; "CCC Youths Work on Range Program," *Nevada State Journal*, June 19, 1940; "County Sets Seasons for Hunting," *Reno Evening Gazette*, August 1941; "Horse Roundup by Plane," *Nevada State Journal*, October 17, 1944; "Plane Is Used on Wild Horses," *Reno Evening Gazette*, October 18, 1944; "Airplane to Help Cowboys Round Up Wild Horses," *Salt Lake Tribune*, April 21, 1946; "Reno Man Dies in Plane Crash during Roundup," *Reno Evening Gazette*, June 24, 1952.

22. James F. Taggart, "An Elusive Crop," *Los Angeles Times*, August 13, 1933; "Food Cannery Proposed Here," *Nevada State Journal*, February 6, 1934; "The Burro's Ultimate Fate," *Reno Evening Gazette*, April 11, 1934; "Button and Gorham Operations in Midas Area Recalled," *Reno Evening Gazette*, March 29, 1938; "Animals: Wild Horse Round-Up," *Time*, February 20, 1939; "Pampered Pets," *Reno Evening Gazette*, June 1, 1939; "Little-Known Industry of Nye County Results in Income for Ranchers," *Nevada State Journal*, December 8, 1939; Margaret Gates, "A Brief History of Commercial Pet Food," Feline Nutrition Foundation, September 28, 2009, http://feline-nutrition.org /features/a-brief-history-of-commercial-pet-food; De Steiguer, *Wild Horses of the West*, 140–41.

23. "Animals: Wild Horse Round-Up," *Time*, February 20, 1939; "Pampered Pets," *Reno Evening Gazette*, June 1, 1939; "Little-Known Industry of Nye County Results in Income for Ranchers," *Nevada State Journal*, December 8, 1939; McKnight, "Feral Horse," 506–25; Wolfe, "Wild Horse and Burro Issue," 179–92.

24. "Wild Mustangs Disappearing Rapidly from Nevada Ranges Commission Report Shows," *Reno Evening Gazette*, November 15, 1933; "Ranges of West Being Cleared of Mustangs," *Reno Evening Gazette*, December 4, 1933; "Deer Show Gain Despite Year of Drought," *Reno Evening Gazette*, January 10, 1935; "Heading for the Last Roundup," *Ogden Standard-Examiner*, July 12, 1936; "Past and Present," *Nevada State Journal*, August 20, 1939; "Forest Game Report Made," *Reno Evening Gazette*, January 27, 1940; "Horse Continues to Hold Place in War," *Reno Evening Gazette*, February 16, 1940; "Cattlemen Hold Meeting in Ely," *Reno Evening Gazette*, April 9, 1940; "Nevada Farm Ramblings," *Nevada State Journal*, September 11, 1940; "Wild Horses Decrease," *Nevada State Journal*, December 11, 1940; "Moorman to Head Livestock Men in Ely Area," *Reno Evening Gazette*, March 31, 1941; "Nevada Sheepmen Elect Officers at Ely Meet," *Reno Evening Gazette*, April 4, 1941; "T-Bone Steaks and Roasts from Nevada Horses Popular," *Reno Evening Gazette*, March 30, 1943; "New Attractions Are Planned for July 4 at Gabbs Valley," *Nevada State Journal*, July 2, 1943; "Grazing Lands Taken for Army," *Reno Evening Gazette*, December 30, 1943; "To Clear Range of Wild Horses," *Reno Evening Gazette*, May 8, 1944; "Wild Horses Rounded Up," *Reno Evening Gazette*, May 23, 1944; "Wild Horses Left Free to Roam Oregon Range," *Reno Evening Gazette*, May 27, 1944; "Mustangs Foil Round-Up," *New York Times*, May 28, 1944; "Wild Horse Roundup," *Nevada State Journal*, November 1, 1944; "Wild Horse Herds Said Diminishing," *Reno Evening Gazette*, November 27, 1947; "Horse Population Declines in West," *Reno Evening Gazette*, December 12, 1949.

25. "Oregon Rancher Rounding Up Mustangs," *Ogden Standard-Examiner*, October 26, 1945; "Horse Meat," *Nevada State Journal*, February 24, 1946; "Big Game Group

Suggests 4 Week Antelope Season," *Reno Evening Gazette*, April 5, 1946; "Horse Meat from Nevada May Be Used to Help Feed Famished Europeans," *Nevada State Journal*, April 16, 1946; "Oregon Sets Roundup for Spring," *Salt Lake Tribune*, May 19, 1946; "Wild Horses on Nevada to Be Slaughtered, Canned to Feed Hungry Europeans," *Nevada State Journal*, June 22, 1946; "Horseman Visits in White Pine," *Reno Evening Gazette*, March 6, 1947; "Wild Horses of West Facing 'Last Roundup,'" *New York Times*, April 18, 1947; "Planes Used with Success as Wild Horses Corralled in Nevada Hills," *Nevada State Journal*, July 15, 1947; "Range Mustangs to be Gathered," *Nevada State Journal*, September 30, 1947; "Five Mustang Wranglers Named," *Reno Evening Gazette*, September 29, 1947; "Idaho Cattlemen Offer to Round Up 4,000 Wild Horses," *Nevada State Journal*, June 4, 1948; "Austria: Canned Cayuse," *Time*, September 6, 1948; "Flying Cowboys Join Round-Up of Wild Horses," *Nevada State Journal*, October 7, 1949; "Horse Population Declines in West," *Reno Evening Gazette*, December 12, 1949; John Brosnan, "Wild Horse Hunt," *Salt Lake Tribune*, April 29, 1951.

26. "Killing Mustangs," *Reno Evening Gazette*, September 3, 1926; "Slaughtering Wild Horses," *Reno Evening Gazette*, November 2, 1928; "Mustangs Given Attention by Assembly," *Reno Evening Gazette*, January 30, 1929; "War Declared on Wild Horse Touches Heart," *Salt Lake Tribune*, February 13, 1927; "Many Seek Jobs Hunting Horses," *Reno Evening Gazette*, April 4, 1931; "Airplane Hunting of Wild Horses Brings Complaint," *Reno Evening Gazette*, April 24, 1947.

27. "Social Notes," *New York Times*, October 15, 1922; Burnett, *Cowboy Never Lies*, 188–208; "Gored by a Steer during Rodeo Stunt," *New York Times*, November 6, 1922; "S.P.C.A. Forbids Steer Wrestling," *New York Times*, November 3, 1922; "Cowboys Do Tricks in Rodeo at Garden: Fancy Riding, Calf Roping and Steer Wrestling with Steers Thrill Spectators," *New York Times*, November 5, 1922; "Protests Rodeo at Fair," *New York Times*, July 18, 1923; "New Fight on Rodeo Act," *New York Times*, November 9, 1922; "Magistrate Sees Steer's Horns Twisted: Watches Rodeo to Determine Whether the Throwing Process Is Cruel or Not," *New York Times*, November 12, 1922; "Cowboy and Girl Injured at Rodeo," *New York Times*, October 20, 1924; "Judge Upholds Sunday Rodeo," *Los Angeles Times*, October 21, 1924; "Wild Horses of West Facing 'Last Roundup,'" *Los Angeles Times*, April 18, 1947; Gladwin Hill, "Report from the Nation: Pacific Coast," *New York Times*, April 27, 1947.

28. Lura Tularski, "Saddle Chatter," *Nevada State Journal*, November 26, 1952; Lura Tularski, "Saddle Chatter," *Nevada State Journal*, April 11, 1954.

29. "Concern over the Wild Horses," *Reno Evening Gazette*, August 30, 1950; Robert M. Hyatt, "Vanishing Horses," *Salt Lake Tribune*, March 4, 1951; Isenberg, *Destruction of the Bison*; Punke, *Last Stand*.

CHAPTER 7

1. Bureau of Land Management, press release, April 15, 1975, Tina Nappe Papers (TNP), 90–34, Box 1, Folder 3; Brendan Riley, "Wild Horses Stampede to Freedom in Nevada Desert," *Nevada State Journal*, August 7, 1975; Brendan Riley, "Nevada Misfits Driven Back into Sage by Government Squabble," *Reno Evening Gazette*, August 7, 1975; Nancy F. Green and Howard D. Green, "The Wild Horse Population of Stone Cabin Valley, Nevada: A Preliminary Report," Summer 1975, TNP, 90–34, Box 1, Folder 13.

2. Brendan Riley, "Wild Horses Stampede to Freedom in Nevada Desert," *Nevada State Journal*, August 7, 1975; Brendan Riley, "Nevada Misfits Driven Back into Sage by Government Squabble," *Reno Evening Gazette*, August 7, 1975.

3. Wild Free-Roaming Horses and Burros Act of 1971, Public Law 195, 92nd Cong., 1st sess. (December 15, 1971); Brendan Riley, "Wild Horses Stampede to Freedom in Nevada Desert," *Nevada State Journal*, August 7, 1975; Brendan Riley, "Nevada Misfits Driven Back into Sage by Government Squabble," *Reno Evening Gazette*, August 7, 1975.

4. Nevada State Water Rights (NSWR) vested water rights V02552 (July 8, 1966) and V02559 (July 8, 1966); "Indian Stops a Big Mining Deal," *Reno Evening Gazette*, February 14, 1906; "Mining Pioneer Is Called by Death," *Nevada State Journal*, April 16, 1916; "Cattle Killing Charged for Waif," *Reno Evening Gazette*, October 25, 1921; "Rumors of Strike Cause Stampede to Stone Cabin," *Reno Evening Gazette*, November 5, 1929; "Treasure Hunt Is Organized at Manhattan to Comb Hills for Strike Made by Clifford," *Reno Evening Gazette*, March 14, 1934; Guy Rocha, "Myth #119: Nevada's Oldest Family-Owned, Working Ranches and Farms," Nevada State Library and Archives, http://nsla.nv.gov/Myth_119/. John Peavine and his wife, Jennie (Minnie), American Indians who worked for the Cliffords, filed suit against the family in 1906 for their failure to pay the agreed-upon sum for locating the Clifford mine. The Cliffords had reportedly required the Peavines to keep quiet about their work locating the rich ore vein, advising them to refrain from showing their written agreement to anyone, especially a lawyer. Just a little more than a decade prior, the Cliffords had adopted an American Indian child they named Cooney, who had appeared on their doorstep in a snowstorm during the early 1890s. Cooney Clifford married a Western Shoshone woman and established his own ranch nearby. However, even bearing the Cliffords' last name, Cooney was not allowed success. In the early 1920s, he was arrested and arraigned for stealing cattle by a neighboring ranch operation.

5. "Rumor of Strike at Ellendale," *Nevada State Journal*, April 10, 1910; "Families Are Tied with Triple Bond," *Reno Evening Gazette*, April 14, 1915; "Range Depletion Causes Stock Sale," *Reno Evening Gazette*, July 9, 1927; Senate Committee on Interior and Insular Affairs, *Administration and Use of Public Lands: Hearings on S. 241*, 79th Cong., 1st sess. (May 23–25, 1945), 5030–31; Chuck Yeager and Leo Janos, *Yeager: An Autobiography* (New York: Bantam, 1985), 16–17; "Storm Does Heavy Damage to Crops Stone Cabin Ranch," *Tonopah Times-Bonanza*, August 10, 1945; "Stockmen Oppose Federal Control," *Reno Evening Gazette*, September 16, 1947; "Hearing Attended by Army Officials," *Nevada State Journal*, February 12, 1948; "Central Nevada Stockmen Elect," *Nevada State Journal*, January 17, 1950.

6. "Central Nevada Stockmen Elect," *Nevada State Journal*, January 17, 1950; Bill Martin, "Long Awaited Nevada Wild Horse Roundup Under Way," *Nevada State Journal*, July 27, 1975; Brendan Riley, "Government Frees Captured Wild Horses," *Reno Evening Gazette*, August 6, 1975; DeSilvia, *Extended Community*, 402–403; Guy Rocha, "Myth #119: Nevada's Oldest Family-Owned, Working Ranches and Farms" Nevada State Library and Archives, http://nsla.nv.gov/Myth_119/.

7. Wyman, *Wild Horse of the West*, 138; Agriculture Division, *United States Census of Agriculture*, vol. 2 (1954), 417, 420, 422, 431; McKnight, "Feral Horse," 519; Fraser, *History of Toys*, 226–27, 230; William Boddy, "'Sixty Million Viewers Can't Be Wrong': The Rise and Fall of the Television Western," in Buscombe and Pearson, *Back in the Saddle Again*, 119–40; "Company History," Breyer Animal Creations, http://www.breyerhorses.com/. The Census of Agriculture did not differentiate between horses

used for work on an agricultural farm and those bred for working cattle or running at a racetrack. It therefore provides a fairly reasonable picture of the growth and decline of horse ownership in the country. As the number of real horses declined, popular westerns on television such as *Hopalong Cassidy, The Lone Ranger, The Cisco Kid*, and the Gene Autry and Roy Rogers shows drew thousands of fans from the ranks of children who wanted to play "cowboy." Filling the role of a fantasy horse, model toy horses launched a whole new market for equines.

8. Cruise and Griffiths, *Wild Horse Annie*, 42–52; Kania, *Wild Horse Annie*, 7–9.

9. Cruise and Griffiths, *Wild Horse Annie*, 42–52; Dobie, *Mustangs*; Wyman, *Wild Horse of the West*; Vesta, "Review," 287–88; Beckwith, "Review," 460–61.

10. "Battle Rages over Protection of Wild Horses," *Reno Evening Gazette*, June 10, 1952; "Storey Issues Order Banning Horse Chases," *Reno Evening Gazette*, June 17, 1952; Kania, *Wild Horse Annie*, 25–29.

11. "Wild Horse Roundup by Air Scored," *Nevada State Journal*, February 24, 1953; "Ban on Horse Drives Proposed," *Reno Evening Gazette*, February 24, 1953; "Wild Horses Taken in Wells Roundup," *Nevada State Journal*, October 20, 1953; Tommy Thompson, "Saddle Chatter," *Nevada State Journal*, April 25, 1954; "About Wild Horses," *Reno Evening Gazette*, March 5, 1955; "Wild Horse Bill Passed," *Reno Evening Gazette*, March 8, 1955; Tommy Thompson, "Saddle Chatter," *Nevada State Journal*, March 20, 1955; Lura Tularski, "Saddle Chatter," *Nevada State Journal*, October 23, 1955; Nevada State Legislature, *Journal of the Assembly of the Forty-Seventh Session of the Legislature of the State of Nevada* (Carson City, Nev.: State Printing Office, 1955), 403–404, 424, 430, 449, 453, 498; Nevada State Legislature, *Journal of the Senate of the Forty-Seventh Session of the Legislature of the State of Nevada* (Carson City, Nev.: State Printing Office, 1955), xx, 136, 235, 236, 268; Cruise and Griffiths, *Wild Horse Annie*, 71–79, 85–88.

12. "Saddle Chatter," *Nevada State Journal*, October 23, 1955; Lura Tularski, "Saddle Chatter," *Nevada State Journal*, October 30, 1955; "Horse Trapping Bill Opposed by Two Groups," *Nevada State Journal*, March 15, 1957; "Horse Killers," *Nevada State Journal*, April 20, 1957; Velma B. Johnston to Robert O'Brien, letter, April 11, 1957, Velma Johnston Papers (VJP), Box 1, Folder 1; Lura Tularski, Velma B. Johnston to Robert O'Brien, letter, August 11, 1957, VJP, Box 1, Folder 1; Velma B. Johnston to Eugene Grunby, letter, December 26, 1957, VJP, Box 1, Folder 1; "Saddle Chatter," *Nevada State Journal*, December 10, 1957; "National Recognition for Nevada Woman," *Nevada State Journal*, December 29, 1957; Lura Tularski, "Saddle Chatter," *Nevada State Journal*, December 21, 1958; "Mustang Matter Up for Hearing," *Nevada State Journal*, December 30, 1958; Cruise and Griffiths, *Wild Horse Annie*, 71–79, 85–88.

13. Seth S. King, "Wild West Scenes Return in Dakota," *New York Times*, May 3, 1954; "To Protect Wild Horses," *New York Times*, May 27, 1955; Alvin S. Trivelpiece, "Desert Wild Horses Face Extinction by Hunters," *Sacramento (Calif.) Bee*, February 21, 1957; "Humane Society Fights Air Slaughter of Horses," *Las Vegas (Nev.) Sun*, March 13, 1957; "Horse Trapping Bill Opposed by Two Groups," *Nevada State Journal*, March 15, 1957; Lura Tularski, "Saddle Chatter," *Nevada State Journal*, March 24, 1957; Velma B. Johnston to Douglas S. Kennedy, letter, April 10, 1957, VJP, Box 1, Folder 1; Velma B. Johnston to Charles N. Barnard, letter, April 30, 1957, VJP, Box 1, Folder 1; Lura Tularski, "Saddle Chatter," *Nevada State Journal*, December 10, 1957; "National Recognition for Nevada Woman," *Nevada State Journal*, December 29, 1957; National Wildlife Federation to Velma B. Johnston, letter, February 19, 1958, Howard Cannon Papers (HCP), 86th Cong., Box 34, Folder 529; Velma B. Johnston, "Mustang

Exploitation," February 28, 1958, HCP, 86th Cong., Box 34, Folder 529; "The Mustang's Last Stand," *True, The Man's Magazine*, June 1958; Cruise and Griffiths, *Wild Horse Annie*, 81–83, 118–19; Carr Childers, "Leisl Carr Childers," 606–11. Velma Johnston had approached the editor of *True, The Man's Magazine* with the concept of the article using Gus Bundy's photographs in April 1957. She hoped to garner national attention for her cause, as had the first piece on the subject in the *Sacramento Bee*.

14. Velma B. Johnston to Douglas S. Kennedy, letter, April 10, 1957, VJP, Box 1, Folder 1; Velma B. Johnston to Charles N. Barnard, letter, April 30, 1957, VJP, Box 1, Folder 1; Lura Tularski, "Saddle Chatter," *Nevada State Journal*, May 25, 1958; Humane Society of the United States to Velma B. Johnston, letter, September 8, 1958, HCP, 86th Cong., Box 34, Folder 529; Massachusetts Society for the Prevention of Cruelty to Animals to Velma B. Johnston, letter, September 25, 1958, HCP, 86th Cong., Box 34, Folder 529; American Humane Association to Velma B. Johnston, letter, November 11, 1958, HCP, 86th Cong., Box 34, Folder 529; Velma B. Johnston to Edward "Tex" Gladding, letter, February 7, 1959, VJP, Box 1, Folder 4; Harold Walter, "Wild Horses West," *Sierra*, July 1959, 10–14; "Animals: Wild Horse Annie," *Time*, July 27, 1959; McKnight, "Feral Horse," 506–25; Cruise and Griffiths, *Wild Horse Annie*, 119–24; Carr Childers, "Leisl Carr Childers," 612–13. Johnston and Bundy developed a tense relationship over the use of his photographs; Johnston failed to credit Bundy and obtain his permission for many of her uses of his images.

15. Velma B. Johnston to Robert O'Brien, letter, August 11, 1957, VJP, Box 1, Folder 1; Velma B. Johnston to Walter S. Baring, letter, December 11, 1957, VJP, Box 1, Folder 1; Velma B. Johnston to Eugene Grumby, letter, December 26, 1957, VJP, Box 1, Folder 1; Velma B. Johnston, "Mustang Exploitation," February 28, 1958, HCP, 86th Cong., Box 34, Folder 529; "Abandoned Horses on the Federal Range," *Our Public Lands*, October 1958, 3, 12; Lura Tularski, "Saddle Chatter," *Nevada State Journal*, April 5, 1959; "Baring Offers Measure, Letter Drive Spurred," *Reno Evening Gazette*, April 7, 1959; Stephanie Godwin, "Wild Horse Bill," *Nevada State Journal*, April 29, 1959; "Magazine Reports on 'Wild Horse Annie,'" *Nevada State Journal*, May 24, 1959; Harold Walter, "Wild Horses West," *Sierra*, July 1959, 10–14; humane affiliates to senators and representatives of Congress, letter, July 5, 1959, HCP, 86th Cong., Box 34, Folder 529; Garden Club of America to James O. Eastland, letter, July 10, 1959, HCP, 86th Cong., Box 35, Folder 529; "Mustang Tragedy," *Salt Lake Tribune*, July 10, 1959; "Wild Horse Annie to Meet Newsmen," *Nevada State Journal*, July 14, 1959; "Wild Horse Roundup Subject of Hearings," *Reno Evening Gazette*, July 15, 1959; "Nevadans Seek Bill to Protect Horses," *Nevada State Journal*, July 15, 1959; House Committee on the Judiciary, *Treatment of Wild Horses and Burros on Land Belonging to the U.S.: HR343, 2725, 4289, 7531*, 86th Cong., 1st sess. (July 15, 1959), 22–72; "Newsmen in Washington See Wild Horse Annie without Shootin' Irons," *Nevada State Journal*, July 16, 1959; "All Hands 'Pull Leather' in Wild Horse Dispute," *Salt Lake Tribune*, July 16, 1959; "Annie Pleads for Protection of Wild Horses," *Provo Daily Herald*, July 20, 1959; Kania, *Wild Horse Annie*, 30–36; Carr Childers, "Leisl Carr Childers," 613. Nevada senator Howard Cannon noted that the vast majority of the letters he received were from supporters of the bill who lived out of state, particularly in New York and California. Most of the letters from Nevada came from the Reno area.

16. House Committee on the Judiciary, *Treatment of Wild Horses and Burros on Land Belonging to the U.S: Hearings on HR343, 2725, 4289, 7531*, 86th Cong., 1st sess. (July 15, 1959), 13–95.

17. "Newsmen in Washington See Wild Horse Annie without Shootin' Irons," *Nevada State Journal*, July 16, 1959; "All Hands 'Pull Leather' in Wild Horse Dispute," *Salt Lake Tribune*, July 16, 1959; "Annie Pleads for Protection of Wild Horses," *Provo Daily Herald*, July 20, 1959; "Solons Approve Wild Horse Bill," *Nevada State Journal*, July 24, 1959; "A Horse Roundup Ban Is Approved," *Reno Evening Gazette*, July 25, 1959; "Mustang Slaughter," *Reno Evening Gazette*, August 12, 1959; "Humane Measures," *Reno Evening Gazette*, August 13, 1959; "House Passes Bill to Save Wild Horses," *Reno Evening Gazette*, August 18, 1959; "Bill to Control Horse Roundups," *Nevada State Journal*, August 18, 1959; "Persistent Annie," *Reno Evening Gazette*, August 26, 1959; "Senate OK's Bill to Save Wild Horses," *Nevada State Journal*, August 26, 1959; "Gets a Reprieve," *Reno Evening Gazette*, September 5, 1959; "President Signs Wild Horse Bill," *Nevada State Journal*, September 9, 1959; "West's Wild Horse Herds Reprieved by New Law," *Ogden Standard-Examiner*, September 9, 1959; "President Approves Bill Making Roundups Illegal," *Reno Evening Gazette*, September 12, 1959; McKnight, "Feral Horse," 506–25; Wild Horse Annie Act of 1959, Public Law 234, 86th Cong., 1st sess. (September 8, 1959); Tom McKnight, "Mustangs, Limited," *New York Times*, January 10, 1960; Humane Affiliates to Senators and Representatives of Congress, letter, July 5, 1959, HCP, 86th Cong., Box 34, Folder 529; Cruise and Griffiths, *Wild Horse Annie*, 81–137; Kania, *Wild Horse Annie*, 37–51; Carr Childers, "Leisl Carr Childers," 613.

18. Velma B. Johnston to Robert O'Brien, letter, August 11, 1957, VJP, Box 1, Folder 1; Velma B. Johnston to Walter S. Baring, letter, May 9, 1958, VJP, Box 1, Folder 3; Nevada Statutes 3978–3989, "Estray Animals," February 19, 1923, in Hillyer, *Nevada Compiled Laws 1929*, 1175; Martin v. Lessee of Waddell, 41 U.S. 367 (1842); Greer v. Connecticut, 161 U.S. 519 (1896).

19. Velma B. Johnston to Eugene Gunby, letter, December 26, 1957, VJP, Box 1, Folder 1; Nevada Wool Growers Association to Howard W. Cannon, letter, May 15, 1959, HCP, 86th Cong., Box 34, Folder 528; Nevada Department of Conservation and Natural Resources to Howard W. Cannon, letter, May 18, 1959, HCP, 86th Cong., Box 34, Folder 528; Nevada Association of Conservation Districts to Howard W. Cannon, letter, May 23, 1959, HCP, 86th Cong., Box 34, Folder 528; Ernest J. Palmer to Howard W. Cannon, letter, August 19, 1959, HCP, 86th Cong., Box 34, Folder 528; Nevada Fish and Game Commission to Walter S. Baring, letter, September 4, 1959, HCP, 86th Cong., Box 34, Folder 528. Ernest J. Palmer emphasized the importance of livestock production to the state's economy; citing the most recent agricultural statistics, Palmer pointed out that 75 percent of Nevada's agricultural income came from meat products, primarily from cattle and sheep.

20. Velma B. Johnston to Eugene L. Conrotto, letter, March 31, 1959, VJP, Box 1, Folder 1; McKnight, "Feral Horse," 506–25.

21. Velma B. Johnston to Eugene L. Conrotto, letter, March 31, 1959, VJP, Box 1, Folder 1; George Hardman to Edward Hoffman, letter, July 30, 1959, Grant Sawyer Papers (GSP), Box 246, Folder 22; "Getting Wild about Wild Horse Hunts," *Salt Lake Tribune*, August 21, 1959.

22. McKnight, "Feral Horse," 506–25; "Hollywood: Marilyn and the Mustangs," *Time*, August 8, 1960; Hedda Hopper, "Disney Mouseketeer to Star in New 'Babes in Toyland,'" *Salt Lake Tribune*, January 30, 1961; "Arthur Miller on Nevada and *The Misfits*," in Reid and James, *Uncovering Nevada's Past*, 168–76; Stillman, *Mustang*, 221–27; Carr Childers, "Leisl Carr Childers," 613–14.

23. Florence Burge, "Round About," *Reno Evening Gazette*, April 22, 1966; "'Wild Horse Annie's' Story Told," *Nevada State Journal*, October 19, 1966; Velma B. Johnston

to Tom Holland, letter, October 2, 1967, VJP, Box 1, Folder 7; Velma B. Johnston to Water-Wearing-Away-the-Rock Pat Woodard, letter, October 3, 1967, VJP, Box 1, Folder 7; Cruise and Griffiths, *Wild Horse Annie*, 147–84; Carr Childers, "Leisl Carr Childers," 614.

24. Robert M. Hyatt, "Vanishing Horses," *Salt Lake Tribune*, March 4, 1951; Paul B. Pearson to Thomas L. Shipman, letter, January 22, 1954, National Nuclear Security Administration/Nevada Field Office (NNSA/NFO); Lura Tularski, "Saddle Chatter," *Nevada State Journal*, July 22, 1962; Office of the Secretary of the Interior, press release, December 27, 1962, HCP, 88th Cong., Box 18, Folder 202; "The Nevada Wild Horse Range Haven for Wild Horses," *Our Public Lands*, January 1963, 12–13; "At Last, U.S. Acts to Save Wild Horse," *Chicago Daily Tribune*, February 11, 1963; Walter Sullivan, "U.S. Creates Haven for Wild Horses in Nevada," *New York Times*, August 21, 1963; James A. Moorhouse and Gene Nodine, "Wild Horse Haven," *Our Public Lands*, Fall 1967, 4–6; Cruise and Griffiths, *Wild Horse Annie*, 142–43; Kania, *Wild Horse Annie*, 82–83. Along with the newly expanded Desert Game Refuge, originally established in 1937 east of the Nellis range, the military base was swiftly becoming a haven for wildlife.

25. Velma B. Johnston to Howard W. Cannon, letter, January 8, 1963; HCP, 88th Cong., Box 18, Folder 202; J. A. Mulvihill to Howard W. Cannon, letter, October 25, 1965, HCP, 89th Cong., Box 11, Folder 109; Howard W. Cannon to J. A. Mulvihill, letter, November 1, 1965, HCP, 89th Cong., Box 11, Folder 109; J. A. Mulvihill to Howard W. Cannon, letter, November 15, 1965, HCP, 89th Cong., Box 11, Folder 109; Howard W. Cannon to Stewart L. Udall, letter, November 24, 1965, HCP, 89th Cong., Box 11, Folder 109; Stewart L. Udall to Howard W. Cannon, letter, December 17, 1965, HCP, 89th Cong., Box 11, Folder 109; Howard W. Cannon to J. A. Mulvihill, letter, January 24, 1966, HCP, 89th Cong., Box 11, Folder 109; J. A. Mulvihill to Howard W. Cannon, letter, January 21, 1966, HCP, 89th Cong., Box 11, Folder 109.

26. National Mustang Association organization and objectives, Paul Laxalt Papers (PLP), Box 352, Folder 23; Cruise and Griffiths, *Wild Horse Annie*, 208–209; Kania, *Wild Horse Annie*, 76–91.

27. National Mustang Association organization and objectives, PLP, Box 352, Folder 23; "Old Whitey Captured, Released," *Reno Evening Gazette*, February 21, 1966.

28. "To Stage Roundup of Wild Horses," *Reno Evening Gazette*, March 23, 1960; "Nye Deputies Study Wild Horses," *Tonopah Times-Bonanza*, November 11, 1966.

29. "Protests Heard on Wild Horse Air Hunt Ban," *Reno Evening Gazette*, January 5, 1960; Karl Landstrom to all BLM employees, memorandum, April 21, 1961, Folder 331, Public Lands Foundation Archive (PLFA); Walter Sullivan, "U.S. Creates Haven for Wild Horses in Nevada," *New York Times*, August 21, 1963; Skillen, *Nation's Largest Landlord*, 49–69.

30. "BLM Ultimatum to Kill Wild Horses on 2-State Range Stirs Discussion," *Provo Daily Herald*, March 30, 1966; "Wild Mustangs May End Up as Dog Food If Order Met," *Ogden Standard-Examiner*, March 30, 1966; Velma B. Johnston to *Denver Post*, April 5, 1966, VJP, Box 1, Folder 7; Cruise and Griffiths, *Wild Horse Annie*, 183–229.

31. Velma B. Johnston to Lloyd and Alana Tillett, letter, April 5, 1966, VJP, Box 1, Folder 7; "Wild Horses Big Problem," *Provo Daily Herald*, April 6, 1966; "Protest Killing Off Wyoming Wild Horses," *Provo Daily Herald*, April 7, 1966; "U.S. Loses Battle of the Wild Horses," *Ogden Standard-Examiner*, April 10, 1966; "Horses Win Battle, U.S. Unglues Rule," *Salt Lake Tribune*, April 10, 1966; "U.S. Studies Fate of Wild Horse Herd Roaming Montana," *New York Times*, April 7, 1968; "Save Wild Horses, Lad Asks," *Ogden Standard-Examiner*, May 5, 1966; "BLM to Protect Mustangs—The

4-Legged Kind," *Salt Lake Tribune*, September 15, 1967; "BLM Acts to Save Mustangs," *Ogden Standard-Examiner*, October 27, 1967; Earl Wallace, "Mustangs Favored by Policy," *Provo Daily Herald*, October 12, 1967; "Wild Horse Band Appears Headed for Auction Block," *Provo Daily Herald*, March 25, 1968; Cruise and Griffiths, *Wild Horse Annie*, 183–229; Kania, *Wild Horse Annie*, 65–75.

32. Velma B. Johnston to Floyd Schweiger, letter, March 27, 1968, VJP, Box 1, Folder 9; Velma B. Johnston to Stewart L. Udall, letter, April 10, 1968, VJP, Box 1, Folder 10; "Wyoming to Shun Controversial Sale of Wild Horses," *Provo Daily Herald*, May 23, 1968; Velma B. Johnston to Dean Bibles, letter, July 15, 1968, VJP, Box 1, Folder 12; Velma B. Johnston to Almer S. Monroney, letter, August 5, 1968, VJP, Box 1, Folder 13; Velma B. Johnston to Lynn Augustine, letter, August 6, 1968, VJP, Box 1, Folder 13; "Mustangs Get Reprieve," *Ogden Standard-Examiner*, August 12, 1968; Velma B. Johnston to Charles E. Most, letter, August 22, 1968, VJP, Box 1, Folder 7; "U.S. Abandons Plans to Trap, Sell Wild Horses," *Ogden Standard-Examiner*, September 15, 1968; George W. Crane, "Reno Woman Helps Save Wild Horses," *Ogden Standard-Examiner*, December 2, 1968; Bureau of Land Management, press release, October 11, 1968, HCP, 90th Cong., Box 18, Folder 295; "Panel Studies Montana-Wyoming Wild Horse Herd," *New York Times*, December 26, 1968; "BLM Announces Wild Horse Policy," *Our Public Lands*, Winter 1968, 3; "Montana Weighing Wild Horses Fate," *New York Times*, March 30, 1969; William M. Blair, "U.S. Urged to Help Wild Horse Herd," *New York Times*, June 21, 1969; John Riley, "The Mustangs," *Los Angeles Times*, July 27, 1969; Department of the Interior, press release, June 20, 1969, HCP, 91st Cong., Box 17, Folder 214V; "Federal Help Asked for Horses," *Nevada State Journal*, June 22, 1969; Charles E. Most, "Wild Horses of the Pryors," *Our Public Lands*, Fall 1969, 18–21; Allan Pospisil, "Where the Wild Mustangs Play," *New York Times*, May 2, 1971; "Secretary Hickel Accepts Recommendations of Wild Horse Committee," *Our Public Lands*, Winter 1970, 3; Charles E. Most, "Little Orphan Annie," *Our Public Lands*, Spring 1971, 12–13; "Herd of Wild Horses in Wyoming Undergoes Saving 'Last Roundup,'" *Provo Daily Herald*, November 12, 1971; "Man Carves Out, Saves 'Wild Bunch,'" *Ogden Standard-Examiner*, November 25, 1971; Cruise and Griffiths, *Wild Horse Annie*, 183–229. There is far more to the story of the Pryor Mountain wild horses than is written here. However, wild horse advocates have written much of the herd's story, so the perspective is heavily weighted against the BLM. For more information, see journalist Hope Ryden, *America's Last Wild Horses*.

33. NSWR applications 14116 (March 17, 1952) and 18760 (April 17, 1960); GLO records NVN 0062155PT (August 20, 1965) and NVN 0062155FD (March 11, 1966); Velma B. Johnston to Baltan P. Mouras, letter, February 21, 1967, VJP, Box 1, Folder 7; Velma B. Johnston to Helen and John Reilley, letter, February 22, 1967, VJP, Box 1, Folder 7; Symanski, *Wild Horses and Sacred Cows*, 43–48; Cruise and Griffiths, *Wild Horse Annie*, 199–207.

34. Velma B. Johnston to Stewart L. Udall, letter, April 10, 1968, VJP, Box 1, Folder 10; Velma B. Johnston to Ernest F. Swift, letter, April 10, 1968, VJP, Box 1, Folder 10; Velma B. Johnston to Joan Blue, letter, April 29, 1970, VJP, Box 1, Folder 20; Velma B. Johnston to Howard Caudle, letter, June 3, 1970, VJP, Box 1, Folder 20; Velma B. Johnston to Walter Clutts, letter, July 1970, VJP, Box 1, Folder 23; Velma B. Johnston to C. Wayne Cook, letter, November 27, 1970, VJP, Box 1, Folder 23.

35. Animal Welfare Act of 1966, Public Law 544, 89th Cong., 2nd sess. (August 24, 1966); Environmental Protection Act of 1969, Public Law 669, 89th Cong., 2nd sess. (October 30, 1969); Endangered Species Conservation Act of 1969, Public Law 135, 91st

Cong., 1st sess. (December 5, 1969); Animal Welfare Act Amendments of 1970, Public Law 579, 91st Cong., 2nd sess. (December 24, 1970); "Moss Aims to Protect Wild Horses," *Provo Daily Herald*, May 18, 1969; "Moss Asks U.S. for Protection of Wild Horses," *Salt Lake Tribune*, May 15, 1969; Velma B. Johnston to Richard W. Faulkner, letter, May 25, 1968, VJP, Box 1, Folder 11; Velma B. Johnston to Tom Gregersen, letter, June 26, 1968, VJP, Box 1, Folder 11; Velma B. Johnston to Lynn Augustine, letter, September 6, 1968, VJP, Box 1, Folder 14; Kania, *Wild Horse Annie*, 92–100; Haynes, *Animal Welfare*, 13–35; Phelps, *Longest Struggle*; Czech and Krausman, *Endangered Species Act.*

36. Velma B. Johnston to Billie Twyne, letter, August 8, 1968, VJP, Box 1, Folder 13; Velma B. Johnston to Joan Blue, letter, August 27, 1968, VJP, Box 1, Folder 13; Velma B. Johnston to Walter S. Baring, letter, August 16, 1968, VJP, Box 1, Folder 13; Melody Kines to Howard W. Cannon, letter, August 25, 1969, HCP, 91st Cong., Box 17, Folder 219; David A. Sklar to Howard W. Cannon, letter, September 11, 1969, HCP, 91st Cong., Box 17, Folder 219; Velma B. Johnston to John Walsh, letter, November 6, 1968, VJP, Box 1, Folder 15; Sherman Gunn to Howard W. Cannon, letter, November 23, 1969; HCP, 91st Cong., Box 17, Folder 219; National Mustang Association, "The Mustang," 1969, HCP, 91st Cong., Box 17, Folder 219; Colleen Cowley to Howard W. Cannon, letter, May 12, 1970, HCP, 91st Cong., Box 17, Folder 219; Mable A. Conelly to Howard W. Cannon, letter, June 12, 1970, HCP, 91st Cong., Box 17, Folder 215; Raymond Golabiewski to Howard W. Cannon, letter, July 28, 1970, HCP, 91st Cong., Box 17, Folder 214; Anthony Ripley, "A Devoted Few Strive to Save Wild Horses," *New York Times*, November 15, 1970; Mildred Plane to Paul Laxalt, letter, November 23, 1970, PLP, Box 352, Folder 23; Cruise and Griffiths, *Wild Horse Annie*, 229–48.

37. Ryden, *America's Last Wild Horses*, 16, 18–20, 24–39, 278.

38. "A Devoted Few Strive to Save Wild Horses," *New York Times*, November 15, 1970; Willa Oldham to Howard W. Cannon, letter, December 1, 1970, HCP, 91st Cong., Box 17, Folder 214; Howard W. Cannon to Willa Oldham, letter, December 8, 1970, HCP, 91st Cong., Box 17, Folder 214; Ryden, *America's Last Wild Horses*, 278.

39. Helen Fallini, interview by Robert D. McCracken, October 25–26, 1987, Nye County Town History Project (NCTHP); Kent Gregersen to Frank E. Moss, letter, December 5, 1969, VJP, Box 1, Folder 19; Velma B. Johnston to C. Wayne Cook, letter, November 27, 1970, VJP, Box 1, Folder 23.

40. Velma B. Johnston to George L. Turcott, letter, July 26, 1969, VJP, Box 1, Folder 17; John Bromley, "Rancher Asserts Horses Captured," *Nevada State Journal*, August 2, 1969; Velma B. Johnston to Curtiss-Wright Corporation, letter, January 23, 1970, VJP, Box 1, Folder 19; "Big Drive Gets Started to Save Mustangs," *Nevada State Journal*, July 12, 1970; "Wild Horse Trap Found, Destroyed," *Nevada State Journal*, July 20, 1970; "Crude Mustang Trap Ripped Apart by Horse Lovers," *Ogden Standard-Examiner*, July 21, 1970; Lura Tularski, "Saddle Chatter," *Nevada State Journal*, July 26, 1970; "Wild Horse Hunters Rumored Working Hills," *Nevada State Journal*, August 6, 1970; "Slatterly Complains of Official Failure to Protect Mustangs," *Nevada State Journal*, August 7, 1970; "Wild Mustangs Trap or Branded Horse Corral?," *Nevada State Journal*, August 15, 1970; Carl Haviland, "Dispute Grows on Wild Horses," *Nevada State Journal*, August 16, 1970; "Builders of Destroyed Corral Seek $65,000 in Damage Suit," *Nevada State Journal*, September 28, 1970; "Lawsuit Filed by Two Reno Men Who Claim Corral Was Destroyed," *Reno Evening Gazette*, September 29, 1970; "New Contract Is Opposed for Professor," *Reno Evening Gazette*, October 2, 1970; Velma B. Johnston to Howard Caudle, letter, October 1, 1970, VJP, Box 1, Folder 22; Velma B. Johnston

to Kent Gregersen, letter, October 2, 1970, VJP, Box 1, Folder 22; Velma B. Johnston to N. Ed Miller, letter, October 6, 1970, VJP, Box 1, Folder 22; Velma B. Johnston to George Lea, letter, October 7, 1970, VJP, Box 1, Folder 22; "Unbridled Symbol of Old West Stands Shakily on Last Legs," *Provo Daily Herald*, October 13, 1970; "Environment: The Fight to Save Wild Horses," *Time*, July 12, 1971; "Time Magazine Features Mustang Story," *Nevada State Journal*, July 9, 1971; "A Week of Successes for Wild Horse Buffs," *Nevada State Journal*, December 5, 1971; Cruise and Griffiths, *Wild Horse Annie*, 235–38. The Curtiss-Wright Corporation owned the land in Storey County on which Jerry "Chug" Utter illegally ran both branded and unbranded horses. Mixing branded animals with unbranded ones gave Utter a legal reason to conduct a roundup. As for Dr. Michael Pontrelli, the University of Nevada, Reno, eventually acquiesced and a judge dismissed the charges against him in 1971.

41. "Wild Horse Annie: We've Won the Battle, but Not the War," *Reno Evening Gazette*, November 5, 1970; "New California Laws Ban Some Sales," *Nevada State Journal*, November 16, 1970; "New California Law to Protect Mustangs Feared Ineffective," *Nevada State Journal*, December 2, 1970; "How to Keep Mustangs from Going to the Dogs," *New York Times*, January 17, 1971; "Measure Asks for Protection of Mustangs," *Nevada State Journal*, February 9, 1971; "Wild Horse Annie's Crusade Making Progress This Year," *Nevada State Journal*, March 7, 1971; Velma B. Johnston to John McCormack, letter, March 8, 1971, VJP, Box 1, Folder 24; Don Lynch, "Land Chief Sees Expanding BLM," *Nevada State Journal*, March 10, 1971; "Land Use Policy Move in Congress Is Predicted," *Reno Evening Gazette*, March 10, 1971; Carl Haviland, "Everyone Rides Mustangs Today," *Nevada State Journal*, March 12, 1971; "Annie Corrals Another Vote for Mustangs," *Nevada State Journal*, March 13, 1971; "Mustang Protection Sought," *Reno Evening Gazette*, March 31, 1971; "Off-Roaders, BLM Pledge Cooperation," *Nevada State Journal*, April 19, 1971. In 1970, several congressional representatives had proposed bills to protect wild horses, but these measures remained in committee during the 91st Congress and had to be reintroduced in the 92nd Congress.

42. Velma B. Johnston to Frances H. Parker, letter, September 6, 1970, VJP, Box 1, Folder 22; Lura Tularski, "Saddle Chatter," *Nevada State Journal*, February 7, 1971; "Mustang Urged as State Animal," *Nevada State Journal*, March 4, 1971; "Please Help!," *Provo Daily Herald*, March 7, 1971; "Case for Mustang Appears Doomed," *Nevada State Journal*, March 23, 1971; "Wild Horse Control, Management Advocated," *Nevada State Journal*, March 26, 1971; Cliff Young, "Nevada Mustang Has Fantastic Bag of Tricks," *Reno Evening Gazette*, March 27, 1971; "Mustang Bill Sent to Death by Committee," *Nevada State Journal*, April 1, 1971; "Expert on Wild Horses Discusses Their Future," *Nevada State Journal*, March 14, 1971; "Legislative Puzzler: What Is a Mustang?," *Nevada State Journal*, March 16, 1971; "Nevada Mustangs Left to Fend for Themselves," *Nevada State Journal*, April 10, 1971; "Mustang Stands Forlorn, Friendless," *Reno Evening Gazette*, April 10, 1971; "Senate Defeats Attempt to Revise Mustang Protection Bill," *Nevada State Journal*, April 14, 1971; Terry Newfarmer, "Is the Mustang Just Fit for Dog Food?," *Salt Lake Tribune*, October 31, 1971. Nevada Senate Bills 41 and 107 made capturing, possessing, or killing wild horses illegal and declared the mustang the state animal, respectively.

43. "Management, Control Called Keys to Nevada's Wild Horse Problem," *Reno Evening Gazette*, March 25, 1971; "Wild Horse Management Advocated," *Nevada State Journal*, March 26, 1971.

44. "Management, Control Called Keys to Nevada's Wild Horse Problem," *Reno Evening Gazette*, March 25, 1971; "Wild Horse Management Advocated," *Nevada State*

Journal, March 26, 1971; "Mustang Protection Sought," *Reno Evening Gazette*, March 31, 1971; "Mustang Fails to Get Help in the Senate," *Reno Evening Gazette*, April 14, 1971; "Letters to the Editor: Hits Lawmakers," *Reno Evening Gazette*, April 21, 1971; "Utah F&G Board Taps Chairman," *Salt Lake Tribune*, April 29, 1971; "Environment: The Fight to Save Wild Horses," *Time*, July 12, 1971; "Case for Mustang Brings Mixed Feelings," *Nevada State Journal*, August 8, 1971.

45. Velma B. Johnston to John McCormack, letter, March 8, 1971, VJP, Box 1, Folder 24; "Baring Plans to Protect Wild Horses," *Nevada State Journal*, March 11, 1971; "Protection Methods Asked for Wild Horses, Burros," *Nevada State Journal*, March 18, 1971; Velma B. Johnston to Chuck Wagner, letter, April 1, 1971, VJP, Box 1, Folder 25; "Bible, Baring, Cannon Support Mustang Plan," *Nevada State Journal*, April 8, 1971; "Hearing Slated for Wild Horses," *Nevada State Journal*, April 12, 1971; Frank Hewlett, "Congress Action Nears on Legislation to Protect West's Wild Horses, Burros," *Salt Lake Tribune*, April 12, 1971; "Western Wild Horse Sanctuaries Are Sought by Bible," *Reno Evening Gazette*, April 17, 1971; "McKay Backs Legislation to Save Mustang, Burro," *Salt Lake Tribune*, April 20, 1971; "Mustang Support Testimony Heard," *Nevada State Journal*, April 20, 1971; "These Guys're Crazy over the Mustangs," *Salt Lake Tribune*, April 21, 1971; "Wild Horse Annie at Senate Hearing," *Nevada State Journal*, April 21, 1971; "'Wild Horse Annie' Continues Her Battle," *Provo Daily Herald*, April 21, 1971; "Save the Mustang, but . . . ," *Salt Lake Tribune*, April 24, 1971; "Wild Horse Annie Continually Fights to Save Mustangs," *Nevada State Journal*, April 25, 1971; "Last Roundup," *New York Times*, May 17, 1971; "Subcommittee Approves Mustang Bill," *Nevada State Journal*, June 11, 1971; "Mustang Measure Passes Hurdle," *Reno Evening Gazette*, June 11, 1971; Charles Hillinger, "Annie Seeking New Name for Wild Horses," *Los Angeles Times*, June 21, 1971; "Mustang Bill Clears Committee," *Nevada State Journal*, June 25, 1971; "Time Magazine Features Mustang Story," *Nevada State Journal*, July 9, 1971; "Environment: The Fight to Save Wild Horses," *Time*, July 12, 1971; "Wild Horse Bill Moves to House," *Nevada State Journal*, July 17, 1971; "The Mountains—A Place for Decision," *Nevada State Journal*, August 29, 1971; Ryden, *America's Last Wild Horses*, 282; Kania, *Wild Horse Annie*, 100–105.

46. Hope Ryden, "On the Track of the West's Wild Horses," *National Geographic*, January 1971, 94–109; House Committee on Interior and Insular Affairs, *Protection of Wild Horses and Burros on Public Lands: Hearings on HR795, 5375*, 92nd Cong., 1st sess. (April 19–20, 1971), 78–117, 134–45; Senate Committee on Interior and Insular Affairs, *Protection of Wild Horses and Burros on Public Lands: Hearings on S862, 1090, 1116, 1119*, 92nd Cong., 1st sess. (April 20, 1971).

47. House Committee on Interior and Insular Affairs, *Protection of Wild Horses and Burros on Public Lands: Hearings on HR795, 5375*, 92nd Cong., 1st sess. (April 19–20, 1971), 117–34; Senate Committee on Interior and Insular Affairs, *Protection of Wild Horses and Burros on Public Lands: Hearings on S862, 1090, 1116, 1119*, 92nd Cong., 1st sess. (April 20, 1971).

48. Wild Free-Roaming Horses and Burros Act of 1971, Public Law 195, 92nd Cong., 1st sess. (December 15, 1971); Terry Newfarmer, "Is the Mustang Just Fit for Dog Food?," *Salt Lake Tribune*, October 31, 1971; Anthony Ripley, "Woman Has Worked for 20 Years to Save America's Vanishing Wild Horse," *New York Times*, November 11, 1971; "Help Is Pressed for Wild Horses," *New York Times*, November 12, 1971; "Wild Horse Bill Passes," *Nevada State Journal*, December 4, 1971; "Bill to Protect Wild Horses Off to President," *Salt Lake Tribune*, December 4, 1971; "A Week of Successes for Wild Horse Buffs," *Nevada State Journal*, December 5, 1971; "Bill to Protect Wild Horses

Goes to President," *Provo Daily Herald,* December 5, 1971; "Group Opposes Bill for Wild Horse Protection," *Provo Daily Herald,* December 6, 1971; "Horse Group Flays Bill; Up to Nixon," *Salt Lake Tribune,* December 6, 1971; "Nixon Signs Bill Protecting Wild Horses," *Reno Evening Gazette,* December 17, 1971; James M. Naughton, "President Signs Bill to Protect Wild Horses on Federal Lands," *New York Times,* December 18, 1971; "Fourth Graders in Oregon Backed Wild Horse Bill," *Reno Evening Gazette,* December 18, 1971; "With a Nod to Kids, Nixon Signs Mustang Bill," *Salt Lake Tribune,* December 18, 1971; "Nixon Signs Bill Protecting Nation's Wild Horses, Burros," *Provo Daily Herald,* December 19, 1971; Cruise and Griffiths, *Wild Horse Annie,* 239–51.

49. "Newark Valley Region Faces Major Problem," *Nevada State Journal,* January 24, 1972; "Multiple Use Advisory Board Plans Reno Session," *Reno Evening Gazette,* January 26, 1972; Lura Tularski, "Saddle Chatter," *Nevada State Journal,* January 30, 1972; Skillen, *Nation's Largest Landlord,* 77–79.

50. Tod Bedrosian, "Nevada Rancher: Put Those Wild Horses behind Bars," *Nevada State Journal,* February 16, 1974; Skillen, *Nation's Largest Landlord,* 77–79; Kania, *Wild Horse Annie,* 105–27.

51. "Bible Eyes Horse Bill Funding," *Nevada State Journal,* March 2, 1972; "Reminder by BLM: Wild Horses, Burros Protected," *Nevada State Journal,* September 6, 1972; "BLM to Stiffen Nevada Rules," *Reno Evening Gazette,* September 30, 1972; "U.S. Investigates Horse Slaughter," *Salt Lake Tribune,* March 4, 1973; "Wild Horse Herd Destroyed; Federal Investigation Begun," *Ogden Standard-Examiner,* March 5, 1973; "Federal Men Probe Scene of Wild Horse Deaths," *Reno Evening Gazette,* March 5, 1973; Kania, *Wild Horse Annie,* 141–66.

52. "Horse Death Raises Legal Issues," *Salt Lake Tribune,* March 6, 1973; "'Nothing Illegal,' Sherriff Claims," *Ogden Standard-Examiner,* March 6, 1973; "Horse Slaughter Charged in Idaho," *New York Times,* March 6, 1973; "Idaho's Missing Horses Found Waiting Slaughter," *Ogden Standard-Examiner,* March 8, 1973; "Wild Horses Still Alive," *Salt Lake Tribune,* March 8, 1973; "Probe Roundup, Legislator Says," *Ogden Standard-Examiner,* March 9, 1973; Helen A. Reilly and Gordon W. Harris to National Advisory Board for Wild Free-Roaming Horses and Burros, letter, March 20, 1973, VJP, Box 1, Folder 31; "BLM Hit with Suit in 14 Horse Deaths," *Ogden Standard-Examiner,* April 6, 1973; "Federal Agencies Drag Feet in Investigation, Utahn Charges," *Salt Lake Tribune,* April 23, 1973; "18 Horses in Idaho May Get Reprieve from Meat Packer," *New York Times,* November 13, 1973; "Slaughter-Bound Horses Shipped Back to Idaho," *Salt Lake Tribune,* November 21, 1973; "Horses Get Chance to Live Anew," *Salt Lake Tribune,* November 23, 1973; "Wild Horse Roundup Illegal, Inhumane, Panel Told," *Salt Lake Tribune,* March 27, 1974; "Board Condemns Idaho's Roundup," *Ogden Standard-Examiner,* March 28, 1974; "U.S. Probe Details Horse Slaughter," *Salt Lake Tribune,* May 12, 1974; "Legs Cut Off, Horse Roundup Report Says," *Ogden Standard-Examiner,* May 14, 1974; "Hearing Could Decide 'Wild Horses' Fate in Idaho Controversy," *Salt Lake Tribune,* June 26, 1974; Anthony Ripley, "Jackson Seeks to Save Horses Captured in Disputed Roundup," *New York Times,* September 26, 1974; "Association and Idahoan Trade Barbs over Wild Horse Issue," *Ogden Standard-Examiner,* December 7, 1974; "Follow-Up on the News: Horse Wrangle," *New York Times,* March 2, 1975; "Horses Still Issue in Federal Court," *Salt Lake Tribune,* March 5, 1975; Cruise and Griffiths, *Wild Horse Annie,* 249–60.

53. American Horse Protection Association, form newsletter, June 1974, TNP, 90–34, Box 1, Folder 23; James P. Sterba, "Revived Killing of Wild Horses for Pet Food Is

Feared," *New York Times*, August 3, 1974; Andrew H. Malcolm, "U.S. Begins Roundup of Wild Horses in West as Their Population Grows," *New York Times*, September 21, 1974; Velma Johnston to Toiyabe Chapter, letter, January 22, 1975, TNP, 90–34, Box 1, Folder 8; Cruise and Griffiths, *Wild Horse Annie*, 249–60.

54. "21 Wild Horses in Nevada, Facing Death, Win Reprieve through Adoption Program," *New York Times*, September 19, 1976; Joyce Brown to James Carter, letter, January 4, 1978, TNP, 90–34, Box 1, Folder 21; Tina Nappe to Joyce Brown, letter, January 1978, TNP, 90–34, Box 1, Folder 21.

55. Velma B. Johnston to George Lea, letter, July 25, 1974, VJP, Box 1, Folder 42; Tina Nappe to Floyd Lamb, letter, March 9, 1975, TNP, 90–34, Box 1, Folder 8; Leslie Stewart to Tina Nappe, letter, August 12, 1975, TNP, 90–34, Box 1, Folder 8; press release, Bureau of Land Management, April 15, 1975, TNP, 90–34, Box 1, Folder 3; Brendan Riley, "Wild Horses Stampede to Freedom in Nevada Desert," *Nevada State Journal*, August 7, 1975; Brendan Riley, "Nevada Misfits Driven Back into Sage by Government Squabble," *Reno Evening Gazette*, August 7, 1975; Nancy F. Green and Howard D. Green, "The Wild Horse Population of Stone Cabin Valley, Nevada: A Preliminary Report," Summer 1975, TNP, 90–34, Box 1, Folder 13; Gene Nodine to Edgar I. Rowland, memorandum, May 19, 1976, Donal "Mike" O'Callaghan Papers (MOP), Box 709, Folder 8; Edgar I. Rowland to Curt Berkland, memorandum, May 26, 1976, MOP, Box 709, Folder 8; John Meder to Norman Hall, memorandum, August 13, 1976, MOP, Box 709, Folder 8; Symanski, *Wild Horses and Sacred Cows*, 123–62.

56. Gene Nodine to Edgar I. Rowland, memorandum, May 19, 1976, MOP, Box 709, Folder 8; Edgar I. Rowland to Curt Berkland, memorandum, May 26, 1976, MOP, Box 709, Folder 8; Bureau of Land Management, press release, July 2, 1976, TNP, 90–34, Box 1, Folder 3; John Meder to Norman Hall, memorandum, August 13, 1976, MOP, Box 709, Folder 8; Helen Fallini, interview by Robert McCracken, October 25–26, 1987, NCTHP.

57. "Army to Pay for Sheep Killed by Gas," *Reno Evening Gazette*, July 10, 1968; Ward Marchant, "Dugway Sheep Incident Changed All—Forever," *Ogden Standard-Examiner*, November 9, 1968; "Horses Opt for Home off Range," *Denver Post*, October 5, 1975; "Wild Horse Auction Protested," *Daily Sentinel* (Grand Junction, Colo.), October 5, 1975; "Army Finds Bodies of 26 Wild Horses at Utah Waterhole," *New York Times*, July 7, 1976; "Death of 26 Wild Horses Puzzles Investigators," *Daily Sentinel*, July 7, 1976; "Wild Horse Death Probe Continues," *Daily Sentinel*, July 12, 1976; "Reports on Wild Horse Deaths to Be Released," *Daily Sentinel*, July 16, 1976; "More Facts Asked in Horses' Deaths," *New York Times*, July 26, 1976.

58. Lynn Simross, "Gentle Women Protect Wild Horses," *Los Angeles Times*, July 24, 1977; Kania, *Wild Horse Annie*, 128–40.

59. See Singer, *Animal Liberation*; Jasper and Nelkin, *Animal Rights Crusade*; Wand, *Animal Rights Movement*. Statement of the American Horse Protection Association, circa 1979, TNP, 90–34, Box 1, Folder 3; Dawn Lapin to Michael Zagata, letter, June 27, 1979, TNP, 90–34, Box 1, Folder 9; Hope Ryden, statement, July 7, 1979, TNP, 90–34, Box 1, Folder 16; Symanski, *Wild Horses and Sacred Cows*, 169–71, 213–15. The animal rights movement heavily impacted later perception of wild horse management.

60. National Sierra Club Board Resolution, May 3, 1975, TNP, 90–34, Box 1, Folder 20; Robert Wright, Reno Wild Horse Forum presentation, circa 1979, TNP, 90–34, Box 1, Folder 12; Tina Nappe to Dean Rhoads, letter, March 2, 1977, TNP, 90–34, Box 1, Folder 31; Toiyabe Chapter Wild Horse Policy, circa 1979, TNP, 90–34, Box 1, Folder 18.

61. Tina Nappe to Bill Reavley, Dawn Lappin, and Russ Shay, letter, August 19, 1979, TNP, 90–34, Box 1, Folder 19; Helen Fallini, interview by Robert McCracken, October 25–26, 1987, NCTHP.

CONCLUSION

1. Environmental Protection Act of 1969, Public Law 669, 89th Cong., 2nd sess. (October 30, 1969); Endangered Species Conservation Act of 1969, Public Law 135, 91st Cong., 1st sess. (December 5, 1969); Kline, *First along the River*, 95–112; Goble, Scott, and Davis, *Endangered Species Act*, 3–15; R. Clark and Canter, *Environmental Policy and NEPA*, 3–14; Cawley, *Federal Land, Western Anger*, 48–53.

2. House Committee on the Public Lands, *To Provide for the Orderly Use, Improvement, and Development of the Public Range: Hearings on H.R. 2835 and 6462*, 73rd Cong., 1st and 2nd sess. (June 7–9, 1933, February 19–21, 23, 28, and March 1–3, 1934), 16; House Committee on the Public Lands, *To Provide for the Orderly Use, Improvement, and Development of the Public Range: Hearings on HR 6462*, 73rd Cong., 2nd sess. (April 20–May 2, 1934), 15; "Grazing Meet Adopts Broad Range Policy," *Salt Lake Tribune*, January 15, 1936; "Stockmen Close Discussion of Ranges in Utah," *Reno Evening Gazette*, January 15, 1936; "Stockmen Want to Pay 5c per Head a Month on Range," *Nevada State Journal*, January 16, 1936; "Stockmen Urge Grazing Fees to Pay Costs Only," *Nevada State Journal*, March 1, 1936; District Advisors' Conference, Division of Grazing, Salt Lake City, Utah, December 9–11, 1936, RKP, Box 92, Folder 4, 51; "Higher Grazing Fees on Toiyabe," *Reno Evening Gazette*, February 22, 1958; Foss, "Determination of Grazing Fees," 536; Foss, *Politics and Grass*, 172–74, 190. In contrast, ranchers who held Forest Service grazing permits paid a little over thirteen cents per head of cattle and more than three cents per sheep in most areas. Most ranchers complained but believed these ranges were worth the cost.

3. This case was Dewar, et. al. v. Brooks, 16 F.Supp. 636 (1936). "Suit in Grazing Act Fees Filed," *Salt Lake Tribune*, June 17, 1936; "Grazing Fee Case Now in U.S. Court," *Nevada State Journal*, June 27, 1936; "Grazing Fee Suit Is Remanded to Washoe Court by Yankwich," *Reno Evening Gazette*, October 21, 1936; "Fee System Termed Legal," *Nevada State Journal*, May 27, 1941; Foss, "Determination of Grazing Fees," 536–38; Foss, *Politics and Grass*, 174–75.

4. "Izaak Walton League Backs Public Interest in U.S. Forest Service Controversy," *Zanesville (Ohio) Signal*, January 23, 1944; Bernard DeVoto, "Two-Gun Desmond Is Back" (March 1951), in Brinkley and Limerick, *Western Paradox*, 116–17; "Grazing Fee Controversy Is Outlined," *Nevada State Journal*, August 11, 1945; "Raise in Grazing Fees Is Promised," *Reno Evening Gazette*, January 26, 1946; "Grazing Fee Price Boost Is Announced," *Nevada State Journal*, February 19, 1947; "Stockmen Facing Fee Hike for Use of Western Range," *Ogden Standard-Examiner*, December 14, 1948; "Grazing Fees Go Up 4c in 59 Areas," *Salt Lake Tribune*, January 15, 1951; "Grazing Fee Waivers Studied for Individuals," *Reno Evening Gazette*, April 14, 1954; Karl S. Landstrom, "Revision of Fees and Charges," *Our Public Lands*, July 1954, 7, 12; "Federal Grazing Fee Policies Are Clarified," *Reno Evening Gazette*, May 20, 1954; "Higher Fees for Grazing Hit by Bible," *Reno Evening Gazette*, February 16, 1955; "Grazing Fees Are Boosted for Nevadans," *Reno Evening Gazette*, January 27, 1958; "Grazing Fees Are Reduced by Three Cents," *Reno Evening Gazette*, January 23, 1961; "U.S. Hikes Range Fees," *Nevada State Journal*, February 16, 1963; "Grazing Fee Boosted on Public Land," *Ogden*

Standard-Examiner, February 15, 1963; Foss, "Determination of Grazing Fees," 540–47; Foss, *Politics and Grass*, 175–93.

5. "Carson District Opposes Federal Grazing Proposal," *Reno Evening Gazette*, January 11, 1962; Leroy Sharp to Howard W. Cannon, letter, January 12, 1962, Howard Cannon Papers (HCP), 87th Cong., Box 19, Folder 234; Gerald H. Sharp, Minnie Sharp, and Norman K. Sharp to Howard W. Cannon, letter, January 18, 1962, HCP, 87th Cong., Box 19, Folder 234; Clair Whipple to Howard W. Cannon, telegram, January 20, 1962, HCP, 87th Cong., Box 19, Folder 234; "Nevadans to Protest Fee Change," *Nevada State Journal*, January 17, 1962; "Board Members Protest Fee Increase," *Reno Evening Gazette*, January 19, 1962; "Postpone Raise in Grazing Fee," *Nevada State Journal*, January 20, 1962; Department of the Interior, press release, January 22, 1962, HCP, 87th Cong., Box 19, Folder 234; John A. Carver, Jr., to Howard W. Cannon, letter, January 20, 1962, HCP, 87th Cong., Box 19, Folder 234; "No Increase in Grazing Fees Now," *Nevada State Journal*, February 7, 1962; Department of the Interior, press release, February 19, 1962, HCP, 87th Cong., Box 19, Folder 234; "Study Group Opposes Fee Boost," *Nevada State Journal*, April 24, 1962; "Support Lacking for Fee Boost, Says Official," *Reno Evening Gazette*, October 26, 1962; "Hike in Grazing Fees Called Economic Threat," *Reno Evening Gazette*, January 8, 1963; "Senator Bible Closes Land Probe," *Reno Evening Gazette*, January 18, 1963; "Statement of John A. Carver, Jr., Assistant Secretary of the Interior, Public Land Management, before the Public Lands Subcommittee, Senate Interior and Insular Affairs Committee," February 7, 1963, HCP, 88th Cong., Box 18, Folder 207; "Senate Refuses Sawyer Request on Udall Chide," *Nevada State Journal*, February 7, 1963; "Grazing Fee Increase Announced; Hearings Start," *Nevada State Journal*, February 7, 1963; "Statement by Senator Howard W. Cannon before the Public Lands Subcommittee of the Senate Interior Committee," February 7, 1963, HCP, 88th Cong., Box 18, Folder 207; "Range Fee Boost Delay Requested," *Nevada State Journal*, February 9, 1963; Department of the Interior, press release, February 15, 1963, HCP, 88th Cong., Box 18, Folder 207; "Protection of Rights Sought by Ranchers," *Reno Evening Gazette*, March 14, 1963.

6. "LBJ Asked: Don't Boost Grazing Fee," *Ogden Standard-Examiner*, December 2, 1965; "Grazing Cost Increase Delay Asked by Baring," *Reno Evening Gazette*, December 3, 1965; "Grazing Fees in Western States to Go Up Three Cents," *Reno Evening Gazette*, February 21, 1966; "BLM to Keep '66 Grazing Fee Formula," *Salt Lake Tribune*, December 15, 1966; "Bible Lauds Delay in Grazing Fee Increase," *Reno Evening Gazette*, December 18, 1966; "Baring Protests against Change in Grazing Fees," *Nevada State Journal*, November 23, 1968; "'Economic Threat' Looms in Grazing Fee Proposal," *Ogden Standard-Examiner*, November 25, 1968; Frank Hewlett, "Protests Fly in Grazing Fee Increase," *Salt Lake Tribune*, November 30, 1968; "Proposed Grazing Fee Increases: 'Darned if You Do . . . or Don't,'" *Ogden Standard-Examiner*, December 1, 1968; "Injunction Filed against Udall in Grazing Fee Hike," *Ogden Standard-Examiner*, January 7, 1969; "Grazing Hikes to Hurt Economy," *Ogden Standard-Examiner*, February 2, 1969; "District Judge Denies Graze Fee Injunction," *Salt Lake Tribune*, February 8, 1969; "Grazing Fee Hike to Cost Utahns $7.5 Million a Year," *Provo Daily Herald*, March 9, 1969; "Hickel to Delay Grazing Fee Hike," *Nevada State Journal*, November 26, 1969; "Officials Agree Not to Increase Grazing Fees," *Nevada State Journal*, January 29, 1970; "Public Land Laws Outmoded, Review Commission Reports," *Nevada State Journal*, June 24, 1970.

7. Public Land Law Review Commission, *One Third of the Nation's Land*, 104–18; "Sen. Bennett Protests Hike in Grazing Fees," *Provo Daily Herald*, December 28, 1970;

"Group Opposes Public Land Grazing Fee Hike," *Ogden Standard-Examiner*, January 31, 1971; "Agency Posts Fee Hike Lid," *Salt Lake Tribune*, January 4, 1972; "U.S. Boosts Fees on Western Land," *Ogden Standard-Examiner*, December 12, 1973; "Halt Grazing Fee Hikes, 5 Governors Ask," *Salt Lake Tribune*, May 29, 1976; "Agreement Reached on Grazing Fee Freeze for One Year," *Provo Daily Herald*, September 30, 1976; "U.S. Won't Raise Fees for Livestock Grazing," *Ogden Standard-Examiner*, November 28, 1976; "Grazing Fee Is Unchanged," *Color Country Spectrum* (Saint George, Utah), September 9, 1977; "Stockmen Protest Proposed Boost in Grazing Fees," *Provo Daily Herald*, October 26, 1977; Molly Ivins, "Andrus's Popularity Washes Away in West," *New York Times*, February 20, 1978; Gaylord Shaw, "Administration in Trouble in West," *Los Angeles Times*, March 13, 1978; "Senate Passes Bill on Grazing Fees," *New York Times*, May 21, 1978; Senate Committee on Energy and Natural Resources, Subcommittee on Public Lands and Resources, *Public Rangelands Improvement Act of 1978: Hearings on S. 2475*, 95th Cong., 2nd sess. (August 9, 1978); "Federal Grazing Fees to Rise," *New York Times*, April 29, 1979; Senate Committee on Appropriations, *Rangeland Management Policy and Wood Energy Development: Hearings*, 96th Cong., 2nd sess. (August 20, 24–25, 30, and October 8, 1979). The Public Rangelands Improvement Act of 1978, sponsored in part by Nevada senator Paul Laxalt, created a compromise grazing fee set between what was considered to be the fair market value of forage and the more immediate cost of livestock production for ranchers. Nevertheless, most public land ranchers were unhappy with the increases.

8. Public Land Law Review Commission, *One Third of the Nation's Land*, 104–18.

9. Ibid.; Federal Land Policy and Management Act of 1976, Public Law 579, 94th Cong., 2nd sess. (October 21, 1976); "National Park Service Organic Act," Environmental and Natural Resources Division, U.S. Department of Justice, http://www.justice.gov/enrd/3195.htm.

10. Emphasis on the terms "highest use" and "exclusive" appears in the original memorandum. "Legal Memorandum on Grazing Rights on Public Lands," circa 1977, Sagebrush Rebellion Papers (SRP) 85–04, Box 1, Folder 3; Voigt, *Public Grazing Lands*; Michael Frome, "Fight for Natural Beauty Access," *Los Angeles Times*, September 2, 1979; Cawley, *Federal Land, Western Anger*, 71–76. The important distinction between the Dann sisters' case and that of the ranchers and politicians involved in the Sagebrush Rebellion centers on indigenous rights. For more information on the Dann sisters and their endeavor to secure recognition of Western Shoshone land rights, see Solnit, *Savage Dreams*, 163–80; Barbara Gurr, "We Are People in the World: Native Americans and Human Rights," in Armaline, Glasberg, and Purkayastha, *Human Rights in Our Own Backyard*, 105–12; and David E. Wilkins, *Hollow Justice: A History of Indigenous Claims in the United States* (New Haven, Conn.: Yale University Press, 2013).

11. "Lamb Privileges Revoked," *Beaverton (Ore.) Valley Times*, March 18, 1977; "Lamb's Permits Revoked," *Nevada State Journal*, March 23, 1977; Al Delagach and George Reasons, "Lamb Is the Name of the Game in Nevada," *Los Angeles Times*, April 15, 1977; Tina Nappe and Rose Strickland, grazing fee hearing, January 11, 1978, Tina Nappe Papers (TNP), 90–34, Box 2, Folder 45; "Joint Hearing Senate Committee on Natural Resources and Assembly Committee on Environment and Public Resources," April 4, 1979, SRP 85–04, Box 1, Folder 7; Tom Matthews, "The Angry West vs. the Rest," *Newsweek*, September 17, 1979; Joseph Ross, "FLPMA Turns 30," *Society for Range Management* 28 (October 2006): 16–23; Skillen, *Nation's Largest Landlord*, 102–32.

12. "Nevadans Charge Fallout Danger," *Los Angeles Times*, June 27, 1957; "Radiation Burns Mark Horses," *Los Angeles Times*, June 27, 1957; Miller, *Under the Cloud*, 247–48,

299–300; Helen Fallini, interview by Robert McCracken, October 25–26, 1987, Nye County Town History Project (NCTHP); Fradkin, *Fallout*, 136; McCracken and Howerton, *History of Railroad Valley*, 283–86.

13. Gracian Uhalde, interview by the author, December 1, 2006, Nevada Test Site Oral History Project (NTSOHP); John S. Coogan, interview by the author, September 15, 2006, NTSOHP; "Treaty Banning Nuclear Weapons Tests in the Atmosphere, in Outer Space and Under Water," U.S. Department of State, http://www.justice.gov/.

14. Southwestern Radiological Health Laboratory, U.S. Public Health Service, "Off-Site Surveillance Activities of the Southwestern Radiological Health Laboratory: From January through June 1964" (Department of Health, Education, and Welfare, January 24, 1966), 1–6; "Nevadans Charge Fallout Danger," *Los Angeles Times*, June 27, 1957; "Radiation Burns Mark Horses," *Los Angeles Times*, June 27, 1957; Miller, *Under the Cloud*, 300–301; Lina Sharp, interview by Robert McCracken, August 14, 1992, NCTHP; McCracken and Howerton, *History of Railroad Valley*, 283–86; Gracian Uhalde, interview by the author, December 1, 2006, NTSOHP.

15. Southwestern Radiological Health Laboratory, U.S. Public Health Service, "Off-Site Surveillance Activities of the Southwestern Radiological Health Laboratory: From January through June 1964" (Department of Health, Education, and Welfare, January 24, 1966), 5; Jerry Le Blanc, "The Radiation Watchers: With Scintillators and Thyroid Counters, Scientists in Nevada Protect Us from the Atomic Age," *Chicago Tribune*, February 4, 1968; DeSilvia, *Extended Community*, 42–43; Carr Childers, "Every Mine, Every Cow Camp, Every Ranch," in Embry, *Oral History, Community and Work*, 294–300.

16. Lina Sharp, interview by Robert McCracken, August 14, 1992, NCTHP; Charles Costa, interview by the author, February 13, 2009, NTSOHP; DeSilvia, *Extended Community*, 42–55.

17. Gracian Uhalde, interview by the author, December 1, 2006, NTSOHP; Donald James, interview by the author, July 12, 2006, NTSOHP; DeSilvia, *Extended Community*, 90–100. For a critical discussion of the framework in which rural residents of the Great Basin raised and consumed their own food, see Fox, *Downwind*, 90–124.

18. Lina Sharp, interview by Robert McCracken, August 14, 1992, NCTHP; Benny Reilly, interview by Rene Corona Kolvet, May 20, 2004, NTSOHP; Patricia George and Virginia Sanchez, interview by March Palevsky, September 11, 2004, NTSOHP; Gracian Uhalde, interview by the author, December 1, 2006, NTSOHP; Virginia Sanchez and Kim Townsend, interview with the author, December 4, 2008, personal collection.

19. For more information on the accident at Three Mile Island, see Walker, *Three Mile Island*. For more information on the people affected by radioactive fallout in the Great Basin, see Gallagher, *American Ground Zero*. Donald Janson, "Radiation Is Released in Accident at Nuclear Plant in Pennsylvania," *New York Times*, March 29, 1979; Richard B. Lyons, "Atomic Plant Is Still Emitting Radioactivity," *New York Times*, March 30, 1979; "The Credibility Meltdown," *New York Times*, March 30, 1979; Richard D. Lyons, "Children Evacuated," *New York Times*, March 31, 1979; David Burnham, "Large Question Mark Hangs over the Future of Nuclear Power," *New York Times*, April 1, 1979; "Nevada Test Site Experts Headed for Stricken Pennsylvania Plant," *New York Times*, April 1, 1979; Alan Richman, "In Plant Vicinity, Suspicion and Doubt," *New York Times*, April 3, 1979; "Nevada Woman Says Nuclear Fallout Made Family 'Guinea Pigs,'" *New York Times*, April 24, 1979; "Millions at Stake in Court Test on Radiation Risks," *Los Angeles Times*, April 29, 1979; Richard D. Lyons, "Radiation Monitors on

the Defensive as Outcry over Nuclear Safety Rises," *New York Times*, May 11, 1979; A. O. Sulzberger, Jr., "A-Bomb Tests: Cold War Fears Stifled Doubts," *New York Times*, May 13, 1979; B. Drummond Ayers, Jr., "Three Mile Island: Notes from a Nightmare," *New York Times*, April 16, 1979; Donald James, interview by the author, July 12, 2006, NTSOHP; Charles Costa, interview by the author, February 13, 2009, NTSOHP.

20. House Committee on Interstate and Foreign Commerce, Subcommittee on Oversight and Investigations, *Low-Level Effects of Radiation on Health: Hearings*, 96th Cong., 1st sess. (April 23, May 24, and August 1, 1979), 14–39, 292–307; Gracian Uhalde, interview by the author, December 1, 2006, NTSOHP; testimony of Governor Robert List of Nevada, U.S. Senate, Environment and Public Works Subcommittee on Nuclear Regulation, January 24, 1980, Robert List Papers (RLP), Box 827, Folder 6.

21. Gracian Uhalde, interview by the author, December 1, 2006, NTSOHP.

22. Department of the Interior, Secretary's Order 3280, December 16, 2008; "Position Statement 2010–16: The National System of Public Lands," September 9, 2010, Public Lands Foundation, http://www.publicland.org/14_position_statements/PLF _2010_16_natl_sys_pub_lands.html.

Selected Bibliography

ARCHIVAL COLLECTIONS

The American Presidency Project. Gerhard Peters and John T. Woolley. http://www
.presidency.ucsb.edu/ws/?pid=14786
Conservation Collection CONS80. Denver Public Library, Denver, Colo.
  Velma Johnston Papers (VJP)
General Land Office (GLO) Records. Bureau of Land Management. http://www.glo
records.blm.gov/
Las Vegas Wash Project Oral History Program. Southern Nevada Water Authority, Las
Vegas, Nev.
National Nuclear Security Administration/Nevada Field Office (NNSA/NFO), Las
Vegas, Nev. http://www.nv.doe.gov/library/testingarchive.aspx
Nevada State Archives, Carson City, Nev.
  Charles Hinton Russell Papers (CRP)
  Donal Neil "Mike" O'Callaghan Papers (MOP)
  Edward Peter Carville Papers (ECP)
  Frank Grant Sawyer Papers (GSP)
  Frederick Bennett Balzar Papers (FBP)
  Morely Isaac Griswold Papers (MGP)
  Paul Dominique Laxalt Papers (PLP)
  Richard Kirman Papers (RKP)
  Robert Frank List Papers (RLP)
  Vail Montgomery Pittman Papers (VPP)
Nevada State Water Rights (NSWR). State of Nevada Division of Water Resources.
  http://water.nv.gov/waterrights/
Nye County Town History Project (NCTHP). Nye County, Nev. https://nyecounty
history.com/
Public Lands Foundation Archives (PLFA). Bureau of Land Management National
Training Center, Phoenix, Ariz. http://www.publicland.org/35_archives_frame
.html
Special Collections, University of Nevada, Las Vegas.
  Howard Cannon Papers (HCP)
  Nevada Test Site Oral History Project (NTSOHP), http://digital.library.unlv.edu
  /ntsohp/
  Nye County Photograph Collection (NCPC)

Selected Bibliography

Special Collections, University of Nevada, Reno.
  Gus Bundy Photograph Collection (GBPC)
  Sagebrush Rebellion Papers (SRP)
  Tina Nappe Papers (TNP)

Newspapers, Periodicals, and Journals

Regional newspapers from:
  Colorado: *Daily Sentinel* (Grand Junction); *Denver Post.*
  Nevada: *Ely Daily Times; Las Vegas Review-Journal; Las Vegas Sun; Reno Evening Gazette; Nevada State Journal; Tonopah Daily Times; Tonopah Daily Times and Bonanza; Tonopah Times Bonanza; Weekly Gazette and Stockman.*
  Oregon: *Beaverton Valley Times.*
  Utah: *Color Country Spectrum* (Saint George); *Garfield County News; Kane County Standard; Ogden Standard-Examiner; Provo (Sunday/Daily) Herald; Salt Lake Herald; Salt Lake Telegram; Salt Lake Tribune.*
National newspapers including the *New York Times, Chicago Tribune,* and *Los Angeles Times.*
National publications including *Time, Life, McClure's Magazine, Our Public Lands, American Forests, Nature, Forest and Stream, Popular Science,* and *National Geographic.*

Books and Articles

Abbey, Edward. *Desert Solitaire: A Season in the Wilderness.* New York: Simon and Schuster, 1968.

Allen, Michael. *Rodeo Cowboys in the North American Imagination.* Reno: University of Nevada Press, 1998.

Allen, Vikki P., Christopher L. Harper, Robin E. McMullen, Susan F. Rose, and Michael S. Kelly. *The Prospects Look Good: A View of 10 Ranching and Mining Sites on Nellis Air Force Range, Nellis Air Force Base, Nevada.* Las Vegas, Nev.: Dames and Moore, 1998.

Amaral, Anthony. *Mustang: Life and Legends of Nevada's Wild Horses.* Reno: University of Nevada Press, 1977.

Angel, Myron, ed. *History of Nevada with Illustrations and Biographical Sketches of Its Prominent Men and Pioneers.* Oakland, Calif.: Thompson and West, 1881.

Armaline, William T., Davita Silfen Glasberg, and Bandana Purkayastha, eds. *Human Rights in Our Own Backyard: Injustice and Resistance in the United States.* Philadelphia: University of Pennsylvania Press, 2011.

Baker, Ray Stannard. "The Great Southwest: The Tragedy of the Range." *Century Illustrated Magazine,* August 1902, 535–45.

Bakken, Gordon Morris. *The Mining Law of 1872: Past, Politics, and Prospects.* Albuquerque: University of New Mexico Press, 2008.

Bancroft, Hubert Howard. *History of Nevada, Colorado, and Wyoming, 1540–1888.* San Francisco: History Company, 1890.

Bartlett, Richard A. *Great Surveys of the American West.* Norman: University of Oklahoma Press, 1962.

Bates, J. Leonard. "Fulfilling American Democracy: The Conservation Movement, 1907–1921." *Mississippi Valley Historical Review* 44 (June 1957): 29–57.

Beckwith, C. G. "Review: Wild Horse of the West." *Revista de Historia de America* 20 (December 1945): 460–61.

Bell, William A. *New Tracks in North America: A Journal of Travel and Adventure Whilst Engaged in the Survey for a Southern Railroad to the Pacific Ocean during 1867–1868*. London: Chapman and Hall, 1869.

———. "On the Basin of Colorado and the Great Basin of North America." *Journal of the Royal Geographical Society of London* 39 (1869): 95–120.

Best, Katharine, and Katharine Hillyer. *Las Vegas: Playtown U.S.A.* New York: David McKay, 1955.

Blackhawk, Ned. *Violence over the Land: Indians and Empires in the Early American West*. Cambridge, Mass.: Harvard University Press, 2006.

Blanton, Ouida. *A History of Tooele County*. Salt Lake City: Utah State Historical Society, 1998.

Borne, Lawrence R. *Dude Ranching: A Complete History*. Albuquerque: University of New Mexico Press, 1983.

Boyer, Paul S. *By the Bomb's Early Light: American Thought and Culture at the Dawn of the Atomic Age*. Chapel Hill: University of North Carolina Press, 1985.

Bradley, Martha Sonntag. *A History of Beaver County*. Salt Lake City: Utah State Historical Society, 1999.

Brewer, William H. "The Great Basin." *Journal of the American Geographical Society of New York* 21 (1889): 197–227.

Brinkley, Douglas, and Patricia Nelson Limerick, eds. *The Western Paradox: A Conservation Reader*. New Haven, Conn.: Yale University Press, 2000.

Bureau of Land Management. "The Taylor Grazing Act of June 28, 1934, with Amendments to September 1, 1955." Washington, D.C.: Department of the Interior, 1962.

Burger, Joel. *Wild Horses of the Great Basin: Social Competition and Population Size*. Chicago: University of Chicago Press, 1986.

Burnett, Dan. *A Cowboy Never Lies*. Hamilton, Wash.: New West Press, 1996.

Buscombe, Edward, and Roberta E. Pearson, eds. *Back in the Saddle Again: New Essays on the Western*. London: British Film Institute, 1998.

Cannon, Brian Q. *Reopening the Frontier: Homesteading in the Modern West*. Lawrence: University Press of Kansas, 2009.

Caras, Roger A. *A Perfect Harmony: The Intertwining Lives of Animals and Humans throughout History*. New York: Simon and Schuster, 1996.

Carpenter, Farrington R. *Confessions of a Maverick: An Autobiography*. Denver: State Historical Society of Colorado, 1984.

Carr Childers, Leisl. "Leisl Carr Childers on the Gus Bundy Photographs and the Wild Horse Controversy." *Environmental History*, July 2013, 606–14.

Carr, Ethan. *Wilderness by Design: Landscape Architecture and the National Park Service*. Lincoln: University of Nebraska Press, 1998.

Carson, Rachel L. *Silent Spring*. New York: Houghton Mifflin, 1962.

Cawley, R. McGreggor. *Federal Land, Western Anger: The Sagebrush Rebellion and Environmental Politics*. Lawrence: University Press of Kansas, 1993.

Chittenden, Russell H. "Biographical Memoir of William Henry Brewer, 1828–1910." *National Academy of Sciences Biographical Memoir* 12 (1927): 287–323.

Clapson, Mark. *Suburban Century: Social Change and Urban Growth in England and the United States*. New York: Berg Press, 2003.

Clark, LaVerne Harrell. *They Sang for Horses: The Impact of the Horse on Navajo and Apache Folklore*. Boulder: University Press of Colorado, 2001.

Clark, Ray, and Larry Canter, eds. *Environmental Policy and NEPA: Past, Present, and Future*. Boca Raton, Fla.: St. Lucie Press, 1997.

Clawson, Marion. *The Bureau of Land Management*. New York: Praeger, 1971.

————. *The Western Range Livestock Industry*. New York: McGraw-Hill, 1950.

Clawson, Marion, and Burnell Held. *The Federal Lands: Their Use and Management*. Baltimore: Resources for the Future, 1957.

Clutton-Brock, Juliet. *Horse Power: A History of the Horse and the Donkey in Human Societies*. Cambridge, Mass.: Harvard University Press, 1992.

————. *A Natural History of Domesticated Mammals*. Cambridge: Cambridge University Press, 1999.

Coleman, Jon T. *Vicious: Wolves and Men in America*. New Haven, Conn.: Yale University Press, 2004.

Commoner, Barry. *The Closing Circle: Man, Nature and Technology*. New York: Alfred Knopf, 1971.

Cronon, William. *Changes in the Land: Indians, Colonists, and the Ecology of New England*. Rev. ed. New York: Hill and Wang, 2003.

Cruise, David, and Allison Griffiths. *Wild Horse Annie and the Last of the Mustangs*. New York: Scribner, 2010.

Crum, Stephen. *The Road on Which We Came: A History of the Western Shoshone*. Salt Lake City: University of Utah Press, 1994.

Czech, Brian, and Paul R. Krausman. *The Endangered Species Act: History, Conservation, Biology, and Public Policy*. Baltimore: Johns Hopkins University Press, 2001.

Dant, Sara. "Making Wilderness Work: Frank Church and the American Wilderness Movement." *Pacific Historical Review* 77 (May 2008): 237–72.

Darlington, David. *The Mojave: A Portrait of the Definitive American Desert*. New York: Henry Holt, 1996.

Denhardt, Robert Moorman. *Quarter Horses: A Story of Two Centuries*. Norman: University of Oklahoma Press, 1967.

————. "The Role of the Horse in the Social History of Early California." *Agricultural History* 14 (January 1940): 13–22.

DeSilvia, Susan. *Extended Community: An Oral History of the Community Environmental Monitoring Program (CEMP), 1981–2003*. Las Vegas, Nev.: Desert Research Institute, 2004.

De Steiguer, Edward. *Wild Horses of the West: History and Politics of America's Mustangs*. Tucson: University of Arizona Press, 2011.

Dobie, J. Frank. *The Mustangs*. New York: Bantam, 1954.

Donaldson, Thomas. "The Public Lands of the United States." *North American Review* 133 (August 1881): 204–13.

Douglass, William A. *Basque Sheepherders of the American West*. Reno: University of Nevada Press, 1985.

Edgington, Ryan H. *Range Wars: The Environmental Contest for White Sands Missile Range*. Lincoln: University of Nebraska Press, 2014.

Ehrlich, Paul R. *The Population Bomb*. Cutchogue, N.Y.: Buccaneer, 1968.

Elliott, Gary E. *Senator Alan Bible and the Politics of the New West*. Reno: University of Nevada Press, 1994.

Ely, Richard T. *Ground under Our Feet*. New York: Arno Press, 1977.

————. *Land Economics*. New York: Macmillan, 1940.

————. *Outlines of Economics*. Meadville, Pa.: Flood and Vincent, 1893.

Ely, Richard T., Thomas S. Adams, Alan A. Young, and Max O. Lorenz. *Outlines of Economics*. New York: Macmillan, 1923.

Ely, Richard T., Ralph H. Hess, Charles L. Keith, and Thomas N. Carter. *The Foundations of National Prosperity*. New York: Macmillan, 1918.

Embry, Jessie, ed. *Oral History, Community and Work in the American West*. Tucson: University of Arizona Press, 2013.

Faragher, John Mack. *Rereading Frederick Jackson Turner: "The Significance of the Frontier in American History" and Other Essays*. New Haven, Conn.: Yale University Press, 1998.

Fehner, Terrence R., and F. G. Gosling. *Atmospheric Nuclear Weapons Testing, 1951–1963*. Washington, D.C.: Department of Energy, 2006.

————. *Origins of the Nevada Test Site*. Washington, D.C.: Department of Energy, 2000.

Fenley, John M., Farrel Branson, Karl Parker, William R. Meiners, and Jim Anderson. "With the Sections." *Journal of Range Management* 5 (November 1952): 430–32.

Fernlund, Kevin J., ed. *The Cold War American West, 1945–1989*. Albuquerque: University of New Mexico Press, 1998.

Flores, Dan. *Horizontal Yellow: Nature and History in the Near Southwest*. Albuquerque: University of New Mexico Press, 1999.

Foss, Philip O. "The Determination of Grazing Fees on Federally-Owned Rangelands." *Journal of Farm Economics*, August 1959, 535–47.

————. *Politics and Grass: The Administration of Grazing on the Public Domain*. Seattle: University of Washington Press, 1960.

Fox, Sarah Alisabeth. *Downwind: A People's History of the Nuclear West*. Lincoln: University of Nebraska Press, 2014.

Fradkin, Philip. *Fallout: An American Nuclear Tragedy*. Boulder, Colo.: Johnson Books, 2004.

Francaviglia, Richard V. *Mapping and Imagination in the Great Basin: A Cartographic History*. Reno: University of Nevada Press, 2005.

Fraser, Antonia. *A History of Toys*. Frankfurt, Germany: Delacorte Press, 1966.

Frémont, John C. *Report of the Exploring Expedition to the Rocky Mountains in the Year 1842 and to Oregon and North California in the Years 1843–44*. Washington, D.C.: Gales and Seaton, 1845.

Gallagher, Carole. *American Ground Zero: The Secret Nuclear War*. Cambridge, Mass.: MIT Press, 1993.

Garreau, Joel. *The Nine Nations of North America*. Boston: Houghton Mifflin, 1981.

Georgetta, Clel. *Golden Fleece in Nevada*. Reno: Venture Publishing, 1972.

Glass, Matthew. *Citizens against the MX: Public Languages in the Nuclear Age*. Chicago: University of Illinois Press, 1993.

Goble, Dale D. J., Michael Scott, and Frank W. Davis, eds., *The Endangered Species Act at 30: Renewing the Conservation Promise*. Washington, D.C.: Island Press, 2005.

Goin, Peter. *Nuclear Landscapes*. Baltimore: Johns Hopkins University Press, 1991.

Gutfreund, Owen. *20th Century Sprawl: Highways and the Reshaping of the American Landscape*. New York: Oxford University Press, 2004.

Gwynn, J. Wallace, ed. *Great Salt Lake: An Overview of Change*. Salt Lake City: Utah Department of Natural Resources, 2002.

Hacker, Barton C. *Elements of Controversy: The Atomic Energy Commission and Radiation Safety in Nuclear Weapons Testing, 1947–1974.* Berkeley: University of California Press, 1994.

Hall, Shawn. *Preserving the Glory Days: Ghost Towns and Mining Camps of Nye County Nevada.* Reno: University of Nevada Press, 1981.

Hamalainen, Pekka. *The Comanche Empire.* New Haven, Conn.: Yale University Press, 2008.

Hardin, Garrett. "The Tragedy of the Commons." *Science,* December 13, 1968, 1243–48.

Harvey, Mark. *Wilderness Forever: Howard Zahniser and the Path to the Wilderness Act.* Seattle: University of Washington Press, 2005.

Hausladen, Gary J., ed. *Western Places, American Myths: How We Think about the West.* Reno: University of Nevada Press, 2003.

Haynes, Richard P. *Animal Welfare: Competing Conceptions and Their Ethical Implications.* New York: Springer, 2008.

Hays, Samuel P. *Beauty, Health, and Permanence: Environmental Politics in the United States 1955–1985.* New York: Cambridge University Press, 1987.

———. *Conservation and the Gospel of Efficiency: The Progressive Conservation Movement 1890–1920.* Cambridge, Mass.: Harvard University Press, 1959.

Hazen, William B. "The Great Middle Region of the United States, and Its Limited Space of Arable Land." *North American Review* 246 (January 1875): 1–34.

Her Many Horses, Emil, and George Horse Capture. *Song for the Horse Nation: Horses in Native American Culture.* Washington, D.C.: National Museum of the American Indian, 2006.

Hibbard, Benjamin Horace. *A History of the Public Land Policies.* Madison: University of Wisconsin Press, 1965.

Hillyer, Curtis. *Nevada Compiled Laws 1929.* San Francisco: Bender-Moss, 1930.

Hirt, Paul W. *A Conspiracy of Optimism: Management of the National Forests since World War II.* Lincoln: University of Nebraska Press, 1994.

Holecheck, Jerry L., Jerry Hawkes, and Tim D. Darden. "Macro Economics and Cattle Ranching." *Rangelands,* June 1994, 118–23.

Hulse, James W. *Lincoln County, Nevada: 1864–1909.* Reno: University of Nevada Press, 1971.

———. *The Silver State: Nevada's Heritage Reinterpreted.* Reno: University of Nevada Press, 2004.

Inter-Tribal Council of Nevada. *Newe: A Western Shoshone History.* Salt Lake City: University of Utah Press, 1976.

Isenberg, Andrew C. *The Destruction of the Bison: An Environmental History, 1750–1930.* Cambridge, Mass.: Cambridge University Press, 2000.

Iverson, Peter. *When Indians Became Cowboys: Native Peoples and Cattle Ranching in the American West.* Norman: University of Oklahoma Press, 1994.

Jackson, Kenneth T. *Crabgrass Frontier: The Suburbanization of the United States.* New York: Oxford University Press, 1985.

Jasper, James M., and Dorothy Nelkin. *The Animal Rights Crusade: The Growth of a Moral Protest.* New York: Free Press, 1992.

Josephson, Paul R. *Motorized Obsessions: Life, Liberty, and the Small-Bore Engine.* Baltimore: Johns Hopkins University Press, 2007.

Kania, Alan J. *Wild Horse Annie: Velma Johnston and Her Fight to Save the Mustang.* Reno: University of Nevada Press, 2012.

Kelso, M. M. "Current Issues in Federal Land Management in the Western United States." *Journal of Farm Economics*, November 1947, 1295–313.

King, Clarence. *Report of the Geological Exploration of the Fortieth Parallel.* Vols. 4 and 5. Washington, D.C.: Government Printing Office, 1877.

Kirk, Andrew G. *Counterculture Green: The Whole Earth Catalog and American Environmentalism.* Lawrence: University Press of Kansas, 2007.

Kirkpatrick, Jay F., and Patricia M. Fazio. "Ecce Equus." *Natural History Magazine,* May 2008, 30.

Kline, Benjamin. *First along the River: A Brief History of the US Environmental Movement.* New York: Rowman and Littlefield, 2011.

Knack, Martha C. "The Saga of Tim Hooper's Homestead: Non-Reservation Shoshone Indian Land Title in Nevada." *Western Historical Quarterly* 39 (Summer 2008): 125–51.

Knudsten, Molly Flagg. *Here Is Our Valley.* Reno: University of Nevada Press, 1975.

Landstrom, Karl S. "Reclamation under the Desert Land Act, 1954–59." *Journal of Farm Economics* 42 (August 1960): 629–38.

Leopold, Aldo. *A Sand County Almanac and Sketches Here and There.* New York: Oxford University Press, 1949.

Leopold, A. S., S. A. Cain, C. M. Cottam, I. N. Gabrielson, and T. L. Kimball. *Wildlife Management in the National Parks: The Leopold Report.* Washington, D.C.: Government Printing Office, 1963.

Limerick, Patricia Nelson, Clyde A. Milner, II, and Charles Rankin, eds. *Trails toward a New Western History.* Lawrence: University Press of Kansas, 1991.

Lister, Adrian M., Carles Vilà, Hans Ellegren, Anders Götherström, Jennifer A. Leonard, and Robert K. Wayne. "Tales from the DNA of Domestic Horses." *Science,* April 13, 2001, 218–19.

McCracken, Robert D., and Jeanne Sharp Howerton. *A History of Railroad Valley Nevada.* Tonopah: Central Nevada Historical Society, 1996.

McKnight, Tom L. "The Feral Horse in Anglo-America." *Geographical Review* 49 (October 1959): 506–25.

Meinig, Donald W., ed. *The Interpretation of Ordinary Landscapes.* New York: Oxford University Press, 1979.

———. "The Mormon Culture Region: Strategies and Patterns in the American West, 1847–1964." *Annals of the Association of American Geographers* 55 (June 1965): 191–220.

Merrill, Karen R. *Public Lands and Political Meaning: Ranchers, the Government, and the Property between Them.* Berkeley: University of California Press, 2002.

Miller, Richard. *Under the Cloud: The Decades of Nuclear Testing.* New York: Free Press, 1986.

Moehring, Eugene P. *Urbanism and Empire in the Far West, 1840–1890.* Reno: University of Nevada Press, 1996.

Morin, Paula. *Honest Horses: Wild Horses in the Great Basin.* Reno: University of Nevada Press, 2006.

Muhn, James, and Hanson R. Stuart. *Opportunity and Challenge: The Story of BLM.* Washington, D.C.: Department of the Interior, Bureau of Land Management, 1988.

Mythen, Gabe. *Ulrich Beck: A Critical Introduction to the Risk Society.* London: Pluto Press, 2004.

Nash, Gerald D. *The American West Transformed: The Impact of the Second World War.* Lincoln: University of Nebraska Press, 1985.

———. *The Federal Landscape: An Economic History of the Twentieth-Century West.* Tucson: University of Arizona Press, 1999.

Nash, Roderick. *Wilderness and the American Mind.* Rev. ed. New Haven, Conn.: Yale University Press, 1967.

Nelson, Judy E. *A Summary of Agricultural Potential for Desert Land Entries in Nevada.* Reno: Bureau of Land Management, 1979.

Nelson, Robert H. *Public Land and Private Rights: The Failure of Scientific Management.* Lanham, Md.: Rowman and Littlefield, 1995.

Nickel, Robert V. "Dollars, Defense, and the Desert: Southern Nevada's Military Economy and World War II." *Nevada Historical Society Quarterly,* Winter 2004, 303–27.

Norcross, C. A. *Agricultural Nevada.* San Francisco: Sunset Magazine Homeseekers Bureau, 1911.

Olson, Brent A. "Paper Trails: The Outdoor Recreation Resource Review Commission and the Rationalization of Recreational Resources." *Geoforum* 2010. doi:10.1016/j.geoforum.2009.11.014.

Olson, Sandra L., ed. *Horses through Time.* Lanham, Md.: Roberts Reinhart, 1996.

Palevsky, Mary. *Atomic Fragments: A Daughter's Questions.* Berkeley: University of California Press, 2000.

Paris, Beltran. *Beltran: Basque Sheepman of the American West.* Reno: University of Nevada Press, 1979.

Pearson, Chris, Peter Coates, and Tim Cole, eds. *Militarized Landscapes: From Gettysburg to Salisbury Plain.* New York: Continuum, 2010.

Peffer, E. Louise. *The Closing of the Public Domain: Disposal and Reservation Policies, 1900–1950.* New York: Arno Press, 1972.

Penny, J. Russell, and Marion Clawson. "Administration of Grazing Districts." *Land Economics,* February 1953, 23–34.

Peterson, Gene. *Pioneering Outdoor Recreation for the Bureau of Land Management.* McLean, Va.: Public Lands Foundation, 1996.

Phelps, Norm. *The Longest Struggle: Animal Advocacy from Pythagoras to PETA.* New York: Lantern Books, 2007.

Powell, John Wesley. *Report on the Lands of the Arid Region of the United States: With a More Detailed Account of the Lands of Utah.* Washington, D.C.: Government Printing Office, 1879.

Proceedings of the First National Water Users' Conference, Reno, February 26–28, 1930. Reno: American Farm Bureau Federation, 1930.

Public Land Commission. *The Public Domain: Its History with Statistics.* Washington, D.C.: Government Printing Office, 1881.

Public Land Law Review Commission. *One Third of the Nation's Land: A Report to the President and to the Congress by the Public Land Law Review Commission.* Washington, D.C.: Government Printing Office, June 1970.

Punke, Michael. *Last Stand: George Bird Grinnell, the Battle to Save the Buffalo, and the Birth of the New West.* Lincoln: University of Nebraska Press, 2007.

Rader, Benjamin G. *The Academic Mind and Reform.* Lexington: University Press of Kentucky, 1966.

Ralli, Paul. *Viva Las Vegas.* Hollywood, Calif.: House-Warven, 1953.

Read, Effie O. *White Pine Lang Syne: A True History of White Pine County, Nevada.* Denver: Big Mountain Press, 1965.

Reid, John B., and Roland M. James, eds. *Uncovering Nevada's Past*. Reno: University of Nevada Press, 2004.

Robison, Russell M. *Our Swallow Heritage*. Vols. 1 and 2. Morrisville, N.C.: Lulu Enterprises, 2006.

Rollins, Philip Ashton. *The Cowboy: An Unconventional History of Civilization on the Old-Time Range*. Norman: University of Oklahoma Press, 1997.

Ross, Joseph. "FLPMA Turns 30." *Society for Range Management* 28 (October 2006): 16–23.

Rothman, Hal K. *Devil's Bargains: Tourism in the Twentieth Century American West*. Lawrence: University Press of Kansas, 1998.

———. "'A Regular Ding Dong Fight': Agency Culture and Evolution in the NPS-USFS Dispute, 1916–1937." *Western Historical Quarterly* 20 (May 1989): 141–61.

———. *Saving the Planet: The American Response to the Environment in the Twentieth Century*. Chicago: American Ways Series, 2000.

Rowley, William D. *U.S. Forest Service Grazing and Rangelands: A History*. College Station: Texas A&M University Press, 1985.

Runte, Alfred. *National Parks: The American Experience*. Lincoln: University of Nebraska Press, 1979.

Ryden, Hope. *America's Last Wild Horses*. 30th anniv. ed. Guilford, Conn.: Lyons Press, 1999.

Sawyer, Byrd Wall. *Nevada Nomads: A Story of the Sheep Industry*. San Jose, Calif.: Harlan-Young Press, 1971.

Scott, James C. *Seeing Like a State: How Certain Schemes to Improve the Human Condition Have Failed*. New Haven, Conn.: Yale University Press, 1998.

Sedjo, Roger A., ed. *A Vision for the U.S. Forest Service: Goals for Its Next Century*. Washington, D.C.: Resources for the Future, 2000.

Sellars, Richard W. *Preserving Nature in the National Parks: A History*. New Haven, Conn.: Yale University Press, 1997.

Shamberger, Hugh A. *Evolution of Nevada's Water Laws, as Related to the Development and Evaluation of the State's Water Resources, from 1866 to about 1960*. Carson City, Nev.: Division of Water Resources, 1991.

Shane, Maxine F. *Taylor Grazing Act in Nevada, 1934–1984*. Reno: Bureau of Land Management, Nevada State Office, 1984.

Singer, Pete. *Animal Liberation*. London: Pimlico, 1975.

Skillen, James R. *The Nation's Largest Landlord: The Bureau of Land Management in the American West*. Lawrence: University Press of Kansas, 2009.

Smith, Thomas G. "John Kennedy, Stewart Udall, and New Frontier Conservation." *Pacific Historical Review* 64 (August 1995): 329–62.

Smythe, William E. *The Conquest of Arid America*. New York: Macmillan, 1907.

Solnit, Rebecca. *Savage Dreams: A Journey into the Landscape Wars of the American West*. Berkeley: University of California Press, 1994.

Starrs, Paul F. *Let the Cowboy Ride: Cattle Ranching in the American West*. Baltimore: Johns Hopkins University Press, 1998.

Steele, Rufus. *Mustangs of the Mesas: A Saga of the Wild Horse*. Hollywood, Calif.: Murray and Gee, 1941.

Steen, Harold K. *The U.S. Forest Service: A History*. Centennial ed. Seattle: University of Washington Press, 2004.

Stewart, Louise B. *The History of Pahranagat Valley*. Provo, Utah: J. Grant Stevenson, 1979.

Stillman, Deanne. *Mustang: The Saga of the Wild Horse in the American West.* New York: Houghton Mifflin, 2008.

Stoddart, Laurence A., and Arthur D. Smith. *Range Management.* New York: McGraw-Hill, 1955.

Stringfellow, Kim. *Jackrabbit Homestead: Tracing the Small Tract Act in the Southern California Landscape, 1938–2008.* Chicago: Center for American Places at Columbia College, 2009.

Symanski, Richard. "Contested Realities: Feral Horses in Outback Australia." *Annals of the Association of American Geographers* 84 (June 1994): 251–69.

———. *Wild Horses and Sacred Cows.* Flagstaff, Ariz.: Northland Press, 1985.

The Taylor Grazing Act, 1934–1984: 50 Years of Progress. Boise: Bureau of Land Management, Idaho State Office, 1984.

Thomas, Heather Smith. *The Wild Horse Controversy.* Cranbury, N.J.: A. S. Barnes, 1979.

Thomson, David. *In Nevada: The Land, the People, God, and Chance.* New York: Alfred A. Knopf, 1999.

Titus, A. Constandina. *Bombs in the Backyard: Atomic Testing and American Politics.* Reno: University of Nevada Press, 1986.

Totoricaguena, Gloria P. *Identity, Culture, and Politics in the Basque Diaspora.* Reno: University of Nevada Press, 2004.

Townley, John M. *Conquered Provinces: Nevada Moves Southeast, 1864–1871.* Provo, Utah: Brigham Young University Press, 1973.

Trexler, Keith A. *Lehman Caves . . . Its Human Story.* Baker, Nev.: Department of the Interior, National Park Service, 1966.

Twain, Mark. *Roughing It.* Hartford, Conn.: American Publishing, 1872.

Udall, Stewart L. *The Quiet Crisis.* New York: Avon Books, 1963.

United States Nuclear Tests July 1945 through September 1992. Oakridge, Tenn.: Department of Energy, Nevada Operations Office, 2000.

Unrau, Harlan D. *Basin and Range: A History of Great Basin National Park.* Washington, D.C.: Department of Interior, National Park Service, 1990.

Vale, Thomas R. *The American Wilderness: Reflections on Nature Protection in the United States.* Charlottesville: University of Virginia Press, 2005.

Vernetti, Michael. *Senator Howard Cannon of Nevada.* Reno: University of Nevada Press, 2008.

Vesta, Stanley. "Review: The Wild Horse of the West." *Mississippi Valley Historical Review* 32 (September 1945): 287–88.

Voigt, William, Jr. *Public Grazing Lands.* New Brunswick, N.J.: Rutgers University Press, 1976.

Walker, Samuel J. *Three Mile Island: A Nuclear Crisis in Historical Perspective.* Berkeley: University of California Press, 2004.

Wand, Kelly, ed. *The Animal Rights Movement.* San Diego: Green Haven Press, 2003.

Watkins, Thomas H., and Charles S. Watson, Jr. *The Lands No One Knows: America and the Public Domain.* San Francisco: Sierra Club Books, 1975.

Weatherly, Megan Sharp. "Transforming Space into Place: Development Rock Climbing and Interpretation in Red Rock Canyon National Conservation Area, 1960–2010." Master's thesis, University of Nevada, Las Vegas, 2010.

Webb, Robert H., and Howard G. Wilshire. *Environmental Effects of Off-Road Vehicles: Impacts and Management in Arid Regions.* New York: Springer-Verlag, 1983.

Webb, Walter Prescott. "The American West: Perpetual Mirage." *Harper's Magazine*, May 1957, 25–31.

———. *The Great Plains*. Waltham, Mass.: Blaisdell Publishing, 1931.

———. "The West and the Desert." *Montana: The Magazine of Western History* 8 (Winter 1958): 2–12.

Westermeier, Clifford P. *Man, Beast, Dust: The Story of Rodeo*. Lincoln: University of Nebraska Press, 1987.

Western Historical Studies, Inc. *Canyonlands National Park, Arches National Park, and Natural Bridges National Monument Historic Resource Study*. Washington, D.C.: Department of the Interior, 1986.

White, Richard. *"It's Your Misfortune and None of My Own": A New History of the American West*. Norman: University of Oklahoma Press, 1991.

Wilson, Richa. *Privies, Pastures, and Portables: Administrative Facilities of the Humboldt-Toiyabe National Forest 1891–1950*. Vols. 1 and 2. Washington, D.C.: U.S. Forest Service, 2001.

Wolfe, Michael L. "The Wild Horse and Burro Issue, 1982." *Environmental Review* 7 (Summer 1983): 179–92.

Workman, John P. "Federal Grazing Fees: A Controversy That Won't Go Away." *Rangelands* 10 (June 1988): 128–30.

Worster, Donald. *Dust Bowl: The Southern Plains in the 1930s*. 25th anniv. ed. New York: Oxford University Press, 2004.

———. *Nature's Economy: A History of Ecological Ideas*. New York: Cambridge University Press, 1977.

Wrobel, David M. *The End of American Exceptionalism: Frontier Anxiety from the Old West to the New Deal*. Lawrence: University Press of Kansas, 1993.

Wyman, Walker D. *The Wild Horse of the West*. Lincoln: University of Nebraska Press, 1945.

Young, James A. "Operation Hay Lift: The Winter of 1949." *Rangelands* 6 (June 1984): 116–19.

Young, James A., and Charlie D. Clements. *Cheatgrass: Fire and Forage on the Range*. Reno: University of Nevada Press, 2009.

Young, James A., and R. A. Evans. "Silver State Rangelands: Historical Perspective." *Rangelands*, October 1989, 199–203.

Young, James A., and B. Abbott Sparks. *Cattle in the Cold Desert*. Expanded ed. Reno: University of Nevada Press, 2002.

Zinser, Charles I. *Outdoor Recreation: United States National Parks, Forests, and Public Lands*. New York: John Wiley and Sons, 1995.

Index

11–14, 211–18; indicators of, 5–7; land classification change, 116–18; map of, 208–209; public interest evolution, 121–23, 206–207, 212; risk misalignment summarized, 217–19. *See also specific topics, e.g.,* grazing *entries;* nuclear weapons testing; wild horses

Multiple-Use Advisory Boards, formation, 115–16, 143

Multiple-Use Sustained-Yield Act, 115–16

Mulvihill, J. A., 184

Murray, Jack, 173

Mustang (Henry), 183

mustangs. *See* wild horses *entries*

Nancy shot, in Upshot-Knothole series, 99

Nappe, Tina, 204

Nash, I. H., 28

National Cattlemen's Association, 195

national monument designation, Lehman Caves, 126, 128. *See also* Great Basin National Park, proposal for

National Mustang Association (NMA), 184–85, 191

national park proposal, Canyonlands, 145–46

National Parks Association, 130

National Park Service, 124, 126–27, 129, 132–33

National Park Service Act, 222n11

National System of Public Lands (NSPL), 219

National Wild Horse Range, 199

National Wild Horse Refuge, 183–84, 189, 191

National Wool Growers Association, 195

Native Americans, reservations, 10, 222n10. *See also* Western Shoshones

NBC Evening News, 94, 247n64

Nellis Range (Tonopah Bombing Range), 55, 57–58, 60–61, 170–71, 183–84, 236n18. *See also* nuclear weapons testing

Nevada: grazing permit statistics, 229n59; homestead application statistics, 107–108; ranch lands percentage,

226n35; water regulation, 23–25. *See also specific topics, e.g.,* grazing *entries;* Great Basin National Park, proposal for; maps of Great Basin; radioactive fallout *entries*

Nevada Bureau of Mines, 140

Nevada Cattlemen's Association, 204

Nevada Farm Bureau, 134

Nevada Federated Sportsmen, 140

Nevada Fish and Game Department, 184, 194

Nevada Foundation for a National Park, 131

Nevada Humane Society, 173

Nevada Livestock Association, 25, 28–30, 40, 42, 129, 225n28

Nevada Mining Association, 133–34, 147

Nevada Outdoor Recreation Association (NORA), 147–48

Nevada Proving Ground: name adoption, 88, 242n43; wild horse incursion, 185–86. *See also* nuclear weapons testing

Nevada Public Domain Survey (NPDS), 148

Nevada State Cattle Association, 134

Nevada State Cattlemen's Association, 116, 118

Nevada Wildlife Federation, 144

Nevada Wool Growers Association, 118, 134, 181

Newark Valley, wild horses, 188

Newlands, Francis, 9

New Mexico, 35, 63–64, 222n10, 229n59. *See also* maps of Great Basin

New York Times, 10, 132

Nixon, Richard M., 149

NMA (National Mustang Association), 184–85, 191

nomadic herders, water regulation impact, 24. *See also* sheep industry

NORA (Nevada Outdoor Recreation Association), 147–48

North Carolina, nuclear testing, 61–62

Northern Paiute Indians, 10, 222n10. *See also* Western Shoshones

noxious weed argument, sheep deaths, 94–95, 96

NPDS (Nevada Public Domain Survey),
148
NSPL (National System of Public
Lands), 219
nuclear power plant, reactor crisis,
216–17
nuclear weapons testing: AEC's
communications with state officials,
65, 237n28; blast effects/damages,
65, 71; continental site search, 61–65;
detonations, 65, 66–68, 77, 78, 89–90,
91, 92; evacuations of residents/
livestock, 49, 71, 79–80; Fermi's risk
calculation, 11–12, 64–65; and grazing
district organizing, 49, 52; increase
in complexity, 87–88; map, 72–73;
public viewing opportunities, 78–79,
90, 242n45, 243n48; site naming, 88,
242n43. *See also* radioactive fallout
entries
Nyala Ranch, Sharp purchase, 115
Nye, Gerald P., 27
Nye County: drought conditions, 34; in
grazing regulation development, 32,
38, 41, 42, 44, 45, 210; and Hoover's
state ownership proposal, 29; livestock
statistics, 48; Tonopah Bombing
Range, 55; wild horses, 162
Nye County Farm Bureau, 43

Oakes, John B., 132
O'Callaghan, Donal "Mike," 149, 152,
199
off-road vehicles (ORVs), 149, 152
O'Harra, John L., 81, 94, 249n72
Old Whitey, the mule, 185
Omaechevarria, Antonio, 143–44
Operation Buster-Jangle, 66–68, 71, 74,
77, 78
Operation Haylift, 136
Operation Outdoors, 124, 131
Operation Ranger, 65–66, 71
Operation Tumbler-Snapper, 77, 78–80,
245n62
Operation Upshot-Knothole, 89–94, 99,
243n48, nn51–52, 244n58
Oregon: BLM's outdoor recreation
beginnings, 126; grazing permit

statistics, 229n59; in grazing regulation
process, 35, 39, 225n28; ranch land
percentages, 226n35; wild horses, 156,
194. *See also* maps of Great Basin
ORRRC (Outdoor Recreation
Resources Review Commission),
124–25, 257n11
Orr Springs, horse deaths, 200
ORVs (off-road vehicles), 149, 152
outdoor recreation: Great Basin's identity,
125–26, 148–49; map of, 150–51; in
new multiple-use framework, 117–18,
124–25; off-road vehicle problems,
149, 152. *See also* Great Basin National
Park, proposal for
Outdoor Recreation Resources Review
Commission (ORRRC), 124–25,
257n11
overgrazing arguments, 20, 36, 40

Pacific Islands, nuclear testing, 61, 62
Paganini, Otto, 243n51
Pahranagat Valley, AEC's warnings, 49.
See also Lamb, Floyd (and family
operations); Sharp, Howard (and
family operations)
Palmer, Ernest J., 181, 274n19
Palmer, Snap, 153–54
Palmer, Vera, 153–54
Palomino Valley, wild horses facility,
198–99
Papoose Lake, cattle deaths, 97
Paradise Valley, 22, 196
Paris, Bertrand, 161, 162
Paris, Peter, 162
Parry, Chance, 163
Pearson, Paul B., 94, 95–96, 246n63
Peavine, Jennie, 271n4
Peavine, John, 169, 271n4
Pelligrini, Steven, 192
Penny, J. Russell, 53, 114
Penoyer Valley, 60, 108–109
Pershing County, grazing district
establishment, 39
Peterson, Gene, 126
Peterson, Gustaf, 235n12
Peterson, Minnie, 235n12
Peterson, William, 28

Printed in the USA
CPSIA information can be obtained
at www.ICGtesting.com
CBHW032126130524
8523CB00011B/120/J